CHINA UNDER COMMUNISM

CHINA UNDER COMMUNISM

THE FIRST FIVE YEARS

by RICHARD L. WALKER

New Haven: YALE UNIVERSITY PRESS, 1955

First published, June, 1955
Second printing, June, 1955

to CELENO, ANNE, GEOFFREY, *and* BRADLEY

who sacrificed so much to enable me to tell others

what I believe is an important story.

CONTENTS

ILLUSTRATIONS

vii

INTRODUCTION

It is obviously impossible to compress all the complicated and diverse events of the first five years of Communist rule in mainland China into a single volume. Further, most historians would rightly affirm that we are much too close to those events to be able to write about them with either perspective or balance. Yet what has happened to China and to the Chinese people is of such importance for all men everywhere that some attempt must be made to tell the story in broad outline, and much of the outline is already clear. The whole of Chinese society together with its long cultural traditions and great legacy of art and learning is being systematically transformed into a modern totalitarian state in which human values are subordinated to a mechanistic philosophy which holds that economic environment and economically determined class relationships are solely responsible for man's thought patterns and concepts of truth.

Because all the great changes in China from 1949 to 1954 cannot be covered exhaustively, I have felt it advisable to concentrate on a few key areas where the apeing of the Soviet "big brother" can be brought clearly into focus and which can serve as an indication of the direction in which the Chinese people are being pushed by their new masters. In almost every case the parallel with the Soviet experience is too obvious to necessitate calling attention to it. Mao Tse-tung and the Chinese Communist party make no secret of their intentions to follow the path blazed by the USSR under Stalin as closely as conditions in China permit, being sure, of course, to avoid some of the Soviet mistakes which later had to be rectified. In this way they believe they can swiftly transform China into an industrialized nation which can be a co-partner with the Soviet Union in bringing about a Communist victory throughout the world. They believe that the pace in China can be faster because of the advantage of the Soviet experience

ix

and the aid of the advanced technicians from the "socialist" center of the world.

As was the case in Russia, China's masters are not concerned about the price of their plans in human terms. Nor do they seem to entertain any notion that some of their plans could be more effectively accomplished by other means. Their rigid adherence to the Moscow party line permits of no such deviations. They are fanatically determined to superimpose upon the Chinese people the blueprint which they have worked out after deep study of the Russian experience of the last thirty-five years, and close cooperation with the leaders of world Communism in Moscow.

China has thus become a test case of whether the Soviet experience in organizing and controlling people under a vast bureaucratic regime can be successfully employed in areas of cultural experience far different from Russia, and in particular in economically underdeveloped areas. If the Communist regime succeeds in China—and the facts brought out in this volume indicate that it is succeeding admirably in some respects—then, the leaders of world Communism feel, they can be optimistic about the eventual victory of the Soviet way of life over the world.

This is one of the reasons why the events in China over the past few years are of utmost importance. The results are being watched eagerly by other people, especially the Indians. The successful creation of a world power center in China holds potentialities for swinging them over to the Communist camp. There are already indications that some Indians, whose standard of living prevents them from being overly concerned about the inhumanity of Communist transformation, are already favorably impressed by what they believe to be the efficiency and large-scale planning of the Mao regime.

China is a far-off place for us, and except for an emotional attachment to some aspects of the traditional Chinese culture, people in the West are little concerned about what happens there. Despite our experiences in World War II, we still tend to measure world events in terms of what takes place in Europe. The cultural roots of the United States lie in Europe, and this fact more than any other prevents the formulation of a truly global foreign policy by administrations Republican or Democratic. Thus, although the lessons to be learned from the experiences of China under a Soviet regime are global lessons, as are those of the satellites in Europe, it is probable that the former will be considered only as they affect the Far Eastern policy of the United States. Given the world-wide ambitions of international Communism, that would indeed be tragic.

The geographical and cultural distance of China from the West also prevents a close following of developments there. Hence many of the individual changes wrought by the Communist masters have escaped our attention and much of their over-all significance has been lost. To some Western businessmen China is still the China of former years, and they continue to hope that as soon as the "current crisis" has passed they can once again carry on business there in the traditional manner. To some diplomats China's foreign relations are still to be understood for the most part in terms of the traditional Western protocol. Again, for some Western scholars China is still the Middle Kingdom whose present is to be understood almost exclusively in terms of the Chinese traditional past.

But China is no longer the China of even five years ago. The changes carried out by the Communists make it impossible for future dealings ever to be carried out on the same business basis or for Western style diplomacy to prove effective in dealing with the regime there. Students can no longer be expected to draw accurate conclusions on the basis of a preponderant reliance on knowledge of the former Chinese culture. The entire Chinese pattern of life cannot be altered completely in so short a time, but the changes under the Communists have already gone deep enough at least to modify such traditional patterns as remain. With the passing years the modifications will increase, and specialists on Communism, not Sinologists, will be better qualified to analyze events within the land which once hailed Confucius as its great teacher.

It is important to understand that the changes brought about by the Communists reach far down into the thought patterns and speech habits of the people. New terms have been introduced, and the Chinese Communist intelligentsia phrase and reorder their thoughts in these terms as the former Confucian gentry molded traditional Chinese thought patterns and speech habits with a specialized set of terms. For this reason it is possible that the Chinese of 1960 may well seem "inscrutable" to a fellow countryman who left his country in 1940. Indeed the Chinese refugee of the 1940's may become as ill equipped to explain his country to the outside world as the White Russian refugee of the 1920's is to explain the Soviet Union of today.

Let us hope this may prove to be exaggeration. Underestimating the extent of the transformation would be to err far more gravely. To deal with the current regime in China in terms of former ideas and a static interpretation of Chinese social patterns would be wholly unrealistic. For this reason I have tried to select some aspects of the Communist rule which will point up the manner in which all social life in mainland China is being permeated by the philosophy and values of the Soviet system.

The cost of the tremendous task of remaking China in the Soviet image has been unbelievable in terms both of human and of cultural destruction. It is for this reason that many feel such a regime can never survive for long. Yet it must be remembered that the very changes already accomplished testify to the ruthless efficiency and the techniques of control developed by the Communists. The manner in which they have reorganized patterns of thought and conduct within the area of their control in itself gives great staying power to their regime. Thus while many residents of the Middle Kingdom, and especially the older ones, may realize that they have been subjected to a form of exploitation and oppression harsher than their country has ever known, these people are rapidly being eliminated and replaced by a generation which will know only that they must submit abjectly to total control.

The Communists have of course been able to utilize some of the great transformations which were already apparent in modern Chinese society in their attempt to create a Soviet type state. Many of the policies and actions of the Mao regime over the past five years are intimately related to recent trends in Chinese history as well as to the whole story of the Communist surge to power. But because there is already a rather extensive literature devoted to the historical background of Communist rule in China, I have decided to concentrate as heavily as possible on the 1949–54 period and to supplement brief background sketches with references to the pertinent literature in the notes.

Despite Communist attempts to curtail the amount of information coming from mainland China, there is a wealth of data to be gathered on a day to day basis. There is in fact so much information that it is impossible for one person to keep up with it. Although I have devoted a great proportion of my time and energy over the past five years to following the developments under the Mao regime, I am well aware that I have missed much. Add to this the exclusions involved in the attempt to compress so much information into the confines of one volume, and the chances for omission of important material or lack of balance are tremendous. The inclusion of one quotation to illustrate a point has in some cases necessitated omitting another point altogether. Thanks, however, to several pioneering studies and the advice and help of many friends closely familiar with the China scene, I hope that I have been able to cover most of the important aspects of China under Communism.

The major source has been the published documents of the Chinese Communists themselves. I realize, of course, that most of their claims and statistics must be subjected to close scrutiny and analysis. For preliminary analysis as well as screening of the great quantities of Communist material I am deeply indebted to the pioneering work of the staff of the United States Consulate

General in Hong Kong, and the work of Howard L. Boorman must be singled out for special mention. Their English language productions of important Chinese Communist documents constitute a basic collection for any study of the Mao regime, and in many cases first-rate scholarly analysis is added. Although I have supplemented these materials by regularly following important Chinese language publications of the Peking regime, I freely acknowledge that this volume could not have been written in its present form without the consulate materials. With the exception of items in the text which are obviously my own interpretations, I believe that, thanks mostly to this great store of materials, every major point made in this book concerning the Mao regime has been documented from the Communists' own statements and publications.

Some of my interpretations are tentative, and I have tried to indicate this. Readers may differ with them: students of China have not been noted in the past for unanimity of opinion. On the other hand these interpretations represent for the most part the result of some years of concentration on the problem of Chinese Communism, and most of them fit into an over-all picture of the regime which I believe is an accurate likeness.

Although I have benefited from the assistance and advice of numerous friends, I would like to single out a few who played a vital role in helping me. I am indebted first of all to Frederick C. Barghoorn and Ralph T. Fisher of Yale University for many stimulating hours of discussion of problems concerning Soviet society. Their knowledge of the history of Soviet Russia has helped me to compare and understand differences and likenesses of Communism as practiced in China and in Russia. W. W. Rostow, Frank Kierman, and Richard Hatch of the Center for International Studies at Massachusetts Institute of Technology contributed hours of fruitful discussion of the problems of understanding Communist China. The penetrating insights of Karl A. Wittfogel have offered much inspiration in interpreting Mao's regime.

A group of friends, James T. Ivy, Howard L. Boorman,

Charles T. Cross, Robert Burton, and the members of the Union
Research Institute assisted me in gathering data in Hong Kong
during the summer of 1952 and again in 1954 and shared with
me their wide knowledge of Communist China. During the 1952
trip to Hong Kong I talked with many refugees from the mainland, an experience which like no other brought home the nature
of the new Chinese despotism. For the trip I am indebted to the
faith of Woodford A. Heflin of the Air University, Maxwell Air
Force Base, Alabama.

During the actual writing many friends gave advice and assistance. Certainly Charles Chu, Tien-yi Li, Fenton Babcock,
Stephen H. Kelly, Edward Manice, and Stephen Hosmer deserve
mention. Abraham Brumberg of the United States Information
Agency assisted me with three of the most important chapters.
Richard M. McCarthy of the United States Information Service
staff in Hong Kong has taken many hours to read the manuscript
and has also contributed much in the way of discussion and valuable advice over the past three years. Thanks are owed to Mr. and
Mrs. Benjamin Cohen for their willingness to work under pressure
on the manuscript and to the staff of Yale University Library for
consistently efficient and friendly help.

Certainly the book owes much of its present form to the editorial abilities of Roberta Yerkes of the Yale University Press,
whose contributions and assistance were far beyond the call of
duty. Above all, however, I am anxious to acknowledge my great
indebtedness to Robert D. Barendsen, a conscientious scholar
and friend. The devotion of many hours of his time has not only
proved an inspiration but also saved me from numerous mistakes.
The section of illustrations is largely his work. Through hours of
informative discussion I have derived many insights and much
information from him.

I am grateful also to the editors of *Problems of Communism*
and of the *Yale Review* for permission to utilize my articles which
they published.

Needless to say, none of these friends is responsible in any way
for the judgments or interpretations in this volume.

1. FIVE YEARS OF COMMUNISM IN CHINA

On 1 July 1949 Mao Tse-tung, the chairman of the Chinese Communist party, published his pamphlet *On People's Democratic Dictatorship,* in which he laid down the general policy which the Communists would follow in ruling China. July 1 five years later Chou En-lai, premier and foreign minister of Communist China, was on his way back to China during a break in the Geneva conference on Korea and Indo-China. He had met with the chiefs of state of India and Burma and was soon to have a three-day conference with Ho Chi-minh, the Indo-Chinese Communist premier. The contrast in China's world position and internal conditions on these two dates represents a change so great and so important that the implications have only begun to be apparent in the rest of the world.

In 1949 China was divided and involved in a bitter civil war. In 1954 she was united under one effective rule, both civil and military. In 1949 China was militarily at low ebb and economically weak, with industrial and food production together reaching hardly more than 70 per cent of the prewar high.[1] Today China, with prewar production mostly restored, has fought a United Nations coalition to a standstill in a major war in Korea, has aided the Indo-Chinese Communists against the French, and is currently speaking in a very threatening manner to the United States over numerous Far Eastern issues. Again, in 1949 China was still open to the West, and some Western nations hoped to play a part in her reconstruction. Now China and her people are separated from the rest of the world by an effective iron curtain.

1

All of these achievements are a testimonial to the amazing energy of Mao, Chou, and their colleagues. They have accomplished what they successfully prevented the Nationalist government from doing. They have extended one effective rule over almost 600,000,000 people, more than have ever been controlled by one government in the history of the world. They have turned China into a world power which, because of its military force in being, is causing grave worries in many capitals of the world, and especially in some of the smaller nations of Southeast Asia.

One other contrast points up the methods by which the Communists have achieved these results. In 1949 they were at the pinnacle of their popularity—the "mandate of heaven" had fallen to them. Five years later they were probably feared and hated by most of the Chinese people, who found themselves in the grip of a new type of despotism they were unable to control.[2]

At the time of the Communists' rise to power in China, many Chinese and foreigners thought them little more than country bumpkins who would fall down helplessly on the complicated job of handling China's cities. And, indeed, some of their early behavior seemed to bear out these predictions. One Communist, sent to balance the books in a bank, is reported to have asked for a pair of scales and begun to weigh them. In a Hankow hospital Red cadres (the term is used by the Communists to describe trained activists), distrusting the former "reactionaries," tore off labels and rearranged all the medicines in the storeroom by size of bottle and color of contents.[3] But such items were hardly a firm basis for predicting failure.

The Communists learned quickly and acted quickly. They seized foreign assets and expelled most foreigners, with the exception of citizens of Communist states. They carried out China's first thoroughgoing modern census. They established a regime which possessed a powerful mechanism for total control of the people. By 14 June 1954 they were so confident of that control that they published the text of a new constitution and at the same time concluded Soviet-style elections at the lowest administrative level in preparation for a national congress which convened in Peking * later in the year.

The Mao regime might seem to have realized Chinese nationalistic ambitions. The goals of power and prestige abroad and unity at home have been in large measure achieved. But any attempt to appraise the Chinese Communist rule must be made with caution, and the actual conditions behind the world propaganda emanating from Peking must be discovered before a judgment can be reached.

The changes wrought between 1949 and 1954 are at the very least testimony to the ability of the Chinese Communist government to organize and control human beings. The Mao regime has demonstrated that it has a plan for China, and to date that plan has proved workable. In essence it is the application of the successful past experience of the Soviet Union to the Chinese scene. In *On People's Democratic Dictatorship* Mao said, "The Communist party of the U.S.S.R. is our very best teacher, and we must learn from it." [4]

In applying the Soviet experience as a model, the Chinese Communists have used ruthless force and have shown a remarkable amount of energy. They have been attempting to capsule over two decades of Soviet history into a few years. The result has been cataclysmic changes in the Chinese mode of life and great destruction of traditional Chinese values. It may be safely asserted that never before have the lives of so many people been so drastically changed in so short a time. The present rulers of mainland China have extended their control into every walk of life. Internal state power has grown to the point of total power.

---

* The Communists established the seat of their government in Peiping (northern peace), which they then renamed Peking (northern capital), as the city had been called under the imperial government. The Chinese Nationalist government, of course, still uses the name Peiping to refer to the city, and by general agreement newspapers in the United States use the "Peiping" spelling.

The "New Democracy" period in China has been far briefer than anyone anticipated. Mao stated in 1940: "The Chinese revolution can only be achieved in two steps: (a) New democracy; (b) socialism; and we should point out that the period over which the first step will extend will be a considerably long one." [5] The "New Democracy" or "People's Democratic Dictatorship" was to be a coalition of "democratic" parties, and "a people's democratic united front composed of the Chinese working class, peasants, petty bourgeoisie, national bourgeoisie and other patriotic elements, based upon an alliance of workers and peasants and led by the working class." [6] It was anticipated that any parties in the coalition with Mao's Communist party would have little autonomy, and events have demonstrated that the "coalition" was hardly more than camouflage, although certainly necessary camouflage at the time when the Communists were surging to power.[7] But few observers in or out of China anticipated such a rapid change in the "united front" class structure of the New Democracy. Private businessmen in China knew that they were doomed eventually, but like even some of the most careful outside observers, they anticipated on the basis of Mao's words a period of from thirty to fifty years before socialism would spell their doom.

By 1954, however, Mao's party had cut short the first step and had interjected what amounted to a new step into the process which Mao had visualized in his *New Democracy*. The Communist government proclaimed a "period of transition to socialism." Accent was placed upon rapid elimination of the non-Communist components of the united front.[8] This meant that the Communists felt their initial goals for the New Democratic period had been achieved and they were ready to move on to a closer approximation of the Soviet system.

The tasks which Mao and his colleagues set themselves in mid-1949, before they had completed their conquest of the mainland, were not modest ones. Basically there were five general goals.[9] The first of these was economic recovery and the consolidation of economic control by the state. This Mao regarded as one of the most crucial and difficult tasks. He pointed out to his fellow Communists:

Some of the things we are familiar with will soon be laid aside, and we will be compelled to tackle things with which we are not familiar. This means difficulties. The imperialists count upon our not handling our economic problems well. They stand on the side-lines and wait for our failure.

We must overcome all difficulties and learn the things we do not understand. We must learn to do economic work from all who know the ropes (no matter who they are). We must respect them as teachers, learning from them attentively and earnestly. We must not pretend to know when we do not know. We must not put on bureaucratic airs.[10]

Solving economic problems implied curbing the inflation which was rampant in China at the time. It meant restoring the communications network, organizing a uniform system of taxation for government revenue, renovating neglected waterworks, improving agriculture, and controlling industry while transferring it from private to state ownership. This last was an especially delicate task because it required obtaining initial cooperation from the "capitalists" until the party cadres could assume the jobs of industrial management. But this was the purpose of the "united front." Mao told the "capitalists": "Our current policy is to control capitalism, not to eliminate it." [11]

The second general goal the Communists set for themselves was to centralize power in the hands of the party. As a first step the regime would have to expand its area of control to include all Chinese territory. Initially this meant winning the support of the people, where possible by persuasion, but Mao made no secret of his intention to be harsh and dictatorial once he felt that his party had sufficient power. His concept of democratic dictatorship, borrowed from Lenin, included Stalin's realistic appreciation of the role of the army, police, and courts.[12] Soviet experience argued that monolithic control by a unified party was necessary for effective state power. This involved a continual and vigorous tightening up of party organization, and even purges. Centraliz-

ing state power also meant that the Communist regime must some-
how solve the problem of minority nationalities in Chinese territory—a matter unsolved by Chinese rulers through many centuries.[13]

A third goal emerged from the second. This was to eliminate
"the enemy" internally and externally. All the major spokesmen
of the Chinese Communist party made it very plain that they
viewed their battle to rule China as a bitter class struggle in which
no quarter would be given. For any remnants of the Nationalist
government on the mainland and their supporters they promised
annihilation. The external enemy was "imperialism." The former
rights of the "imperialist powers" in China were to be abolished.

The Peking regime was very open about its fourth general goal
too. It shared Stalin's appreciation of military power in being
and saw in military strength a means of winning prestige abroad.
The *People's Daily,* official organ of the Chinese Communist party
in Peking, stated the aim succinctly for the Chinese: "By conscientious effort China can become a first class world military
power like the Soviet Union." [14]

A final general goal involved the completion of agrarian reform, the program which had helped the Communists to power
among the peasantry and which was a part of their over-all program for transforming what they called the "semifeudal and semi-
colonial" old society of China. They sought to transform the
thoughts, habits, and value patterns of traditional Chinese society
and even launched a direct attack on the Chinese family. All human life should, they felt, be channeled into support of their
monolithic and all-embracing philosophy.

The Communists faced many difficulties in addition to the immediate postwar situation referred to above. They came to power
in a vast country. China is one-sixth again as large as the United
States and far more divided by natural barriers. A very small
percentage of the people were literate, and the language is cum-
bersome and difficult. Even the reading of simple texts requires
more time than the peasants can spare. Again, much of the tradi-

tional Chinese social order in the countryside remained unaffected by the changes of the last century, and the suddenness of the Communist victory left the party without the trained manpower to operate the administration at the level of the peasant villages.

On the other hand, the Communists possessed advantages which many of those who predicted failure did not take into account. The first of these was a unified doctrine which taught no compromise with the old society. Although they gave lip service to the preservation of some of the culture of the past, the Reds never had to pretend that they wanted to preserve any of the basic structure of old China. Through three decades their doctrine had been permeating Chinese literature, and much of their program had struck roots in intellectual circles.[15] They had also gained more than three years' experience in Manchuria, the industrial heart of China, and when victory came suddenly in 1949 were not entirely naive about problems of urban control. In Manchuria they had mastered many of the techniques of propaganda which were to prove invaluable to them later. They had many supporters and high-ranking members in the Kuomintang administration and in the British Crown Colony of Hong Kong.[16] An invaluable asset was the support of the Chinese youth, especially the organized student groups. And lastly they had the advantage of Soviet backing and experience.

Let us examine in detail some of the major aspects of the first five years of the Communists' rule, analyze where they have succeeded and where they have failed, and finally attempt to discover some of the effects of their control upon the Chinese people. A brief historical survey of these five important years will provide the general setting.

The first five years of Communist rule in China may be divided into two periods according to the timetable Mao laid out in his speech of 6 June 1950. The period of "Reconstruction" was to take about three years.[17] At the end of that time the regime declared that the damage of the second World War and the civil war had been repaired and China was ready to start on its first five-year plan for "national construction," with the accent on building heavy industry.[18] Although this division of these first years of Communist rule does have some meaning, it can also prove misleading, for it tends to obscure Peking's continuous and consistent policies of building military power and consolidating internal state power in order to control every facet of Chinese life. Nevertheless, there is real value in attempting to characterize the outstanding features of a period by some identifying phrase. In the chronological review which follows, the designation for each of the five years is an attempt to grasp the prevailing tone of the year.[19]

1949–50. THE FLUSH OF VICTORY

On 1 October 1949 Mao Tse-tung, as chairman of the Chinese Communist party and chairman of the "Chinese People's Government," read a proclamation before a cheering crowd of more than 200,000 in Peking in which he announced the formation of the Central People's Government of the People's Republic of China and declared it to be the "sole legal government representing all the people of the People's Republic of China." [20] This proclamation followed on the heels of the meeting of 662 delegates of the Chinese People's Political Consultative Conference (CPPCC), 21–29 September. The CPPCC had passed three basic pieces of legislation which were to serve as the Constitution of the Chinese Communist government until the convening of a duly elected people's congress in September 1954. These documents, the Common Program, the Organic Law of the Central People's Government of the People's Republic of China, and the Organic Law of the CPPCC, followed the line which Mao had spelled out in *On People's Democratic Dictatorship*. On the surface the CPPCC body was a united front group representing the various groups and political parties in China, with the exception of those parties closely associated with the Kuomintang. In actuality it was a Communist-controlled group.

The Communist leaders exuded confidence. During 1949 their

armies had scored great successes on every front. South China was rapidly falling to them, and they seemed to have the support and enthusiasm of the people wherever they went. Many of their public statements compared the triumph of the Communists in China favorably with the October Revolution in Russia.

The leaders were serious and intense. They settled down to the task of passing basic laws for governing their large country. By the end of 1950 most of the major laws and decrees had been promulgated, including the Organic Law of the Great Administrative Areas' Government (16 December 1949), the Agrarian Reform Law (30 June 1950), the Trade Union Law (29 June 1950), and the Marriage Law (1 May 1950). A collection of the major ones occupies 660 pages of a very large volume in Chinese.[21]

During this period, in the flush of victory, the Chinese Communists also laid the basis for their conduct of foreign relations. Diplomatic relations were established with the Soviet Union, which recognized the Mao regime the day after it had been declared. Within the first year relations had been established with sixteen other countries, including most of the European satellites of the Soviet Union as well as the Communist regimes in North Korea and Viet Nam and several other states, especially the Asian neutral group. Eight other countries had expressed a willingness to enter into formal diplomatic relations.

Almost immediately after the setting up of the Peking government, the leaders established the pattern for one of the major aspects of their conduct of foreign relations: the holding of large-scale conferences to the accompaniment of much propaganda fanfare. A Trade Union Conference of Asian and Australasian countries opened in the newly proclaimed capital on 16 November with 114 representatives from nineteen countries attending; and another large world Communist organization, the Women's International Democratic Federation, sponsored an Asian Women's Conference on 10 December in Peking.

By all odds the most important event in foreign relations during this period was Mao Tse-tung's visit to Moscow, where he arrived 16 December 1949. The stay was an extended one including many lengthy talks with Stalin, and he did not return to his own capital until 4 March 1950.[22] The nature of the conversations with Stalin and the decisions reached have never been made public, but the rest of the world has been able to see the results in the subsequent pattern of Sino-Soviet relations. It is quite possible that during the Moscow talks the launching of the Communist offensive in Korea was decided upon. The only open result of the Mao-Stalin meeting was a series of treaties and agreements which guarantee the Soviet Union a vital role in Communist China's future.

By 30 July 1950 the optimism of the Communists seemed to have been justified, for they were able to claim the "liberation" of all of China (including Hainan Island) with the exception of Taiwan (Formosa) and Tibet, and they launched their drive to "liberate" the latter on 7 October of that year. Their Land Reform program was aiding them in gaining control of the countryside, although at the end of the year they were running into some opposition in central and south China.

On the first anniversary of the establishment of the regime Chou En-lai was enthusiastic in his report to the National Committee of the CPPCC, claiming that no government in China's history had accomplished so much in one year. He stated that the Chinese Communist army had annihilated 8,070,000 enemy troops since July 1946; real unity had been achieved for the first time in Chinese history; inflation had been conquered by March 1950; almost 90 per cent of the railroads had been opened to traffic; and many other great victories had been scored.[23]

Less than one month later, on 25 October, the Chinese People's Volunteers had entered the Korean War and were driving the United Nations troops south in headlong retreat. This external war provided ample excuse for tightening up internal controls, and by the start of the new year the outward attitude of the government manifested a great change. There had been indications earlier of what was in the wind. For example, throughout the first part of 1950 foreign missionaries remained optimistic about chances for getting along with the new government, but by summer the situation had changed drastically. They were beginning to be subjected to persecution, and members of their congregations began to avoid them.[24] The *People's Daily,* in a 26 December 1950 editorial entitled "The deviation of 'generous policy' must be radically corrected," indicated that former concepts of law would be abandoned. It stated that some of the cadres "have funny theories which they apply to counterrevolutionaries. They speak of an 'attempt' when the counterrevolutionary failed to execute his plan; they release such a person on the plea of 'self-defense.' They soften their hearts when the delinquent is a minor."

1951. THE YEAR OF VIOLENCE

Until 1951 the Chinese Communist party had always claimed that it learned from the masses, but the decision announced on New Year's Day 1951 to establish a Party Propaganda Network indicated that from that time on the party would not attempt to conceal the fact that it was doing the teaching and the masses must learn.[25] Refugees who streamed from China in late 1950 and during 1951 revealed that far more coercion had been applied during the seemingly welcome flush of victory period than outside observers had realized, but in 1951 the totalitarian terror in China was manifest to everyone.[26]

Two of the most drastic aspects of the shift to violence were the activities of the "people's tribunals," set up to carry out the Land Reform program in the newly won areas, and the "people's courts," which carried out the party-directed Campaign against Counterrevolutionaries. Evidently by this time the Communist leaders felt they had learned sufficiently well the jobs of the members of the former administration whom they had kept in office, and were now prepared to eradicate all traces of the Nationalist government. Under the Regulations for the Punishment of Counterrevolutionaries passed on 7 February by the Government Administration Council, the highest executive body of the Mao regime, and promulgated 21 February, mass trials were staged throughout the country and thousands were sentenced to death each day. In a statement before the United Nations in Paris on 12 November, Dr. T. F. Tsiang quoted Communist sources to show that more than a million and a half Chinese had been executed in the previous twelve months.[27] Those "counterrevolutionaries" who were not executed were subjected to "reform through labor," a euphemism for slave labor, and participated in the intensive work which began on railway and road construction and water conservation schemes. The most important of the latter was the vaunted Huai River flood control project, which has been the subject of praise in all the accounts of fellow travelers who have visited China.

The Campaign against Counterrevolutionaries was linked with an intensive program to subordinate religion to the state. In March a ruthless drive against Taoist societies was launched.[28] Christian missionaries became the target of fantastic charges. Mission hospitals and orphanages were accused of planned murder of thousands of Chinese children.[29] On 2 December, for example, at a mass rally held in Canton two French Catholic nuns were given five-year jail sentences and three others ordered deported for "willfully murdering" 2,116 Chinese babies at Canton's Holy Infant Orphanage.[30] Peasants' associations in the rural areas and security forces in the cities kept the populace stirred up in a constant state of fear and high tension. There was little time to attend to the serious famine which P'eng Chen, vice-chairman of the Government Administration Council, acknowledged in a speech on 11 May.[31]

The inexorable extension of the power of the state was partly obscured by the violence. In his report of the first two years' progress on 1 October, Tung Pi-wu, vice-premier, indicated that four-fifths of heavy industry was state-operated, that state control of foreign trade had been centralized, that state banks and trading companies had "become a powerful instrument for state control," and that the control of the Communist government extended into all phases of Chinese cultural life.[32]

In its conduct of foreign relations also Communist China displayed an intensification of violence. A Hate America Campaign was linked with the Korean War. Charges of bestiality and even cannibalism were launched against the United States, which became "the most deadly enemy of the peace-loving people of the world." General Wu Hsiu-ch'uan had laid down the general line for rewriting the history of Chinese relations with the United States in his speech at the United Nations on 28 November 1950, which pictured "American imperialism" as the enemy of the whole world. Inside China almost every execution or mass meeting linked the activities of the counterrevolutionaries with American "special agents." America and other Western powers were accused of "cultural aggression" against China. The Communists accused the Westerners of having forced the Chinese to learn Western languages and in the next breath demanded that more energy be devoted to the study of Russian.

The Korean War occupied the center of attention in international events. On 2 February the United Nations declared Communist China an aggressor in Korea and trade restrictions were imposed. Truce talks were started 8 July, but it was soon apparent that the Communist side was using them mainly for propaganda purposes and to get a breathing spell. Although the Korean War went against the Communist side in 1951, the Chinese were able with Soviet help to achieve a real modernization of their armed forces.

In early September Chinese troops entered Lhasa and the "liberation" of Tibet was proclaimed. There was also violence in other aspects of China's foreign relations. During 1951 the practice of extorting ransom from Chinese living overseas to prevent the torture and killing of relatives on the mainland reached its peak. Millions of dollars poured into China every month in this hopeless cause despite attempts by the outside governments to prevent it.[33]

One aspect of foreign relations involved no violence; that was, of course, the Sino-Soviet tie. Here everything was peaceful and orderly. Kuo Mo-jo, the cultural commissar, was awarded the International Stalin Peace Prize, and hundreds of millions of signatures were obtained for "peace" appeals. China's trade with the Soviet Union and the European satellites jumped from 26 per cent of her total trade in 1950 to 61 per cent in 1951.[34] Manchurian produce was being sent to Soviet Asia in increasing quantities.[35] At the great festive celebration of the thirtieth anniversary of the founding of the Chinese Communist party on 1 July most of the high statesmen lauded the Soviet Union and pledged to learn from its experience.[36]

By the end of the year China's position abroad was stronger than ever and the Communists through a campaign of violence had created an atmosphere of fear which guaranteed that there would be little resistance within the country. Now the task was to take advantage of the situation and organize a systematic control over the people.

1952. THE YEAR OF REGIMENTATION [37]

Actually there was little abatement in the violent attitude of government policy in 1952 although the number of counterrevolutionaries executed was curtailed. The Ministry of Propaganda of the Chinese Communist party turned its full attention to a chain of purges and drives which reached unprecedented intensity during the first half of the year. The now infamous combination "3-anti 5-anti Movement" (see Chapter 4) was directed toward purging the ranks of the party and the bureaucracy and extending control over private business. An Ideological Reform Movement elicited endless confessions and recantations from intellectual leaders. In addition there were the campaigns for judicial and party reform and a continuation of the Agrarian Reform Movement.

By the end of 1952 the Communists could claim that their Land Reform program had been virtually completed. It had been a bloody affair costing untold numbers of lives and enabling the party to extend its power into the countryside as no Chinese government had ever done before. On the third anniversary of the regime Po I-po, vice-chairman of the Committee on Financial and Economic Affairs, declared: "Up to August 1952, about 300 million peasants and their families who formerly possessed little or no land were given a total of 47 million hectares of arable land that had belonged to the landlords. The landlord class and the feudal system of land ownership are eliminated from China's countryside." [38] Actually these figures are open to serious question. No comprehensive survey of China's arable land or land tenure had ever been undertaken. There was some inconsistency between Po I-po's announcement and Tung Pi-wu's October 1951 statement that the Land Reform had been 75 per cent completed with the distribution of 12,000,000 hectares to 90,000,000 peasants and tenants.[39] The statistical work of the Mao regime was beginning to show some of the serious flaws which were to be discovered later and admitted by the Communists themselves. Nevertheless, testimony and even pictures which reached the outer world indicated that the Land Reform had been comprehensive as well as brutal. As a follow-up to the intense pressure of the drives the Communist government proclaimed its Provisional Regulations Governing the Organization of Security Committees. These security committees were clearly being set up to aid in the control of the masses.

The Red government wound up its first three years in office with a series of reports claiming great progress for the regime in every activity, and especially in the economic field, which Mao had said was so important.[40] New railroad lines had been opened, including the 318-mile line between Chungking and Chengtu. At mid-year the economic experts claimed that the budget had been balanced. All in all, the flush of victory seemed to have extended throughout the first three years, and the leaders exuded more confidence than ever when they staged their mammoth parade in Peking on 1 October.

Meanwhile, in anticipation of what was to come, a government reorganization was carried out. A State Planning Commission with the leader of the Northeast Regional Administration, Kao Kang, at its head was established and the government ministries were reformed to correspond more closely to the Soviet model. On 15 November reforms were carried out in the organization of the regional groupings of provinces in order to bring them more closely under the supervision of the central government.[41] In retrospect it is easy to see that everything was being prepared for Chou En-lai's 24 December announcement of China's first five-year plan. This was to start heavy industrialization and lay the basis for modern military power. Chou also declared that 1953 would witness the convening of the first duly elected All China People's Congress.

In foreign relations the former trend continued. The USSR and the European satellites now accounted for more than 70 per cent of China's foreign trade. Chou En-lai went to Moscow for several days in September for negotiations which resulted in a statement that contrary to the 1950 agreement the Soviets would continue to hold their extraterritorial rights in Port Arthur and Dairen but would turn the Chinese Changchun Railroad over to the Peking government at the end of the year. The accusation and expulsion of foreigners continued, and an economic squeeze forced most of the Western powers to abandon their assets in China. The British gave up over $800,000,000 of assets and closed out some of their oldest firms.

The Chinese attitude of hostility and hatred toward the United States was stepped up with the launching of the "germ warfare" campaign, which was also designed to alienate the neutral and Asian states from the United States and to support the Soviet position on how to deal with the weapons of mass destruction.[42] In the war against the United Nations forces in Korea the Chinese troops showed impressive improvement in training and equipment.

In fact, the army's advancement in mechanization and improvement in discipline was but a reflection of the regimentation of the whole population. Little wonder, then, that the leaders decided they were ready to start a five-year plan on the Soviet model.

1953. THE YEAR OF RETRENCHMENT [43]

The previous optimism quickly abated in 1953, which was not a good year for Communist China. This was the year of Stalin's death, of floods, famines, typhoons, late frosts, blights, and natural disasters on an unprecedented scale. By October the food situation was so serious that the government cut down on famine relief and told the people they would have to work their own way out of the problem. Some observers estimated that ten million people were starving by the middle of the year.[44] The rulers launched a drive for economy, austerity, and cutting expenditures and combined it with a drive against "bureaucratism," making an example of the case of Huang Yi-feng, a high-ranking party member who was purged.[45] Despite the tightened controls of the year before, there were evidently such intense signs of passive resistance that in July the "5-too-many" Drive was launched against too many meetings, too many tasks, too many organizations, concurrent posts, and official documents and forms.

Quite obviously there was still some slack to be taken up in the matter of control, and there was a pause while the Communists reassessed the situation. The five-year plan was reduced on 7 May by as much as 34 per cent in some items. It suffered further reduction in mid-September following Minister of Heavy Industry Li Fu-ch'un's return from Moscow with details on the limited amount of economic aid the Soviets were actually prepared to give. Nevertheless, the cadres of the party continued intensive study of the documents connected with the period of economic construction in the USSR, especially Chapters 9–12 of the *History of the Communist Party of the Soviet Union (Bolshevik)*.

As part of the program for retrenchment and tightening control practically every major Communist mass organization held a congress in the nation's capital during the summer and fall, and

most of their constitutions were revised to give more centralization and more direct control by the party. The All China Federation of Trade Unions met from 2 to 11 May; the New Democratic
Youth League held its second national congress from 23 June to
2 July; and numerous other groups met to discuss their roles in
the urgent task of economic construction. A hush-hush Civil Affairs Conference was held from 22 October until 13 November.
Its decisions called upon the civil affairs committees to exert closer
control of the masses.

There were other aspects of the regime's attempt to intensify
control of the people. A decree by the Ministry of Public Security
of 30 July set out the regulations for the appointment of "people's
supervision correspondents." This elevated spying into citizen's
private affairs to the level of state policy. As a part of the increasing financial centralization the Customs Administration was
brought under the control of the Foreign Trade Ministry.

The other major undertakings of the Mao government were
continued. By the beginning of 1953, 15,048 miles of railroad
were in operation, with almost 400 more miles scheduled to be
opened before the end of the year. Water conservation and road
building (including a military road into Tibet), items for which
the major resource needed was manpower in the mass, were continued. Retrenchment did not affect the armed forces either. By
the end of the year the modernization program had been carried
out and China was estimated to have at least five million mobilized
men, including the secret police.

In three of the major programs for the year the Communists
were forced to pause and delay completion. On 1 March Mao
issued a proclamation calling for national elections which were
to be completed by September. These elections, which were linked
by decree with the national census on 3 April, were postponed
again and again. Even Mao Tse-tung and his old comrades did
not get around to casting their own votes until 8 December.[46] The
election decree itself provided for a further means of organizing
control over the people and accounting for every citizen. As in

the Soviet Union the results were preordained by the method of
nomination.[47] Another program which was delayed was the campaign to propagandize the benefits of the Marriage Law, a law
that directly attacked traditional Chinese family institutions.[48]
This campaign was temporarily interrupted by Stalin's death, and
soon after its resumption it was quietly dropped because of increased popular resistance. Yet another program delayed during
1953 was the move toward collectivization following the completion of the Land Reform (see Chapter 6). In March a temporary halt was called to the pressure upon the peasants to enter
into collective type units. Party cadres were criticized for blind
and adventurist deviations in forcing collectivization on the
peasants.

Despite famine conditions and other troubles at home, the
regime continued to export foodstuffs to the Soviet Union and
other states in return for military hardware. In spite of dependence
on military aid from the USSR, the propaganda advantage of having held off the most powerful states of the West was given real
force with the conclusion of the 27 July truce in Korea, which the
Peking spokesmen regarded as a clearcut victory. Satisfaction
was short-lived, however, for the refusal of more than 74 per
cent of the released Chinese prisoners of war to return to their
homes and their families in Communist China was the biggest
setback the government had yet received. The choice of the prisoners made it all too plain to the world that the popular approval
of the flush of victory period was over. The attention of the internal press was quickly diverted to the Chinese support of the
cause of Ho Chi-minh and his fight with the French "imperialists"
in Indo-China. A Sino-Korean treaty negotiated in Peking and
signed 23 November was obvious proof that the Chinese did not
intend to see Korea united under any but a Communist government and that the government of Mao had staked out a long-range
claim to a decisive role in the internal politics of that country.

In this year of retrenchment Mao's government stepped up
its expulsion of foreigners and repatriated approximately 25,000

Japanese who had been held since the end of the second World
War. By the close of the year the Chinese were beginning the mass
expulsion of the White Russians from Manchuria, and very few
foreigners outside of the omnipresent Soviet advisers were left in
China.

China's year of retrenchment was hardly the glorious year of
the first five-year plan which had been so boastfully proclaimed
on 1 January. In a way the troubles were a reflection of the un-
certainties manifest in the Soviet Union following the death of
Stalin, the man whom Mao termed "China's greatest friend."
There was a slight wavering and uncertainty, a tightening of the
already binding belts, a taking up of what slack remained in
establishing complete control of the people. But by the beginning
of the next year the decisions had been reached, and the Chinese
Communists decided to surge forward on the path of Stalin.

1954. THE YEAR OF DECISIONS

By New Year's Day 1954 propaganda on China's "general line
of the state for the period of transition to socialism" had become
a major part of the required study for all the Communist party
activists. Newspapers called for more and more education work
in the villages and cities, austerity became more austere, and
food rationing started in earnest.[49] Before the year was half over
it was very clear that the New Democracy period had drawn to a
close. The Communists were moving into direct control in all
fields. A series of major events and decisions foretold the end of
private enterprise, of the "united front," and of any illusions about
Maoism being some sort of special ideology.

The first important decision of the year was the publication by
the Communist party (not the government) of the decision to
collectivize the land.[50] Despite Khrushchev's admission in September 1953 in Moscow that collectivization in the Soviet Union
had been a failure from the point of view of production (see Chapter 11), the Chinese comrades decided that they must use this
method for ensuring control of the peasants.

The second major decision of the new year was to launch a

party purge in order to restore unity and eliminate centrifugal tendencies. Liu Shao-ch'i announced the decision in a speech before the meeting of the Fourth Plenary Session of the Central Committee of the party 6 to 10 February, when he presided in Mao's absence. Implicit in this decision was the abolishing of the great administrative areas, for Liu talked of divisions and factions inside the party and of some high leaders who looked upon their own departments or regions as personal property or an independent kingdom. Those who would not reform were to be subjected to severe punitive action.[51] On 19 June the Government Council decreed the abolition of the regional administrations and reduced the number of provinces from thirty to twenty-six. The provinces are now the unit immediately under the central government at Peking. This third major action spelled the end to certain tendencies toward autonomy which were the result of the separation of areas of Communist control during the second World War.

The Chinese completed their local elections and census count sometime in the spring, but the results were not announced until the same meeting of the Government Council which abolished the administrative areas.[52] Teng Hsiao-p'ing, secretary of the Election Committee, announced that China's population (including Taiwan, which he estimated as having 7,000,000, and the overseas Chinese with 12,327,532) was 601,912,371 as of midnight 30 June–1 July 1953. This figure, which at once necessitated a reappraisal of the ratio of land (and food) to population, threw into doubt many of the previously published Communist statistics and indicated that some serious rethinking of plans might be in order. It confirmed the population estimate made many years earlier by J. L. Buck.[53] The party's chief ideological journal had prepared the party cadres for this tremendous figure in its March issue, the contents of which indicate that the Election Committee had the results for more than three and a half months before making them public.[54] One of the many possible explanations for the delay may have been that the government wanted to wait for an opportunity to use the figure to advance its power position at the Geneva conference.

The completion of the elections at the local level meant that the major preparations could be made for summoning the People's Congress which had been postponed from 1953; it convened in Peking on 15 September. Prior to this, however, the Chinese Communist party published the draft of the New Constitution on 14 June. The issuing of this constitution was yet another important decision. Like the other decisions of 1954, it represented the consummation of all previous trends toward copying the Soviet model. Although the constitution does not provide for direct elections like the 1936 Stalin constitution, many of its articles are taken word for word from the Soviet counterpart. A distinction formerly possible between China and the European satellites of the Soviet Union is in part eliminated by a passage which equates the system of the People's Democracy with the New Democracy.[55] Implicit in the summoning of the People's Congress which adopted the constitution on 20 September is the virtual abandonment of the united front of various parties. Although the constitution makes provisions for parties other than the Communist party, and a few non-Communist political parrots were elected, it was obvious that the Communist party has the only local level organization capable of putting forth candidates.

To parallel the political decisions which marked the movement to a transitional stage between the original government proclaimed in 1949 and a socialist state, the Peking masters moved rapidly in the economic field in 1954. On 1 March they published the Order for Planned Food Buying and Supply, and a Temporary Ordinance on the Management of Food Markets. These decisions nationalized all major food materials. They were followed by a decision on 23 March by the Committee on Financial and Economic Affairs for advance purchase of eight major agricultural products used in industry. A concerted effort was made to convert such private enterprise as remained to the temporary joint public-private form which the Communists had evolved.

The high points of the year in international news were Chou En-lai's performance at the Geneva conference, his joint statement with Nehru on 28 June [56] (a magnificent world propaganda move), his success in driving deeper a wedge between the American and British allies, and finally the Indo-China truce of 20 July which guaranteed the Communists complete control of northern Viet Nam and offered them a good possibility for extending control over all French Indo-China within a few years. There was general agreement that the Chinese Communist premier had scored a major victory against his hated enemy, the United States.

Nineteen fifty-four was the year of consummation of many of the goals which Mao had announced in 1949 and of crucial decisions to follow the path blazed by Stalin regardless of the cost. Of course, Taiwan had yet to be "liberated," but Communist China was a major military power with probably the second largest standing army in the world.

In their methods for bringing about this tremendous change in China during their first five years the Chinese Reds have conscientiously tried to follow the teachings of Lenin and Stalin and the experiences of the USSR. There have, to be sure, been differences because of the special characteristics of the Chinese scene, and many of the measures would be typical of any totalitarian regime; but in general the pattern of rule in China bears strong resemblances to the Soviet pattern. It is probably not an exaggeration to say that it is the pattern which is closely associated in the eyes of the world with "Stalinism" as a particular brand of Communism: it resembles the latter in the increasingly bureaucratic and hierarchical nature of the regime, the type of constitution, the methods of election, in collectivization, thought control and recantations, slave labor, iron curtain, five-year plan designed for forced industrialization and militarization, labor heroes, emulation drives, and so on.[57] These are the measures we must examine in order to appreciate the significance of Communist rule in China, and must understand if we are to appraise what Communism has done for China and what continued Stalinist Communism means for China's future.

2. HOW CHINA IS RULED

"You are dictatorial." My dear sirs, what you say is correct. That is just what we are. All the experiences of the Chinese people, accumulated through the course of successive decades, tell us to carry out a people's democratic dictatorship.

This means that the reactionaries must be deprived of the right to voice their opinions; only the people have that right.

Who are the "people"? At the present stage in China, they are the working class, the peasantry, the petty bourgeoisie and the national bourgeoisie. . . .

Our present task is to strengthen the people's state apparatus—meaning principally the people's army, the people's police and the people's courts—thereby safeguarding national defence and protecting the people's interests. Given these conditions, China, under the leadership of the working class and the Communist Party, can develop steadily from an agricultural into an industrial country and from a New Democratic into a Socialist and, eventually, Communist society, eliminating classes and realizing universal harmony.

Mao Tse-tung
On People's Democratic Dictatorship
July 1949

Communist China is a totalitarian dictatorship. In all the smooth flow of words which emanates from the Peking regime, this is one fact which Mao and his colleagues do not attempt to conceal. They do, however, maintain that all the Chinese "people," a somewhat ill-defined group, participate in the dictatorship; those who are not specifically included in the definition of "people" are

dictated to (that is, those who are not "people" have no rights).
The trend has been for a gradually lessening number of the Chinese
population to be included in the category of "people." As Mao
indicated in the passage quoted above, there has been a realistic
appreciation of the role of force. Indeed, with such a large and
disparate area as China the "strengthening of the people's state
apparatus" was a vital task for any regime planning to maintain
itself in power.

The use of force and the threat of force in China today cannot
be ignored. Communist China is a Soviet-style police state, and
behind every decision and every act lies an ability to apply military
and police force. In the discussion which follows it is necessary to
keep this fact constantly in mind. Most of the leaders of Communist China are military men, used to the role of command and
accustomed to dealing in terms of raw power.[1] They have organized and run their country in such a way as to assure complete
compliance with their wishes, to absorb and direct the time and
energy of any natural leaders who might otherwise oppose them,
and to provide a system of checking and supervising on as all-
pervasive a scale as possible. On the other hand, they continue to
place great stress on winning voluntary support of the people
through propaganda and "education."

Studying the formal structure of the Chinese Communist government is worth while only if one appreciates the manner in
which it is utilized and controlled by the real rulers. The formal
structure, once erected, constitutes a framework within which
the Communist leadership maintains its fiction of legality and
"democracy," but it is usually not involved in the vital process of
decision making.

The real rulers of Red China are the members of the Central
Committee of the Chinese Communist party, especially its Politburo, and a few other key Communists who have come to the
front since the present Central Committee was formed at the
Seventh Party Congress in 1945. These men have worked together
as armed revolutionaries for decades and constitute a tightly knit

body cemented into unity above all by their respect for their leader Mao Tse-tung.[2]

— Mao is revered as one of the leading theoreticians of world Communism and has shown a remarkable ability to hold together the top leadership. Since his assumption of undisputed leadership of the party during the period 1932–34 there have not been the open schisms which have marked the Communist party of the Soviet Union.[3] Mao is both respected and powerful, and his popularity among many of the Chinese people, who frequently tend to disassociate him from the harsh measures of the regime, has remained high.[4]

Mao's close associates during the first five years, who constituted the Politburo, are Liu Shao-ch'i, the austere party theoretician and disciplinary specialist; Chu Teh, long-time comrade in arms and head of the Communist armies; Chou En-lai, versatile international public relations man; P'eng Chen, a party organization leader; Ch'en Yün, the economics authority; Kao Kang, former head of the Manchurian region (now probably no longer a Politburo member); and two of the party elders, Tung Pi-wu and Lin Tsu-han. These men and their colleagues who constitute the seventy-two regular and alternate members of the Central Committee have shown a remarkable amount of stamina and energy. For all their long years of struggle and desperation they do not seem, as do many of their past opponents, to be tired or listless. In discipline, unity, and direction they reflect the position recently adopted from the Soviet Union following the death of Stalin, that "Collective leadership is the highest principle of party leadership." [5]

These are the men who sit on top of the whole structure of political control in China today. They occupy every major position. All basic policy decisions are handed down by them to administrative or military organs. For example, these leaders of the Communist party presented the draft of the New Constitution for acceptance in 1954; they issued the Agrarian Reform Law; they promulgated the Decision on Agricultural Collectivization.

CHAINS OF COMMAND IN COMMUNIST CHINA

This graph attempts to convey in rough form how the decisions and control emanating from the Communist leaders in Peking make themselves felt by the individual Chinese. The arrows indicate supervision, pressure, and control.

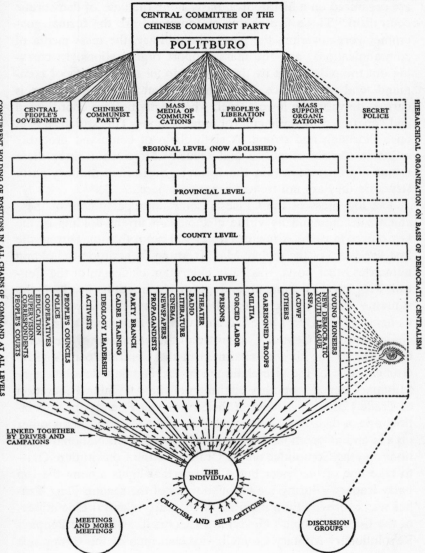

Beneath this central decision-making body are five separate chains of command, including the Communist party, all of which are organized on a hierarchical basis along the lines of democratic centralism.[6] These five chains of command are the formal government organization, the party, the military, the mass media of communications, and the mass support organizations. In carrying out the policies set by the leadership all these chains of command tend to reinforce each other so that a unified process is carried down to the lowest level, where activities are coordinated and supervised by basic control organizations. This structure is at once thorough and strong. A sixth chain of command probably exists in the secret police and security forces, but since these nominally operate within the formal government-military-party structure they are not treated separately here.

The top brass of the Chinese Communist party control these chains of command by virtue of their concurrent holding of the key offices in each. A few examples will point this up. During the first five years of the regime Mao Tse-tung, in addition to holding numerous other posts, was party chairman, chairman of the Central People's Government and at the same time head of the supreme military body, the People's Revolutionary Military Council (PRMC). Liu Shao-ch'i was at the same time vice-chairman of the Central Committee of the party and of the Politburo, one of the six vice-chairmen of the Central People's Government, one of the vice-chairmen of the People's Revolutionary Military Council, honorary chairman of the All China Federation of Trade Unions, president of the Sino-Soviet Friendship Association, one of the party's chief publicists, and a leader in many other organs and associations such as the Committee on National Elections and the Committee on the Drafting of the Constitution. Or— to take one of the lesser but still important lights among the top party leaders—during the first five years of the regime Teng Tzu-hui was concurrently a member of the party Central Committee, of the Central People's Government Council, and of the People's Revolutionary Military Council, vice-chairman of the Committee

on Financial and Economic Affairs of the Government Administration Council, and one of the key figures in the Central-South
Region, where he held top party, military, and administrative posts
and was a leader in mass organizations. Again, Hu Ch'iao-mu
was editor of the *People's Daily*, organ of the Central Committee
of the party, deputy director of the party Propaganda Department,
director of the government press administration, an executive
member of the New Democratic Youth League, and one of the
group chairmen of the Sino-Soviet Friendship Association.

This concurrent holding of posts extending down to the lowest
level has guaranteed that one of the major goals of the party
would continue to be fulfilled; that is, the presentation at all times
to the people within the country and abroad of a monolithic unity
on all problems. To date the Central Committee has been able to
conceal any antagonisms or rivalries within its membership. Such
an organization of control has also meant that the Central Committee has been able to keep its fingers on the pulse of all aspects
of national life and to control the many front organizations which
were set up in the name of the New Democracy.

The formal government administrative machinery under which
the Mao regime initially operated was established by the Chinese
People's Political Consultative Conference (CPPCC), which met
from 21 to 29 September 1949. This remained the supreme
legislative body until the completion of national elections and the
convening of the National People's Congress 15 September 1954.
The CPPCC was, of course, the united front body composed of
representatives of other "democratic" political parties and other
large organizations such as labor and cultural groups. Its total
membership was 662. The control was obviously in the hands of
the Communists. The CPPCC established the Central People's
Government Council (CPGC), sometimes referred to simply as
Government Council, with Mao Tse-tung as its head. Actual administration centered in this body, which contained a sprinkling
of non-Communist members—for example, Soong Ching-ling
(Mme. Sun Yat-sen) and Kuo Mo-jo, the chairman of the Cul-

ture and Education Committee of the government. The executive body was the Government Administration Council (GAC or cabinet) under the leadership of premier Chou En-lai. Under the GAC were the numerous ministries grouped together under three committees: Political and Legal, Financial and Economic, and Cultural and Educational. Various commissions, such as Overseas Chinese Affairs, Nationalities Affairs, and the Committee on People's Control, were also subordinate to the GAC. On a level with the GAC were the People's Revolutionary Military Council with Mao as chairman, the People's Procurator-General's Office, and the Supreme People's Court.

Until their abolition in June 1954, the "great regional administrative councils" were the next subordinate unit in the administration. Under the regions came the provinces (*sheng*) and special cities (*t'e-pieh shih*), then the special districts (*chuan ch'ü*), then counties (*hsien*), then districts (*ch'ü*), and finally the villages (*hsiang*). This complicated organization has been streamlined in the 1954 Constitution adopted in Peking on 20 September by making provincial and special city administrations directly subordinate to the central government, then in order of authority the county administrations, and finally the villages; other administrative units have been eliminated. The number of provinces (including Taiwan) was reduced from 30 to 26 by the 19 June 1954 meeting of the CPGC. There are more than 2,000 counties and some 214,000 electoral units, mainly villages, throughout the country.

At the lowest level in this administrative hierarchy are the "people's representative conferences" or, as they are now called, "people's congresses." These units, which correspond to the Soviets in the USSR, elect "people's councils" which are the executive organs at this low level. Actually, the system of nominations and the presentation of slates of candidates stack the deck from this level on up in favor of the Communist party. Government organs at this level are subject to the orders of the next higher level and so on up to the top. As Minister of the Interior

Hsieh Chüeh-tsai put it tersely in 1951, the duties of the local conferences or congresses are "to transmit orders, to report results and to guide the work." [7]

In many respects the military chain of command in Communist China has been more powerful and important than the formal administration. Nominally, of course, the People's Revolutionary Military Council was subordinate to the Central People's Government Council; but since in most areas of China military control by the so-called People's Liberation Army (PLA) came first, the military actually retained their predominance. The system of "great administrative areas" or regions established in 1949 was but a reflection of this fact. Indeed, many of the early administrative arrangements in Communist China stemmed from the long civil war period. For example, Ping-yüan, a new province established in 1949 and abolished late in 1952, was a carry-over of an independent wartime guerrilla base.

The decision to abolish the great administrative areas on 19 June 1954, was one of the most important indications of the Communist ability to centralize and control. Until a government decision of 15 November 1952 began the process of elimination, the executive organs in these six great groupings of provinces were known as administrative areas' people's governments. They had their own ministries and were in many respects independent of the central authority in Peking. After November 1952 the civil governments in the regions were known as councils. The top leaders in these regions were the great military leaders who had led the Communist armies to victory over the Nationalist government. In some cases the boundaries of the administrative areas seemed to coincide with the areas assigned to the field armies of the Communist war machine. Thus, the extinction of the regional level administration was a step designed to shift the weight of authority in the central government toward the economic planners and away from the military, and at the same time a method of eliminating the traditional Chinese tendencies toward local and regional autonomy. The most important of the regional groupings of provinces had been the Northeast (Manchuria). Here the Soviet advisers were most numerous and most of the policies which were later applied in the rest of the country were tested.[8]

The military chain of command played a vital role in the carrying out of the decisions of the Chinese Communists during the first five years of the regime. The PLA units aided in the Agrarian Reform, they have supervised some of the great mass labor construction works, and they continue to be the main components of government in the more remote areas such as Tibet, Sinkiang, and Sikang. The PRMC (now the National Defense Council under the New Constitution) is in charge of a system that extends down to the militia units which are being organized in all the villages of China, and its commanders are also the leaders of the public security troops. The aim is to develop the present militia forces, which number more than five million (in addition to the regular army of more than five million), into a force which will constitute more than 5 per cent of the population.[9]

The regime has been very successful in its program of modernizing and developing the Chinese Communist army into one of the major fighting forces in the world today. Not only does the garrisoning of the more than five million troops, a large proportion of whom now possess modern weapons, throughout the Chinese countryside serve as a reminder of the strength of the regime among the people, but the members of the armed forces participate in propaganda and leadership activities in the localities where they are stationed. They constitute the second largest component of the membership of the Communist party.

The third chain of command, extending down to the lowest level throughout the country, is the party. At the level of the factory, office, or village there is a party branch composed of three or more members. The party is organized in almost every detail along the lines of the Communist party of the Soviet Union. It insists on discipline, obedience, and conscientious activity from its members. It is actually the basic power organization in China today, for individual loyalty is given above all to the party. Be-

cause of the complete integration in all of these three major
chains of command—government, military, and party—made
possible by the concurrent holding of posts, many of the complications of command channels are avoided: at most levels one man
holds the top post in all three.[10]

According to Liu Shao-ch'i's speech at the Fourth Plenary Session of the Central Committee of the party (6–10 February
1954) the Chinese Communist party now has 6,500,000 members.[11] As in the Soviet Union, about 10 per cent of the members
are women. Since the Communist seizure of power, there has been
a concentrated effort on the part of the top leadership to make the
party correspond more closely to Communist theory; that is, to
make it the party of the urban "working class." Party purges and
drives resulted in reducing the rural component from 90 to 80
per cent by 1951, but the peasants are still predominant.[12] This
fact has worried the leaders greatly. Many of the peasant party
members have slipped from party discipline and have relapsed
into habits of independence and abuse of power (see Chapter 4).

During the 3-anti Movement, one of the many campaigns of
1952, the year of regimentation (see p. 14), the party attempted
to reorganize its more than 180,000 rural branches. An Tzu-wen,
one of the rising young lights of the party and deputy director of
the Organization Department of the Central Committee, revealed
in February 1953 that the process had been very slow and that a
very small proportion of the rural branches had been affected.
In branches where reorganization had been carried out, An reported that 10 per cent of the members had failed to qualify for
continued membership and were read out of the party.[13]

The Chinese Communist party, like any highly disciplined organization, is extremely rank-conscious. The higher the rank, the
more comprehensive and absolute the power. This leads to abuse
of power and occasionally to poor morale. The method for avoiding this is the process of criticism and self-criticism developed in
the Soviet system and insisted upon constantly in China. Stalin
and Malenkov are quoted in detail on the necessity for maintain-

ing criticism from bottom to top within the party ranks.[14] But it
has proved difficult to encourage criticism from the lower ranks
when their members have been made acutely aware of the disciplinary power which exists above them. Nevertheless, the Chinese
Communist party has, during its first five years in power, managed
to keep a fair amount of the initial vigor and sense of dedication
alive, especially among the youth, by means of a continuous series
of reforms, drives, and campaigns.

At its top level the party has, in addition to its Central Committee and Politburo, a Secretariat of which Mao is chairman.
The Central Committee has five main organs: an Organization
Department headed by Liu Shao-ch'i, a Propaganda Department
with Lu Ting-yi as its head, a United Front Work Department
directed by Li Wei-han, a Social Affairs Department under Li
K'o-nung, and an Administrative Office. The Social Affairs Department is the dread secret police organization whose activities
remain clothed in mystery. It is never officially referred to in
present Communist sources, but its network parallels the party
network and extends throughout the armed forces. The whole
party organization parallels the administrative machinery of China
down to the provincial and county levels, where the party organs
are known as bureaus and subbureaus, and to the villages, where
the party branches merge with the village government.

A fourth major chain of command in the political control of
Communist China exists in the mass media of communication.
Here the control of the party is more obvious, for all newspapers,
radios, motion pictures, comic books, and other organs take their
cues from the Propaganda Department of the party. The official
line on any issue or internal government program is established
by the *People's Daily* in the capital. Its editorials are read over
the radio and issued daily, though sometimes in abridged form,
by the New China News Agency. This agency (and its affiliates),
like Tass in the Soviet Union, is the only official and recognized
channel for disseminating news within the country or abroad.

On 1 January 1951 the decision was announced to set up a

propaganda network of the party throughout the country, with the aim of having at least one articulate official spokesman for every hundred people. Two years later, in January 1953, over 3,790,000 propagandists had been organized.[15] In addition to receiving official statements of policy through the *People's Daily* and the radio, the propagandists at the local level, who hold meetings and lecture to the people, are aided by handbooks which offer effective methods of explaining to the peasant why he should contribute more grain, to the worker why he should work longer hours, or to the small peddler why he should abandon his capitalist enterprise. Such handbooks are the *Current Affairs Handbook* (circulation over 700,000), the *Propagandist's Handbook*, the *Illustrated Propagandist Handbook,* and many others. Comic books have also assumed great importance to the propaganda machine.

The Communist leaders consider propaganda a dignified profession, and they make no distinction between propaganda and education. As a part of their attempt to remake the whole of Chinese society they have insisted that every aspect of life, including the work of doctors or painters, must contribute to the building of "socialism." Therefore they believe that every realm of activity comes within the purview of the propagandist. The ranking of the propagandists depends upon their effectiveness, and they frequently vie with each other to do a better job of convincing the masses.

According to a party directive, "Reporters are propagandists of a higher rank and therefore are the directing personnel among the propagandists." [16] Propagandists have been taught that all news must be political news and that their duty is to keep the masses engaged in intense discussions of the issues determined upon by the top party leadership.

Any deviations from the correct line or methods established by the party Propaganda Department are quickly noted. The party journal of ideology, *Hsüeh-hsi (Study)*, usually informs the higher ranking propagandists what special precautions must be taken in their work. For example, in reviewing the propaganda work which had been carried out to celebrate the occasion of the thirtieth anniversary of the party, *Study* had many critical comments to make about numerous publications. The editors stated:

All portraits and photographs of chairman Mao used by the newspapers and periodicals should undergo strict selection. On July 2, the Northwest *Masses Daily* printed a painting by Liu Kuang with the caption "Chairman Mao in the Self-Defence Battle of North Shensi." This is a very poor painting, as a reader's critical letter published in the newspaper half a month later pointed out: "What angers one most is the representation by the painter of Chairman Mao as a man with an expressionless and melancholy face, disproportioned stature and leaning as if about to fall and gazing helplessly at the grayish sky." Such hasty and careless printing of portraits of comrade Mao should be strictly avoided.

The propagandizing of the leader of the party is a necessity, but the propaganda must be consistent with the facts and have high ideological and educational content. In no case should it be incorrect, vulgar, hasty, and careless.[17]

The fifth chain of command linking the top Communist leaders with the people they control consists of the many mass support organizations. These serve as sounding boards for intensifying support for government and party policies. All are under the leadership and direction of the party. They are organized in most cases along the lines of democratic centralism, which in effect means that the lower organs give unified and unwavering obedience to dictates passed down from the top.[18]

There is a mass support organization tailored to fit almost every possible social grouping. This is, of course, an effective means for the party to supervise the many social activities which in a non-Communist state would not be considered political. These organizations also serve to absorb the energies and time of people who might otherwise be directing their attention to matters outside of the narrowly prescribed area, and thus be, to a Communist regime, suspect. It is safe to say that practically everyone in China today belongs to one of these organizations.[19]

During 1953, when internal problems were causing a great amount of soul-searching among the Communist leaders, every one of the major mass support organizations held a congress. These congresses revised constitutions so as to provide even tighter control by the central organs and to accent duties and responsibilities of members rather than rights and privileges. The series of congresses also served to emphasize the common goals of all the organizations and reinforce their interlocking nature. In order to gain some idea of the great numbers of people involved in these organizations, it is perhaps desirable to list some of them.

Undoubtedly one of the most important of the mass organizations is the highly disciplined New Democratic Youth League (NDYL) which Liu Shao-ch'i has termed the "reserve force of the party." [20] This group, which held its Second National Congress from 23 to 28 June 1953, revised its constitution to tie it more centrally to the party and bring it more closely into line with its Soviet model, the Komsomol. Like the Komsomol, its membership is open to all young people, male and female, between the ages of fourteen and twenty-five. Its higher officers, including all of the central committee, must be members of the Communist party. It has its own publications, which frequently carry elaborate articles on the work of the youth and its relationship to the work of the party.[21] According to the *People's Daily* of 5 May 1954, the membership of the league was more than 12,000,000. These members are scattered in more than 470,000 cells or branches, which exist wherever there are three or more members in the same block, school, village, factory, or other location.[22] Like its Soviet counterpart, the NDYL also sponsors a junior organization, the Young Pioneers. This is for children from nine to fourteen years of age who show leadership qualities. By May 1953 there were already 8,000,000 in this organization.[23] The *Chinese Young Pioneers' Journal* is issued for this group and its contents are devoted to the same general themes as all of the mass media in the country. In appraising this journal the *People's Daily* said:

During the 3-anti and 5-anti campaigns, the journal contrasted the good characters to bad characters, thus arousing the children's strong love and hatred. The children love the Chinese People's Volunteers, love the Korean people and army and hate American imperialism. The revolutionary heroism of the CPV influences the children's thoughts and feelings. The stories of how Lo Sheng-chiao saved a Korean child by sacrificing his own life and how CPVs practice austerity on the front exert great effects on their daily life.[24]

The members of the Youth League and the Young Pioneers have been inspired with the "five loves": love for fatherland, people, labor, science, and public property. As one Indian observer adds, there is no mention of love for parents.[25]

The important point about these youth organizations is that they aid the regime in enlisting the enthusiastic devotion of those young people who early show capacities for leadership. The net result is that after a few years these youngsters find that their own interests, by the sheer amount of time invested, are wholly bound up with the future of the party. They come to lean heavily on the party for moral support and to expect, and as they grow older demand, discipline. Little wonder then that Hu Yao-pang, the newly selected head of the Youth League in 1953, stressed the party's concern for the youth of China: "Comrades, the youth movement in modern China has always developed under the leadership of the Communist Party of China. The Communist Party of China and Chairman Mao always show extraordinary concern for the Chinese youth movement. Our Party and Chairman Mao consider the Chinese youths to be 'an important front army' in the revolutionary struggle of our country ever since the May Fourth Movement." * [26]

Hu went on to say that "the past four years' experience tells us that the subordination of the NDYL to party leadership has decisive significance for the NDYL work." He proceeded to lay out such future tasks for the Youth League as "to rally the whole body of young workers to labor emulations," "to mobilize young

* A movement of protest against the concessions to Japan by the Paris peace conference in 1919, led by the students and a few young teachers and hailed by the CCP as one of the great forerunners of its development.

peasants to take an active part in the patriotic production-increase movement," "to teach NDYL members to observe school discipline and fulfill pedagogical plans," and "to further the campaign for learning from the Soviet Union among the League members and all the youths of China." [27] Hu Yao-pang also stressed the need for united front work and leadership by the NDYL in other youth organizations. These include the All China Federation of Democratic Youth (of which the NDYL is one of the member groups) with a membership of 18,000,000 and the All China Students' Federation with a membership of 3,290,000 in early 1953.[28]

Another important mass organization is the Sino-Soviet Friendship Association (SSFA), which was founded 5 October 1949 under the leadership of Liu Shao-ch'i. By February 1954 this organization could boast, according to the statistics of the regime, more than 58,000,000 members in 1,830 branches and 213,150 subbranches.[29] This association serves as one of the major media for dissemination of pro-Soviet propaganda. It sponsors student training in the Soviet Union, promotes mass Russian language training, organizes meetings and cultural exchanges, and publishes and distributes periodical literature and pamphlets. By the end of 1953 it was issuing 74 periodicals. As Dr. K. C. Chao observes, "The list of the 203-member Executive Committee of the SSFA reads like a 'Who's Who in Communist China.' " [30] There is reason to question the significance of some of the figures and enthusiastic claims of the SSFA—for example, all the members of the Chinese Communist army were automatically made members —yet as a propaganda agency for cementing an international alliance it is probably unmatched in the history of international relations.

A third vitally important mass organization is the All China Democratic Women's Federation (ACDWF). This organization, which like the others is organized along the lines of democratic centralism, consisted of more than 76,000,000 women when its Second National Congress convened from 15 to 23 April 1953. It addresses itself to the long-standing grievances of Chinese women, to which they have been awakened in recent decades, and enlists their support by offering positions and much propaganda about equality. The talk of equality is, for the most part, all in terms of equal opportunity to participate in the various drives, campaigns, and other duties of the Communist state. Probably no description of the type of work involved in the promotion of women's activities is more eloquent than an NCNA dispatch from the 17 April 1953 session of the All China Women's Congress:

> Living proof of what Chinese women can do in all phases of national construction was provided by a roster of 14 speakers at today's plenary session . . . 23-year-old Sun Hsiao-chu, China's first woman railway traffic controller, held the audience in great attention as she told how she started her work on the railways as a coupler and later became a model dispatcher. Ridicule by her male colleagues was not the only obstacle in her way—even her mother was against her working as a coupler. This tall lively young woman told the audience, "To be a coupler, you must be able to catch up to and jump down from running engines which at their slowest run as fast as the cars on Peking streets. But I learned to do it." And she became a model coupler. . . .
>
> She also told the audience how the Communist Party backed her up whenever she met difficulties and that this help was indispensable in improving her work.[31]

One of the main reasons for organizing the women is to get them away from the home and into production and defense work. These efforts have not met with uniform success, and indeed, as the *People's Daily* admitted in 1954, the women in the country-side have been in the forefront in resisting socialization. The campaign to publicize the new Marriage Law and equality of the sexes has, according to a competent observer, been a signal failure.[32]

The All China Federation of Trade Unions is another organization of major importance within Communist China.[33] By 2 May 1954 the membership of the ACFTU was reported to be 11,-000,000 Chinese workers.[34] It held its Seventh Congress from 2 to 11 May 1953, at which time the revised constitution was adopted by the 813 representatives present. The ACFTU is now run by a presidium of 24 members and an eight-man secretariat.[35] It sponsors emulation and Stakhanovite campaigns among the workers, selects labor heroes, and attempts to enforce labor discipline in the interests of the policies of the party and the state. Its members are assured that they are indeed the true leaders of the Chinese people. Undoubtedly some of them find this a little hard to believe when they are told in the next breath that their duty is to heighten labor discipline, cease overemphasis on the welfare of the workers, and practice austerity.[36] Part of the activity of the Federation of Trade Unions is probably reflected in a Christmas Day 1953 letter from the workers at the Anshan Iron and Steel Company to comrade Mao:

Beloved Chairman Mao: We know that the beginning of production in the Heavy Rolling Mill, the Seamless Tubing Mill and the No. 7 Blast Furnace is but a start in our country's first five-year plan. Ahead of us lie still more complex and bigger tasks. We will resolutely follow your teachings, eagerly learn from the Soviet Union and try our best to raise our technical level and political consciousness to strive for the successful realization of Anshan's five-year plan and China's first five-year plan.

We pledge to you that in order to carry out the general line to build our country into a mighty and prosperous Socialist society, we will fulfill all the tasks given to us by our motherland. We will answer your call by achieving greater and more successes in our production and construction.[37]

Another one of the mass support organizations of the regime is the All China Federation of Industrial and Commercial Circles, which was set up at a congress in Peking from 23 October to 12 November 1953. Its purpose was to bring the remaining sectors of the private economy under the control and supervision of the Communist party and prepare them for their elimination. The leaders at the congress made no bones about their purpose in urging China's few remaining independent commercial and industrial leaders to accept the new "general line of the state." [38]

Mass organizations in Communist China are legion. There is an organization for almost every conceivable social interest: academic groups, artists, actors, authors, and various religious groups.[39] Through direction from the Central Committee of the Communist party, whose members hold key positions in them —although in many cases the figure-head officers are nonparty members—the mass support organizations can develop regimented support for the various drives and programs launched in China. For example, they compete with each other to organize the most effective displays and best disciplined marching units in Red China's interminable series of parades and demonstrations.

Two other organizations which develop mass participation on a large scale are the "cooperatives" and peasants' associations. The cooperatives, which in September 1953, according to Communist figures, boasted a membership of 141,000,000, are actually state-run monopolies in which little choice remains to the peasant with regard to membership.[40] The peasants' associations boast a membership as high or higher.[41]

The Communist regime also organizes its own functionaries or cadres into groups according to function in order to make the work of controlling the people more efficient. At the periodic conferences and congresses of these cadres shortcomings and difficulties being encountered are frequently revealed to the outside world. There is always a speech of harsh criticism in addition to the long speeches on great achievements which serve as window dressing. For example at the Second National Conference on Procurators' Work held at Peking from 17 March to 10 April 1954, the government authorities revealed that public prosecutors' offices had been established in only one-third of the administrative units of county or higher level.[42]

At the Civil Affairs Conference held from 22 October to 13 November 1953 representatives of the Ministry of the Interior were urged to get the masses mobilized. It was quite apparent that affairs were not going well in the villages. An unusual aspect of the meeting was an address by the Soviet expert Runev, who explained "the advanced Soviet technique" for building state power at the local level.[43] Resentment and resistance were plainly growing, and the penetration of the whole apparatus of control still left much to be desired from the point of view of local control.[44] The *People's Daily* editorialized on the day that news of the conference broke: "The building of state power in cities and factory and mining areas does not mean relaxation of the building of state power in the countryside. The state power in the country is confronted with an ocean of individual small peasants farming with about 100,000,000 farms. These individual small peasants, if not organized and guided, will spontaneously take the capitalist path." [45] Thus there continue to be indications that there are many areas where the control process at the lowest levels has yet to be consolidated by the Mao regime. On the other hand, achievements in the first five years were remarkable, and the Communists are aware of the tasks ahead. With each passing day the coordination of the various chains of command improves in efficiency at the lowest level.

At the base of the pyramid constituted by the five chains of command in those areas where the organs of Communist power have already been consolidated, the "fearsome Orwellian State glares through the whole façade." [46] Force, supervision, spying, and propaganda are integrated in such a way as to bear out Trotsky's grim description of the Soviet system as a "hitherto unheard-of apparatus of compulsion." [47] The real meaning of the whole political structure is not clear without examination of its relation to the individual Chinese in the village or city where it is imposed.

At the level of the individual, force is very apparent. The regime swiftly adopted Mao's injunction to strengthen the army, police, and courts. Garrisoned troops of the People's Liberation Army are quartered in almost every county, where in cooperation with the Ministry of Public Security they help to organize militia forces. In addition to the militia there are the public security (*kung-an*)

forces, which supervise prisons and correctional institutions and
are in charge of forced labor battalions. They are organized in
military formations and at the higher levels are under the command of the military. As in the Soviet Union under Stalin, these
security troops perform such tasks as guarding frontiers and internal communications networks. The public security police form
an organization apart from the regular police forces of the large
towns and cities, and their members, whose authority is unques-
tioned, are quartered in some of the smallest villages. In addition
there are the undercover agents of public security who operate
under the Social Affairs Department of the party. "Special agents"
from this organization have infiltrated all government organizations, the army, and the mass organizations.[48]

All of these police organizations function in cooperation with
a system of courts and law which "exists to protect the regime
and advance its policies." [49] The formal courts of the land are set
up at three levels—county, province, and national—but they have
been hopelessly behind in trying cases, and the courts which reach
the level of the individual Chinese are the "people's courts" and
special "people's tribunals." These are carefully staged mass meetings which are convened by the political leaders for immediate
disposal of cases connected with the security of the "people's state
apparatus." [50] There is no aura of professional justice about these
mass trials, but then, as the *People's Daily* maintained: "The view
held by some people that trial proceedings can only be conducted by
professional judicial workers, and not by other persons, is entirely
erroneous. The law of the people's state is a weapon in the hands
of the people to be used to punish subversive elements of all sorts
and is not by any means something mysterious and abstruse to be
controlled by a minority separated from the masses." [51] Here, indeed, is one of the basic differences between the Communist
system and the non-Communist world. During the first five years
of the Communist regime in China there was no codified system
of laws. Article 17 of *The Common Program* adopted by the
CPPCC abolished all the laws and statutes of the Nationalist

government; and in none of the four major statutes under which the courts operated in Communist China was there any provision for the rights of the defendant.[52] Both the people's tribunals and the people's courts have had the power to impose the death sentence. In fact, under the law passed 21 February 1951 for the Punishment of Counterrevolutionaries, death or life imprisonment was specified in over 95 per cent of the cases. Further, this law made punishment applicable retroactively to any crimes ever committed by an individual. The only legal interpretation necessary was the whim of the crowd led on by the agitators.[53]

Practically every individual in China has been obliged to witness or participate in one of the mass trials staged in connection with the Land Reform or the suppression of counterrevolutionaries. He knows what his fate will be if his activities make him undesirable from the point of view of the regime. To this is added his awareness of being continually supervised and spied upon. He must account for all his movements to the association with which he is registered. If he is a peasant this means reporting to the head of the Peasants' Association; if he is a city resident, to the block warden. He is not free to move his residence, to stay out after a certain hour in the evening, or to travel beyond a certain radius without prior permission from the local public security bureau where he is registered.[54]

Further spying into the affairs of the individual is provided by the system of "security committees" set up by the Ministry of Public Security 10 August 1952. These committees have been based generally on "[government] organ, factory, enterprise, school and street as the units in cities and the administrative village as the unit in rural districts." They comprise three to eleven members who "have a clean history and are upright in working style, adept in linking up with the masses and enthusiastic in security work"— in other words, loyal supporters of the regime. Their job is to follow the activity of all people in their area of supervision and to report any activity contrary to the interest of the regime. Needless to say, these committees operate in secrecy.[55]

Another method for checking on and controlling every individual in Communist China was provided by the combined elections and census conducted in 1953–54. Under the regulations established by the party all those who were to vote had first to be screened, and only the reliable were given cards entitling them to vote. There were four classes of unreliables: 1) the still unreformed landlords (although they were supposed to have been completely eliminated in 1952); 2) counterrevolutionaries; 3) those deprived of their rights as citizens; and 4) the insane.[56] The combining of the census with the election gave the regime a fine opportunity to penetrate every household in order to determine political reliability. In connection with the election campaign, once again special people's courts were formed to punish the politically unreliable who were discovered. The census-election also gave the party an opportunity to check up on the local cadres and bring them under the strict discipline of the organization if they had strayed out of line.[57]

Despite the careful screening, which revealed more than 9,000,-000 unreliables, the election system still provided for open voting by show of hands at the lowest levels, and at higher levels a slate of candidates was presented by the party, with one candidate for each office. In the usual "people's democracy" style the voters had an opportunity to vote "yes" or "no." [58] Teng Tzu-hui in giving the figures for the election and census indicated that 2,570,000 specially trained cadres had guided the process in which some 278,000,000 people had voted. He gave the following figures for the population of China: [59]

Direct investigation	573,876,670
Estimated	
National minorities excluded from election	8,708,169
Taiwan	7,000,000
Overseas Chinese	12,327,532
Total	601,912,371

Exercising control over a population of this size from a centralized headquarters of necessity involves careful supervision over

those actively engaged in administration. In addition to the infiltration of the secret police through the whole administrative
structure, the regime has also established a system of supervision
which has roots deep in the Chinese past political system: the
Censorate.[60] The Communist leadership has employed the system
on a mass basis by setting up people's supervision committees at
the county level and above and appointing people's supervision
correspondents at all levels in the administration. The job of supervision is to encourage criticism from "the masses" and to aid the
regime in keeping some of its active members under restraint.
Actually, the system has not always worked out too well, as one
careful observer has noted. The supervisory organs do not have
sufficient power, their decisions are frequently not respected, and
there is a general reluctance to expose the shortcomings of the
party except for specific party purposes.[61] Nevertheless, the system
of people's supervision correspondents provides a system for mass
mutual spying on both the people and the lower level leaders. For
example, if a village party member failed to punish an old man
caught in an "anti-state" act, an enemy of the old man could denounce him for neglect of duty to a correspondent who in turn
would denounce him to the higher level of the party.

In addition to the above methods of supervision and spying at
the local level, there are the manifold activities of the party cell
and the mass support organizations. All people of like occupa-
tions or with like interests are called together for regular discussion
meetings under the leadership of the party cadres. Discussion
groups of ten to twenty people are constantly engaged in political
studies, including Communist theory and current events. They
discuss their work and their contributions to the drives of the government. At these small discussion sessions of all sorts of people,
the party leaders are able to check further upon the political reliability of all of the people. The individual peasant or urban
dweller, having observed the methods of force in action, easily
decides in favor of enthusiasm; apathy toward the policies of the
regime is considered a sign of noncooperation.

Buttressing the whole structure of control at the level of the individual is the propaganda and organization framework. The party has its local propagandist, newspapers and magazines, wired radio system, motion pictures, lantern slides, and song and dance groups. An important aspect of control here is the fact that county and provincial news is localized and only a limited number of centrally supervised publications are permitted to circulate freely through or out of the country.[62] The activities of the children, the women, and the town leaders are all directed toward discovering more persuasive means to bend everyone to the will of the Communist party. At the local level the individual finds himself enmeshed in an intricate network of controls and bombarded by a strange-sounding jargon which remains a mystery to him and which seems to be the key to promotion only for party members.

The *Propaganda Handbook* for 21 July 1951 gives its readers a sample of an approved method for whooping up enthusiasm and organizing the village populace:

After attending the meeting of representatives of all propaganda workers throughout the county, propaganda worker Wu Ch'i-hai of Tung-t'ai Hsien laid down his own plan as to how to respond to the June 1 appeal of the Resist America, Aid Korea Headquarters. This is his scheme:

1. I pledge to make use of the evenings, asking Hsü to play his Chinese violin to attract a crowd, and then I will sing and speak, alternately, and in this way thoroughly publish the three great appeals of Resist America, Aid Korea Headquarters.

2. I can organize two small administrative groups, 14 families in all, to help people draw up Patriotic Pacts definitely to be completed before the 10th (my own household included). From wages I will earn by repairing other people's stoves, I pledge to contribute ¥10,000 —in two instalments of ¥5,000—during the period July 30 to August 30. I shall also persuade the masses to increase production for the purpose of contributing.

3. Regarding care for soldiers' families I pledge to go regularly to their homes and comfort them and also to supervise the group in charge of working for them. I shall myself check the cultivation of their fields, which is to be done for them by others.

4. I shall do more studying, more inquiring, and more propagandizing. I shall go to the Peasant School and the Newspaper Reading Team for studies, shall subscribe to the *Current Affairs Handbook,* erect a propaganda signboard, and pledge not to propagandize by empty meaningless words.

5. On return, I pledge to publicize in my village the selling and depositing in public warehouses of cotton, to raise the people's patriotic knowledge, and to induce those who hold stocks of cotton to sell them before the 10th of July. I shall promote the policy of suppression of counterrevolutionaries and pledge to organize militia men of our group, who will train once every three days and stand guard at two places in the village.

Obviously propagandist Wu was filled with enthusiasm after his return to his village from the meeting at the county seat. He typifies in a way the pattern of political control in Communist China today: a combination of persuasion and coercion, organized, supervised, checked, enforced, and reinforced. The scientific gadgets of the age of Orwell's Big Brother are missing, but most of the other ingredients are there.

The individuals in the most precarious position in this whole structure of political control are the lower level party members and activists—the cadres. While they hold some power in the villages and small urban groupings, they are nevertheless subjected to continual disciplinary action from the top leadership, which at all times maintains a position of infallibility. Thus, if there is serious resistance to a government measure, the blame is always placed upon the lower cadres, who are accused either of having advanced too rashly (a sign of "leftist deviationism" or "adventurism") or of not having advanced rapidly enough (a sign of "incorrect attitude" or "bourgeois standpoint") in their work. If the poor cadres seek more guidance on the recommended rate of progress, they are likely to be told that it is all very simple: advance at the "correct" pace, which is usually defined as "neither too fast nor too slow." The lot of these low-ranking cadres many times proves gloomy, yet it is upon them that the whole system of political control depends.

3. PSYCHOLOGICAL CONTROL

> *The cadres of the Party are the nucleus of the party leadership and of the Chinese revolution. Everyone knows that "cadres decide everything." . . . They are, as Comrade Mao Tse-tung puts it, "the treasures of the nation and pride of the whole Party."*
>
> Liu Shao-ch'i, 1945 [1]

To consolidate power and keep their vast political machine in operation in a country as large and populous as China the Communist leaders require a tightly knit and loyal group of subordinates. The party by nature of its structure and ideology requires also that these lower level leaders be devoted and unquestioning enthusiasts. Developing such militant bearers of the party doctrine in China, a country where tradition has always been strong, has been no small task. Communist achievements in the last five years, at least in the field of political control, testify to the success with which it has been accomplished.

The membership of the Chinese Communist party has grown very rapidly since the end of World War II, in spite of an almost continual state of purge to weed out undesirable elements. [2]

Year	Party Membership
1937	40,000
1945	1,200,000
1948	3,000,000
1950	5,000,000
1951	5,800,000
1953	6,000,000
1954	6,500,000

Bringing all the new party members, as well as others serving in the bureaucracy, into a pattern of conformity and discipline required intense indoctrination and involved changing thought patterns and social habits on an unprecedented scale. The growth in party membership figures between 1945 and 1948 indicates the Communists had already tackled the problem of creating cadres before their army overran China, and helps to explain the disciplined success of the Communist forces when they engulfed the mainland in 1949.

As used by the rulers of China the term cadre (*kan-pu*), which is applied to individuals as well as groups, does not necessarily mean a member of the Communist party, although at most of the lower levels all party members are referred to as cadres.* Walter Gourlay defines a cadre as "an 'activist,' a dynamic element, who serves as the transmission belt between the party, the state, and the masses. He may be the leader of a group, or merely a rank-and-file member, but he is at all times connected with the activity of the party and expresses the point of view of the party." [3] The method for creating cadres stems from training techniques developed by the Communist party of the Soviet Union and is being applied everywhere in the Communist orbit today—from Romania and East Germany to the jungles of Malaya and the battle-scarred towns of North Korea.[4]

At the level of creating cadres the Communists have arrived at a system of conversion and changing of thought patterns which in many ways constitutes a new dimension of power in the world today. It is of course possible to overestimate the effectiveness of this system, but the development of psychological control techniques has contributed far more to the thoroughness and success of the Communist regime in unifying China than has been apparent in accounts published in the West. The feats of Mao Tse-tung and

* The use of "cadre" for the individual as well as the group dates back to the early days of the Chinese Communist movement and has become customary. It probably stems from the fact that the Chinese make no distinction between singular and plural.

his colleagues were accomplished not so much by force of arms as through a superiority in disciplined organization. It is necessary therefore to examine closely the process as well as the tools involved in mass control in China.

This new dimension of political power which has been applied in China and which is probably best described by the phrase *psychological mass coercion* is not a simple process which can be isolated and analyzed by the traditional methods of the social and political scientist in the West. It is not only a system of political authority and social control; it is a method of linking all aspects of life in a Communist state. For example, psychological mass coercion links internal security with education and is at the same time a part of both of these systems.

There are many reasons for the rather widespread failure to describe the Communist rule in China in terms of such a method of control. Our methodological tools are not as yet sufficiently developed to analyze such a phenomenon. There is a general lack of appreciation of its importance, and tendency to dismiss it as sensationalism or an ephemeral development. And finally this process of control involves an attack upon the human mind, a subject unpleasant to the West, where tradition and religion affirm that the human mind is sacred and therefore cannot be regimented or controlled. Most of the literature to date has been descriptive and journalistic. The only start at analysis, *Brain-washing in Red China* by Edward Hunter, is still dismissed in some academic circles as mostly fiction.[5]

Brain-washing or *hsi-nao* is the phrase which the Chinese have applied to the most thorough aspect of psychological mass coercion: that part which focuses with intensity on the individual. Actually the loose use of the term has tended to prevent differentiation among four separate processes: 1) creating cadres, 2) converting enemies, 3) controlling masses, and 4) extracting confessions.[6] Although all of these are a part of the control pattern, and although all blend into one another and share many techniques in common, they must be carefully separated in any attempt to understand the psychological control pattern in China today.

Certainly the creation of the cadres is the most important part of psychological mass coercion. To date, however, most of the attention of the West has been centered on the attempts by the Chinese Communists to convert or extract confessions from the rather sophisticated products of Western civilization among their prisoners in Korea. The significant fact that there were thousands of dedicated cadres who dealt with United Nations troops in Korea, who were fanatically devoted to their tasks of converting or extracting confessions, and further who felt that they would succeed, is all too frequently overlooked.

People's China, the English language propaganda magazine of the Chinese Communist, has explained clearly what the Communist high command was attempting to do with its trainees in the first year of the regime:

The breath-taking rate at which the People's Liberation Army freed China's mainland led to many new problems. One of the most urgent was the problem of sufficient cadres to introduce the policies of the people's government in the newly liberated regions and to mobilize the population for all-out production.

The government has adopted the principle of making the greatest possible use of students, government personnel and other intellectuals of the old society. But the minds of such people are thickly encrusted with the ideology of the feudal gentry and the bourgeoisie. And as long as these people retain the viewpoint of the former ruling classes, they cannot adequately carry out the program of the new government, which is based on the interests of the laboring classes.

This problem was met by setting up people's revolutionary colleges in all newly liberated sectors of the country. These educational centers specialize exclusively in transforming old-type students and intellectuals into the new-type of cadre willing to place all of his talent and energy at the service of the people. Utilizing the experiences of earlier political retraining schools in the Old Liberated Areas, these colleges now carry out their task so efficiently that the great bulk of their students have virtually become new people at the end of a six-month course.[7]

The cadre training process has been applied in China with great flexibility, and its quality and effectiveness have been uneven. In some cases it has involved only part-time study; sometimes courses last for more than two years. In general, however, it is the most effective type of brain-washing and has been carried out by schools like the North China People's Revolutionary College near Peking, which by March 1950 had trained more than 18,000 cadres. Over 200,000 cadres had been trained in such schools by that time.[8] Minister of Personnel An Tzu-wen stated on the third anniversary of the regime that the number of cadres had reached 2,750,000, about four times the number in 1949.[9]

Much of the process of cadre training owes its origins to Moscow training schools for Chinese Communists, which have been in operation at least since 1920. One such school, expressly devoted to the training of young cadres, has not been mentioned in Western literature to any great extent. It has been graduating almost 500 a year since 1931, including the war years. Throughout the war carefully selected young Chinese, sent from the Communist areas of China to the many Moscow schools, learned in them some of the basic psychological techniques of mutual spying and group responsibility.[10]

The really important development in cadre training in China took place during the war, as part of the Party Reform Movement of 1942–44. It was at this time that Liu Shao-ch'i came into his own as chief deviser of the party's indoctrination program and brain-washing methods. Liu was a discipline specialist, and during the Party Reform Campaign he managed to introduce Soviet psychological techniques on a mass basis. As Boyd Compton points out, the "purpose was the type of intensive indoctrination and training which would allow the party to operate with unanimity in a situation where close administrative control and inspection were out of the question." [11] In this period the works of the Soviet Communists of the Stalin era made an indelible impact on the Chinese Communist party. By the postwar period, twelve of the thirteen books of required reading for cadres were Chinese translations of Russian books.

The Party Reform Movement of 1942–44 was the first of the

great drives of the Chinese Communist party which have now become one of their methods of governing. The Soviets had already contributed their organizational techniques. During this wartime Party Reform Movement Mao Tse-tung turned to Stalin's version of Marxism for his basic concepts and methods.[12] This "organized indoctrination by means of criticism, self-criticism, discussion, and the continual study of selected Marxist writings" aimed at "steeling" the cadres to all sorts of violence and hardship and at the same time making the complete obedience of each one a spontaneous move.[13] The process is one which Liu Shao-ch'i labeled "self-cultivation."

Liu could draw on many aspects of the Chinese tradition for such a phrase as this, and the meaning behind it. This was the expression which the Chinese philosopher Hsün-tzu had used in developing a doctrine which in part underlay an almost equally totalitarian state two thousand years before. Liu quoted Confucius to the trainees in answering the question "Why Must Communist Party Members Undertake Self-cultivation?" [14] "Confucius said: At fifteen, I had my mind bent on learning. At thirty, I stood firm. At forty, I had no doubts. At fifty, I knew the decree of Heaven. At sixty, my ear was an obedient organ for the reception of truth. At seventy, I could follow my heart's desire, without transgressing what was right." The goal was to make obedience to the will of the party so natural and automatic that it would at all times be the heart's desire of the trainee.

Here is where Confucius, Liu Shao-ch'i, and the Russian physiologist Pavlov are all blended into one. Pavlov held that man integrates impressions from his environment into his reflexes. This seemed to fit ideally with the Communist conviction of economic environmental determination. Thus, by an extension of Pavlov's theories, when they prevailed over those of voluntarism in the USSR, Soviet psychologists have held that given the proper conditioning the human being could be turned into the ideal new Soviet man. Pavlovian psychology holds that the human physique cannot resist the conditioning, and Soviet scientists have since been attempting to perfect Pavlovian techniques so that any focus of resistance in the individual can be overcome. All of this is not too far from the final phrase in the Confucian saying quoted by Liu or from the situation in China where in the course of many centuries the formal ceremonials imposed by the Confucian ideology had become almost automatic reflexes to the Chinese.[15] Of course the big difference is in the underlying philosophy, which for Confucianism is eminently humanistic.

The basic element in conditioning in Soviet discipline is the process of criticism and self-criticism. That is the "key weapon" in the cadre training procedure. When Mao Tse-tung listed the assets of the Communist party in China in *On People's Democratic Dictatorship,* he put this before the army or the united front: "a disciplined party armed with the theory of Marx, Engels, Lenin and Stalin, employing the method of self-criticism and closely linked with the masses." [16] Criticism and self-criticism constitute in effect an open method of mutual spying and form the basis for the emulation campaigns and the volunteering. They are responsible for much of the grim fear and lack of humor which are a part of China today. *People's China* says about them:

It is not easy for old-type intellectuals, particularly those from feudal backgrounds, to learn to use this essential weapon for self-improvement in a correct manner. At first there is often the liberal tendency to spare the feelings of one's fellow-students by softening one's criticisms. Some students take criticism meetings as an occasion for attacking others in a non-constructive and uncomradely manner. Still others tend to rattle off a lot of "leftist" sounding phrases and thus ward off any real analysis of their own short-comings. However, in a remarkably short time, most students have learned to apply criticism and self-criticism in the correct spirit of seeking the truth, recognizing both merits and defects with equal frankness in order to encourage the one and eradicate the other. It is in this way that the students are gradually able to raise their political level.[17]

The intense application of the experiences gained during the war has been continued in a never-ending schooling of the cadres.

The revolutionary universities set up in 1949 for the rapid brain-washing of tens of thousands of young Chinese were dissolved in 1953. In their place the formal school system of the country carries on the function of cadre training. Here the most interesting development has been the opening of the new building of the People's University on 4 October 1953, in the Western Hills outside Peking. This high-level school in Marxism for Chinese Communist party cadres was organized and its curriculum laid down in toto by a group of Soviet advisers.[18] Here, as in all the cadre training centers and small discussion groups, learning Communist theory and memorizing long passages of Marxist phraseology constitute the main task.

But the import of psychological mass coercion does not really become clear until we examine the details of what is involved in creating a cadre for the party.[19] Here the Chinese Reds have undoubtedly made some new contributions to the methods they learned from the Soviet "big brothers."

For creating cadres, the Communists approach humans with a manipulative attitude. The trainees constitute just so many bodies to be transformed into parts of the organizational structure which will function automatically yet with enthusiasm and almost fanatic devotion to the cause of the party. It is probably because of the Communist demand for fanaticism that most of the trainees are youths between the ages of eighteen and twenty-four.

The training process usually lasts from nine to twelve months—in some cases more, in others less. Although there is wide variation depending on the intellectual level of the trainees, the same general program is used for all. The Communist leaders prefer young people who have had at least one year of middle school. After they took over the mainland they concentrated heavily on this group, skipping over their former source of numerical strength, the illiterate peasant youngsters.

Throughout the training at least six factors are kept constant. First, the training takes place within a controlled area or camp. The only reason the trainees leave the reservation is for conducted "field trips." Ties with former friends and family are severed almost completely. A second constant factor is fatigue. Students are subjected to a schedule which maintains physical and mental fatigue throughout the training. There is no opportunity for relaxation or reflection; they are occupied with memorizing great amounts of theoretical material and are expected to employ the new terminology with facility. Coupled with the fatigue is a third constant: tension. This comes not only from knowing a complete break is being made with the past but also from not being able to keep up with the work assigned. In numberless classes and through long hours of reading and discussion sections the trainee must force himself to stay alert or be prepared to face serious consequences.

Uncertainty is a fourth factor throughout the process. Almost immediately the prospective cadre finds himself isolated from his fellows by a feeling of uncertainty. He is never sure whether he is behaving properly, whether he may be whisked away to the fate which awaits unsuccessful trainees, whether he is going to be denounced by one of his associates. Trainees who conspicuously fail to comprehend the camp pattern in the first few weeks disappear overnight, and there is usually a well-sown rumor concerning their fate. One refugee reported: "I found out later that my friend Liang who had disappeared from the camp one night during the second month of training had been sent to one of the labor battalions, where he almost died. He has returned home now and is still so weak that he stays home in bed." [20]

A fifth constant factor is the use of vicious language. The future cadre learns almost immediately that vocabulary is divided into glowing words reserved for the "new" pattern of life and invectives which are to be applied to all phases of his previous life. The final factor is the seriousness attached to the whole process. Humor is forbidden and consigned to the "decadent and rotten values of the old society."

The training process, whether carried on in the revolutionary colleges, in training centers for captured Nationalist soldiers, or in the formal universities, also employs a set of common techniques. There are first of all the small discussion groups of about ten or twelve into which all trainees (and for that matter most of the people in the country) are divided. In the camps the future revolutionaries stay in the same group throughout the entire training process. They have not known the other members of their group previously. It is within these small groups that the really intense part of the training takes place. As one young Chinese woman points out:

> The purposes of these small groups were explained as follows: "To make our fellow students better accustomed to collective life, to give them more opportunities to inspire and encourage one another, to render their lives fuller and more significant." But the most important purpose was left untold: To make the students form a network of espionage so that they may watch one another, and to breed a spirit of espionage, and to teach spying techniques in a totalitarian state.[21]

Each of the small groups has one informer planted in its midst. Most trainees are aware that the spy is there, but they are usually unable to identify him. The small group is led through its training by a deeply devoted and already well trained cadre. The major work of the small groups is criticism, self-criticism, and discussion of training materials. Here the trainee first learns the technique of the "struggle meeting," the term the Chinese apply to group meetings at which members accuse each other, sins are confessed, and the values of the "old society" are destroyed in the process of "struggle."

Next there are the large group meetings, in which an entire training class within the revolutionary school gathers relatively frequently to hear long lectures by high-ranking party officials. These are then discussed in the small groups and all trainees are held responsible for details of their contents. It was before such large group meetings that Liu Shao-ch'i delivered the series of lectures which were later published as books: *How to Be a Good Communist, On Intra-party Struggle, On the Party*, etc. The large groups also hear model confessions and criticisms, examine group progress, and witness demonstrations. One ex-trainee in Hong Kong in the summer of 1952 described a trip by the whole school to a nearby village to watch and participate in the beating to death of an old woman "landlord" who was hung up by her wrists before a mob of over a thousand people.[22]

A third training technique is the required writing of autobiographies and diaries, which are exposed to the glare of group criticism and continuously revised and rewritten. A former trainee explains: "A straight narration of your past life was not enough. For every action you described you had to give its motive in detail. Your awakened criticism had to be apparent in every sentence. You had to say why you smoked, why you drank, why you had had social connections with certain people—why, why, why." [23] This technique of autobiographies and diaries was employed on United Nations troops in Korean prison compounds. The thousands of Japanese who returned to Japan in 1953 and 1954 had also been subjected to it.[24]

The autobiographies or diaries are mostly confined to ideological life histories and constitute a process of deep self-analysis. Required content includes "principle," "stand," criticism of family and friends, class self-analysis, and correct "content." They are read in the small groups and sometimes in the large groups, and then criticized. After being rewritten many times in line with the criticisms, they become a part of the dossier of the trainee. His soul becomes public property.

Through the technique of questioning, trainees are forced to participate in discussion. There is no remaining outside of the program; no trainee dares to remain silent. If he does not take part in correcting his fellows, he is not alert; if he does not engage in self-criticism, he is not learning properly and is subject to "reassignment." Students as well as instructors participate in constant questioning of each other, with such queries as: "Did I see you gazing around instead of paying attention at the lecture?" "You did not seem to sleep peacefully last night; was there something on your mind?"

A fifth technique utilized during training is that of "volunteering." Throughout the period the trainees participate in emulation campaigns. One small group challenges another by volunteering to devote an extra hour to studying. Soon everyone in the camp is studying the extra hour in order not to be "backward" or ungrateful to Chairman Mao for the opportunity to study his great works. The emulation campaigns always serve to make the work load harder and the training more intense and thorough. Another aspect of this is volunteering signatures to petitions, declarations, and other documents which carry with them deep involvement.

A final important technique, which stems from the others, is the isolation of the individual. Doubts and fears create an inner battle which the individual must fight for himself. Thus an end result of the training is the seemingly paradoxical isolation of the individual at the same time that he is losing his individuality to the group.

All of the training techniques and their effectiveness depend in large measure upon the ideology of the training period. The ideology is, of course, Marxism and Mao. The trainees are made aware that their training and future career have been planned and forecast under the superior dialectic of Marx as interpreted by Stalin, Mao, and, since 1953, the collective leadership. The Organization is infallible because it has a monopoly of the correct interpretation of Communist dogma as well as of history.

One of the key ideologists in the cadre training process is the popularizer of Marxism in China, Ai Ssu-ch'i, whose name is not too well known outside of China, but whose relatively simple books have been very effective in explaining Marxism to the Chinese. Ai Ssu-ch'i is the founder and editor of *Hsüeh-hsi (Study)*, the magazine which guides the ideological lives of the cadres and is one of the leading journals in China today.[25]

Ai Ssu-chi's contributions to "thought changing" and to the popularization of Marxism for the Chinese masses have been neatly summarized by Walter Gourlay:

"Philosophy," wrote Ai, "consists not only of the ability to speak pretty words, it must also be able to lead us to activity." The correct

philosophy is therefore the one which enables us to engage in constructive activity. Since there is only one correct philosophy, it follows
that there can be no constructive activity unless one accepts this philosophy. It is worth noting that this line of reasoning leads directly to
the conclusion that the Communist party, which alone possesses the
correct philosophy, is alone capable of engaging in the correct activity,
and that those who do not accept the party's philosophy are, *ipso
facto,* engaged in incorrect activity.

Since constructive activity is socially desirable, it follows that acceptance of Communist philosophy becomes an ethical question. Here,
in embryo form, is the concept later used in the hsüeh-hsi movement,
that acceptance of Marxist theories would lead to greater happiness in
one's personal life.[26]

The key doctrines of Marxism necessary for understanding its role
in China are contained in the series of required readings for cadres
which Ai has helped to interpret. These originally included *The
Communist Manifesto, Socialism—Utopian and Scientific, Imperialism—the Highest Stage of Capitalism, Foundations of
Leninism, The History of Social Development,* Leontiev's *Political
Economy,* and *The History of the Communist Party of the Soviet
Union (Bolshevik).*[27] The list is constantly being added to and
revised.

Stalinist Marxism then is the major ingredient of the themes
which are stressed during the training period. Ai Ssu-ch'i maintains
that the rank and file of the people do not have to be concerned
with subtleties of Communist ideology—they can leave these
for the bigwigs of the party. He maintains that the bulk of the
population need to know but three basic theories in order to adopt
the correct mental attitudes, namely: 1) labor created the world,
2) class struggle, and 3) the Marxist theory of the state.[28] These
three theories are indeed the background for the training.

The first theme stressed in the revolutionary schools is the unimportance of the individual. By himself he is nothing. He amounts
to something only when he is united in spirit with the masses and
expresses himself through mass action. Many projects are designed

to demonstrate to the trainee in the course of camp life that as an individual he is powerless, that only as part of an organization whose discipline he accepts does he come to have strength. Another theme linked to this is the power and force of the Organization—that is, the state led by the party. This is stressed both positively and negatively. Positively the trainee is made acutely aware how effective and efficient the Organization is. An abstraction, and intangible, it yet has immediate meaning for everyone in the camp. *The Organization* orders this and plans that. Negatively the Organization places limits upon the actions and ambitions of the trainees, who soon learn to conform.

A third theme stressed is old versus new. All of the vocabulary and indoctrination are set up to make a clear distinction between the two. The past life of the students is dark, feudal, corrupt, degenerate, etc.; everything about the party and the country under the party's rule is bright, progressive, cooperative, democratic, and moral. Of course patriotism, a fourth theme, is brought in. Nationalistic overtones can be discovered in all the speeches. The coupling of the ideology of the party with the party's rule of the land makes it possible to regard any negative attitude as treason. The training itself is viewed as a method for reviving the spirit of the ancestral land and setting it in motion along the right path after centuries of "feudal betrayal." The theme of service to country makes the training much more palatable to some of the most cynical of the revolutionary students.

The power of the Chinese Communist party and its sweeping victory over China make the fifth theme—inevitability—easy for the trainee to accept. The cadres in charge of the camp insist that there is no sense in holding back; the party will win in any task it undertakes, whether it concerns an individual, a group, or an external enemy. Trainees are told to confess their reactionary thoughts in self-criticism sessions, for the party will inevitably find them out.

Of course, the theme of class consciousness and class struggle is an essential ingredient of the ideological training. Every trainee is expected to have examined closely his own and his associates' class backgrounds. He is expected to develop the habit of assessing the class status of everyone he encounters. Since in Marxian theory all history is the history of class struggle and the trainee is to represent the side of the final victor in this long historical process, he is expected to be able to distinguish between friend and enemy, to know whom to hate and whom to love. There is no middle ground, and clear lines must be drawn in dealing with others. Trainees must express hate and contempt for the enemies of the Organization, who are their enemies. They must love Mao and their comrades. The more enthusiastic the extremes of hate and love, the clearer the class consciousness. Neutralism thus becomes a contemptible position. An important part of cadre training involves explaining whom to hate and for what reasons and whom to love and for what reasons. Each trainee must by the end of his course be able to identify friends and enemies and to explain his reasons in proper terminology.

From class struggle the theme of "steeling" naturally follows. In order to hasten the inevitable victory the trainees must "steel" themselves so as to be able to fight their class and national enemies without showing such bourgeois emotions as pity and sympathy. They must steel themselves in order to be able to participate in struggle meetings and to denounce and execute others. Steeling involves the ability to dispense with conscience. Sentiments, emotions, esthetics, love—all must be subordinated to the battle conducted by the Organization. Even romance is consigned to the dated values of the "old society." Liu Shaw-tong reports that one of the trainees was told:

"Our dealings with female lovers are exactly the same as our dealings with any other comrade, with the exception of the sex act. Our lovers are first comrades, then lovers. Any extra emotions or private affections are really subversive, because then the temptation to place the Revolution on a secondary level of importance becomes too great to be resisted. It is undisciplinary to forsake the concept of the classes even for a moment, and we must always strengthen the propertyless-class standpoint, cultivate the correct working attitude, and nourish our good antiliberal ways. The correct view of love must ever conform to a positive thought standard and the proper political recognition that the Organization comes first in all matters." [29]

With this background in mind, let us turn to the actual training process itself. As pointed out above, the amount of time involved, of course, varies from camp to camp and also depends upon the character of the trainees and the purposes for which they are being trained. Those who are marked as potential high-level cadres train longer hours and for a longer period. The training for those whose major work will be in metropolitan and more sophisticated centers is longer. Actually a course is continuous, the stages blending into each other, but for the purposes of analysis the cadre training at the revolutionary colleges divides conveniently into five stages.

The first stage is physical control, which begins the minute the trainees have been recruited. Major methods for recruiting trainees, both male and female, are calling for volunteers from regular educational institutions, recommendations from party members who have observed the candidates in their home atmosphere, and local pressure exerted through unemployment agencies, etc.

Immediately after shipment to training schools, cadre candidates become aware that there is no retreat. At least one case of punishment for attempted escape is brought to the attention of the class before the end of the first week. Physical restriction is imposed "voluntarily" at the suggestion of the hidden party members who are planted among the trainees and who agitate for enthusiastic volunteering of services so that the training will be more effective. Trainees are immediately divided into the small groups, led by a training activist assigned to them as soon as they are formed.

This period of physical control lasts about two months. During this time the trainees are allotted all sorts of physical tasks, often of a demeaning nature, connected with the housekeeping of the camp. Long hours of physical exercise combined with propaganda are designed to show the trainee the meaning of the tasks of proletariat and peasants at first hand, so that he can appreciate why the revolution is being carried on for the people who do and who understand this type of work. Grandiose physical labor projects demonstrate the importance of group effort for real achievement. The parallel is drawn between camp problems and the national problems which the cadres will face.

During this period of physical exhaustion, training themes are designed to instill a maximum of disillusionment in the mind of the trainee. He is disillusioned with his past; he is disillusioned with his training. Disillusionment with the training allows respect for the whole procedure to be built up gradually; respect for former social values is never revived.

Although physical tasks constitute at least two-thirds of the load during this stage, the other third is regarded as far more important. It is during this time that the pattern for the next stage is established. The small groups meet once a day for at least two hours for purposes of "study." Initial study is devoted to analysis of each trainee's background, his ideas, his family, past friends, ideals, and so on. This gives the leader and the secretly planted cadre opportunity to become intimately acquainted with each member of their group and to note weak spots for later exploitation. Criticism and self-criticism play an important role; there is competition to determine which recruit can be most successful in uncovering the mistakes of his past. Initial criticisms come as a shock to many who find their parents and deep personal values attacked as "feudal," "reactionary," "selfish," etc. The one who can pry deeply into the background of his fellows is quickly marked as a good prospect. Even during this initial stage some of these are withdrawn to be assigned to a more specialized and intensive program which lasts almost a year with six working days from 5:00 A.M. to 11:30 P.M.

Although the lives and backgrounds of the trainees constitute the main subject matter of this first stage, much attention is given to camp behavior. Each is expected to observe and criticize the conduct of his associates. If he cannot find items for criticism— such as relaxing on a work detail or showing too little enthusiasm —he in turn is criticized for not showing sufficient concern for the members of his group who are presumably anxious for his aid.

During this stage there are one or two large group meetings each week, devoted either to a long lecture in Communist theory or to confessions. Here specially selected trainees bare their past sins as examples for the several hundred in the audience. They know that they dare not hold anything back from the assembled throng, for their small group has already heard the full confession.

Food and accommodations are especially poor in this stage. Trainees are told they must come to appreciate the position of the "propertyless classes" in order to understand the necessary violence of the class struggle.

The main achievement of this first stage from the point of view of the party is teaching the value of mutual spying. All must be convinced that the new society rewards those who feel concern for the "ideological lives" of their associates. Pointing out errors of one's fellows is the type of duty required everywhere in the "people's state." Sometime during the initial stage of training the individual becomes aware that he can have no secrets. His life and his thoughts are to be public property. If, for example, he is morose or worried, he knows that the fact will be brought out in his group and he will be obliged to state the reason.

After about two months of physical control, the camp authorities decide that the time has arrived for the second stage of training: intense indoctrination. Although entrance into this stage may be gradual, it is usually marked by an important change in the day-to-day routine. The physical work is cut to a minimum, and the number of small and large group meetings is more than doubled. In most cases the small groups now meet three times a day. Physical accommodations and meals are improved. This indicates to the trainees that in return for their diligence and enthusiasm they are being rewarded as they will be when they take their role of active leaders in the new society. The following is the schedule of a typical training day:

5:00 A.M.	Reveille
5:30 A.M.	Camp duties and work
8:00 A.M.	Small group meetings to discuss the morning's work experience
9:00 A.M.	Breakfast
9:30 A.M.	Large group meeting—four lectures per week
12:30 P.M.	Lunch
1:00 P.M.	Study period—lecture notes and preparation of afternoon discussion
2:30 P.M.	Small group discussion
5:30 P.M.	Supper
7:00 P.M.	Small group discussion
9:30 P.M.	Taps

Such a schedule six and sometimes seven days a week guarantees utter mental and physical fatigue at the end of each day. The major subject matter at this stage is basic Marxist theory and its application in China. In general, trainees find themselves memorizing quantities of terms and long passages which have little meaning for them. The discussion groups apply the theoretical material to concrete situations, but this is a process which at first seems to have little meaning. Comprehension comes later. Camp authorities encourage wall newspapers in which members write accounts of their progress and give their "correct" views.

The group struggle meetings, both large and small, are now devoted to writing autobiographies and diaries. The autobiography is an account of each trainee's ideological development. It helps him come to the conviction that all that has gone before was evil, and to decide that peace of mind can come only through wholeheartedly throwing in his lot with the Organization. Each confession or conclusion becomes group property, and eventually the accumulated weight of the confessions already extracted shows the futility of trying to hold back any doubts or thoughts. The meetings become more intense. Having given up so much of his own privacy, each feels justified in making the others in his group do the same. The day-to-day diary serves as a link between the struggle meetings and the sessions devoted to Communist ideology. If a trainee feels sleepy during a lecture, he dare not fail to mention it in his diary, or he will be caught by one of his comrades who wishes to "aid him" to be a more valuable asset to the new society.

During this period the intense strain becomes obvious to all, yet there is no escape. Tension mounts within discussion sessions; tempers are short in living quarters; social competition is keen in all activities. In camp details, for example, the piecework method is used and emulation campaigns are launched.

This is the period in the training when most of the reclassification takes place. Those trainees who have shown themselves to be vigorous and enthusiastic and have abandoned any reservations are sent along for advanced training. Those who are obviously too upset to be valuable members of the Organization are sent elsewhere to undergo longer periods of training through physical labor. Many are never heard of again.

A major subject during the intense period of indoctrination is "current events." Here the regular themes of enemy-friend and inevitable victory are carried over into the national and international political scenes. The dichotomy makes possible a simple portrayal of the complexities of international life. The "democratic camp" led by the Soviet Union versus the "imperialist camp" led by the United States is the chief theme. The student begins to see parallels in the analysis of his own life and problems, those of his country, and those of the world. Eventually he projects onto the world scene the unbeatable "Organization" and its telling victory over every small barrier he erected. His experience confirms for him the validity of the claim that victory on the world scale is inevitable.

The other important part of the period of intense indoctrination is the field trips. The small groups go into the surrounding country under supervision and observe "concrete situations." Back at camp they discuss what they have seen, methods for coping with the problems they uncover, and possibilities for work by the Organization, attempting to apply the theory they have learned. In many cases field experience includes participation in violence against enemies of the state. The trainees are reminded that they will have to compensate for their youth and inexperience by firmness and vigor against the old class enemies, whose ideas are so entrenched they can never be reformed.

At some point, usually after about six months of training, each trainee passes through an emotional crisis. This is the third stage in the process. It may come after participation in a field trip execution or prior to reading a confession before the large group. Or it may come without apparent reason after about three months of the intense indoctrination and high tension. The crisis usually starts with hysteria and sobbing at night, which go on during the small group meeting the next day and are immediately discussed. One former trainee interviewed in Hong Kong in 1952 claims, though probably with some exaggeration, that in his camp almost one-fifth of the trainees went out of control and their minds broke down completely when the crisis was reached. Some ended up babbling maniacs. These were usually taken from the camp immediately.

The crisis usually comes at about the same time for all the members of a small group. Apparently the breakdown of one of the members launches a chain reaction. A few descriptions of the crisis have been published, but the party's methods for handling the situation and what is involved are still not clear.[30] In some cases, of course, it is much more violent than in others. The cynics and those with a sense of humor seem to survive best; those with strong emotions or deep religious or other convictions frequently break first.

Apparently each recruit reaches a stage when his consistent denunciation of his whole past life and value patterns weighs heavily on his conscience. Strong doubts are created by the atmosphere and methods of the camp. He must decide whether to give up his past individuality completely or attempt to retain it by deceiving his fellow group members and the staff. Usually all doubts are resolved, and the trainee gives himself enthusiastically to every task posed by the Organization. Most refugees indicate that after the crisis has been passed the trainees act as if a great weight has been lifted from their shoulders.

The crisis period is also associated with what the Chinese Communists call "tail-cutting." The "tails" are ties with the old society such as family, friends, old values, and so forth. Following the crisis trainees are able to put an end to all these old associations and values. One refugee tells how a trainee who had successfully passed the crisis stage refused to see his mother when she came to camp, because he knew she would try to win him back with tears.[31] Tears are considered a product of the old society. The good cadre does not give way to such sentimentality.

After the crisis the students of the revolutionary schools are ready for the next stage: final convincing. Life now becomes easier. By this time the trainee is ready to turn wholeheartedly to the doctrine which he has been learning and to the routine of the camp. All former associations and values have melted away or been successfully dismissed from mind. In a search for something solid to grasp he begins to discover the applicability of the Communist terminology.

Up to the period of crisis, most of the Communist jargon was relatively meaningless. It was just a new language to be memorized, played with, and rearranged in patterns. Now he begins to find that it does have some pertinence to his problem. He sees why it was necessary to eliminate his former "bourgeois" social values and cut his ties with the old society. He comes to understand language of violence because his own experiences and crisis have been violent. In place of his feeling of guilt he is now fired with the conviction that he must publicize his newly found security and help others find peace of mind through service in the Organization.

At this period in the training the staff launches many campaigns among the trainees and uses them in the countryside to help with national drives currently in progress. This sort of activity gives body to the doctrine expounded in Mao's *On Practice,* which all have studied. The convert fills with a new dedication the void left in his life following the crisis. He seizes upon every word of Communist gospel and learns to apply it to his past, which he now has a vested interest in denouncing. He tries to make himself one of the camp models for emulation.

It takes at least another four months of intense work to consolidate the hold on the now willing mind. Some rewards are given for enthusiasm and in appreciation of the conversion of the trainee. Discussions are now channeled into facing problems which will confront the graduates. They are told of the difficult tasks which will have to be undertaken; for example, that their work may involve living and working with the peasants in order to bring them into the planned economy of the new people's democracy. At this time most of the trainees are willing to volunteer for any assignment which may be proposed. All are impressed with the fact that the success of the Organization depends upon their applying to the groups into which they move the same type of training that they have received. But the experience of most of the students has been so intense, so dramatic, and so vital that they now feel the only hope for them and for their society lies in turning to the Organization.

The final stage in the process is assignment. This depends upon the current demands and drives of the regime. At least one-fourth of the graduates are scheduled for further schooling. Others are assigned to different sections of the society as activists, propagandists, party leaders, or planted students. In all cases the first few months of work are carefully supervised, and the process of small group criticism and self-criticism continues throughout active party life.

By the use of these brain-washed cadres, the Chinese Communists carry the general techniques learned in the cadre schools into the whole of the society. Practically all the Chinese population has been or is being organized into small discussion groups led by trained cadres. These discussion groups usually meet three times a week and are organized from people with similar backgrounds and professions. Thus college professors have their small groups, as do the maintenance employees on college campuses. The process of ideological spying and assistance from the group in problems of conformity continues.

The following excerpt from a statement of a grade school teacher indicates how basic to the whole process of controlling the country the techniques of the cadre training can be, and how they are carried over into the mass arena:

During these present studies I came to realize all these defects and got ready to reveal my mentality right to the bottom, but then I became doubtful again and thought nobody would notice if I hid my errors. Wouldn't I be losing a lot of face by telling everything? Once revealed it could not be taken back again. How ridiculous it would look among the whole school, so many people, that I, a person who has received higher education, could still be so backward! Then I thought that if I let this opportunity pass uselessly, I would not be able to receive further assistance. Just when I was undecided like this, the director of our school saw the outline of my speech (in which I had put down my ideological life) and dispelled my doubts and made me reveal myself courageously in front of my comrades.

After having revealed all my ideological problems, I felt very much lighter. The comrades gave me very valuable suggestions and confirmed me in my resolution to reform myself. I came to realize that the problems were not a question of superficial mistakes, but were a question of maintaining a petty bourgeois standpoint. Without a resolution to change my standpoint and to gain the proletarian standpoint, I cannot attain to the glory of being a people's teacher.[32]

The methods of mutual spying and the attitudes engendered in cadre training have no limits. They penetrate into the innermost privacy of the home and family. In the China of Mao Tsetung every action is political. The 1 March 1952 issue of *New*

China Women, for example, carried two accounts of how women had prevailed upon their husbands and fathers to make public confessions of past bourgeois sins. One woman writes:

When the San-fan * Movement was first launched, I thought that it had nothing much to do with us women, but after I heard the report concerning the significance of the movement and the role of us women in it, I changed my view. I thought of the corrupt acts of my husband Chen Yu-ming, a technician of a certain municipal warehouse, and felt ashamed of them. I felt that I should motivate him to make a confession and to start anew with a clean slate. . . . he was hesitant about making a confession. I sensed his caution, and reasoned with him . . . saying that if he would sincerely repent, the government would be lenient with him. . . . Finally he promised that he would make a confession to his organization on the morrow.

Another woman describes her methods for making her father confess his past sins and concludes:

Father is a happy man after making a clean breast of his problems. He now heads the San-fan study group of his trade association. The government has saved my father and I have done what is beneficial both to the country and the people.[33]

It must not be assumed, however, that psychological mass coercion or the cadre training has met with uniform success. Although in many cases a permanent change has been made in the lives of the trainees, many of them re-evaluate their training after they have had time for reflection following assignment. Some become disillusioned as they see that the Organization operates for its own self-perpetuation rather than for the happiness of the masses. Others are disappointed to find that power has corrupted many of the old cadres who are seemingly above the process of criticism and self-criticism.[34] The individualism of the Chinese peasant represents a hurdle which the party has yet to overcome. The marked shift away from the persuasion of the flush of victory period to increasing emphasis on the compulsion of the police state

* The 3-anti Movement discussed in Chapter 4.

indicates that the brain-washing process is still far from being completely effective.

Nevertheless, working through the political structure of present-day China, psychological mass coercion has achieved results which justify studying it as a new dimension of political power. In the first place, wherever it has been imposed in the Communist orbit, including China, the outside world has been denied access to the people. The system of mutual spying and the organization of every aspect of life make penetration of the printed word from outside or the existence of organized groups devoted to a democratic way of life practically impossible. Underground resistance is effectively checked. Passive resistance seems the only hope for undermining Communist power.

Secondly, psychological mass coercion makes possible as never before the mobilizing of great numbers of people. Its successful imposition through time promises to change all the values of the society and raise a new generation for whom the subtler shadings of human life are obscured by extremes of hate and love. Throughout the Chinese press today runs the theme that mercy and compassion are concepts of the old society which can have no place in the class struggle.

Finally, psychological mass coercion working through the five-fold chain of command in China has produced a rigid pattern of conformity and unity. The country today is a drab prison for the mind, which discourages any hopes of Chinese originality finding a way out. For maintaining the conformity the mass media of communication are most important. Every word published bears out the indoctrination of the training and works for uniformity. Warfare and the class struggle are the themes of all literature dealing with any act of the government. The Chinese people are being uniformly conditioned to think in terms of violence. For example, here is how *People's China* describes the movement to teach the masses the difficult Chinese written language with its thousands of characters: "The 'shock attack' on the characters is carried out with the same spirit and determination, leadership and organizational discipline as if it were a military operation in the style of the People's Liberation Army. To the workers and peasants, learning means fighting the enemy of ignorance—an enemy that has cost them untold suffering in the past. 'If we can capture an enemy who can run,' said one worker student, 'why can't we catch a character which has no legs?' " [35]

Psychological mass coercion is bringing about the dehumanization of Chinese civilization. In China it is perhaps more thorough than Stalin's attack on the human qualities of the Russians. According to Raja Hutheesing, Nehru's brother-in-law, who was a visitor with an Indian "cultural delegation":

. . . New China is dogmatic, harsh and cruel.

I saw this cruelty in the nursery school at Shanghai run by Mme. Sun Yat-sen. There were more than two hundred children between the ages of three to seven. . . . The children put on a show for the guests. In the show, they marched as the People's Liberation Army, their toy guns pointed at "American" planes above. They learned to hate and kill. . . . There was no love for parents or family, and these little children sorely missed it. They clung to the visitors and wanted to be fondled and kissed. Some had tears in their eyes as they were picked up and patted. I knew then what cruelty meant.

. . . There are no friendly faces in New China. . . . now the faces are set and grim. A friend described the crying of Chinese children under the New Democracy as shrieks of anger.[36]

4. THE ROLE OF THE DRIVE

The editor of the *Times of India,* Frank Moraes, observed following his trip to Communist China, "In India, as in other democratic countries, the government passes a law when it wants something done. In China it starts a movement." [1] Indeed, the whole history of the first five years of Communist China might be written in terms of the great mass movements or drives carried on under the direction of the regime. The drive (*yün-tung,* also translated "campaign" and "movement"), like cadre training, is a method of consolidating control by the party Central Committee in order to facilitate the ruling of this vast land in an all-pervasive manner. The drive provides an opportunity for setting tasks as well as taking stock.

Actually almost every major task in China today is carried out in the form of a movement. Some of these movements are brief; for example, the special celebration of Sino-Soviet Friendship Month from 7 November to 6 December 1952. Others, such as the campaign against bureaucratism, are carried on all the time but in different forms. The drive may be focused on just one segment of the population, like the 1952 5-anti Movement, which had private businessmen as its target, or it may be directed toward the whole population, as the Hate America Drive has been. It may be designed to bring about action such as raising money, or to influence thinking, as was the Ideological Reform Movement, carried on among the intellectuals. In any case, these drives follow on, blend into, or overlap one another in such a way as to provide a steady supply of projects and maintain a state of tension for the Chinese people, who are kept in an almost perpetual condition of mass hypnosis. [2]

Certain drives have far outclassed all the others in intensity and

scope of application. Some of these will never be forgotten by
Chinese living today even if they are forced to endure hundreds
more of these Communist mass movements. These large drives
follow what appears to be a well-established and regular pattern.
They are usually started in an outlying area. Most of the big
nationwide drives during the first three years were first tested in
the Northeast (Manchuria) before being applied nationally.[3] The
Northeast is considered an "old liberated area," and because of
geography and the existence of an almost independent regional
government it constituted relatively good testing ground. Other
areas, however, were also used, even during the early period, to
trigger various campaigns.

The usual method is for a model case to be uncovered by a local
or provincial paper. For example, a series of stories and an editorial in the *New China Daily* in Chungking started the nationwide
Campaign against Chaos in the Schools during the summer of
1951.[4] The case is then taken up either by a major government
figure such as Mao himself or by the official party organ, the
People's Daily (or both). This constitutes a call for a nationwide
campaign. Immediately all the mass media of communication go
into action, and the mass support organizations join in the appeal.
Following the call for a Resist America, Aid Korea Campaign
when the Chinese Communists entered the Korean War, the Publications Administration of the government announced that more
than one billion copies of publications on Resist America, Aid
Korea would be turned out in 1951.[5] Every major organization
in China made this campaign a key task that year.

Meanwhile, every small discussion group throughout the land
is organized to hold struggle meetings, parades, demonstrations,
or to carry out whatever activity is required by the campaign. After
the initial launching of the nationwide campaign the administrative organs of the government usually formalize the movement
with a series of decrees. For example, although the 3-anti 5-anti
Movement was well under way in January 1952, it was not until

11 March that the Government Administration Council issued the formal measures for disposing of such cases of graft and corruption as were uncovered. The drive then continues until a formal halt is called or until the party organs cease to mention it. The tapering off of publicity without calling a formal halt usually indicates that the rulers plan to revive the campaign at some future date.

After a formal halt has been called, there comes a period during which the party leaders appraise their efforts. Those local leaders and organs which have contributed enthusiastically are praised, the mistakes of others are pointed out. The party's ideological journal, *Study,* usually makes the most thoroughgoing appraisal of the contributions and shortcomings of the cadres. Actually the movement may go on for some time after the formal halt. One reason for this is that most of the big drives move geographically from north to south, and frequently the work of the drive is not so expeditiously handled in south China, where the regime's hold on the people is not yet as effective as in other areas.[6] By way of illustration, although the 5-anti Campaign was called off in mid-1952, the termination and appraisal meeting was not held in Canton until 8 February 1953.[7]

A final aspect of the pattern established for the various drives is the constant emphasis on the relationship of each drive to others simultaneously in progress or subsequently initiated. The Communist dialectic is used to show how all are really part of the same process of consolidation of the "people's state power" or of the same class struggle. Thus, the peace campaign is linked with the Korean War, Sino-Soviet Friendship is linked to Hate America, the Campaign for the Implementation of the Marriage Law is linked with Ideological Remolding, and they all are regarded as a part of the over-all goal of moving toward "socialism." The major movements in progress at a particular moment are always linked to the regime's over-all goals, and the leaders indicate that they are quite aware of the importance of these great campaigns for achieving these goals. Thus Mao Tse-tung in his report to the Third Session of the National Committee of the CPPCC on 23 October 1951 stated:

The three great movements which were developed in our country during the past year—resistance to American aggression and aid to Korea, land reform, and suppression of counterrevolutionaries—have achieved great victories. The remaining counterrevolutionaries on the mainland will shortly be in the main eliminated. Land reform will be completed in 1952, except for a few areas where national minorities live. . . . As a result of the victories already achieved by these great movements . . . our country has attained a unification that is unprecedented.[8]

Perhaps full understanding of the important role played by the various drives in Communist China can best be grasped by following one of them through and seeing how the various chains of command swing into action, how the drive itself is also an important part of the explanation of how China is ruled. As an example let us choose a campaign which has received relatively little attention as yet in the outside world: the 1953 Campaign against Bureaucratism, Commandism, and Violation of Laws and Discipline. This drive constitutes a valuable example not alone because it was one of the important major drives but also because it illustrates the extreme emphasis which the top leaders place upon constant self-criticism and the maintenance of discipline within the administration. It also indicates how much we can learn about the problems and shortcomings of the regime through one of these internally focused movements.

During 1953, the year of retrenchment, as a part of taking up slack, enlisting the support of the people where possible, and striving toward efficiency, the Communist authorities decided to launch this all-out campaign against their chronic problems. "Commandism" is defined as the blind use of compulsion on the masses, and it is viewed as a manifestation of "bureaucratism." Mao pointed out that the latter consisted of failure to "get down to the masses" by cadres who were "satisfied with sitting in their offices, writing out decisions and issuing directives." The campaign was designed to enable the regime to check up on the functioning of various local officials and carry on where the former 3-anti Campaign of 1952 (anti-corruption, anti-waste, and anti-bureaucratism) had left off. The sequence of events indicated from the beginning that the strategy had been well planned by the party leaders.

The way was prepared by the publication in the *People's Daily* of 23 January 1953 of materials on the case of Huang Yi-feng, a high-ranking Communist cadre in the East China Regional Administration in Shanghai. He had suppressed criticism in the Department of Communications, of which he was the director, and had exhibited the worst of "bureaucratic tendencies" by retaliating against those who had dared to criticize him. Huang was eventually relieved of his posts and expelled from the party, and his name became a by-word in all propaganda in the drive which followed. The printing of the details of this case in the organ of the Central Committee of the Communist party was followed on 7 February by a speech in which Mao Tse-tung called for a campaign against bureaucratism.[9] Mao's speech, before no less important a body than the National Committee of the CPPCC, was timed to coincide with a report by An Tzu-wen, party organization specialist, calling for a nationwide struggle against these three worst sins within the administration and party.[10]

Thus both party and government organs were prepared for the new drive. The army was for the most part to escape participation, because it was still deeply engaged in the Korean War. But An Tzu-wen gave notice that the mass organizations were to participate and that the press should not only publicize the campaign with fanfare but also check up on its own work. The general strategy for the campaign he laid out as follows:

During 1953, we shall first start such tasks as dealing with letters from the people, inspection of work, education of universal cadres, and further development of criticism and self-criticism through the medium of the press, and coordinating these works with the franchise, and other tasks, in order to expose thoroughly bureaucratism, commandism and breaching of laws and discipline, and develop a fierce struggle against them.[11]

The *People's Daily* then began the mass campaign with its editorial of 11 February in which it said that

Only by strengthening supervision and carrying out check-up from top to bottom and by coordinating criticism, suggestions, prosecution and denunciation, can all kinds of undesirable elements and bad things be discovered and stamped out in time. This is the only way to deprive bureaucratic elements guilty of commandism and who disregard the suffering of the masses of any opportunity to hide within our organizations.[12]

Two days later another editorial declared:

in order to wage a serious struggle against bureaucratism among the leading organs and leading cadres, it is very necessary to commence the struggle among the leading organs and leading cadres in the Central People's Government, administrative regions, provinces, administrative districts and *hsien*. It is necessary because occurrence and growth of commandism and breaching of law and discipline among primary organizations and basic-level cadres are inseparable from bureaucratism on the part of leading organs and leading cadres. . . .

In the course of this struggle, the leading organs and leading cadres should make a special point of strengthening the work of the party disciplinary committees and people's supervision committees. First of all, they should start with examination and disposal of letters from the people and the unfolding of criticism from below in the press. They should select serious cases of bureaucratism and breaching of law and discipline from among the denunciations, particularly cases of bureaucratism where suppression of criticism has been committed, and proceed with serious disposal of such cases and publish results of the disposal in newspapers, in order to arouse the serious attention of the cadres, to encourage the masses to denounce boldly, and to develop criticism and self-criticism, particularly criticism from below. Further, it is necessary for the party and government departments to dispose of letters from the people through people's representative conferences in order to develop criticism from below on a broader basis. Just as stated by Comrade Malenkov in his report at the Nineteenth Congress of the CPSU, "Only when anyone who puts forward healthy criticism is sure of support from our organizations and sure of genuine elimination of the defects pointed out by him can criticism from below be developed and expanded." Popular criticism from below is the door to opposition against bureaucratism and newspapers are the key to the door.[13]

The campaign was under way. The formal government organs followed up the call by organizing inspection teams to tour the country and check up on the work of their subordinate offices. Practically every major ministry of the Government Administration Council was involved. By the middle of March more than one hundred inspection teams were touring the country, and their findings were being reported in the press.[14] The ministers and vice-ministers themselves were included as members of the teams. Some of the reports published indicated the depth and intensity of party power in relatively nonpolitical posts and the nature of the terror involved. For example, in its inspection of its subordinate branches the People's Bank found two bank managers who had had an innocent cadre imprisoned for one year and seven months on trumped-up charges, with the result that he was nearly sentenced to death. Another bank manager in Hunan province "set up a tribunal without authority and flogged and tortured over fifteen cadres." In reporting this the vice-manager of the People's Bank stated: "The branch of the People's Bank in Hunan province paid no attention to such bad men doing such evil things for a long period, and the Head Office knew nothing about such cases. This showed that because of bureaucratism the phenomenon of violating law and discipline has been intolerably developed." [15]

By the end of March the Ministry of Foreign Trade announced that it had concluded its anti-bureaucratism movement in its top-level offices. Some of the discoveries announced by Li Che-jen, vice-minister of foreign trade, hardly bear out the glowing reports on China's foreign trade management in the materials released for consumption abroad. Li pointed out that

The China Import-Export Company has found out that several kinds of supplies purchased in May 1951 have not been sold even now, thereby incurring a loss of over ¥210 billion in payment for storage, interest, and depreciation. In 1952, owing to the overstocking, the China Animal Products Company incurred a loss of ¥123 billion in payment for interest alone. . . . The China Industrial Chemicals Import Company has found out that in March 1952 the rubber-vulcanizing materials ordered by the East China Department of Industry were incorrectly allocated to the Northeast Regional Company, and the dyestuffs ordered by the Ministry of Textile Industry were incorrectly allocated to the China Supplies Company, thereby directly influencing the supplies for production organs and wasting much freightage. . . . A letter from the people was held up for seven months. It was a letter from a merchant . . . requesting assistance in the export of fresh eggs. Arriving in the Ministry of Commerce, the letter passed through nine units, gave birth to 16 documents, which altogether were handled by 400 people, yet no reply has till now been made.[16]

Such revelations might well leave some doubts in the minds of the Chinese audience as to whether bureaucracy, inefficiency, and oppression were evils of the old society alone! Further, if such irregularities were uncovered at the highest levels, where presumably the most capable party cadres were in power, it is not difficult to understand Mao's insistence that the campaign "reach right to the bottom," where some of the cadres were somewhat less capable. Interestingly enough, in few of the revelations coming from the top government ministries was there any suggestion that anything more than bureaucratism was involved. It is difficult to avoid speculating that the more subtle methods of passive resistance may have come into the picture.

By April 1953 the various regional administrations had organized teams for checkup work; and the drive began to make itself felt at most of the lower levels of government. Checkup teams began to report back on their work and draw up reports at the regional level before the end of the month.[17]

An Tzu-wen had of course indicated that the party was to be included in the drive, and party cadres were quickly alerted to the necessity for carrying out thorough criticism and self-criticism at the meetings from branch level on up. Top leaders of the regional party bureaus met within two or three weeks after Mao's call and drew up plans for mobilizing all party members to conduct the drive with utmost intensity. For example, top members of the Northeast Bureau met in Mukden on 21 February, and on 26 February the Northwest Bureau of the party called a meeting in Sian to carry on the process of criticism and self-criticism.[18]

The mass support organizations were expected to contribute their part to the drive too. In fact, some of them such as the All China Federation of Trade Unions were called upon to attack the three new evils in their own structure as well as contribute to cleaning up the formal administration of the government.[19] The Youth League especially was called upon to launch a drive to clear out the evils of bureaucratism, commandism, and violation of laws and discipline. The 1 February 1953 issue of *China Youth* argued: "As masters of the country, the youth of China should manifest a high degree of political initiative and responsibility and should show concern for various kinds of work involving national interests." But, it pointed out: "As everybody knows, mistakes and defects at present exist at various levels of Youth League committees and basic-level organizations as well as league cadres at various places." [20]

One month later the same Youth League journal began to reveal some of the results of investigations. Once again it became evident that some of the statistics coming out of Communist China on such matters as periodical circulation might not be entirely meaningful. In an article entitled "Practice of Commandism toward the Masses is a Criminal Act" *China Youth* stated:

The working style of commandism expresses itself in two forms. In one, cadres in undertaking any work resort to compulsion, cheating, and arbitrary allocation of tasks. In another, they pretend to be democratic and hold meetings with the masses but they reject public opinion and restrict free expression of views. They have everything fixed up beforehand and want the masses to do what they are told.

Here it is possible to sense the frustration which must seize some of the younger cadres who are given impossible assignments in the various drives and competitions and must bear the brunt of criticism from both directions, since the top authorities will never admit to using or advising methods of compulsion. Yet the background of the cadre training sponsored by the same top authorities shows through in some of the examples of commandism which follow in the article. About one group of cadres it states:

They had to resort to forcible methods in order to fulfill their tasks. Consequently, they forced the aged to subscribe to the *China Youth* journal and the illiterate to buy *Hsüeh-hsi* (*Study*). They even compelled a factory with only 161 workers to subscribe to 443 copies of newspapers. In order to push the sale of stamps, they popularized the insurance value of registered mail. This made the public believe that the post office was just a "merchandizing house run by bureaucrats." [21]

By the time government, party, and mass support organizations began to get down to the local level, it was apparent that there was ample reason for the drive. A total power structure such as the Mao regime is bound to feel the corrupting influence of its power. The *People's Daily* began to publish such accounts as the following about some lower level cadres who

manipulated the village government and the people's militia, cruelly oppressed the masses, fined the farmers at will, raped women and even young girls at the point of a bayonet, and beat up, insulted, detained, put under surveillance and assaulted the families of servicemen and workers. As a result, seventeen families were detained and put under control, two persons were forced to commit suicide, and four persons died of injuries resulting from beatings. [22]

Even the mass media of communication and especially the newspapers were subjected to extensive criticism and investigation during the campaign. Correspondents had been instructed to write letters to the newspapers denouncing examples of bureaucratism, commandism, and violation of laws and discipline which they observed in their factories and other basic units. It was found, however, that some of the editors were informing the superiors of these worker-reporters and suppressing the criticism, and that revenge was being taken. The *People's Daily* came out with a strong editorial entitled "Fight the Barbarous Acts of Suppression of Criticism." [23] A few weeks later it was again urging other papers to conduct the publicity on the anti-bureaucratism struggle in a correct manner.[24]

At the lowest level in the society, where the various chains of command are linked together by the security police, the party propagandists, the small discussion groups, and other methods of intimate personal control, the drive was felt much later. The cabinet called a Second National Supervision Work Conference from 19 to 26 February, during which the tasks were laid out for the people's supervision correspondents; but it was mid-July before the *People's Daily* could report that "In the struggle against bureaucratism, the people's supervision correspondents have developed a positive function in mobilizing the masses, exposing problems, and assisting leaders in pushing through the struggle." [25] Thus although the campaign was designed primarily to tighten up discipline and efficiency within the growing party and government organizations, it eventually made its impression throughout the society.

After reaching the local level, this 1953 Drive against Bureaucratism, Commandism, and Violation of Laws and Discipline was allowed to blend into the other campaigns of the year and pass quietly out of existence. It was, however, mentioned at all the meetings of the mass organizations held during the summer and fall and was reflected in the tightening up of their constitutions. The manner in which it ended indicated that some version of the same thing would be revived soon in order to keep control over the cadres and improve their efficiency. This campaign was not so spectacular as some earlier ones, yet it was important because one of its major targets was the party itself. Mao and his colleagues on the Central Committee have never relaxed their concern for party discipline, unity, and reform; and although such drives as this do bring to light the inefficiencies, brutality, and other shortcomings of the regime, they also indicate one of the major strengths of the Communist party of China today: its determination and ability to keep its resilience.

Other drives not focused primarily on the Communist party organs have demonstrated another strength of the regime in China today: its ability to penetrate and consolidate its control over every aspect of life. A few major movements have been spectacularly successful in this respect. Probably the most important of these is the Land Reform Movement, which was already in full swing when the Mao regime was inaugurated.[26] The Land Reform program of the Chinese Communists was designed to extend their control to the village level. Prior to this, the effective control of Chinese governments had stopped at the county level. This drive had, of course, many other purposes, and one of the most important of these was an attack upon the whole system of traditional Chinese society. The program had been essentially completed by the time of the third anniversary of the regime, when Liao Lu-yen reported that a rural population of more than 420,000,000 had been affected.[27] By 4 February 1953 Chou En-lai indicated that the Agrarian Reform had reached 450,000,000 people and only a few minority areas had yet to be dealt with.[28]

The whole of the Land Reform was marked by violence. Land was confiscated and redistributed and "landlords" killed. By the time the movement had passed its height in 1951, the year of violence, a stable element in the Chinese society—the village gentry—had been eliminated and the Communist cadres had moved into the resulting political vacuum. Mao's injunctions had been followed in the setting up of the people's militia and the people's tribunals. The violence and mob hysteria proved a valuable means for the regime to warn the peasants of the consequences of resistance. At the same time, the redistribution of the land evoked temporary enthusiasm and support from many within the rural segment of the population. Those peasants who would be most likely to lead in resisting the Communist attempt to transform the whole of Chinese society into the Stalinist pattern were effectively eliminated. Those who were not executed by the people's tribunals called together by the cadres were subjected to "control and reform," with forced labor sentences up to five years and sometimes more.[29]

Another important Communist drive, which up to the present has probably been as unsuccessful from the point of view of Mao and his colleagues as the Land Reform Movement was successful, has been the campaign to implement the Marriage Law.[30] This was the first important law passed by the Mao regime—it even preceded the formal passage of the Agrarian Reform Law—and constituted an attempt to revise the basis of Chinese society by an attack on the family system. It was advanced, to be sure, in the name of eliminating the feudal status of women and promoting their economic and political equality and free marriage.[31] Yet the Peking government allowed no doubts to remain in the minds of the cadres as to what was to be involved. By the end of 1950 certain irregularities were beginning to appear in the application of the law, and the following year the Government Administration Council launched an investigation into its implementation. The instruction read in part:

marriage reform is not merely the task of the Courts and the local women's associations; every organization must cooperate in it. There is work to be done in schools, youth organizations, workers' unions, and cultural organizations. The people must be brought together at public accusation meetings to expose those who have failed to live up to the standard of the new law. There must be huge mass trials. The marriage reform is to go hand in hand with land reform. The same technique is to be used for both.[32]

The ostensible purposes of the law were to eliminate the Chinese custom of arranged marriages, do away with concubinage and prostitution, make divorce easy, and raise women's status. It was also an appeal for the support of China's women and an attempt to make them give first loyalty to the party and state rather than the family. The cadres were urged to take up the task of marriage reform with enthusiasm and vigor. The result was a wave of divorces, suicides, and violent deaths. The *People's Daily* reported the sharp rise in divorce rates: 186,000 for 1950, 409,000 for 1951, and 396,000 for the first six months of 1952; the people on the mainland began calling the Marriage Law the "Divorce Law." [33] Meanwhile the parallel development of violent deaths required explanation. At first they were blamed on the feudal attitude and marriage system. For example, the New China News Agency released the following story: "In Minchu village in the 13th district of Shaotung county, Hunan, a woman activist Ch'en Tuan-hsiu was killed by her husband with a spear because she dared to pledge to overfulfill the task of accumulating 1000 catties of night soil [human excrement used as fertilizer] at the village production conference." [34] However, on 11 October 1951 the *People's Daily* apologized for not having previously reported abuses by the Communist cadres themselves. Some had maintained the former attitude of male superiority and others had taken advantage of their power positions. It also appeared that China's women were not as anxious for equality and marriage reform as their Communist leaders. One capable analyst summarizes as follows the results of the investigations into the implementation of the law by lower ranking cadres:

What these little despots in the villages did with the women was so low and contemptible that it shocked the not-oversensitive leaders in Peking. Party members ordered husbands and wives to separate, and if any resisted, they were sent to jail as counterrevolutionists, or were handed over to the village militia, which soon became notorious for its licentious behavior. . . . Those not themselves philanderers indulged in the nation-wide sport of "fornicator catching," confessions being extracted from women by physical torture. No wonder suicides and violent deaths amongst women showed a rapid increase.

Enquiry into family sex-life, abhorrent anywhere, is intolerable in

China, where tradition of domestic and sexual reserve is extremely strong. Thus the publicly organized mob trials of those who resisted the new Law, created not only terror, but also resentment amongst the people. In the city of Chungking, 40,000 people were obliged to attend one such meeting.[35]

In February 1953 the Communists stated that the Marriage Reform was of quite a different character from the Land Reform and that no violence should be involved.[36] They decided to launch another all-out campaign, this time with the stress on education. The campaign was to last through the month of March, but Stalin's death on 5 March disrupted the schedule, and it was May before the New China News Agency could state that the publicity campaign had been "basically concluded." [37] However, the summary report on the "Movement for the Thorough Implementation of the Marriage Law," delivered to the Government Administration Council on 11 November 1953 by Liu Ching-fan, indicated that only 15 per cent of China's population have accepted the Communist version of what marriage and the family should be.[38] Family and social ethics have not yet succumbed entirely to Marxism. Because their doctrine allows no social grouping to take precedence over the party's wishes, it can be anticipated that the Communist leaders will persist in their attempt to implement the Marriage Law.

A third major drive has been the Resist America, Aid Korea Campaign, which got under way on 4 November 1950, as soon as it was officially known that Chinese Communist troops were fighting in Korea. This campaign illustrates one of the methods used by the regime to draw off any dissatisfactions and at the same time stir up Chinese nationalism. As has so frequently happened in world history, the creation of an external threat served as an excuse for strengthening not only military power but internal state power as well. The Mao regime has used this campaign to great advantage on many scores.

The Resist America, Aid Korea Movement became one of the major methods for dissolving all ties with the West. It was used to accentuate traditional Chinese xenophobia and thus served as an excuse for expelling foreigners from the Middle Kingdom, eliminating United States and Western influences from the educational system, and attacking Christianity. The whole movement was tied to a doctrinaire acceptance of Lenin's theory of imperialism. The main effort was to picture the United States as the deadly enemy of the whole world, because by Lenin's definition the United States is the chief imperialist power in the world today.[39] Since 1951 this campaign, which has been kept alive by such fuel as germ warfare charges, has been a main concern of the Chinese people. Continuation of the Resist America, Aid Korea Campaign was the first of the three major tasks which Chou En-lai listed for 1953 in his address to the Fourth Session of the National Committee of the CPPCC 4 February 1953.[40]

Some indication of the extent to which this drive was used to embrace many other mass movements can be gathered from a report on the achievements of the first three years of the Communist regime published in the *Current Affairs Handbook* in September 1952:

In the course of the various movements the whole nation has gradually enhanced its political consciousness and, particularly in the course of the Resist America, Aid Korea Campaign, has greatly elevated its patriotism and internationalism. The whole nation has basically cleared away the worship U.S., fear U.S., and pro-U.S. ideas and established national self-respect. This great change in ideology helped to bring about a new appearance in all phases of work in our country. For example, during the patriotic donation campaign in 1951 the whole nation donated over ¥5,500,000,000, equivalent to 3,710 fighter planes, which greatly increased the national defense strength of our country. In the course of the patriotic health campaign in 1952, over 10,000,000 tons of garbage were disposed of, over 30,000,000 rats were captured, 1,600,000 catties and 18,500,000,000,000 heads of mosquitoes and flies were wiped out, in addition to numerous ditches repaired and numerous cesspools and ponds filled up, according to incomplete returns compiled in June. This highly elevated the health level of our country and greatly reduced the incidence of epidemics. In other movements such as demonstrations, the signature campaign in support of world peace, and the signature campaign against remilitarization of Japan, over half the population of China took part. Also very broad was the public which signed patriotic compacts. All this shows how strong is the determination of the people to construct the fatherland, safeguard peace, and resist aggression.[41]

This report indicates that in addition to their already high taxes in 1951 the Chinese people were "persuaded" to contribute the equivalent of U.S. $230,000,000. The Soviets received U.S. $61,770 per fighter plane. It is impossible to resist adding a story current in Hong Kong during the height of the clean-up campaign referred to. In one Chinese city every male head of a household was required to bring a dead rat to the clean-up headquarters every day. Those failing to do so were subject to fine or imprisonment. The never-ending stream of rats turned in led authorities to investigate. They found several enterprising Chinese in business breeding and selling rats to harassed heads of households. Thus does Chinese capitalism flourish in spite of Mao!

A fourth major drive conducted by the Communist authorities was the Campaign against Counterrevolutionaries. This drive developed in December 1950, after some of the leaders had denounced the deviationist policy of "boundless magnanimity" which had been developing. On 20 February 1951 the government issued its Provisions for the Suppression of Counterrevolutionaries. During the next ten months public mass executions took place everywhere throughout China. A conservative estimate would be that at least one million people were silenced forever during this campaign. Other estimates run much higher.[42] The scope of this movement was indicated in a report by Minister of Public Security Lo Jui-ching on 27 September 1952 which claimed that counterrevolutionaries had been practically eliminated:

This campaign was an unprecedented one whether in terms of the effect of elimination of counterrevolutionaries, in terms of the scope and extent of mobilization of the masses or in terms of the soundness

of the development of the campaign, and won a great victory in stamp-
ing out large numbers of counterrevolutionaries. . . . the broad
masses of the people of town and country have set up millions of security organizations and are now applying their rich experience gained
in the campaign for suppression of counterrevolutionaries to the protection of production and construction.[43]

If the Land Reform and the behavior of the cadres in connection with the Implementation of the Marriage Law had not
succeeded in striking terror in the hearts of the Chinese people,
this campaign did. Refugees poured into Hong Kong during 1951
with stories of brutality, torture, and murder.[44] Although the
Campaign for the Suppression of Counterrevolutionaries carried
over into 1952, like the Land Reform most of its violent aspects
were felt in 1951. Minister Lo warned that the campaign would
continue as long as counterrevolutionaries existed, which meant
of course so long as there was opposition to the regime. It was
not surprising, therefore, that toward the end of 1953 and during
the first months of 1954 there was an increasing number of reports in the press on the suppression of counterrevolutionaries.
The *People's Daily* of 9 March 1954 reported the elimination of
more than forty members of the Green Lance Society in Canton,
a secret society which like all former Chinese secret societies is
by definition accused of being counterrevolutionary.

Yet another drive of major proportions was the Ideological
Remolding or Thought Reform Movement, which although aimed
at only a small segment of the population, the intellectuals, was
considered by the regime to be vital to its whole program. The
movement was launched with a five-hour speech by Chou En-lai
on 29 September 1951. Soon afterward some of the foremost
scholars and writers of China were writing public confessions
and criticizing each other in public view. The movement brought
about the regimentation of the intellectuals and persuaded them
of the wisdom of severing connections with the "bourgeois ideologies" of the West. It was, in effect, "a thorough-going attempt to
implement party control in the field of the creative arts rather

than a mere attempt on the part of the regime to force 'liberal writers' into step." [45]

Since the party is viewed as possessing a monopoly of all that is good and progressive, Chinese intellectuals were called upon to denounce former affiliations with the non-Communist world. A special attack was made against Hu Shih, former ambassador to the United States; many of his colleagues and friends and even his son were forced to denounce him. Hu stood as a symbol of non-Communist liberalism in modern China, and the Communist leaders (especially Mao, a former student of Hu's) felt called upon to demolish the symbol.[46] Another famous Chinese liberal intellectual, Ch'ien Mu, was also the center of attack. Of course, a major leader in this whole movement was Ai Ssu-ch'i, now professor of Communist ideology. In an article published in *Study* in 1952, when the Ideological Remolding Campaign was in full swing, Ai pointed out that criticism of the "ideology of the bourgeois class" was the basic program of the movement.[47] The campaign was designed to lay the basis for acceptance of the "advanced" Soviet ideology and scholarship and guarantee that no deviationist ideas would be implanted in the heads of the new rulers of China—the youth. Although Ideological Remolding reached its zenith in 1952, the year of regimentation, it has continued and will continue. Independent thought, as the Soviet masters have found out, is hard to eliminate. Mao and his colleagues follow the Soviet example, however, and maintain the effort. For instance, in July 1953 more than 6,500 professors and staff members of universities and colleges in Peking underwent another new course in "thought change" under the direction of Professor Ai, whose works many of them used to characterize as "trash." [48]

A sixth major movement which demonstrated the ability of the Communist regime to consolidate control over every facet of life was the much publicized 3-anti 5-anti Movement.[49] This was really a combination of two drives and was essentially urban in character. The 3-anti Drive (anti-corruption, anti-waste, and anti-bureaucratism) was launched to clean up government and party organs and businesses. The 5-anti Drive (anti-bribery, -tax evasion, -fraud, -stealing state property, and -theft of state economic secrets) was directed against the business and commercial groups in China. Like the Land Reform and many other movements, it started in Manchuria and moved south, lasting officially from October 1951 until 13 June 1952, when the Government Administration Council issued instructions to bring it to a close.

This movement had all the trappings of the other major movements: accusation meetings, confessions, recantations, and people's tribunals. It was designed to remake Chinese industry and commerce in the Communist-approved form and extend state control over them. Inspection teams were organized to examine the books of companies as well as of individual businessmen. Po I-po, minister of finance in 1952, reported that in nine cities alone more than 450,000 industrial and commercial establishments had been investigated and more than 76 per cent of them found guilty of malpractices.[50] As a result of these investigations the Communists were able to gain virtually a complete understanding of the inner workings and trade secrets of the nation's private enterprises.

Old Chinese methods of doing business were brought to trial and found unworthy. Squeeze, carelessness, bribery: all these were judged acts against the state, and their perpetuators were punished. Actually, it was not until 11 March 1952 that the government got around to issuing formal measures for disposal of the cases uncovered. Under these, merchants fared worse than industrialists, but all were subjected to fines, imprisonment, and sometimes death. During the intense part of the drive business ground to a halt, many urban leaders fled China, and there was a wave of suicides.[51]

The real motives of the regime for launching the 3-anti 5-anti Movement have been appraised in various ways, but there seems to be general agreement on several items. The movement was probably most significant in terms of its economic implications. As a result of the denunciations by employees and children of its victims, the Communists collected large sums in various forms; e.g. between one-half and one billion United States dollars in back taxes; hoarded cash, gold, and other valuables; refunds from businessmen; and fines. This enabled them to meet the increased budgetary demands of the Korean War.[52] Further, in the economic sphere the 3-anti 5-anti Movement enabled the Mao regime to extend state control and absorption of private enterprise in China. Businessmen were made acutely aware that the New Democracy period was practically over and were prepared for the "use, restrict, and transform" policy enunciated toward them in the New Constitution made public in June 1954. Some indication of the transformation wrought during the campaign was revealed in Finance Minister Po I-po's announcement that state enterprise would produce 67.3 per cent of the nation's industrial goods in 1952 whereas it had accounted for only 43.8 per cent in 1949.[53] Most aspects of the private sector of the Chinese economy which were not taken over by the government were brought under strict state control. Government and party also used the occasion to purge undesirable members and assert discipline. That they were not entirely successful is borne out by the new 3-anti Campaign launched during 1953, which has been described above in detail.

One result of the 3-anti 5-anti Movement which was of serious consequence to the Communist government in Peking was the alienation of most of the "overseas Chinese" in Southeast Asia. The movement brought about a rapid shift of sentiment away from Peking and toward the Nationalist government on Taiwan among these people, whose primary interests are commercial. The campaigns of 1952, the year of regimentation, such as the Ideological Remolding, the 3-anti 5-anti, and Resist America, Aid Korea, demonstrated the determination of the Communist authorities not to allow any segment of the population to remain outside the iron control of the state.

Two other major movements which should be listed are that to publicize the "general line of the state for the period of transition to socialism," and the drive to complete the elections and census.

Numerous other campaigns connected with the launching of the
first five-year plan and the study of the New Constitution were
linked to the publicity on the "general line of the state." [54] Because heavy industry was viewed as one of the chief goals of the
period of transition, it was to be expected that the Chinese rulers
would call on their people for increased sacrifices. By September
1953 a Production Increase and Austerity Movement was in full
swing; and in connection with this 1954 brought harsh rationing
measures.[55] The combination census-elections, completed in mid-
1954, which were described in Chapter 2, had all the characteristics of some of the earlier intense drives.

To select eight major drives from among the many carried
on by the government is, to be sure, somewhat arbitrary. The first
five years of Communist rule in China were filled with drives.
There were for example the Drive for National Construction
launched by Chou En-lai in a speech of 24 December 1953; the
Drive for Judicial Reform and the Sanitation Campaign, both
1952; the Peace Appeal, announced 28 April 1950; and numerous
party reforms including a very important Campaign for Party
Unity launched by Liu Shao-ch'i on 4 February 1954.

It is not surprising, therefore, that in mid-1953 the rulers in
Peking were forced to call for what in effect was a drive against
too many drives! This was the 5-too-many Movement of June and
July 1953, directed against too many assigned tasks, too many
meetings, too many organizations, too many concurrently held
posts, and too many official documents and forms. Actually the
regime used this short campaign to blame some of the lower ranking cadres for pressures put on the people for which it was itself
solely responsible. The drive against the 5-too-many was also
used to combat the favorite enemy, bureaucratism. Investigations
into the management of the Tientsin railway station, for example,
revealed:

There are as many as 27 kinds of organizations in the railway station. . . . Li T'ing-p'u, assistant stationmaster in charge of personnel, holds 9 posts concurrently. . . . There are 58 kinds of meet-

ings according to their nature, such as regular meetings, irregular
meetings, extension meetings, discussion-of-living-conditions meetings, informal discussion meetings, joint representative meetings,
"Come and meet people" meetings, reports compilation meetings,
work planning meetings, change of shift meetings, etc. For instance,
Li Yu-lin, chief of the East Freight Yard, attended altogether 17
meetings in the 5 days from May 11 to May 15. The meetings take
up an average of about 7 hours each day.[56]

Despite such obvious disadvantages, however, the drives which
the Communists have used to carry on their rule in China have
aided the regime in many ways. In the first place, they have served
to integrate the whole apparatus of state compulsion. All the
various chains of command and the means that link them have
been kept in constant operation. Thus the regime has been able to
flex its muscles, so to speak, and keep in trim. Again, these mass
campaigns have tended to discourage the growth of opposition to
the Communist rule. The sheer weight of the bandwagon tactics
is enough to convince the psychologically isolated Chinese that
his resistance would be useless when so many people are supporting the efforts of the leaders.

Third, the drives have proved one of the most effective methods
for meeting the current needs and demands of the state. Financial,
military, production, and social programs of seemingly impossible
dimensions have been laid out and apparently met by means of
mass mobilization and mass hypnotism. The regime has been able
to extract even greater sacrifices from the people it rules. Fourth,
the drives have enabled the party to approach achievement of its
goals of perfecting unity, conformity, discipline, power, and intellectual monism. And fifth, they have served and continue to serve
as the most effective means both of weeding out any individuals
or groups within the population who are opposed or indifferent
and of turning up promising new activists. The drive has enabled
Mao and his colleagues to follow the injunction laid down by
Saint-Just and the Jacobins in the French Revolution: "You must
punish not only the traitors but also those who are indifferent;

you must punish all who are passive in the Republic and do nothing for it." [57]

A sixth function of the drives has been to maintain a high emotional pitch among the people. To this the violence of the class struggle, the many people's tribunals, the mass parades, mass demonstrations, and violent language of the controlled media of communication have all contributed. And finally, these great movements with their tactics of mass participation have served to undermine personal human values and extend the regime's control into every reach of human activity.

On the other hand, the mass drives of the Chinese Communists have served to expose the nature of the regime to the outside world. While self-criticism and self-examination keep the huge bureaucracy active and alert, many of the facts brought to light during the drives bear out Lord Acton's warning of the corruption inherent in absolute power.

5. ECONOMIC CONTROL

Given the basic thesis of economic determinism which underlies all Marxist theory, and the very doctrinaire approach of the Chinese Communists, it is understandable that they view economic matters as of vital interest and economic control as the key to all control. It is impossible in a general treatment of the Chinese Communist regime to cover all the major aspects of economic development, but the measures for economic control taken by Mao and his colleagues are such an important part of their program of Sovietization for China that some attempt at summary, however inadequate, must be made.[1]

On 24 December 1952 Chou En-lai announced to the meeting of the National Committee of the CPPCC that China's first five-year plan for economic construction would start in 1953. This did not come as a surprise to the Chinese people, who had been prepared all through 1952 for the start of "capital construction." In fact on 9 January of that year, the cabinet's Committee on Financial and Economic Affairs had promulgated Provisional Measures for Capital Construction Work, in which it carefully defined just what capital construction was and the methods to be followed for drawing up plans. Included under the term "capital construction" were such items as building schools and geological exploration as well as the projects usually considered as falling within that field.[2] In August 1952 six new economic ministries were formed and on 15 November a State Planning Commission was named, with Kao Kang, the head of the Manchurian Region, as chairman. This made the governmental setup for launching the plan correspond almost exactly to that of the Soviet Union. Meanwhile, throughout the year various plants in China had been making out plans to be "fulfilled and overfulfilled."

The basis for the plan was faithful to the teachings of Stalin throughout, although on the surface there seemed to be one slight difference. At the time the Soviet Union started its first five-year plan, the NEP period was over, whereas in China the mixed economy of the New Democracy still existed at least in name. Nevertheless the Chinese plan for "building socialism in one country" bore the trademark "Made in the USSR." Chinese cadres were told to study and restudy Stalin's theories as the indispensable means for the successful building of a "socialist society." [3]

Though still in a stage of mixed economy, the Chinese were starting their five-year plan far ahead of where the Soviets had started in at least one respect: they had the advantage of the Soviet theories and techniques for subordination of all aspects of life to the great economic plan. Within the framework developed by Stalin economics and politics have been fused as never before. Economic resistance, economic failure or inefficiency, or even economic apathy became treason and sabotage of the worst sort because theoretically the coming of socialism depends upon the realization of the economic plan. Stalin had written down the formulae for the plan in his *History of the Communist Party of the Soviet Union* (*Bolshevik*), so that the Chinese comrades at least had a guidebook for what they term the "advanced experience of the Soviet Union."

In announcing the goals of the first five-year plan the Government Council stated its determination to concentrate on the "development of heavy industry for the establishment of the foundations of the industrialization of the state and the modernization of national defenses." [4] The Chinese were doctrinaire not only in accepting the Soviet accent on heavy industry at the expense of the sectors of the economy which might contribute to greater long-range industrialization but also in justifying it on the basis of Stalin's thesis of capitalist encirclement and the resultant need for military power and on the basis of Lenin's interpretation of imperialism. One Chinese Communist writer put it as follows:

Obviously a country not economically independent cannot be considered an industrialized country. Stalin had given the example of India, where there was general industrial development, and which could not be considered industrialized. India has many industrial undertakings, industry continues to be developed there, but only enterprises which do not produce capital goods, and such capital goods as are needed are imported from Britain. Accordingly India's industry is totally subservient to Britain's industry. Some people see the fact that industry has been developed to a definite stage in India and consider that country to be industrialized. But India's economy is still colonial economy and not industrialized economy.[5]

Thus from the outset the Chinese Communists announced their intention to substitute guns for food and to move toward industrial self-sufficiency in a plan which necessitated complete state control of the economy.

In addition to coping with some major problems of the Chinese economy and society itself, the Peking authorities had to face at least three major tasks before a five-year plan of such proportions could be launched: 1) they had to restore the war-shattered economy, 2) they had to ensure that the state could control the economy, and 3) they had to develop technical proficiency in the economics of the plan. These were sizable tasks to be handled in the short space of three years. To what extent were they in fact accomplished?

According to the statements released by the Chinese Communist authorities on the third anniversary of their regime, 1 October 1952, restoration of an economy which had suffered through twenty-five years of international and civil war was complete.[6] Yet a closer examination of some of the higher levels of self-criticism reveals that the restoration actually lagged far behind the expectations of the regime. The industrial targets for 1952 on the whole were not met; and one of the few exceptions, coal production, was still far below the prewar peak. In fact, such essential items as electricity and steel were among those which failed to reach the "restoration goals" for that year.[7] But, as Rostow points out, Mao and his colleagues already showed aptitude for the Soviet and satellite practice of camouflaging failures and exaggerating achievements.[8]

It was to be expected, however, that the Communist government would succeed to a fairly high degree in restoring the Chinese economy to the prewar levels. In many cases this would not involve much in the way of capital outlay, but mainly the organizing and putting back into operation of already existing capital equipment. From 1946 to 1949 the United States had supplied much in the way of economic assistance to China, and most of the items reached the Communists intact with the rapid collapse of Nationalist resistance. The three years from 1950 through 1952 were favorable ones for agriculture, which in most respects had been unaffected by the civil war, and further, the Communists possessed an asset which they had succeeded in denying to any other Chinese government for a quarter of a century: internal peace and effective control.

On the other hand, the problems of restoration were not small, and the accomplishments should not be minimized. According to the United Nations Economic Commission for Asia and the Far East, China's industrial production in 1949, when the Communist regime took over, was only 56 per cent of the prewar peak, and food production was about 75–80 per cent.[9] In addition in Manchuria, the center for Chinese heavy industry, the Soviet had destroyed or carried off over half of the industrial capital equipment.[10] The problems in the field of transportation were truly great. Railroad bridges were out, and only about 60 per cent of China's railways were operative when the Communists took over; highways had not been maintained and they too had suffered great war damage. Yet by the end of 1952 the rulers claimed to have restored all railroads and built some 1,400 kilometers of new lines, and they stated that highway transport had passed prewar figures.[11] On the other hand the *People's Daily* warned:

It is undeniable that the foundation of our communications and transportation is very weak. The steamships and motorcars left by Old China are not many and moreover are in bad shape in most cases; only after overhaul have these sole means of modern transportation been enabled to play their due part and, together with the numerous civilian means of transportation—mule carts, junks, etc.—basically to meet the needs during the rehabilitation stage of the national economy.[12]

Another aspect of China's economy which demanded immediate attention was the repair and restoration of flood control and irrigation projects which had been neglected for over a decade. The dikes of the major rivers had been broken by both sides in the civil war, and most of China's millennia-old water control works were of a sort that demanded constant attention. Here the Communists were at a distinct advantage, for this work, like that of repairing transportation lines, depended for the most part on mass unskilled labor, and their methods for mobilizing mass labor forces were indeed adequate. By the end of 1952 the Ministry of Water Conservancy under Fu Tso-yi, former Nationalist commander in Peking, claimed to have done earthwork the equivalent of digging twenty-three Suez canals.[13]

Restoring the economy also involved conquering China's problem of inflation, which had caused the Nationalist government so much difficulty in its last years on the mainland. This meant in part restoring confidence in the government's fiscal machinery. The goal was achieved by March 1950; by then open inflation had disappeared, only to be replaced by hidden inflation under a system of economic controls. Because of rationing and rigid controls prices of essential commodities remained stable and were not even drastically affected by the Korean War. In August 1952 the government boasted that the 1951 budget had been balanced, but critical economists looking behind the figures and the claims pointed out that the Peking government had simply ignored all debts and obligations, maintained an inconvertible currency, depended upon barter agreements for international exchange, and relied on fines, forced loans, and "voluntary" donations—not to mention strict rationing and price controls. The national economy was not quite as healthy as the claims of the spokesmen made it appear.[14] In agriculture the Communists claimed to have passed the prewar peak in both food and industrial crops; the fact that they began exporting great quantities of foodstuffs in 1952 seems to bear out their claim.

For both internal and external consumption the claims of the Communist regime in the field of recovery and progress toward modern industrialization were given much attention by the government's propaganda organization. Frank Moraes and Raja Hutheesing, two Indian visitors to China, tell for example of a Mukden Industrial Exhibition in 1952 where generators, turbines, heavy lathes, and many other items were displayed as the products. of the "new China." They were both amazed until they saw exact duplicates with Soviet markings and realized that most of the products they saw had had their markings changed for propaganda purposes. The Chinese were not producing such products after all. Both visitors give a rather sobering appraisal of the recovery as it appeared to objective observers.[15]

Nevertheless, the Mao regime had probably achieved a fair degree of economic recovery by the time it was ready to launch its five-year plan, in spite of the fact that this was rather a test of organization and control of existing resources than of ability to industrialize or to carry out capital construction.

With regard to this control problem, which constitutes the second major task faced by the Communist regime, success had been far greater. The mass movements carried out through the first three years had helped to lay the foundation for nationalizing the economy. To be sure, further measures for state economic control were developed after the start of the plan, but by the end of 1952 the basis for a state monopoly of the economy had been laid. In its formal estimate of the extent of nationalization the regime gave the following figures:

by October 1952 nationalization extended to about 80 per cent of the heavy industry, and 40 per cent of the light industry; the government operated all of the railways and about 60 per cent of the steamships plying the home waters; it controlled 90 per cent of all loans and deposits through the People's Bank; finally State trading companies were responsible for about 90 per cent of imports and exports, for about half of the wholesale trade and for about 30 per cent of the retail trade.[16]

Under the New Democracy there were to be five sectors in the economy: individual handicrafts and farms, private capitalist enterprise, cooperatives, combination public-private companies, and nationalized enterprises. These forms continue, but the private sector of the economy is rapidly being overwhelmed and absorbed into state enterprises. Where private business continues to exist it is so closely controlled that the word "private" is little more than a euphemism.

The Peking government has used an imposing array of methods to bring the private sector of the economy under control. One of the most effective has been the very high rate of taxation. Then there were the many fines and penalties in connection with the 5-anti Movement. The government monopoly over many raw materials and services needed by the private sector of the economy is utilized for control by discriminatory pricing. Since most of the private economy produces consumers' goods it is to a large extent at the mercy of the government wholesalers who can force the sale of goods at government-fixed prices. All of the private industrial and commercial firms operate under a series of strict regulations which provide for sentences up to death in case of breach. For example, numerous reports came out of Shanghai in the spring of 1954 of merchants and manufacturers receiving the death sentence for "swindling" the state. "Swindling" in some cases consisted of overcharging the state or mistakes in figures.[17] Private entrepreneurs can be arrested for not fulfilling contracts with the state or for not merging with other private businesses at the state order. One set of regulations for private firms published in the *Southern Daily* in Canton stated that "production and purchase orders must be accepted, cannot be refused or transferred." Such orders may come from "state-owned undertakings, government offices, military units, schools or social organizations," and any private factory failing to fulfill these obligations is subject to criminal law.[18]

Most of these measures are designed to drive private industry and commerce so far into the red that the only resort is to apply for a loan from the State Bank. This is readily given and the result is the establishment of the "joint private-public enterprises." Under the regulations governing these enterprises 75 per cent of the profits go to the state, and dividends, bonuses, and managerial salary must come out of the other 25 per cent.[19] Such joint concerns represent one further step along the road to nationalization. The state insists on this method rather than allowing the firms to go out of business, for it makes possible the retention of private managerial skills. Thus bankruptcy like silence is a privilege which businessmen no longer enjoy!

These many restrictions on the nonstate enterprises under the New Democracy were supplemented after the start of the five-year plan by inauguration of the Federation of Industry and Commerce. When this held its first congress, from 23 October until 12 November 1953, it had over 1,913 local chapters.[20] The purpose of the organization is to apply propaganda pressure to get the remaining private enterprises to join "warmly and enthusiastically" in their own socialist transformation. It was at this congress that Li Wei-han, vice-chairman of the administration's Committee on Financial and Economic Affairs, announced the principles for private enterprise which were later embodied in the New Constitution of 1954: "use, restrict, and transform." [21]

As a result of the earlier restrictions and the policy announced by Li, private businessmen began to appreciate that the end of even their nominal private status was at hand, and many of them sought during the winter of 1953–54 to dispose of what remaining liquid assets they had by purchasing consumers' goods such as clothing, wristwatches, fountain pens, jewels, and even fancy coffins for themselves, or by paying bonuses to their employees. The state was forced to step in as prices on noncontrolled items soared. While the official organs stated that the rise in prices represented the increased purchasing power of the people, the cadres began lecturing to these men about their "anti-state attitude." In

Chungking, for example, over 30,000 had to go through an in-doctrination course designed to convince them that they should maintain their enterprises with full capital assets until time for the socialist economy to take over.[22]

Other sections of nonstate economy have traditionally been the rural handicrafts and village stores. Here too the Communists have taken over. The rural industrial cooperatives developed during World War II are now Communist monopolies. Government stores, called cooperatives, now monopolize rural commerce, and the handicrafts have been subject to organization into producers' cooperatives. Peking admitted in 1953 that 37 per cent of the government's rural stores were running in the red and warned them that they would still have to supply 60–80 per cent of the peasants' demands by tapping local industry during the plan.[23]

Thus in nationalization and state control of economy, the Peking regime of 1953 was really much closer to the Soviet starting point than would appear on the surface. From the viewpoint of mobilizing the essential parts of the economy for the first five-year plan, the techniques of control made any distinction between state and private enterprise more nominal than real. By the end of 1952 most of the economic aspects which made the New Democracy of Mao appear something distinctive seemed to have disappeared in fact if not in name.

With regard to its third major task, that of learning the techniques of the plan, Mao's regime showed an early aptitude, but later events demonstrated that success was not as great here as in the restoration and control of the economy. Factories and other state enterprises were preparing their plans before the government was a year old, and even before the Communists came to power their leaders in Manchuria had shown a marked ability to speak in terms of percentages rather than concrete figures. In Manchuria the Chinese comrades received a background training in Soviet economics from thousands of Russian advisers. The timing of Chou En-lai's visit to Moscow on 17 August 1952, prior to the announcement of the plan, and all of the official government and party statements indicated that the Soviets were not only inspiring but also playing a key role in the course of Chinese economic development. The need for Soviet direction and technicians in all fields was acknowledged, and the large part which the Soviets would play in China's five-year plan was borne out by the change of ambassadors to Peking in March 1953. Kuznetsov, a specialist in economic planning, replaced Panyushkin.[24] (Kuznetsov was replaced later in the year by ideologist Yudin when the problem of explaining the Soviet "collective leadership" principle became more pressing.)

The decision to launch the five-year plan thus involved an important shift in the educational pattern in China. Beginning in 1952 there was a marked tendency for the cadre schools to emphasize training in economics and the techniques of the plan. The whole of the higher educational system of China went through a revamping along Soviet lines and under Soviet direction. Ma Yin-ch'u, president of Peking University, declared that the true goal of higher education henceforth would be "to train advanced technical personnel and principal cadres for national construction." [25] A vital element here has been learning the Russian language, since most of the key textbooks on Communist economic planning are in Russian. "The Soviet-directed five-year plan," one Japanese observer states, ". . . cannot possibly be undertaken without some knowledge of Russian. . . . anyone not able to understand the Russian language cannot play an important part in the forthcoming five-year plan activities." [26]

Yet despite Soviet guidance and assistance the early aptitude and enthusiasm of the Chinese comrades soon faded. The complexities of drawing up an economic plan were greater than the regime had apparently realized. Before the first year of the plan was three-quarters over, the original goals for that year had been reduced twice.[27] The program for training technical personnel proved far from adequate.[28] And although the Chinese had apparently learned such Soviet techniques as hiding military expenditures under the heading of appropriations for the Second Ministry of Machine Building Industry, there were many shortcomings in the budget for the first year of the plan as announced by Po I-po on 17 February 1953.[29] No over-all figures for the whole five years were released in China, and one limited list of percentage figures published by *Pravda* hardly constituted a plan.[30] The first few months' experience indicated that the problems of launching a Soviet-style five-year plan in China involved more than merely completing the tasks of economic reconstruction, ensuring state control, and learning the techniques of the plan.

In attempting to industrialize their country on the Soviet pattern the Chinese are forced to face up to some very grim realities of the present Chinese situation. From the releases of the New China News Agency it is easy to gain the impression that Chinese production has been growing by leaps and bounds and that China is capitalizing at an amazing rate; but most of the figures given are based on estimated 1949 production. Even though Chinese production may have approached the prewar peak by the end of 1952, the situation at the start of the plan presented none too promising a picture.

The most important fact which confronts the regime in this connection is the size of China's population. The Chinese Communists have boasted of this in claiming great-power status; and indeed in "limited" wars such as that in Korea the never-ending ranks of Chinese infantrymen constitute real power. But in the long run China's population problem is the greatest hurdle in any attempt to industrialize the country or raise the standard of living.[31] In spite of this, the Chinese Communists as well as the Soviets are strictly doctrinaire on this subject, maintaining the Marxist position that there is no such thing as overpopulation. According to them, there is only underproduction and underconsumption.

The Peking regime announced the results of the census on 19 June 1954, claiming: "This is the first time in the history of our country where correct population figures have been arrived at as the results of universal investigations." Given the tightness of the Communist control network and their utilization of the census as a method for further political consolidation, it is quite probable that the figures are reliable. They show for the mainland a total of 582,584,839 people.[32] Previous releases had revealed other interesting facts. For example, a survey of fourteen of the special municipalities and five provinces revealed that 64.1 per cent of the population was below the age of twenty-eight.[33] The population of Tientsin has grown from its largest prewar total of 1,800,000 to 2,620,000, of whom more than one-sixth have been born in the last five years. The regime attributes this increase to improved living conditions.[34] These figures indicate the extent to which population pressure can increase in an area like China under conditions of internal political stability and some improvement in medical facilities, and they also suggest that the rapid turnover of a youthful population may assist the Communists in supplanting a former ideology and former values.

The significance of these figures becomes plain when they are compared with China's output of major products, shown in Table I.

TABLE I. ESTIMATED PRODUCTION OF SELECTED COMMODITIES IN MAINLAND CHINA [35]

Product	Unit	Peak	1949	1950	1952
Pig iron	000 metric tons	2,000	210	827	1,589
Crude steel	"	900	144	551	1,215
Rolled steel	"	500	90	259	740
Coal	"	59,000	26,000	35,000	53,000
Crude oil	"	330	125	207	389
Cement	"	2,140	663	1,412	2,311
Paper	"	120	108	101	264
Flour	"	2,450	1,911	1,200	3,087
Sugar	"	410	164	198	328
Cotton yarn	000 bales	2,400	1,728	2,040	2,784
Cotton cloth	000 bolts	41,000	29,930	3,230	56,580
Cigarettes	000,000 sticks [individual cigarettes]	82,000	47,000	54,520	102,500
Electric power	000,000 KWH	6,900	3,600	3,800	5,700
Rice	000 metric tons	48,600		46,900	55,890
Wheat	"	24,000		19,300	22,800
Soybeans	"	10,000		5,890	8,900
Cotton	"	1,115			1,290

For example, China is producing less than 4 lbs. of steel per capita at the start of her five-year plan, whereas the Soviet Union started its first five-year plan with a per capita steel production of more than 64 lbs. Given the size of the country, the relatively low level of industry, and the near-subsistence level of living, the problems involved in industrialization are indeed tremendous. As a starting base for development, the Peking government can obviously count on present industry for only a minor share of the capital goods it needs. Obviously, most of the resources for China's industrialization will have to come from outside her borders through the earnings of foreign trade.

This in turn means that the determining factor in China's ability to industrialize is the preponderant agricultural sector of the economy. Here the importance of the population figure for China is even more plain. According to a report of the State Statistical Bureau, there were 330,980,000 acres of land under cultivation in mainland China in 1952.[36] About one-tenth of this amount was devoted to industrial crops and the other nine-tenths to food crops. In all China, including the wide and relatively sparsely populated grain areas of Manchuria, therefore, there is only 0.57 acre of cultivated land per person and only 0.52 acre of food-producing land per person. In the south of China the figure approaches 0.30 acre of cultivated land per person.[37] The cultivation of the land occupies almost 80 per cent of the population, which by intensive labor methods extracts almost as high a yield per acre as do the farmers of any other country.

That this agricultural sector of the economy must bear the brunt of China's industrialization stems from the fact, as indicated in the 1952 trade statistics, that more than 70 per cent of China's exports are agricultural.[38] China has shifted from a net food-importing country before the war to a food-exporting country under the Communists. For example, she exported 66,000 tons of rice to India in 1951, and the next year continued the export of rice to India and began an annual exchange with Ceylon of 240,000 tons of rice for 50,000 tons of rubber. Again, rice is mentioned as one of the main articles of export to the Soviet Union.[39] Such food exports have been consistently stepped up despite admissions of serious famines in some areas every year and general famine conditions in 1953.

The rulers in Peking have adopted numerous methods for accumulating food for export, and at no time have they indicated that any consideration for famine conditions among their people would deter them from their purpose. At the meeting of the Central Committee of the party 6–10 February 1954 Liu Shao-ch'i announced the establishment of a state food monopoly, which was proclaimed by the government on 1 March. This move nationalized all important agricultural crops including eight nonfood crops, and was an answer to the refusal of the farmers to sell enough of their grain to the state in 1953.[40] Prior to this the Communist authorities had introduced a comprehensive system of food rationing. The people have been forced to accept what is known as "92 rice" and "81 flour," meaning 92 pounds of rice and 81 pounds of flour from every hundred pounds of unhusked grain. Although they were assured that this roughly husked grain is more nutritious, there have been indications in the press that people are not happy over this sacrifice in quality.[41] Refugees and expelled missionaries from Communist China began in 1952 reporting shortages in such items as cooking oil, rice, and even the bean cake needed for fertilizer, and the serious shortage of these essentials was more evident in 1953. "We should realize that short supply of commodities will be a protracted phenomenon in our country," the people were warned, "particularly during the transition period in which the main forces are concentrated on the development of heavy industry. . . . *only after the building of heavy industry can food industry be developed considerably.*" [42] In view of the great dependence on agriculture, this might seem to be putting the cart before the horse.

In the first year of the five-year plan grumbling over the export of much-needed foodstuffs to the Soviet Union was reported by the press. Complaints about lack of meat were countered with the reply that "the supply of frozen pork to brother nations [i.e. members of the Communist bloc] is important as payment for urgently needed industrial machinery." [43] In view of the near-subsistence level of the population it was unlikely that many of the readers of the *People's Daily* would accept the argument advanced for increasing still further the export of foodstuffs:

Looking at a few of China's exports in 1953, we can see that the volume of exports did not constitute a large proportion of the volume of production; thus it is definitely possible to increase our exports. According to statistics, the amount of pork exported in 1953 constituted only 1.52 per cent of the number of pigs reared, and 2.15 per cent of the number slaughtered in the country throughout the year. The quantity of eggs exported constituted approximately 7 per cent of the total output. [44]

The authorities do not often give out such figures as these. They indicate, for example, that at going international market rates the Chinese were earning more than U.S. $50,000,000 annually from the Soviet Union by the export of pork alone.

The prospects for increasing China's food production are not bright. The land already in use includes marginal land with irrigation and terracing up the mountain slopes of the many valleys in south China, where two and sometimes three crops per year are raised. Compared with a frequently quoted estimate of 357,000,000 acres of arable land, the Communist figure of 331,000,000 acres under cultivation indicates that there is little unused land yet to be opened up. [45] The other possibility for increasing food production involves the intensive application of chemical fertilizers in the pattern established by the Japanese. But on this score the prospects are even dimmer. All of mainland China used approximately 350,000 tons of chemical fertilizers in 1952—a little over half the amount applied in the island of Taiwan, which is about $\frac{1}{230}$ the size of China. [46] The Communist figures indicate that only 11 per cent of the total capital investment for 1953 was applied to forestry, agriculture, and water conservation. Obviously no major attempt is being made to increase production of chemical fertilizers.

In view of the serious situation in respect to agriculture and population pressure, some of the other Communist methods of a more or less desperate nature for accumulating capital become more easily understood. The government has pursued a policy of imposing forced saving on the people by numerous devices. They have been "asked" to buy government bonds, in drives which are always, according to the *People's Daily* and other publications, "warmly supported" and "eagerly and enthusiastically oversubscribed." In these drives quotas are always assigned and party activists are employed to guarantee the "enthusiasm" of overfulfillment. Communist self-criticism, for example, revealed the common practice of round-the-clock meetings, not to be broken up until the quota of savings bonds had been bought.[47] With the National Economic Construction Bonds which the Peking regime floated at the end of 1953, quotas were made out for various segments of the population. The quota for private businessmen was two-fifths of the total despite the fact that private business, already overtaxed, provided only 22.36 per cent of the government's tax revenue.[48] Other methods of forced saving have included compulsory deposits in the People's Bank and "voluntary" donations for the various drives of the state. In a way, taxation itself becomes a method of forced saving for the state.[49]

The Peking authorities look to two other major sources for the additional capital needed for industrialization. The first of these is the institution of a more intense labor discipline and regimentation in order to increase the present rate of production.[50] The other is, of course, the "great unselfish and advanced" help of the Soviet "big brother." [51]

In addition Mao and his colleagues have turned to such expedients as the blackmail of overseas Chinese for remittances, seizure of foreign investments and equipment, and fines imposed during the many drives. The latter, however, have proved only temporary, and measures of desperation. The chronic problem of agricultural overpopulation and the comparatively low present state of modernization and industrialization remain the major obstacles in the path of the Chinese Communists' plans.

These are not the only problems of major proportions that the regime faces at the outset of the plan. There is the condition of the transportation network mentioned earlier. Although the Chinese have restored it to prewar status, it is not designed to support an industrialized economy, and transportation over long land distances is still exceedingly expensive despite cheap labor. During the Chinese New Year Holiday (which the Communists now call the "Spring Festival") in 1953, the Shanghai Military Control Committee issued the following notice to the people:

During the Spring Festival large numbers of residents of Shanghai will want to return to their home towns to see their families, relatives, or friends. Though communications have been restored in China, there is still a shortage of transportation facilities, and no large-scale increase can be made at present. With a view to avoiding the jam at a period when production increase and austerity are being implemented, those who can manage not to return to their home towns are being requested to postpone their trip temporarily.[52]

Since residents must always get special passes from the security police before leaving the city, this was tantamount to a polite announcement that no such passes would be issued. In transportation facilities the Chinese economy is far behind that of the Soviet Union when it started its first five-year plan or even at the time of the revolution. Whereas Russia had 36,550 miles of railroads in 1913 and 47,721 in 1928, China's railroads totaled only 15,045 miles at the end of 1953, and almost half of that was in Manchuria.[53]

The educational and technical level of the Chinese populace is another matter of concern for any government planning modern industry. The Chinese language is not ideally suited either for rapid learning or for modern scientific work, and to date no way has been found to shorten the time-consuming work of teaching and learning the Chinese characters. There is an acute shortage of skilled labor in China, and despite the boasts of the regime about the schooling of the workers and cadres and the help of Soviet specialists in "advanced Soviet techniques," the problem is causing serious concern. The *People's Daily,* for example, stated that "among 10,000 workers in the building industry in Anshan, only 1.27 per cent are listed as skilled and the skill of 77 per cent of these is questionable." [54] Anshan is supposedly the main showplace of the most advanced "proletarian experience" in China.

Probably nothing reflects the problem of the educational and technical level of the Chinese population better than the government's very startling revelations with regard to statistical work. In the Soviet system of drawing up the national plan, everything depends upon accurate statistical information about the various sectors of the economy. Before the plan can be drawn up every individual plant must make up estimates of production in line with control figures released by the central government. These in turn must be coordinated by the final over-all plan in such a way that movement of goods equals the capacities of the transportation network and provides efficient mobilization of local resources. Work must be allocated so as to fit in with the capacities of local labor forces, etc.

The Third National Congress on Statistical Work was held in March 1954, and as at the previous two conferences government authorities revealed through their criticism that all Communist statistics, and not alone those given in percentages, are open to grave question. At the start of the plan, some provinces and cities had not even set up statistical offices. Those offices which had been set up by the various ministries had bombarded the lower level cadres with such an assortment of forms that they could not possibly fill them all out. For example, the Office of Hygiene in Peking sent out an 87-column questionnaire on child welfare to local cadres engaged in health work, with such questions as "How does the child play?" and "In what position does he sleep?" In its Health Campaign the government demanded statistics from the cadres on the exact number of flies and mosquitoes killed. The result of all this was a directive by the government in September 1953 requiring the clearing of all forms with the State Statistical Bureau.[55]

The *People's Daily* editorialized on 31 March following the Statistical Congress that the statistical data in China were "far from sufficient" for planning work and that the quality was very low. "Statistical work connected with capital construction is still less adequately attended to than statistical work connected with industrial production, and there is still no adequate guarantee for the correctness of the data compiled to date." Meanwhile throughout the years 1952–54 Communist papers reported that the filing of false statistical reports on production records had become a common phenomenon. The organ of the Youth League called upon its members to "Correct the Undesirable Habit of Filing False Reports." [56] The figures released by the Communist government on China's population in mid-1954 threw into doubt all of their former figures involving ratios of population to resources (they were usually based on a population of 475,000,000); and the use of the year 1949 as a base for stating achievements in production, despite the admission by the regime that statistics for that year were merely estimates, threw doubt upon the statistical ability, not to mention the honesty, of even the top-level members of the Statistical Bureau. Li Fu-ch'un, vice-chairman of the State Planning Commission, told the Statistical Congress in March 1954 that, to be of value to the state, statistical work should 1) collect reliable material, 2) analyze the collected material, and 3) propose solutions for the problems revealed by the statistics. He then pointed out that the first item was not being well attended to.

The editor of the *China News Analysis* concluded a survey of the statistical situation in Communist China by pointing out:

It is disappointing and disturbing to realise that hundreds of millions in China are ruled by men who are prepared to introduce planned economy without having a clear picture of the problems they are facing, and who are now going ahead with a radical readjustment and transformation of the whole economic structure of the nation without the means necessary for forecasting the economic results of their action. The government in Peking seems to be moved by emotional appeals and political motives rather than economic reasons; it is taking a great risk in blindly carrying out its own slogans instead of measuring facts, and taking economic realities into account.[57]

Despite these many long-range and immediate problems, the Chinese Communists have gone inexorably ahead with their plans for industrializing the country after the pattern of Stalin's first five-year plan. The Central Committee of the Chinese Communist party early in 1953 issued a directive for the "Theoretical Education of the Cadres during 1953–1954," which laid down as the basic text chapters 9–12 of Stalin's *History of the Communist Party of the Soviet Union* (*Bolshevik*), and listed for the advanced cadres selected supplementary readings from Stalin, Lenin, and Malenkov.[58] All of these texts were primarily concerned with the problems of industrialization and economic construction in the Soviet Union under the five-year plan. At least in China there were to be no disputes such as Stalin had with Trotsky and Bukharin.

The ostensible reason for the failure of the Communist authorities in Peking to reveal the scope of their five-year plan for 1953–57 has been that they were awaiting its approval by the People's Congress, which was postponed from 1953 to 1954. The following are the major features of the five-year plan as derived from a *Pravda* article and other sources by the United Nations Economic Commission for Asia and the Far East (amounts involved can be calculated by reference to Table I, p. 112 above):

1. Steel production will be 4 times, and rolled steel production 2½ times as great as in 1952. Two large metallurgical plants will be built, one in Tayeh, an iron mining center 50 miles southeast of Hankow, and the other in Paotow in North China near the border of Outer Mongolia.
2. Coal production will increase by 60 per cent over 1952 through the building of new mines and new fuel processing plants.
3. Power output will be doubled through (*a*) expansion of the hydro-electric power plant at Hsiao Fengman on the Sungari River and

of the steam electric plants at Fushun, Harbin, Fushin, and Dairen in the Northeast, and (b) construction of new steam power plants at Taiyuan, Sian, Lanchow, Tayeh and Paotow.

4. Non-ferrous metals. The most important projects seem to be (1) expansion of the existing aluminum production at Fushun in the Northeast, and (2) reconstruction of a tin combine at Kochinu, Yunan [sic] province.

5. Others include (a) construction of a new large oil refinery in Kansu province, (b) building of the first synthetic rubber plant, and (c) building of several new fertilizer and pharmaceutical plants.[59]

A sixth item which can be added is the projected 30 per cent increase in grain output over 1952 revealed by Teng Tzu-hui as the agricultural target for 1957.[60]

The State Budget for 1953 as given by Po I-po was probably a good barometer of the relative amount of intended investment in the various sectors of the economy: [61]

	Per Cent
Industry	46.0
Agriculture, forestry, and water conservancy	11.4
Railways and communications	14.3
Trade and banking	4.3
Unspecified	24.0

Heavy industry and war industry are the "necessary" items of concentration, and emphasis on these is a key item in the theory of the "general line of the state for the period of transition to socialism," which the cadres are called upon to propagandize especially to the peasants.[62] Peasants are shown large propaganda posters and pictures of such things as the constructing of "China's First Automobile Factory" near Mukden on which work began on 15 July 1953 along the lines of "Soviet up-to-date designs." [63]

In another important respect the Chinese first five-year plan follows that of Stalin. The country is divided into regions which concentrate on certain items of production. Manchuria is termed the "base of heavy industry," Central-South China the "home of supplies of fish and rice," etc. The People's Daily of 6 June 1954 reported, for example, that Kwangsi province was to be divided along the lines of the government's policy of economic regionalism, with the southeast reserved for fishing and the rest for agriculture. Those not engaged in fishing in the southeast part of the province were urged to move out.[64]

The Peking regime has hastened to employ all the incentives the Soviet has developed for carrying out the plan. It has its own Stakhanovite movement, a technique which the "big brother" did not invent until the Soviet second five-year plan, and citations for model workers, model peasants, labor heroes, etc. On Christmas Day 1952 the Wusun Factory in Manchuria was the first factory to be awarded the title of "model factory." [65] There are "emulation campaigns" in which workers challenge each other to competition in production, and drives to "volunteer" extra hours to the state for capital construction. Needless to say, there are also all the negative incentives developed by the Soviet: labor discipline, a system of responsibility (introduced in 1954), the enforcing of economic control by the courts, and the threat of slave labor and extinction.[66]

Many observers have interpreted the Soviet destruction and removal of Manchurian industry as a sign of lack of confidence in the future of the Chinese Communists. While this may or may not be so, one thing is certain: in rebuilding Manchuria under China's five-year plan as the industrial heart of China, the Soviet is gearing it entirely to equipment of Russian standards and replacing the Japanese influence in industry in the area. The Soviet impact on the Chinese industrial economy is of dimensions that have not generally been appreciated by students in the West. At the Anshan steel center in Manchuria, a full-time staff of more than three hundred translators is required for the No. 1 plant alone, to translate the various Russian language orders and directions from the Soviet "advisers." [67] Peking stated on 8 October 1953 that "All 85 major industrial plants under construction this year have been designed either in the Soviet Union or with the help of Soviet experts. . . . the essential equipment of completed factories is supplied by the Soviet Union." [68] Until 1 January 1955 joint Sino-Soviet companies carried on the development of Chinese Turkestan, and Communist China's contact with the outside world by airplane was through the joint Sino-Soviet Aviation Company.

But the consequences of launching the plan have not merely been greater subordination to the Soviet Union (discussed in Chapter 11) and subordination of all aspects of life to the dictates of the state. The initial consequences in human terms and in waste have been enormous, although some gains in production were undoubtedly registered. Failures to achieve production goals during the first year of the plan brought about two curtailments of the initial year's goals, and even then only three of thirteen major quotas in seven industries were fulfilled.[69] Coal production dropped in some mines to as little as 10 per cent of former totals in the first months of 1953 as a result of damage to equipment and injury to workers from Soviet-type "shock operations" introduced in mines to meet targets at the end of 1952.[70] The Ministry of Light Industry reported that capital construction tasks were fulfilled by "only 61 per cent in the first half of 1953 (constituting 26.5 per cent of the tasks for the whole year), while the quality of some works was very poor." [71] During this year of retrenchment the report of almost every government ministry disclosed the disruption caused by the implementation of a poorly prepared plan. On 15 April the *People's Daily* reported that the lack of concrete planning had cost the people over 152,000 working days and ¥2,400,000,000 on the new railway lines between 15 January and 15 March, and laid the blame at the door of the Ministry of Railways. Workers were blamed for lack of labor discipline, officials for "adventurism" and irresponsibility, cadres for erroneous concepts, and everyone for bureaucratism; the state's concept of planning was blamed for nothing.

Self-criticism in government and party organs indicated that the forced pace of change from a free economy has caused great losses to the Chinese people. A cotton-packing plant built under Communist direction at Loyang turned out to be useless because too far away from the cotton centers where it was needed.[72] The loss was ¥11,500,000,000. Bureaucracy and corruption caused a heavy loss of funds allocated for a fertilizer plant in Canton which never went into operation.[73] A survey of wholesale centers of the All China Federation of Cooperatives revealed "that because of poor management, conditions are serious in that commodities have become rotten and overstocked." [74] Because of "poor guidance by the cadres in the party's railway bureaus," some 140 tons of rice out of 352 tons being shipped to the Soviet border at Manchouli were spoiled by rain and the remaining rice was in very bad condition.[75] The China Technical Development Company went from Peking to Chahar to purchase alcohol which had originally been imported from Tientsin and had passed through Peking on its way to Chahar.[76] These are but a small sampling of the reports which began to pour in during 1953. The situation was neatly summarized by an inspection report of the First Ministry of Machine Building Industry which listed the following shortcomings: lack of competent engineers, disorganized management, shortage of materials, few skilled workers, unreliable and incomplete plans, and lack of proper guidance at all levels.[77]

The results of the first months of movement from economic reconstruction to capital construction confirmed the gravity of the problems which the Peking regime faced in any attempt to follow the methods for industrialization laid down by Stalin in the documents which the cadres were studying. It was understandable that the leaders should turn to the Soviet for even greater help.

This was, however, a year when the Soviet itself was having difficulties. The result of protracted negotiations carried on in Moscow by Li Fu-ch'un, vice-chairman of the cabinet's Committee on Finance and Economics, was the firing of Po I-po, author of the budget for the first year of the plan, and the sharp reduction to modest figures of the published targets for 1953.

Li reported that as a result of the negotiations the Soviet Union had agreed to build or rebuild by 1959—two years after the end of the first five-year plan—a total of 141 enterprises, including iron and steel plants, nonferrous metal enterprises, automobile and tractor works, hydraulic and thermal power stations, and coal and petroleum enterprises. These projects, which included those already started in the previous three years, involved 91 new and 50 existing enterprises. Some idea of what was involved was provided at the formal ceremony opening three plants at Anshan, Manchuria, on 26 December 1953—a seamless tubing mill, a heavy rolling mill, and a blast furnace. Kao Kang declared at the ceremony that these were "three important projects out of the 141 projects which the Soviet Union is helping China to build or renovate. With the sincere, selfless and highly technical assistance of the Soviet Government, they were successfully built at rapid speed and will shortly play their important role in China's industrial construction." [78]

No official figures on the amount of money involved in this aid were released by either the Soviet or Chinese Communist governments, although one Japanese newspaper printed what it claimed to be a New China News Agency dispatch stating that the aid consisted of one billion roubles (approximately $250,000,000) a year for seven years.[79] What was plain was that in order to pay for Soviet aid the Chinese would have to tighten controls even further.

Thus it was that by mid-1954 major decisions had been made in China with regard to such measures as food rationing, a government food monopoly, increase of food exports, and stepped-up collectivization. All of these measures indicated Peking's recognition that industrialization could not be accomplished by political control and propaganda alone and that the major part of the cost would have to be borne by China's agriculture.

The haphazard course of events in 1953 makes it seem quite probable that no formal plan of the Soviet type had been formulated that year; 1953 can probably be viewed more accurately as a year of experimentation and preparation. By the following year the stated goals of the regime had become much more cautious; the planned rate of industrial production increase had been reduced from the 23 per cent figure for 1953 to 17 per cent for 1954.[80] The budget presented by Teng Hsiao-p'ing for 1954 was admittedly an austerity budget, yet even he, like his predecessor Po I-po, was relieved of his post as minister of finance after its presentation, possibly an indication that economic planning for the second year still left much to be desired.[81] In March 1954 the major financial newspaper in Communist China admitted: "At present planning is in its infancy in our country, and the economic situation is confused; it is difficult, therefore, to draw up estimates expressing the objective phases of coming developments." [82]

Nevertheless, the Chinese Communist government has expressed its firm determination to proceed with its five-year plan along the lines laid down by Stalin in his *Short Course*. This decision marks a drastic break with China's past economy, and its repercussions will be felt in every field of activity. For example, it may be that the need for foodstuffs to export to the Soviet Union and the European satellites in exchange for the industrial capital needed under the plan may prove the additional and decisive factor sparking a drive by Communist China to control the rice-export areas of Southeast Asia. Undoubtedly, given the political and economic control exercised by the regime, and the restoration of China's former productive capacities under conditions of internal peace, the Communist government will be able to channel a relatively high proportion of the gross national product into industrial investment. Rostow estimates that in 1953 approximately 10 per cent or about U.S. $3,000,000,000 constituted investment. But, as he observes, the long-run question "is not whether the Chinese Communist economy will grow at all, but whether the rate of growth will be sufficiently rapid so that forces of the industrial revolution will be in a position to defeat the Malthusian counter-revolution." [83]

Some results of the tightening of Communist economic control in China and the submission of that country to the dictates of a Stalinist five-year plan are already apparent. China has been tied economically to the Soviet Union by patterns which involve the subordination of Chinese interests and which are becoming increasingly hard to change. To one who follows the Peking press closely it is only too apparent that the cost in terms of brutality and human suffering have already been, and will continue to be, vast. In addition, the Communist method involves the economic waste characteristic of bureaucracy, poor allocation of resources, high military expenditures, and the trappings of thought control and the police state.[84]

But the waste and human cost of Peking's economic control can be adequately understood only by examining the fate of the two groups within the population which must eventually bear the brunt of any effort to develop China: the peasants and the urban workers. To their life under the rule of Mao Tse-tung we now turn.

6. THE PEASANTS

Winston Churchill tells in *The Hinge of Fate* of a conversation he had with Stalin concerning collectivization in the Soviet Union:

"Tell me," I asked, "have the stresses of this war been as bad to you personally as carrying through the policy of the Collective Farms?"

This subject immediately aroused the Marshal.

"Oh, no," he said, "the Collective Farm policy was a terrible struggle."

"I thought you would have found it bad," I said, "because you were not dealing with a few score thousands of aristocrats or big land-owners, but with millions of small men."

"Ten millions," he said holding up his hands. "It was fearful. Four years it lasted." [1]

Anyone who lived through the Soviet struggle of collectivization could not help having the nightmarish feeling, if he studied the documents coming from Red China today, that he was living through the whole experience again.

The economic importance of land redistribution in China has been exaggerated. Official Communist figures on the amount of cultivated land in China and the amount of redistributed land now confirm what qualified authorities have pointed out but what many have failed to appreciate: land redistribution though surely desirable was not the single most important reform needed in China. Mao Tse-tung and his comrades cynically deceived the Chinese people and the world on this issue which played such a crucial role in their seizure of power. Mao, at least, has frequently been pictured sympathetically as having the interests of the Chinese peasants at heart, but figures released by his own regime reveal him as the fabricator of one of the most brutal and bloody hoaxes in Chinese history.

On Christmas Day 1947 Mao Tse-tung set down in his pamphlet "On the Present Situation and Our Tasks" the figures on land tenure in China which were eventually to be incorporated in every major statement on agrarian reform issued by the Communists. He stated that of the rural population "landlords and rich peasants . . . make up only approximately 8 per cent, reckoned by families. However, the land they hold . . . makes up 70 to 80 per cent of all [cultivated] land." [2] The official elaboration and interpretation of these figures was presented by Liu Shaoch'i in his formal commentary on the Agrarian Reform Law which was promulgated by the Peking regime 30 June 1950:

> The essential content of agrarian reform is the confiscation of the land of the landlord class for distribution to the landless and poor peasants. Thus the landlords as a class in society are abolished and the land ownership system of feudal exploitation is transformed into a system of peasant land ownership. This is indeed the greatest and most thorough reform in thousands of years of Chinese history.
>
> Why should such a reform be made? In a nutshell, it is because the original land ownership system in China is extremely irrational. In general the land situation in old China is roughly as follows:
>
> Landlords and rich peasants, who constitute less than 10 per cent of the rural population, possess approximately from 70 to 80 per cent of the land and brutally exploit the peasants by means of their land.
>
> Poor peasants, farm labourers, middle peasants and others, however, who make up 90 per cent of the rural population, possess in all only 20 to 30 per cent of the land. [3]

These figures on land tenancy and exploitation in China have been repeated so often by every major Chinese Communist spokesman that even critical observers outside of China have unwittingly treated them as fact and aided in promoting their further acceptance. [4]

There are three very basic distortions of fact in Liu's statement, and it is important to see through these distortions in order to appreciate the agrarian reform strategy of Mao and his colleagues. In the first place, there has been no feudalism, by Communist or any other definition, in China since the formation of the first Chinese Empire some two centuries before the birth of Christ.

Chinese land has been freely bought and sold since then, and the intervening centuries have seen the rise and fall of Chinese rural families in a cyclical pattern somewhat similar to the rise and fall of dynasties. Yet in his *New Democracy* Mao maintained that Chinese society was feudal until the Opium War, 1839–42, after which it became a "semicolonial semifeudal society."

The point may seem relatively minor to one not trained in Communist theory, but the "feudal" argument becomes the critical item in the application of the Marxist theory of historical evolution to such oriental type societies as China. Only by projecting the Marxist "feudal stage of society" onto the Chinese scene are the Communists able to justify a class war in which the antagonists are the landlords and the peasants.[5]

This leads, of course, to the second basic distortion in Liu's statement. There are no class divisions in rural China corresponding to the artificial categories he sets up: landlord, rich peasant, middle peasant, poor peasant and farm laborer. After a careful study of the Chinese scene the English economist R. H. Tawney demonstrated that both the class conflict and the feudal argument were inapplicable to China.

Whatever her [China's] rural problems may be, they are not complicated by the existence of a landless proletariat. The typical figure in Chinese country life is not the hired labourer, but the land-holding peasant.

. . . She possesses no landed aristocracy, no dominant class of *junkers* or squires, and few beasts. She is not afflicted by the complicated iniquities of feudal land law; manorial estates worked by *corvées,* if they ever existed, have left few traces; since animal husbandry is of secondary importance, the conflict over the use of common pastures and meadows, which kept European villages simmering for over a thousand years, presents no problem. Landlord and tenant are parties to a business contract, not members of different classes based on privilege and subordination.[6]

With regard to the various "classes" in rural China mentioned by Liu, a Chinese long associated with rural reconstruction work,

S. T. Tung, has stated that "never has the rural population been classified, or classifiable, into these categories. China has no 'landlord' class . . ." [7]

This brings us to the third and most crucial distortion, the matter of the landlords. If the Chinese system of landholding were as inequitable as Mao's and Liu's figures seemed to indicate, with 10 per cent of the people owning 70–80 per cent of the land, there might have been some excuse for waging a bitter class struggle for change. But where did the figures come from? There had never been a census of land ownership in China. The closest thing to it was a survey conducted by the Nationalist Land Commission before World War II. "It covered 1,750,000 families," Tung Shih-tsin reports, "in 163 *hsien* [counties] over 12 provinces. Nearly 80 per cent of the land was shown to be in the hands of owners of less than 100 *mou* [about 16 acres]. Almost 99 per cent of the families were such small owners, while 1.34 per cent of the families owned 100 *mou* or more, and only 18.32 per cent of the land belonged to such owners." [8] These figures were borne out by the studies of such scholars as J. L. Buck, who conducted a survey of some 17,000 farms in 22 provinces of China.[9] Buck found that 54.2 per cent of the farmers were owners of their own land, 39.9 per cent were part owners, and 5.9 per cent tenants.[10] He also found that only 28.7 per cent of the cultivated land was rented. This compares rather favorably with figures released by the United States government on farm tenancy in America in 1940 when landlordism was certainly not considered a major problem. In the United States 42.3 per cent of the farm land was cultivated by owners and managers, 28.3 per cent by part owners, and 29.4 per cent by tenants.[11] After exhaustive study and years of first-hand experience in rural China Gerald F. Winfield concluded that "well under 10 per cent of China's total farm production is used to pay rent, and even much of this rental crop goes to landlords who are themselves farmers and would be classified as 'poor' by American standards." [12]

The Communist authorities claimed to have based their figures upon a "comprehensive investigation and computation" by the "Chinese Institute of Rural Economic Research" published in 1936; but as S. T. Tung has pointed out, such an institute probably never existed, and no such "comprehensive investigation and computation" was ever conducted.[13] The conclusion would seem to be that the Communist figures were doctored to support the application of Marxist dogma to China.

Some people conversant with the works of Buck, Winfield, Tung, and others have withheld judgment as to the land tenure situation, however, because of uncertainty as to what long years of war had done to the picture. Also there is little question that there were absent landowners; and many malpractices by some of the large landowners in the Chinese countryside were outrageous. These conditions were undoubtedly aggravated by the war, and postwar observers attested that in most areas there were usually one or two landlords whose conduct made it easy for the Communists to use landlordism as a symbolic explanation for the pitiful condition of many of the peasants. In spite of all this, landlordism was not the basic agrarian problem except in the statistics originally cited by Mao.

Now the Communist Land Reform has been "basically completed," and a total of 47,000,000 hectares of cultivated land redistributed.[14] This is only 35 per cent of the 134,000,000 hectares the Communists said were under cultivation at the time,[15] or about one-half of the amount of cultivated land that would have been subject to redistribution as excess land of landlords and rich peasants according to the statistics of Mao and Liu.* Thus the Communists must either have failed to redistribute a great part of the excess land of landlords or have grossly overstated the amount of land in the hands of this group to begin with. The basic problem in the agricultural sector of the Chinese economy remains

* Mao and Liu had stated that about 10 per cent of the population owned 70–80 per cent of the land. Since the size of this group would entitle it to only about 10 per cent of the land as its fair share, there would be land available for redistribution equal to 60–70 per cent of the total.

what it was before the Communists started redistribution: too
many people and too little land. According to the Communist
figures for Kwantung in south China, for example, where population pressure is extreme, the per capita ownership of the land after
land reform is 0.22 acre for the rich peasant, 0.21 for the middle
peasant, and 0.167 for the poor peasants and former "landlords." [16]

Certainly there were many other reasons for the unhappy lot of
the Chinese peasants. One of these was the long absence of any
form of political stability. The peasants were never sure of the cash
value of their crops or indeed whether they would be able to
market them at all because of the constant disruption of transportation facilities. Again, changes in political control led to arbitrary,
capricious, and sometimes double and triple tax exactions. The
lack of a uniform and stable system of taxation was in a way a
reflection of a generally disrupted national economy under which
the Chinese peasants had suffered for decades. All of these factors
coupled with the general lack of physical security placed the
peasants in an intolerable position. And yet most of these conditions were in large measure attributable to the Communist strategy
for seizing power by means of armed struggle.

In view of the level of subsistence imposed by the accumulated
disruptions of international and civil war and the basic demo-
graphic problem in China, it is not surprising that the peasants
should be happy to share the land, animals, and equipment of
some of the more fortunate among their number or that many
of them who were near starvation should join in mass hysteria
and believe that the destruction of "feudalism," a term which
most of them had never heard before and did not even understand, would solve their problems. Nor, perhaps, is it to be wondered that so many outsiders, seeing the desperate poverty of
China and feeling that something must be done, believed the
Communists should be given a chance. The more sober proposals
of agrarian experts and agencies (the Joint Commission on Rural
Reconstruction, for example) for such steps as improving seed

strains, putting emphasis on the production and application of chemical fertilizers, making long-range plans to augment transportation facilities, and so forth could never match the claims or the appeal attached to the panacea of Land Reform by the Chinese Reds.

Communist policy toward the peasants during the first five years of their rule can be divided into four phases, and Land Reform was the first of these. It moved from north to south in a deliberate manner, like many of the great Chinese drives, though the methods varied from place to place. The Agrarian Reform Movement was declared to have been completed in southernmost Kwangtung in April 1953, leaving untouched only a few minority areas, Tibet, and the Nationalist-held island of Taiwan. In areas conquered before the establishment of their government, the Communists had pursued a policy of taking over the land of the wealthiest 15 per cent of the landowners for redistribution. Over 100,000,000 people were reportedly concerned in the areas of north China and Manchuria affected by this first drastic reform, and probably close to half a million heads of families were executed as "feudal bullies." [17] With the coming of formal political power, however, the policy changed, and instead of indiscriminate violence and rural disorder the Red leaders substituted a determined effort to establish political control and stability backed by slightly more selective liquidation of opposition.

The whole process of Land Reform became standardized by a series of regulations passed by the government in June and July 1950. These included the Agrarian Reform Law, the Decisions Concerning the Differentiation of Class Status, and Regulations Governing the Organization of Peasants' Associations. Under these regulations a team of three or four trained cadres enter a village and talk with the various peasants, gathering information. They then begin to hold a series of mass meetings at which the government's determination to expropriate the land and possessions of the "landlords" is explained to the assembled throng. The poor oppressed peasants are urged to speak out their bitterness. A few selected landlords are displayed before the shouting mob, and people hasten to tell of their "crimes." Then the people's tribunal meets to pass sentence on the victims.[18] Meanwhile the adults of the village meet, under the direction of the cadres, to determine "class status." The status of each must be settled according to a very detailed series of regulations drawn up by the government. Landlords have all their property confiscated, rich peasants part of their property, and so forth. Finally comes the redistribution, which includes land, buildings, tools, stored grain, and farm animals. Meanwhile the cadres have utilized the "enlightened elements" to form a village or peasant association, and have sponsored women's organizations and recruited potential members of the Youth League.[19] A village militia, responsible to the party and the army, is organized to carry out the sentences of the assembled "village congress."

All the while every possible medium of propaganda is utilized to explain to the peasants that they are participating in a necessarily brutal class struggle in which there can be no mercy. They have been identified as taking part in a "People's Government" by their very act of expressing their will in the class struggle. It follows that anyone opposed to the wishes of the government is opposed to them and must be exposed. "Blood debts" must be collected from such enemies.

The whole of the process of Land Reform in the villages was openly and purposefully brutal. The regime made no effort to cloak this brutality in the propaganda it published for the benefit of the outside world. Apparently the Peking leaders were determined to convince outsiders that a Marxian class struggle was involved, no matter what the facts were. The following excerpts from a book length story by a supposed eyewitness of the Land Reform in action give some idea of what was presented to the outside world by the Communists:

Her face was white with fury. She pointed an accusing finger at Peng Erh-hu. Tears of sympathy trickled down the cheeks of the militia members standing nearby.

With raised fists, the audience below shouted in one voice, "Down with reactionary landlords!" "We demand that Peng Erh-hu be shot!" . . .

The masses again shouted in unison. "Down with criminal landlords who hide and disperse their properties!" "Long live the unity of the peasants!"

It had started raining. But the tense atmosphere did not in any way lessen . . .

By four o'clock over 20 peasants had poured out their grievances from the platform. Mass sentiment had surged to the boiling point. Over and above there was a curious hush of expectancy. Not one person left or took shelter in spite of the terrific downpour.

[Then the people's tribunal meets to deliberate.]

"Peasant comrades!" The Judge's voice was grave. "We have just heard some of the accusations made by local peasants. From these accusations, it ought to be clear to everyone how the landlord class has always worked hand in glove with the enemy of the peasants— whether it was Japanese imperialism or the KMT [Kuomintang]—to oppress the peasants themselves. The same motive has prompted them to act as fawning lackeys to American imperialism, since American imperialism is directly opposite to the people's interests too.

"Our verdicts on the three criminal landlords are as follows: . . . Peng Yin-ting, age 49, native of Hsinlu Village, has caused the deaths of patriotic youths during the Resistance War. After liberation, he organized superstitious societies and spread rumours to delude the public. Also he has hidden firearms with the intent to plan for an uprising. The sentence for him is—death. Do you all agree?"

The sound of applause that came from below the platform was deafening. . . .

With one arm sheltering his tear-stained face, Peng Yin-ting was hurried along. . . . When Grandma Li, with her bony fist clenched, edged her way through the crowds and tried to hit him on the shoulder, the guards immediately stopped her. A cordon was quickly formed by them around the prisoners as more blows were about to shower from all directions. . . .

The prisoners were escorted to the graveyard south of the temple. From the back of the graveyard came the sound of several shots.

The sound shrilly pierced through the thick, moist atmosphere en-

veloping Huilung *hsiang*. Sighs of relief were heaved as justice was
meted out to the convicted.

"Down with reactionary landlords!"
"Long live the emancipation of the peasants!"
"Long live the Communist Party!"
"Long live Chairman Mao Tse-tung!"
The masses, for the first time, freed from their dread and restraints,
let out these slogans with a voice stronger than ever.[20]

These mass trials which took place throughout China reached
an intense pitch during 1951, the year of violence. By the time
the Land Reform had been completed even the most conservative
estimates were that at least a million and a half people had been
executed under the guidance of the cadres, and that another 35
to 45 million had been stigmatized as "exploiters" and "class
enemies." [21] This was in addition to the great numbers of "counterrevolutionaries" executed, for the most part, at the same time
(see Chapter 4). Untold numbers of peasants committed suicide
rather than face further Land Reform struggle meetings. The
cadres were urged to convince the "backward peasants" that
suicide was "reactionary" and "illegal anti-state activity." [22] In
their press and through the cadre training process, the Peking
leaders have made clear their view that "class status" is hereditary
and that children of "reactionary classes" must achieve merit by
turning against their families and being doubly enthusiastic in
serving the new society.

The purposes of the Chinese Communist Land Reform Movement are all too clear. The first was the complete destruction of
the traditional pattern of rural life, including family ties. The
political and social stability of the Chinese villages was thoroughly disrupted, and into the vacuum created the Communists
projected their organization. This, of course, was the second
main purpose of the reform: to extend the centrally controlled
apparatus of the Communist state to the lowest possible level. In
place of the informal, individualized village structure the cadres
erected the great impersonal organs of state power.

In addition to the people's tribunals (which continued to operate after the Land Reform, for the punishment of counterrevolutionaries), the peasant associations, the local militia with its security police, and the party branch, the Communists have the system of rural cooperatives, the state monopolies already mentioned, which are subordinate to the Ministries of Commerce, Food, and Finance. In some villages there are separate state credit cooperatives and more are being established, but their functions were still carried out by the marketing and supply cooperatives in most of the 31,953 rural districts where cooperatives had been established by 1952.

The cooperative provides a basic method of economic control, reinforcing the political control of the party over the villages. It "overshadows the whole life of the farmers: it lends or sells seed, prescribes methods of cultivation, determines the time of harvest, buys up the crops, fixes the prices, sells salt, fertilizer, and industrial products which the farmer needs and when funds run short, lends him money." [23] The policies of the cooperatives are directed by the party cadres; these organizations can thus discriminate against "backward" peasants in order to fulfill their primary task of service to the state. The interests of the consumers are secondary. The peasant has naturally found these representative organs of the state much harder tax extractors and taskmasters than the landlords ever were. [24]

Of course, the Land Reform helped to establish the Communist-directed mass organizations at the village level. Through these the villagers have been forced to attend the endless meetings, participate in discussions and criticism sessions designed to set members of families against each other and at the same time show the power of the government. Through these meetings the party implements its attack on religion, the custom of ancestral shrines, family celebrations, and "feudal" marriage practices.

Thus it turns out that Lenin's slogan of "land to the tiller" proved an effective strategy for establishing initial control over the Chinese peasantry. Mao's method of application of the class struggle theory made it doubly powerful. The most forceful de-

no private property

fenders of traditional Chinese society and likely sources of future possible opposition were liquidated. Land Reform, Communist style, laid the necessary foundation of terror and fear which would enable the party to consolidate the control it had set up. Further, by their very participation in the violence of the rural class struggle the peasants shared in the guilt of the Communist party and felt themselves identified with it. By the time they found out that they had been deceived they had little choice but to support the Communists, for always hanging over their heads was the fear of retribution from their victims if Communist power should be upset.[25]

As C. M. Chang points out,

The [Land Reform] program as carried out by the Communists makes sense only when it is regarded as blazing a trail for Socialism . . . The Chinese Revolution cannot, of course, be permitted to halt short of the final stage of Marxist-Stalinist theory—the collectivization of agriculture. To press on thus is not only an article of faith with the Communists; it is a practical necessity, for they can never feel secure so long as an overwhelmingly large section of the population clings to the idea of private property.

This is exactly what happened. Sometime about the middle of 1951 the Peking rulers began to emphasize that Land Reform was only the first step in the Communist program.

This switch in emphasis marks the second phase in the Mao government's policy toward the peasants. It lasted until March 1953. Stalin had quoted Lenin as saying, "as long as we live in a country where small-peasant farming predominates, there is a firmer basis for capitalism in Russia than for Communism." [26] This was precisely the position taken by Mao's government. The cadres were now instructed to push toward collective types of work in the countryside.

A large movement for the creation and development of the various stages of peasant "cooperation" preliminary to socialized agriculture was launched in August 1951, in a manner typical of many of the great movements. A provincial paper, the *New*

Hunan Daily, printed an attack on what was called the "Li Ssu-hsi mentality." Li was made a symbol of undesirable attitudes on the part of the village cadres. According to the story which was later played up in party journals and papers throughout the land:

Li Ssu-hsi was a poor hired farm laborer who had worked for over ten years and all the time suffered bitter hardship. Only after liberation did he marry and have a son. During land reform he was extremely active and was elected secretary of the youth corps branch. But after he had obtained land, he did not want to go on working but wanted to go home to devote himself solely to production. When the cadres admonished him, he cried out with passion: "All my life I suffered hardship and had no land. Now I have land and am completely satisfied. Why still carry on revolution? What for? [27]

The official party line on the issue was that here was an example of the dual nature of the peasants, who were progressive in one aspect, backward in the other:

The peasants want to oppose imperialism and feudalism; they have actively taken part in the struggle against imperialism, feudalism and bureaucratic capitalism. This is their progressive side. But the peasants are small producers representing individual economy. This determines their selfish, conservative, complacent and politically short-sighted character. Village cadres who do not want to work for the revolution after the completion of land reform fully reflect this backward character.[28]

Soon the cadres were under fire from all directions. They were accused of reflecting the Li Ssu-hsi mentality by relaxing in the wake of the Land Reform. Communist cadres who had come from urban areas to help out in the Agrarian Reform were charged with reviving their "bourgeois backgrounds" by wanting to get back to the cities and bright lights before the revolution had been completed in the countryside.[29] The cadres were urged to explain, explain, and explain again to the peasants the advantages of the socialist methods of agriculture. They were told to increase the number of meetings and make sure that more people attended them. *Study* magazine pointed out that in some places where meetings drew more than two hundred during the Land Reform they now drew only a few dozen.[30]

From this time on, even in propaganda, the peasants were no longer the favored members of Mao's revolutionary alliance of proletariat and peasants. They were to be led gradually, by propaganda and by examples, toward final abandonment of the land for which they had participated in the execution of untold numbers of their fellow men. The ideologists on high talked in terms of a formula for developing an individual peasant economy and a collectivized economy at the same time.[31]

The various steps toward collectivization set up by the Peking authorities parallel to some extent the pattern used in the European satellites.[32] First there are the mutual aid teams. These draw on a practice common in many parts of the Chinese countryside of pooling labor during busy seasons. Under the direction of the cadres these labor pools are converted into permanent mutual aid teams, which require organized direction and management for the accomplishment of tasks during the slack season. The peasants retain the title to their land and the produce from it. Naturally quarrels develop, but the Communists view these as opportunities for propagandizing the next higher form of organization, the agricultural producers' cooperatives. These are the key development from the point of view of collectivization. Agricultural producers' cooperatives are formed by merging several well established mutual aid teams. The peasants pool their land and most of their equipment, retaining for themselves only a hut and possibly a small plot and an animal or two. Theoretically membership in the cooperatives is voluntary; the peasant retains title to his land and is free to withdraw. Actually, the peasant is at the mercy of the cadres, who can exert pressure on him by discriminatory pricing and interest rates in the village cooperative stores and through denunciation at meetings.[33] These agricultural producers' cooperatives correspond to the artels which Stalin

characterized as the key to the whole collectivization movement
in the Soviet Union.[34]

Above the level of the cooperatives are the collectivized farms,
owned not by the member-peasants but by the collective as a
unit, the state farms, owned by the state and manned by peasants
working as employees at regular wages, and the machine tractor
stations, state-owned units which farm out tractors to the collectives. These were set up during 1951 and 1952 mainly to provide
examples for the peasants who, it was anticipated, would immediately begin to see the advantages of collective agriculture. By
the end of 1952 there were 545 state farms in Manchuria, with
more than 43,000 employees; more than 40 per cent of these
farms were reported to be mechanized. Communist figures on the
number of collective farms are contradictory, but to date their
number is apparently small. Under continuous pressure from the
government, provincial cadres were urged to set up one or two
model collectives in each province. Communist reports by the end
of 1952 claimed the establishment of such models as far south as
Fukien and Kwangtung provinces.[35]

With the exception of a few areas such as the Manchurian
plains, Chinese farming is not suitable for collectivization in the
usual Soviet sense of thorough mechanization. For this reason the
agricultural producers' cooperative is the decisive form of collectivization in China. The Chinese collective farms will probably
not involve much more than the peasants' formal abandonment
of their ownership of the land; in other respects they will remain the same as the cooperatives; and for this reason the latter
are, as in the Soviet Union, the key to the collectivization process.

Throughout this second phase of Communist policy the cadres
were urged to employ every possible method for persuading the
peasants of the advantages of collectivized agriculture. The papers were full of accounts of how the collective farms excelled
the producers' cooperatives in production per acre, how the latter
excelled the mutual aid teams, and these the individual farmer.
"Spark," the first collective farm in Manchuria, was hailed as a

great success, and the press told stories of how peasants from all over China had eagerly volunteered to join it.[36] Peking publicized the honors bestowed on model peasants, model mutual aid teams, and model producers' cooperatives. Incentives were made so attractive that cadres and peasants turned in false reports of harvests "in an attempt to gain glory." [37]

The Communist party and the Sino-Soviet Friendship Association organized trips for Chinese peasants to the Soviet Union to see the collective farms there. They returned with glowing accounts, which were prominently featured in the propaganda handbooks, of what was to be expected in China's future.[38] Band wagon tactics were employed. The newspapers assured the people that women were flocking to join the cooperative movement in agriculture.[39] Meanwhile with each passing month the figures for the number of agricultural producers' cooperatives organized throughout the country were boosted. Kao Kang stated in June 1952: "It is expected that in five years the agricultural producers' cooperatives will occupy a dominant position in the rural economy." [40] The peasants' "winning back of their own soil" was hardly mentioned any more.[41] In his report to the Fourth Session of the National Committee of the CPPCC on 4 February 1953 Chou En-lai summed up the work:

> The reform of the individual economy of the peasants and handicraftsmen has begun and there is a great expansion in the agricultural mutual-aid and cooperative movement. In the old liberated areas, organized peasant households now average more than 65 per cent of the whole, and in the newly liberated areas they generally account for some 25 per cent. Throughout the country, nearly 4,000 agricultural producers cooperatives have been set up, and more than ten experimental collective farms, over 2,000 state farms, and more than 2,600 handicraft producers cooperatives have been organized.[42]

But if the peasants, as the regime claimed, were shortsighted in some respects, how was it that such "progressive" changes were made? Some of the criticism which came out later revealed the methods and the intensity of pressure applied by the cadres.

One report described a county where 83 mutual aid teams were organized, comprising 92 per cent of the total peasant households,

but among them 35 teams, constituting 42.2 per cent of the total number of peasants' households, were formal and false mutual aid teams. In such districts there have been instances where *discrimination was practiced against individual peasants who were subject to isolation politically and economically.* Among the amalgamated large teams, many have collapsed due to difficulty in management and *absence of free will of peasants.*[43]

The extent of growing peasant resistance throughout the second phase did not become apparent to outside observers until the next phase of Communist policy toward the peasants.

This third phase matched the year in which it occurred; it was a period of temporary retrenchment—at least on the surface. It lasted from March 1953 until the publication of propaganda for "the general line of the state" in November of that year. Apparently great resistance on the part of the peasants forced the government to call a temporary halt to the pressure for collectivization. Despite the many controls established and the constant pressure, the peasants were refusing to sell their grain to the state and were showing little enthusiasm for the many campaigns employed by the regime to redirect their antipathy. The result was that in March 1953 the high party officials accused the lower cadres of "adventurist deviationism" and demanded stronger guidance by their immediate superiors to halt the "present tendency of blind advance in the mutual aid and cooperative movement." Making an object lesson of Shantung province, the *People's Daily* pointed out:

Due to the impatience of a few rural cadres and activists many districts violated the law of objective development in promoting mutual aid and cooperative organizations to higher levels. They blindly organized agricultural producers' cooperatives and expanded mutual aid teams, advocated amalgamation of small teams into large teams, made announcement that teams with five households and less are not to be reckoned as teams and that it would be an honor to join large teams, and blindly built up public property without regard to practical conditions of mutual aid teams and agricultural producers' cooperatives and the practical requirements of the peasants. In a single winter Yangku *hsien* established 32 cooperatives but *many peasants did not join the cooperatives voluntarily.* Nor did the amalgamation of a number of mutual aid teams into 26 large teams in No. 8 *ch'ü* of Chiaochi hsien genuinely correspond to the demand of the masses. Moreover, in blindly building up public property, 205 mutual aid teams in the above ch'ü without regard to objective conditions *transferred their livestock and farming tools to public property.*[44]

Obviously the party, which must at all times remain infallible, was not going to take any of the blame for the resistance of the peasants.

History was repeating itself much too closely for the comfort of the Chinese peasants. It was in March 1930 that Stalin, after about two years of driving toward collectivization, temporarily slackened the lines, while maintaining his position of always being correct by denouncing the actions of the lower Soviet cadres. Many sections of the Chinese Communist directives of March 1953 might have come directly from his "Dizziness with Success," in which he accused these cadres of "rash advance," and from his "Reply to Collective Farm Comrades," in which he pointed out that the principle of voluntarism had been violated, that a diversity of conditions had not been allowed for, and that too many of the Soviet cadres were trying to skip the incomplete stages in the collective movement. It was at this time that Stalin pointed to the artel as the key to the whole problem.[45]

But just as in the Soviet Union, this temporary release of pressure did not mean any really basic change in policy in China. The party still maintained its goal of the socialization of agriculture. In July 1953 in an address to the Second National Congress of the Youth League, party Central Committeeman Teng Tzu-hui stated: "We cannot allow our rural economy, after the conclusion of agrarian reform, to remain forever on the present stage of individual economy and small production and small private ownership. Neither can we allow the growth, on the foundations of the economy of the small peasant, of the capitalist development on a free basis." [46] The cadres were, however, ordered to expose each other's mistakes through criticism and make the development of mutual aid and cooperation correspond to the "objective situation."

The collectivization program at this point bore one other resemblance to the Soviet situation which deserves mention. The Soviet leaders attempted to turn attention away from their own mistakes and channel resistance against "foreign intelligence services" and "anti-Soviet elements." One of the accusations made was repeated by Andreev at his speech before the Eighteenth Party Congress in 1939:

The masked wreckers carried on a large-scale infection of the collective and state farms with glanders, plague, and other infectious diseases, and by means of the livestock they infected the people also. Instead of preparing remedies in the biological laboratories the enemies who had established themselves there prepared poisons for the livestock which artificially gave rise to lack of fertility in order to bring about a large-scale decline in livestock.[47]

Stalin had accused the "anti-Soviet elements":

They organize wrecking activities in the collective farms and state farms, and some of them, including certain professors, go to such lengths in their zeal for wrecking as to inject germs of plague and anthrax into the cattle on the collective farms and state farms, help to spread meningitis among horses, etc.[48]

It was in Manchuria, the territory where collectivization was most advanced and being pushed with most vigor, that the United States was accused in 1952 of launching germ warfare.

After Peking had accused the Chinese cadres of "dizziness with success," the party papers began to report corrective measures, inadvertently revealing some of the symptoms of peasant discontent which lay behind the move. The measures were supposedly aimed at counteracting the blind haste of the cadres, the infringing on private property, and failure to allow full development of the mutual aid teams. By July it was reported that 2,600 of the 9,000 * agricultural producers' cooperatives had been turned back into mutual aid teams.[49] In Szechwan province only 19 producers' cooperatives were permitted to remain out of over 100.[50]

The symptoms, which had caused Peking to tell party activists to move more deliberately, grew more pronounced throughout 1953, a year of natural calamities. The *China Agriculture Fortnightly* revealed that the great mechanized state farms had been running consistently in the red and were far behind in production quotas.[51] By May 1953 the news dispatches from mainland China were filled with accounts of famine caused by "natural disasters." There was a late frost, a blight, floods, and locusts. Ironically enough, the most extensive famine was reported in those provinces which constitute the basin of the Huai River, where the Communists had boasted of their greatest achievements in flood control and irrigation.[52]

In April the *People's Daily* began to talk about the "blind influx" of peasants into the cities which had been reported from all administrative regions. More than 20,000 peasants had entered Mukden and Anshan alone.[53] Behind this influx was obviously the lack of food in the country. But the situation in the cities was no better. Communist papers complained that not enough food could be got from the peasants to feed the cities; the peasants did not seem to understand the "correct relationship between industry and agriculture" and had adopted the "one-sided viewpoint of neglecting agricultural production." [54] They were accused of failing to take into account the needs of the state and not selling enough of their grain to the government. The Canton *Southern Daily* pointed out: "The peasants fear that since they have increased production their burdens will be increased correspondingly. They fear collectivization and communization of

* March figure.

land and property. They are afraid to be regarded as rich and are proud to be poor. Thus middle peasants dare not expand their enterprise; rich peasants and landlords, afraid of struggles against them, dare not produce at all." [55]

By September the food problem had become one of major proportions for the Mao regime. The *People's Daily* complained about peasants who "are not interested in collecting the harvest. The cadres must convince them of the importance of harvesting for the sake of the country and of the masses, for the present and for the remote future." [56] In Hupei province it was reported that the farmers were cultivating only a minimum, knowing that because of taxation and government-fixed prices they would get little return from larger production.[57] From many other parts of the country came reports of peasants refusing to sell their crops to the cooperatives.

To explain away its troubles the Communist government turned to tales which would have been humorous if it had not been for the tragic facts behind them. Wild beasts were reported to be roaming the countryside and devouring the crops. Bands of seven or eight hundred tigers were accused of destroying the farmers' grain. Officials in the capital talked of a "beast calamity." [58] In addition, the government revived its campaign against counterrevolutionaries, which led observers in Hong Kong to believe that the "beasts" were probably two-legged.

Peasant resistance was helping to put the Peking government far behind with its plans. A report by P'eng Chen in September spoke of peasant relief costing the government ¥1,670,000,000 for four provinces alone. Yet the next month the Ministry of the Interior ordered drastic reductions of grants of money and grain for famine-stricken areas. The sufferers, it said, would have to find their own way out of their distress through "self-aid by production." [59]

Meanwhile, disquieting news came from the Soviet Union in the form of Khrushchev's September revelations that from the point of view of production twenty-five years of collectivized agriculture in Russia had been a failure.[60] There seems to have been a slight period of hesitation on the part of the Peking authorities. They evidently realized that peasant resistance was curtailing their collection of the grain which would pay for industrial equipment from the Soviet Union.

But by November 1953 Mao and his advisers reached their decision, and Chinese Communist policy toward the peasants entered its fourth phase: accelerated collectivization. The regime evidently decided that the five-year plan, then nearing the close of its first year, necessitated a thorough control over the agricultural sector of the economy no matter what the demands on—or reactions of—the peasants. It is also possible that the Communists, aware of their growing unpopularity (demonstrated about this time by the decision of almost 75 per cent of the Chinese prisoners in Korea not to return to their homeland under Communism) felt the need to extend political control over the peasantry as rapidly as possible. Whatever the reasons behind the shift, the fate of the peasants was unrolled in a series of decisions and actions extending into the spring of 1954.

The *People's Daily* of 16 November 1953, in an editorial entitled "Lead the Peasants to Take the Path of Prosperity for All," spelled out the manner in which the "toiling peasants" were to play their part during the transition period. Party activists were told that since March they had abandoned the active and energetic direction of the peasants; they must now fulfill their duties of leading the peasants along the road to mutual aid and cooperation. Once again the poor lower level cadres were to bear the brunt of a change in policy in Peking. The editorial stated that the peasants "are to be gradually organized to carry out large-scale production with new implements and new technology on the basis of *common ownership of land and principal means of production, and to distribute the yield according to the principle of 'distribution according to labor.'*" (Italics added.) The era of Mao's "land to the peasants" was over four years after his government had come into power!

On 24 December the Communists boasted that there were more than 14,000 agricultural producers' cooperatives, fifty times as many as in 1951.[61] There was no talk of "blind advance" now, although this represented more than twice as many as the government had decided to be the "correct stage" in March.

It was not until 8 January 1954 that the Communist party— not the government—got around to publishing its decision to move inexorably ahead with collectivization. This decision, which still maintained that the advance was to be measured and rational, set the goal of at least 800,000 agricultural producers' cooperatives, involving more than 20 per cent of the population, by the end of the first five-year plan.[62] In a special article written for *Pravda* of 11 July 1954 Liao Lu-yen predicted that 35 per cent of China's farms and 40 per cent of the cultivated land would be collectivized by 1957 and that collectivization under the agricultural producers' cooperatives would be complete within a decade.[63] Chou En-lai in his report of 23 September to the National People's Congress on the government's work for the first five years indicated that the pace would be even more rapid: "We hope that, by the end of the first five-year plan, over one half of all peasant households throughout the country will have joined in agricultural producers' cooperatives, and over half of the cultivated land will be pooled in cooperatives." [64]

The decision to speed up collectivization was followed rapidly by public announcement of some other decisions vitally affecting the lives of the peasants. On 19 November 1953 the cabinet had passed regulations setting up a government monopoly of all major food materials. The decision made no secret of the fact that more grain was needed to make industrialization possible. This decision was made public on 1 March 1954, and two days later the *People's Daily* asserted that the whole system of controlling agricultural products was modeled on Soviet methods used under the first five-year plan.[65] On 23 March the cabinet's Committee on Financial and Economic Affairs issued a decree on advance government purchase of eight major nonfood agricultural products.[66]

Every organization and every method have been called into action to enforce these decisions. Throughout the early months of 1954 major attention in the Communist press was devoted to urging more and more education for the peasants to "awaken their political consciousness" and overcome their individualistic tendencies. No propaganda effort was to be spared to convince them of their duty to produce grain for the state.

Meanwhile, in talking of the opposition of the peasants, Communist leaders began to turn on the "rich peasants," whose economy Mao had originally said must be preserved. Peasants in this unenviable category are referred to by the term used to express the Soviet word *kulak*. For the cadres studying Stalin's *History of the Communist Party of the Soviet Union (Bolshevik)* the implications are plain.[67] The marketing cooperatives and equipment supply stations are giving priority treatment to mutual aid teams and producers' cooperatives in the distribution of scarce farm equipment, fertilizer, and seed. Discriminatory interest rates on loans and discriminatory tax assessments are used to persuade the peasants of the advantages of collectivization.[68] The *People's Daily* has reported that in estimating crop yields for tax purposes some cadres have been putting the figures so high that the tax is more than the total yield of the peasant's farm.

The tax burden under the Communists has already become far greater than the rent formerly paid to landlords. Some idea of it can be gained from a dispatch concerning the famine areas of Honan in the summer of 1953. Taxes were to be collected on all land where crop yields were more than 35 per cent of normal, although where the yield was as low as only 20 to 30 per cent 40 to 60 per cent of the tax would be collected.[69]

Thus the fate of the Chinese peasants has been sealed. By the end of May 1954 the *People's Daily* claimed the establishment of more than 95,000 agricultural producers' cooperatives,[70] and in September Chou En-lai stated that the regime expected to have more than 500,000 involving 10,000,000 peasant households set up by the spring sowing of 1955. Eleven new machine tractor stations were reported to have been set up since the beginning of the year.[71] Rationing was being strictly enforced throughout the land, and people in the urban areas were being forced to accept lower quality.

In December 1952 Communist peasant policy had been stated bluntly: "There is only one way for the rural villages of China. They must, like the rural villages of the Soviet Union, be collectivized." [72] Yet few anticipated that the process would be so rapid or so drastic. Throughout the process Mao and his comrades have maintained the position stated in the 8 January 1954 decision to collectivize: "precipitate haste and adventurism must be avoided. We must use persuasion, set examples and render state assistance in order to make the peasants join together voluntarily." [73] At the same time they issued plans for the number of agricultural producers' cooperatives to be set up, which meant that the various areas of the country were assigned quotas.[74] The result has been again that the lower level cadres have been caught in the middle.

It must be pointed out that the decisions to speed up collectivization and establish a state food monopoly followed the conclusion in mid-September 1953 of a Moscow-Peking agreement exchanging Soviet industrial assistance for a number of Chinese exports. The subsequent increase in food shipments and publicity about the necessity for shipping meat and other food to "brother nations" may indicate that the Soviet had aided in pushing the decision. If, as Stalin admitted, the cost had been terrible in Russia, there was no reason why the Chinese Communists should expect to avoid paying a similar price.[75]

Thus the policy of the Chinese Communists toward the peasants, who, they have asserted, are the rulers in China, has followed the line originally dictated by Stalin for the USSR down to some of the most minute details. From a cynical "land to the peasant," through an initial pushing of preparatory steps toward collectivization and a brief period of easing the pressure while cadres, wild beasts, foreign agents, and everyone but the party was blamed for resistance, the Chinese have moved to the final decisions for wiping out the individual peasant economy.

In China, where the level of subsistence allows practically no margin such as Russia had, the cost in terms of starvation and further bloodshed is likely to be even greater. This probability is enhanced by the fact that the plans for economic development in Mao's China concentrate almost exclusively on building heavy industry and war industry and neglect almost completely the agricultural sector of the economy which must perforce bear the burden of development costs. As in the Soviet Union these costs are to be met by collective control rather than increased production.[76]

After an analysis of Mao's economic theories one economist recently maintained that agriculture was the *only* field in which "Maoism" deviated from "Stalinism," because there was as yet no decision to collectivize.[77] It is now plain that with regard to the treatment of the peasants there is no such thing as "Maoism." For the sake of an outmoded doctrine maintained by a few people in power, the Chinese peasant is to be brought under a system which according to figures released by Stalin's successors has failed to solve the problem of increasing agricultural production.[78] And this will be and has already been at a cost in human destruction which staggers the imagination.

7. THE WORKERS [1]

Article 1 of the 1954 Chinese Communist Constitution reads: "The People's Republic of China is a people's democratic state led by the working class and based upon the alliance of workers and peasants." [2] This is, of course, a strictly Leninist-Stalinist formula for the role of urban labor in government and for the official government attitude toward this minute portion of Chinese society. Also in a Marxist-Leninist tradition, the Chinese Communist party claims that it "is the organized vanguard of the Chinese working class and the highest form of its class organization." [3] In view of this professed special status for the "working class," the Communist treatment of this group can be taken as one of the most important indications of the nature of the regime. Developments in the labor field over the past five years are important also for another reason. The increase in numbers of Chinese workers and in control over them assumes major importance in any plans for industrialization. Has the worker half of Mao's revolutionary alliance fared any better than the peasant half?

Actually, the stretching of ideology that was necessary in the application of Marxist-Leninist formulae to the Chinese scene becomes clear when we consider the size of the Chinese industrial proletariat. There are only 3,000,000 industrial workers in China, 0.51 per cent of China's 582,584,839 people. [4] Adding in technical and administrative personnel, other workers such as telecommunications personnel, and certain government employees and schoolteachers performing specialized functions within industry, the official figure for the Chinese labor force for 1954 is 15,000,000 or approximately 2.6 per cent of the Chinese population. This represents a gain of only 2,000,000 over the figure given four years before. [5] An accurate breakdown of the labor force in each industry is not available, but three of the

154

largest groups and their numbers in 1953 were railroad workers, 504,000; textile workers, 594,000; and coal miners, 460,000. Among these workers are several thousand full-time trade union officers and secretaries.

There is only one union organization for Chinese workers, the All China Federation of Trade Unions (ACFTU), which has exerted great effort to make itself one of the major members of the Communist-led World Federation of Trade Unions.[6] The regime's Trade Union Law of 29 June 1950 states explicitly (Article 4) that all bodies not members of the ACFTU "shall not be called trade unions, and shall not be entitled to the rights laid down in this law." The law also states plainly that the first duty of the trade unions is to "educate and organize the masses of workers and staff members to support the laws and desires of the People's government; [to] carry out the policies of the People's government in order to consolidate the people's state power, which is led by the working class." [7] In effect, the unions perform a dual function: 1) as a control mechanism for mobilizing and directing the productive activities of the labor force within the state-controlled industrial nexus; and 2) as a complex framework for the dissemination of propaganda to reinforce worker morale and to propagate Communist teachings. This concept of the role of the trade union was pointed up in an article published May Day 1952, in the Peking *Daily Worker* (the organ of the ACFTU), which stressed that a union's main task was to aid the government and the party in controlling industry.

The ACFTU is under the direct supervision of the Ministry of Labor and under the control of the Chinese Communist party. It is organized both regionally and according to basic industries, and its policies are supposedly determined by a National Congress which appoints an executive committee, which in turn appoints the presidium and the secretariat. These latter handle the affairs of the federation on the day to day level.[8] The organization is responsible for propaganda by activists or agitators among the trade union members. It also takes credit for most of the workers' achievements and for any benefits which may be extended to them. The member unions are responsible for organizing and carrying through the many drives and emulation movements which the government has demanded. They must instill "labor enthusiasm" and are responsible for "labor discipline."

According to a Peking dispatch of the New China News Agency of 2 May 1954, there are over 11,000,000 trade unionists in 180,000 basic trade unions. It is probable that about one-twelfth of these are Communist party members.[9] The growth of the ACFTU and the expansion of its activities, though slow at first, have been quite impressive. Previous membership figures cited by the mainland press were: 1,440,000 in July 1948; 5,130,000 in February 1951; 7,297,000 in April 1952; and 8,500,000 in December 1952. Lai Jo-yu became chairman of the Presidium at the Seventh Congress of the ACFTU held in Peking from 2 to 11 May 1953, replacing Ch'en Yün and the Moscow-sponsored Li Li-san. He credits his organization with most of the alleged gains in China's industrial recovery. Such gains as have been made are in part attributable to "emulation drives" sparked by the ACFTU—that is competitive campaigns between individuals and groups of workers to speed up production. According to ACFTU figures, for example, over 80 per cent of the workers took part in emulation campaigns in connection with the 5-anti Movement in the first half of 1952.

On the other hand, the ACFTU must take the responsibility for failures on the part of the workers to live up to their role of the most politically enlightened members of "new China." When it became evident in mid-1953 that national production plans were not going to be fulfilled, a slackness in labor discipline was blamed as being chiefly responsible, and the result was a decision by the ACFTU on the Strengthening of Labor Discipline.[10]

Given the central role assigned to the working class in a Communist state, it is not surprising that problems concerning the workers have received priority treatment in China.[11] The foremost of these problems has been to increase the size of the "working class"; this in turn is related to other basic problems such as industrialization, changing the traditional Chinese social attitude toward the worker class, etc. Under the autarchic policies of the regime, the Lilliputian labor force faces a tremendous task. Besides meeting the minimum needs of the vast peasant population and the growing bureaucratic apparatus of "non-productive military and administrative personnel," the laborers are expected to produce surplus enough to buttress plans for new capital construction and to carry on the major military activities undertaken by Peking.[12]

The first step of the regime was to establish relatively complete control over the labor force. Measures toward this end were carried out for the most part through the ACFTU. By the end of 1952 the more important of these measures could be summarized as follows:

1. Workers cannot get jobs without first passing through a Communist-dominated screening group.

2. Persons entering the labor market for the first time (for example, college or technical school graduates) are assigned jobs.

3. Workers are subject to arbitrary transfer by authorities if necessary for a "unified distribution of laborers among the various enterprises, within provinces and between provinces."

4. Hiring and firing of personnel require the permission of local labor bureaus or trade union representatives.

5. Employers cannot hire laborers from other districts or regions without letters of permission from the Ministry of Labor.

6. Workers cannot be hired from the staffs of other organizations without the government's permission.

7. Unemployed laborers must present a prospective employer with registration cards issued by one or more of the following: the local relief committee for unemployed workers, the local labor unemployment office, the local committee for the place-

ment of unemployed intellectuals, the ch'ü [district], or higher
government bodies.

In the next two years the regime added the final touches to pat-
terning the life of the workers after that of their big brothers in
the Soviet Union. In 1953 it began an intensive campaign for
improving labor discipline; and in 1954 it began setting up
workers' courts (discussed p. 173). These last two years saw the
launching of a mass education campaign among the workers to
convince them of the necessity for iron discipline in the new
society. Small discussion and criticism sessions were held; and
although the top leadership stressed that improved labor discipline was to be achieved by "education alone," punishments were
instituted in many factories.[13] "Education" included required
attendance at political discussion meetings until the worker's
proletarian appreciation of his "leading role in the direction of
the state" was enhanced to the point where he no longer committed breaches of discipline. As in the Soviet Union, by the fifth
year the Chinese Communists had developed legal sanctions
which extended to such matters as the attendance, punctuality,
sick leave, and general attitude of the factory and mining
workers.

The problem of developing a reserve of skilled labor and
technicians has been more formidable for the Communists than
the matter of controlling the already existing labor force. Many
of the most highly trained people fled and are now refugees in
Hong Kong or serving the Nationalist government on Taiwan.
Mao's regime has admitted its shortage of skilled workers in all
industrial and commercial centers, and has devised several
methods to train technicians as rapidly as possible. First, most of
China's universities have been turned into technical and political
training schools. The major recruitment of students has been
among the workers; for example, the ACFTU reported in late
1952 that during the year over 26,400 workers had been released
from production for technical training.[14] "By mid-1953, one-
third of China's college and university students [or 68,000 ap-

proximately] were in engineering schools. With the addition of 29,610 new engineering students enrolled in the fall of 1953, China now has a total of 97,610 engineering students at the college level." [15] All this, of course, according to Communist figures.

Secondly, the party has encroached upon the spare time of the laborers for additional technical training on the job as well as for political indoctrination. Lai Jo-yu reported in November 1952 that there were 8,900 spare-time schools with an enrollment of more than 3,000,000 workers. A critical problem in this respect is the high rate of illiteracy among the Chinese workers. Liu Lan-t'ao, chairman of the North China Administrative Committee in 1952, estimated that in his area more than 80 per cent of the workers were illiterate or semi-illiterate.[16] A major reason is the difficulty of the Chinese written language, which contains more than 40,000 different characters, 3,000 to 7,000 of which must be mastered for minimum practical literacy. In its attempt to meet this problem, the regime has experimented with its "shock attacks" on characters and the publication of large quantities of simple and illustrated technical training literature. In May 1954 Peking claimed that more than 400,000 workers had learned to read during the past year.[17]

As a further means of increasing the number of skilled technicians, Mao's regime has "borrowed" large numbers of Soviet specialists for instruction purposes and has sent Chinese workers to Soviet technical schools. The New China News Agency reported on 15 August 1954 that more than 13,000 students were leaving China for advanced study in the Soviet Union; and undoubtedly a large number of these were laborers. There are no figures available on the number of Soviet technicians in China, but some estimates run as high as 150,000; although such a figure is probably exaggerated, the number is certainly great. Rostow thinks that 15,000 is a closer approximation.[18]

The problem of elevating the laborer to a high prestige position in Communist China is probably less formidable. Traditionally the peasant ranked far above the laborer in the Chinese social framework, but the Communists have enlisted all their propaganda resources to glorify the worker in the best Marxist-Leninist manner. The shift away from Mao's early emphasis on the peasant started much sooner than most outsiders realized. It was in March 1949 that the Central Committee of the Chinese Communist party decided to transfer the party "center of activity from rural to urban districts." Since then the peasant has been relegated to an inferior status. One bit of propaganda in October 1952 asserted that Chinese farm girls now prefer to marry workers instead of peasants. "As the working class is the glorious class, why shouldn't the girls change from the peasant class to the working class?"

Following the Soviet example, the regime has utilized material incentives as well as propaganda to make the working class the most attractive group in Chinese society. It has advertised rest homes, orphanages, homes for the aged and disabled, workers' cultural palaces, libraries, and nurseries for workers' children. It is quite probable that the success of this propaganda has been in part responsible for the large influx of rural labor into the cities from the countryside, a problem which has been troubling Peking authorities since 1952. As early as August of that year measures were taken to halt the "blind flow" of surplus agricultural labor and to order resettlement on uncultivated land of a marginal nature being opened up in the northeast, northwest, and southwest of China.[19] In many cases the Communists admitted that resettlement was forced, and its major purpose would seem to be to prevent any evidence of industrial dissatisfaction from becoming evident within Communist territory or from leaking to the outside.

As for the rest homes, vacations, and other workers' benefits of which the Communists have boasted so loudly, Peking's figures indicate that to date they are little more than propaganda promises. In mid-November 1952 ACFTU figures for the whole of China included only 37 sanatoria, 14 homes for the disabled and aged, and 3 orphanages. Laborers escaping to Hong Kong reported that most of the rest and vacation places are reserved almost exclusively for party functionaries, trade union officials, and labor heroes. They also stated that most of the news pictures of happy workers in sparkling places of work and in "workers' cultural palaces" are as "carefully staged as movies."

But far more important are the actual conditions of work in China under the Communists. What about wages, hours, safety, health, etc.?

On 16 August 1952 the Central-South Administrative Council issued Provisional Regulations Concerning Wages in State-operated Factories, Mines, and Communications Enterprises. These regulations were part of a program of wage reform launched by the Peking government early in 1952. The Central-South Region was the first area to promulgate a complete series of regulations, but a similar system had already been in operation in north China and Manchuria for some time.[20] These regulations inveighed against the "serious equalitarianism in wages" which had been developing, and established a complex system of wage determination. The wide differentiation in wages is an obvious imitation of Soviet wage policy since 1931, when Stalin rectified the regime's former "mistake" of relying on socialist incentives alone to spur production.[21] As early as November 1949 Li Li-san had stated the regime's position: "We oppose equalitarianism and adopt various methods and systems of awards to encourage technical progress and labour initiative." [22]

The wage regulations passed by the Central-South Region may be assumed to be the standard applied to China as a whole. They set up eight industrial categories with five wage groups in each and with seven or eight wage grades in each group. Economic-financial commissions are established to determine into which category factories within the region fall. The different wage groups correspond to different types of work within the same plant. According to the regulations, piecework and time bonus systems should be adopted wherever possible. Technicians and managing personnel may receive up to 30 per cent of their wages in bonuses. Actually, the regulations may be viewed as a sort of bridge to the establishment of a piecework system which the Communists have universally decried in the capitalist societies and which has become a major part of the Soviet wage system.

Under the Chinese Communists most of the wages in industry are now paid under either a "parity unit" or the "fen" system. The parity unit is presumably a unit of constant purchasing power based upon the wholesale price of five daily necessities and varying from one locality to another. Thus in Hankow the parity unit is equal to the wholesale price of 1.65 lbs. of white rice, 4 inches of cotton cloth, $\frac{1}{32}$ kilogram of sesame oil, $\frac{1}{32}$ kilogram of salt, and 3.3 lbs. of coal briquettes. The fen is also based upon the prices of staple commodities from city to city. This unit was introduced expressly for the use of state industries, but it has spread into the few remaining "private" enterprises. The value of the fen is published regularly by the State Bank of the district involved. On 8 September 1952, for example, the rates for one fen were ¥2,551 in Shanghai, ¥2,268 in Peking, and ¥2,796 in Canton. At that time an American dollar equaled ¥22,490 at the official pegged rate of exchange.

The Peking government claims that wages have risen steadily during its rule. It asserts that average wages of the workers are 60 to 120 per cent above 1949 levels, while the price index was 5 to 10 per cent lower in the first half of 1952 than in the same period in 1949.[23] While these claims may have some validity, they must be balanced against the many drains on the worker's pay in the form of "volunteered" hours, "voluntary" donations, "aid" to various campaigns and other contributions, and greatly increased taxes. In Shanghai it is estimated that workers in general received the equivalent of 160 parity units per month before the Communists took over. In February 1952, after one of the "voluntary" wage reductions which the party cadres stage so well, the average wage fell to less than 100 parity units, a drop of more than 37 per cent—this despite the fact that the workers were putting in an average of ten hours more per week than in 1949. The *People's Daily* reported in the spring of 1954 that the highest wage in a factory where the piecework system had been adopted was ¥575,000 per month. Some idea of the actual value involved— not based on government-established exchange rates—can be conveyed by the cost of a bicycle in China today, more than ¥7,000,000.[24]

According to the Shanghai *Liberation Daily,* while the regime was boasting of the rise in wages, a miner was getting the equivalent of U.S. $4.25 a month for working 14 hours a day and 30 days a month. This hardly more than paid for his food, which cost him 13 cents for two meals a day. The wage of the average worker, according to one source, is just about half what he got under the Nationalist government or what his counterpart on Taiwan gets today.[25]

The Communist record with regard to hours would seem to be even more damning, especially in the light of past resolutions and promises. Article 32 of *The Common Program* states that "an eight- to ten-hour day should in general be enforced in publicly and privately operated enterprises . . ." While reports are, of course, difficult to substantiate, available evidence indicates that in most areas workers still average a 12-hour day. In addition, they must participate in many supervised activities, such as current affairs discussion groups, which add a minimum of two more hours per day to their schedule. According to Chinese defectors, workers still labor 13 to 14 or even 17 to 18 hours a day in some enterprises. But sometimes Communist sources themselves are more eloquent. The *People's Daily* stated that "railway workers in Shihchiachuang on the Peking-Hankow line usually work up to 24 hours consecutively. In September 1951 thirty-six workers worked for over 24 hours at a stretch; eleven worked for 27 hours at a stretch; three worked for 30 hours; and one worked for over 39 hours at a stretch." The last man was made a "labor hero." [26]

One group of refugees in Hong Kong describes Shanghai conditions in the fall of 1952 as follows:

Under the slogans of so-called "work for the people" and "work for our own working class," they demand the workers to increase their working hours in order to increase "class consciousness." Through such agents as "radicals" and "progressive elements," a series of voluntary requests were being made for the prolongation of working hours as a display of the awakening workers' "class consciousness." Up till now, the working hours have been raised to 12 hours per day. In reality it is even worse. Owing to the introduction of "emulation," "challenge," "increase production and conservation," "inspection system," and "methods of increased production," following each other in waves, the workers, in general, must work 14 hours or even more to achieve the required quota.[27]

Soviet style "emulation drives" have become one of the major methods for persuading the workers to contribute extra hours and work for less pay. Despite the claim by Liu Ning-yi at the Trade Union Congress in Vienna that "labor competitions show the firm determination of the masses of Chinese workers," the regime has had to launch emulation campaigns on a periodic basis.[28] These campaigns, which had been started before the inauguration of the regime, were called for on a nationwide basis by Li Li-san on 1 July 1951; they were made one of the major concerns of the ACFTU at its congress in May 1953; they were called for by the People's Daily in November of that year; and again in April 1954 the same paper reported an ACFTU Directive Concerning Further Development of Emulation Drives in State-Operated Industrial and Mining Enterprises.[29]

In far too many cases these emulation drives have had disastrous effects upon the workers as well as on long-range production. In one factory, workers were forced to carry a weight of 180 pounds uphill instead of the prescribed maximum of 80 pounds. Many were so exhausted after the competition month that they were unable to continue working.[30] The People's Daily of 13 July 1953 reported that as a result of "shock production" and the neglect of upkeep entailed in meeting the fourth quarter quota for coal mining in 1952, production had dropped sharply during the first quarter of 1953. "Taking the output of December 1952 as 100, it dropped to 38.1 per cent in January, to 9.7 per cent in February and to 27.2 per cent in March 1953." [31]

For the most part, wage and hour conditions are determined by "the plan" which is drawn up by each enterprise with guidance from the ministry under which it operates. In the "private" enterprises plans are drawn up by joint labor-capital consultative councils in which party cadres and activists take the lead. The necessity of meeting the goals of the plan, if possible ahead of schedule, frequently dictates long hours of work and "volunteered" hours. Plans in some cases demand production increases of up to 100 per cent in one year. Since the workers "participate" in drawing up the plan, they share in the rewards of success—such as a special mention by Chairman Mao—and in the shame and blame for failure. The number of plans for individual factories increased steadily through 1952, and most of China's workers labored under them by 1953.

The increase in hours to speed up production under the plans has had its effect on industrial safety. In a country where many of the machines are admittedly obsolete and where equipment has been more highly valued than lives, the effect of such exclusive concentration on production quotas can be costly. The *People's Daily* reported that there had been almost 3,000 industrial casualties between March and August 1952 in the North China area alone. According to the same paper on 26 August 1952, Liu Lan-t'ao admitted that injuries and deaths in factories in Tientsin had shown a 42 per cent increase between January and June. In September 1953 the *People's Daily* reported again: "During the first half year accidents were not only not reduced, but were actually more serious compared with the same period in 1952." [32]

Table II gives figures of the Shanghai General Labor Union for workers' hospitals. These figures do not include cases treated at the factories or by independent physicians. It is worth noting that the first big emulation boom reached its peak in Shanghai between August and November 1951: [33]

TABLE II

	Deaths in Hospitals	Patients	Accidents Causing Disabilities
January 1950	92	550	8
April 1950	70	625	7
July 1950	130	700	15
October 1950	132	550	18
January 1951	105	700	12
April 1951	118	600	14
July 1951	170	800	23
October 1951	255	2,050	77
January 1952	260	1,700	65

The Shanghai *Liberation Daily* admitted in an article devoted to self-criticism that "Salt workers in Hweipei [northern Kiangsu province] die like flies. Between January and June, 1951, over three hundred workers died of malnutrition and exposure alone. Most of the workers' sheds have no roofs. They sleep outdoors under a tree if they can find one. There is no fresh water supply either for drinking or cooking. There is no supply of fresh vegetables. No medical service is provided for the needy salt workers." [34] At the Tangshan Iron and Steel Works in Hopei, 41 per cent of the workers developed tuberculosis as a result of the production speed-up.[35]

In an attempt to meet this problem, the Government Administration Council instituted safety training programs and inspection systems in factories and mines in September 1952, but so far these measures have failed to alleviate a serious and steady growth in the incidence of disease and accidents among the workers.[36] As usual, lower cadres among the workers bear the brunt of the blame both for failure to speed up production and for the consequences of too rapid speed-up.

The production speed-up has been one of the factors contributing to a fairly widespread and persistent unemployment problem in Communist China. In August 1952 Minister of Personnel An Tzu-wen reported that the unemployment figure had reached more than 3,000,000 or almost one-fourth of China's working class.[37] This was a rather strange admission in view of earlier claims by the Communists that they had eliminated the unemployment problem in China. Previous official unemployment statistics had been: June 1950, 1,660,000; December 1950, 613,-000; and July 1951, 450,000.[38]

At a meeting in July 1952 the cabinet issued a statement attributing unemployment to: 1) a rise in per capita production due to industrial reforms; 2) the elimination of many of the "decadent and extravagant industries" of the past bourgeois regime; 3) the application of a large number of housewives for employment in the cities; and 4) the influx of a "surplus labor force" from the rural areas.[39] This attempt to explain growing unemployment in terms of the regime's efforts to modernize and rationalize industry (as in points 1 and 2) neglected certain obvious contributing factors. One basic cause is the regime's inability to restore prewar industrial activities which are dependent upon overseas trade and markets. The report also neglected to mention the effect of such campaigns as the 3-anti 5-anti Movement which caused the shutdown of numerous enterprises.

According to figures released by the Ministry of Labor at the end of April 1954, regular employment had been secured for some 2,063,000 workers over the past four years.[40] This would leave, after five years of Communist rule, a minimum of 1,000,000 unemployed plus seasonal unemployment and the possibility of returning soldiers. Thus, it is improbable that Mao's regime has been able to keep unemployment below 20 per cent of the non-agricultural working force of 15,000,000.

The Peking government has adopted several measures in an attempt to cope with the unemployment crisis. As mentioned above, it has forced the migration of large numbers of Chinese to some of the less populated regions of the country. "Absorption of unemployed workers" has been adopted as one of the criteria for assessing the excellence or poorness of a factory's record. Factories which effect labor economies are no longer permitted to discharge employees, and public works have been encouraged in rural areas in order to absorb workers. The cabinet has expressed a determination to achieve in the near future a "centralized system of labor distribution," again adopting a Soviet solution to the problem.

Not only are the various enterprises forced to keep workers, but they must maintain a large overhead of managerial personnel. The extent to which bureaucracy has become a part of industrial enterprise in China was revealed in a *People's Daily* editorial of 11 March 1954. It reported that a survey of 195 factories had revealed only seven in which the managerial staff was less than 10 per cent of the workers. In 50 factories the managerial staff was from 10 to 20 per cent of the number of workers and in 138 it ranged from 20 to above 50 per cent of the workers. This is a rather telling admission of the high price which the Chinese workers are paying for their supervision, political control, and education in a state where they are presumably the favored class.[41]

The matter of industrial disputes has become an almost academic question in Communist China. In state industries there are no disputes. In "privately owned" factories labor-management disputes reached a peak in May 1950, but following the introduction of party-controlled "labor-capital consultative councils" in most of the concerns, there has been no report of trouble. Machinery for collective bargaining exists, but the real decision-making power in factory management rests with trusted Communists, the "active elements" among the laborers. These activists who constitute the party committee or party branch within the state-owned factories have the duty of guaranteeing and supporting the authority of the factory director, whose position is similar to that of the director of the Soviet factory.[42]

Workers' benefits have fallen far short of the regime's extravagant propaganda promises. But since the low-wage group is presumably the leading element in Chinese politics, some enactment of workers' benefits was to be expected. One measure which the Communists claim has worked out is labor insurance. Labor Insurance Regulations, first promulgated on 26 February 1951, were revised by a proclamation of 2 January 1953.[43] Under the amended regulations, certain categories of workers are awarded benefits including aid in sickness and injury, old age pensions, maternity care, compensation to families in case of death, and disability subsidies. The regulations discriminate against nonunion members, however, and are limited to the following enterprises: 1) state or private factories or mines with workers and staff of over one hundred; 2) railways, navigation, postal, and telecommunications organizations; 3) capital construction units of industrial, mining, and communications organizations; and 4) state-operated building and construction companies. The latter two categories were added in the revised version of the regulations, undoubtedly in anticipation of the first five-year plan. Enterprises under labor insurance pay the equivalent of 3 per cent of the workers' wages into a Labor Insurance Fund which is deposited in the People's Bank in the name of the ACFTU.

Actually the distribution of registration cards for possible benefits under the Labor Insurance Regulations was accompanied by the most careful screening, with violent "struggle meetings." In Hankow, where the workers had been registered with too much haste, the ACFTU ordered that the whole process be repeated with "democratic struggle meetings" so that no politically unreliable elements would be able to participate in benefits.[44] That the Labor Insurance funds will be used without hesitation to advance the political goals of the regime was confirmed in 1954 when the ACFTU issued a notice allocating funds for the "comforting" of People's Liberation Army units.[45] This was, of course, done with the "whole-hearted, unanimous, warm and enthusiastic support of the workers."

Among other incentives for the workers, the government boasts large-scale construction of housing projects. For example, NCNA reported from Shanghai on 20 November 1952 that over two

million square meters of housing for workers had been erected
in the East China Region since "liberation." Once again, however, the self-criticism columns of the papers reveal that this has
been almost exclusively for party and trade union officials among
the workers.

In addition to such methods as the emulation campaigns, the
Chinese Communists have developed the use of the Soviet technique of "model worker." Model workers are those who set
production records or perform other feats which are exemplary
from the point of view of the regime. They are awarded prizes,
given special privileges, and prestige trips and vacations which
are highly publicized among the workers. An indication of how
attractive the "model worker" category is made was a case which
came to light in August 1952. Two railroad employees had
doctored railroad books to prove themselves "model workers."
They enjoyed labor hero benefits for quite a while before they
were discovered and expelled from the party. Their case was
publicized throughout the country as a lesson for other workers
who might harbor such "bourgeois ambitions." In December 1952
(as mentioned in Chapter 5) the Communists proclaimed the first
"model factory," and publicized its achievements to other workers
for copying. One of the achievements was the so-called "rational
distribution" of four extra hours per day for political study, technical instruction, and meetings.

But even the life of the labor hero is fraught with difficulties.
The Shanghai *Liberation Daily* of 15 July 1951 talked of the
strain put upon labor heroes and singled out the case of Yüan
Kai-li as an example. According to the paper Yüan heads his
group at the shop and has the following concurrent duties: he is a
member of the executive committee of the factory's trade union,
a member of the production committee, member of the factory
management committee, propaganda officer for the party, vice-
director of a committee for the elimination of counterrevolutionaries, workers' representative at the People's Representative
Conference of Shanghai, people's representative of the New

Municipal Center, district vice-chairman of the Consultative Council of the New Municipal Center, and district people's representative of his residential district of Yangtzepu. Yüan had to participate in meetings which lasted sometimes ten hours and in addition was called upon to speak at mass meetings. At one point he had to attend meetings for four full days and had no opportunity for sleep between his twelve-hour night shifts. Finally he had to have at least five glucose injections each month to keep him going. Meanwhile his team dropped to Grade C and the "glory of the model worker was tarnished." The paper further revealed ill feeling which developed among Yüan's fellow workers toward him. They began to call him a "model attending-meetings worker." [46]

Despite such benefit and incentive measures as have been enacted, and also despite the priority treatment given the working class in the propaganda of the regime, reports in the Chinese Communist press have indicated growing dissatisfaction among China's workers. During the first half of 1952 a purge was conducted within the labor unions in an attempt to weed out "bourgeois elements" which had "infiltrated" them. In Hankow there were charges that the "bourgeois class has sabotaged the trade unions by disintegrating the unity of the workers." [47] By mid-1952 the regime began to report cases of sabotage among the workers, though always attributed to bourgeois infiltration. In July, for example, a disastrous mine blast in Kwangtung province was laid to sabotage. In north China, Liu Lan-t'ao complained that "the amount of bad or inferior quality products is still high, while the phenomenon of waste and defective work is also serious." [48]

By 1953, however, such incidents began to assume major proportions. This was when, as mentioned above, the regime launched a campaign to take up what it called "excessive slackness in labor discipline." The campaign began with the publication of facts and figures on the industries in Tientsin in the spring. By July the *Daily Worker* in Peking reported that throughout the country state and municipal enterprises seldom achieved 90 per cent attendance of workers.⁴⁹ The 8 July *Daily Worker* listed numerous examples of slackened labor discipline, which it admitted was a far more common phenomenon than before. It reported that absenteeism, sick leave, and leave of absence had cost Tientsin's 99 state-operated units 196,149 working days in the first two months of the year. Workers were reported arriving late and putting their tools away early and some were working at low speed. "A worker in the Central-South Motor Factory could finish grinding an iron barrel in 10 minutes but took 2 hours and 15 minutes to finish one." Again, workers were accused of not taking care of their machines, some of them not being oiled or repaired in time to prevent breakdown. Defective pieces and rejects were produced. Some workers even disobeyed the chief of the workshop or their party cadres.

The NCNA reported from Shanghai on 16 July 1953:

A number of workers in some factories have even resorted to all sorts of irregular means to get a sick leave slip from the doctor. They pretend to be afflicted with headache, abdominal pain and general malaise, which are difficult to diagnose, or even take some hot pepper and hot water before they go to the clinic for temperatures to be taken. . . . In the Shanghai Electric Bulb Factory, where the working hours terminate at 5:00 p.m., many workers go to the toilet room at around 4:50 p.m. to wash their hands and get ready to leave. . . . the workers eat candies and water melon seeds, talk and laugh just as if they are attending a tea party. Instances like this are too numerous to mention.

The low degree of political consciousness on the part of workers is one cause for the relaxation of labor discipline. . . . They lack a sense of responsibility as masters of the nation. Some only see the position of the working class but fail to realize that to observe labor discipline is their duty toward the nation and the society.⁵⁰

Even fellow Communists, if they had followed the Chinese press, would have had some difficulty in accepting the statements made by Lai Jo-yu in a special article written for the Cominform journal *For a Lasting Peace, for a People's Democracy!* in April 1954, entitled "Working Class of China Carrying Out Country's General Line in Transition Period." Lai states that "The 1953 emulation drive . . . helped not only to increase output but also to improve the quality of products, reduce production costs, and lighten manual labor." According to him, "The Chinese workers possess a high degree of political consciousness; they fully understand their own responsibility to the country." [51]

In fact, the increasing concern for the state of political consciousness of the workers led to the establishment of "comrade workers' courts." These courts were set up in accordance with a resolution of the Second National Judicial Conference in 1953. According to the *People's Daily:*

The workers' court is different from the people's court in that the latter is an organ to carry out the duty and right of judgment on behalf of the state while the former is one organized by the workers and staff members themselves. But the workers' court also differs from the practice of criticism and self-criticism as generally conducted, because the disciplinary education and actions taken by the workers' courts are of a forcible nature and those who are brought under its sanction are obligated to comply.[52]

By 5 June 1954 the regime reported that more than seventy such courts had been set up to cope with labor indiscipline and that the results had been uniformly successful.[53] Yet the *People's Daily* still talked of the need to consolidate labor discipline and urged the cadres to exert their utmost efforts to educate the workers and strictly punish all offenders.[54] In August 1953 the Peking *Daily Worker* reported the beating and torture of workers by the cadres in the factories. The cadres were accused of "rash methods" and an "impatient mood." It explained to these cadres, who were as usual caught in the middle: "It must be made clear that in the work of strengthening labor discipline, we must determinedly prevent the occurrence of this method of punishment, but this does not mean that the adoption of necessary punishment measures is rejected." [55]

Mao's regime faces a difficult propaganda problem in trying to persuade the Chinese working class that despite increased hours, lower wages, and almost total control over their every movement, their lot has been improved. Whatever success has attended the efforts thus far is due in large measure to the party and trade union activists who have kept the laborers so occupied with meetings and "political" studies that there has been little time to express dissatisfaction.

The lot of the Chinese worker has never been an easy one, and the Chinese are capable of enduring great hardships. Yet with their life now harder than ever, workers are still loath to leave their home areas or to risk movement without authorization, and many have realized that they dare not complain against the regime. Their only hope—and a dubious one—for bettering their increasingly miserable situation is to achieve model worker status, which means staying on the job, working harder than ever, and endorsing the propaganda line of the party with enthusiasm, all of this sometimes at the risk of enmity from fellow workers. The deterioration of conditions among this "favored" class in Communist China has become evident from their increasing proportion among the refugees slipping into Hong Kong from 1952 onward.

The lot of women among the workers has not been appreciably different. Women were afforded equal rights under *The Common Program,* and the Marriage Law in form at least underscored those rights. Although women still constitute only about 9 to 10 per cent of the Communist party membership, their number in industry has shown a decided increase. Teng Ying-chao, vice-chairman of the All China Democratic Women's Federation, reported that in 1952 there were almost one million women in industry or nearly 74 per cent more than in 1950. Women constituted 8.6 per cent of the model workers in 1951.[56] The increase in women workers is due in large part to the propagandizing of increased benefits which have been extended to them under the ACFTU and Labor Insurance Regulations.

Presumably child labor has not been a problem for the Communists. They have merely changed the term to "apprentices" or "youth workers." There are no reliable statistics on the number involved, but there are indications in Communist publications that child labor continues. One source in 1952 described the work of youth workers six or seven years old in the silk industry in southern Kiangsu. They work 12 hours a day for the equivalent of eight cents worth of rice. This would seem to be in defiance of directives limiting the work day for children under 14 years to six hours, and guaranteeing that the minimum wage for the youth worker should be enough to live on.[57] These children are getting an early introduction to the glories of belonging to the "leadership class in Chinese society."

Any capital surplus for industrial construction can accumulate only through further deprivations imposed upon both workers and peasants, and this presents the regime with a formidable problem of maintaining workers' morale, which has already shown signs of breaking. The criticisms of their attitude in the press and the increasing number of control measures indicate that the Chinese workers are beginning to realize that they, like the peasants, are the victims of a great hoax.[58] During the first two years of the five-year plan the regime has stepped up propaganda and control measures to a new intensity, and this has involved the extension of control over "private" industry and a consequent subjection of the interests there to the overriding dictates of state interest. This has meant advances for certain workers, but in general hours are longer, wages are lower, and conditions of work are increasingly hazardous.

An examination of the relationship of the Chinese Communist party and the labor force, therefore, shows that as in the Soviet Union under Stalin the party has become a bureaucratic status group which, though operating in the name of the workers, is controlling and exploiting them with techniques learned from its Soviet counterpart. Apparently the Communist party of the Soviet Union has been an excellent teacher.

We may agree—though hardly with enthusiasm—with a group
of factory workers in Communist China who sent a fraternal note
to Soviet workers and concluded it by saying, "All of us understand that your today means our tomorrow."

8. CULTURE AND THE INTELLECTUALS

At present . . . many of our comrades fail to understand even the most fundamental concepts of Marxism-Leninism. It is, for example, a fundamental concept that objective conditions determine the subjective, that objective conditions of class struggle and national struggle determine our thinking and our sentiments. They say that everything begins with "love." Speaking of love, there can only be love of a class, or class love, in a class society. Yet these comrades seek a love that stands above all class distinctions; they seek abstract love, abstract freedom, abstract truth, abstract human nature, etc., and thereby prove how deeply they have been influenced by the bourgeoisie. We must uproot this influence and bring an open mind to the study of Marxism-Leninism.

Mao Tse-tung, Talks at the Yenan
Literary Meetings, *May 1942.*[1]

As early as 1942, in talks at Yenan, Mao Tse-tung indicated that Communism in China, as in the Soviet Union, would involve the complete subordination of all phases of life to the dictates of the Communist party. The ideology of Marx, Lenin, and Stalin was to be the instrument for an all-pervasive political control. The Party Reform Movement of 1942–44, of which Mao's talks to the meeting of literary and art workers were an important part, was an intensive period of political training with struggle meetings and mutual criticism designed to reform the thoughts of party members and leftist intellectuals. It was the first comprehensive attempt by the Chinese Communists to pattern thought control after the Soviets and to prepare the party for the application of these principles to all of China after military victory in the civil war. Under the influence of this movement the cult of Mao Tse-tung and of the "thought of Mao Tse-tung" was inaugurated, and the "mass line and class line in art and literature" were laid down, Stalin's pet phrase "the union of theory and practice" became basic doctrine, and the various techniques for ideological remolding were adopted from the Soviets.

It is ironical that the Chinese intellectual and artistic leaders failed to see the implications of the "struggle" at Yenan. They continued to support the Communists, who represented the most vocal leadership in protesting conditions in postwar China. But they were not alone in missing the significance of the first large-scale Ideological Remolding carried on under the Communists. One searches the State Department's 1949 *White Paper* on China in vain for any indication of what was going on in Communist areas during this very important purge.[2] The first thorough treatment of the Party Reform Movement in Communist areas during World War II did not appear in the United States until 1952, long after the portents had been replaced by fact in Red China.[3]

To understand the significance of the 1942–44 Party Reform Movement for subsequent Communist policy toward the various aspects of Chinese culture, one must appreciate how Marxist dogma and the Communist structure of control buttress each other. In the Marxist world view, environment determines everything, and the most important aspect of environment is the class struggle. Not even the natural or physical sciences can be separated from the class struggle. In fact, to a Marxist the term "science" is synonymous with Marxist-Leninist theory, which is viewed as the purest of all sciences. Every activity or thought of man is determined by the class structure of his environment. Therefore, in Communist theory, no activity can be nonpolitical because all politics are determined by the class struggle. The frequent Communist phrase "politically conscious" means being aware of the class struggle.

This view gives the Communists the assurance of infallibility and authority, since they see themselves as the leaders in the final phase of the great world class struggle. It justifies them in asserting authority in every field of activity once the party is in control of an area. Any failure to accept such authority would by logical extension of the reasoning be equivalent to sabotage of the state and of the highest interests of the people as embodied in the Communist leadership. This leads in a circle, for the further a regime extends its supervision, the more fearful it becomes of any activities which are beyond its purview. Thus intensification and further penetration of control follow, until no field remains outside the scrutiny of the interpreters of Communist doctrine.

Because the Communists view all other fields as subordinate to Marxist "science," the leaders of the party regard themselves as being at the same time the leading scientists and intellectuals. As leaders of a party whose mission they see as historically predetermined, they feel called upon to supervise any field of human intellectual or artistic endeavor. This is part of the rationale behind the leader myth created for Stalin in the USSR and in a similar manner for Mao in China. As the highest embodiment of the aspirations of the "working class" both Stalin and Mao could within the Communist framework be regarded as all-sapient.[4]

In the Soviet Union under Stalin the invasion of some new field by the regime usually brought about recantations and acceptance of the official line laid down by Stalin. For example, in the summer of 1948 the Soviet geneticist Lysenko won Stalin's support over all opponents for his promotion of the late T. H. Michurin's theory that acquired characteristics are inherited. He announced to the Lenin Academy of Agricultural Science that the Central Committee of the Communist party had approved of his theories. *Pravda* described the scene as follows: "This communication by the President aroused general enthusiasm in the members of the session. As if moved by a single impulse all those present arose from their seats and started a stormy, prolonged ovation in honor of the wise leader and teacher of the Soviet people, the greatest scientist of our era, Comrade Stalin." This was followed by a series of recantations by many geneticists who had been bold enough to disagree with Lysenko.[5]

Other fields of science in the Soviet Union have suffered the same fate. In physics Einstein's theories of the universe have been attacked; in psychology Pavlov has been enshrined and Freud and other Western psychologists discarded; in linguistics Marr was repudiated and Stalin himself propounded the official doctrine. Communist orthodoxy in the USSR also "invaded the cultural sphere, laying down the party line, and banning all 'bourgeois' ideas, in philosophy, music, drama, and art." [6]

The story of all cultural and intellectual activity in China in the five years of Communist rule has been for the most part identical. Since the years of the Party Reform Movement Mao has been regarded as the oracle in all phases of Chinese thought and culture. The "thought of Mao Tse-tung" is one of the essential ingredients of Chinese Communist doctrinal training; it is the highest science and basic philosophy. According to the official interpretation of Mao's intellectual leadership:

For 30 years Comrade Mao Tse-tung has waged unceasing and irreconcilable struggles against various reactionary ideologies outside the Party and against opportunism which took various forms inside the Party. . . . Without doubt, the very fact that the Chinese people under the leadership of the Chinese working class rose to struggle and have recently won great victories is a fresh confirmation of the large-scale, outstanding victory of Marxism-Leninism in the East; a confirmation that the teachings of Marx, Engels, Lenin and Stalin are a universal, all-powerful science applicable everywhere without exception; and a confirmation that Comrade Mao Tse-tung, the leader of the Communist Party of China, has applied this science to the conditions of China and developed it with very brilliant success.[7]

Like Stalin, Mao has become more of a myth than a public figure. No one is sure where he lives, and he is seldom seen except at the most important functions in Peking. Yet everyone is made acutely aware that his is the guiding hand for China under Communist rule. His picture adorns every home and every room in public buildings. His name is invoked by people of every profession as the all-knowing leader in their field. Young children chant poems and songs dedicated to him. Every public utterance ends with a *"Mao Tse-tung Wan-sui* (Long live Mao Tse-tung)!" The national favorite song of China according to the Reds, "The East Shines Red," is in praise of Chairman Mao:

> The East shines red,
> The sun arises,
> Mao Tse-tung appears in China,
> Toiling for the happiness of the people,
> The savior of the people! [8]

Mao's writings are studied exhaustively and committed to memory. In many ways Mao has come to fill the symbolic position of the Chinese emperors of old who not only were heads of state but were also regarded as the first scholars of the land, the leaders in all matters affecting Chinese society, and the symbolic representatives of the unity of the people.

The use of the cult of the leader is just one of the party's many techniques for achieving the goals which have been set for "cultural and educational work in the new China." [9] In general these goals are the same as in the political, military, and economic activities of the party. The first is complete party control. This means enforcing subordination of all interests to those of the Marxist state. The second major goal, that of conformity, follows from this. Heresy, or in Communist parlance "deviationism," cannot be permitted. Pressure for orthodoxy and unanimity is unrelenting. These two goals are dependent in great measure upon achieving the third goal, that of eliminating "undesirable influences." This entails examining religion, art, literature, music, education, and every other form of cultural activity with roots deep in the past. Those aspects of Chinese culture which cannot be made to serve the interests of the state are slated for destruction.

In eradicating "undesirable influences" Communists were at a distinct advantage when they seized power in China. From the outset they had openly stated their determination to do away with those aspects of the former Chinese culture which they labeled "feudal." [10] They could accept those aspects of traditional Chinese civilization they deemed desirable from the point of view of their political power and could be utterly ruthless about destroying the rest. Of course, temporary concessions had to be made to long-established customs, but there was no need to compromise with regard to their ultimate objectives. For example, the Communists advocate cremation of the dead as means of freeing some of the large plots of arable land used in China for grave sites; but this involved a drastic attack upon the whole Confucian pattern of family life and ancestor worship. When in 1952 the regime ran into difficulty because some of the cadres were forcibly expropriating grave sites, the *People's Daily* urged them to proceed slowly: "the government cannot for the time being enforce cremation as the only form of burial, but the cadres should enhance the awakening of the masses and leave it to the masses themselves to take the initiative in effecting reform." [11]

One "undesirable influence" in present-day Chinese culture has been the impact of the West, and this the Communists are determined to wipe out. All Western influence in China is viewed by Mao and his colleagues as imperialism, and according to their theory of social development its elimination is one of the most important parts of the class struggle in China.

A fourth major goal of cultural and intellectual control by the Chinese Communists is the creation of "true patriotism." According to one of the party's guidebooks for patriotic education in the Chinese schools, patriotism involves the following:

1. absolute opposition to imperialism (primarily American);
2. belief that the Fatherland is great, lovable, and has offered great inventions to the world;
3. absolute support of the present government, the New Democracy, the *Common Program*, and the Democratic Dictatorship;

4. love of the people, of work, of science, and of the protection of
the collective properties of the country;
5. support for the association of China with the USSR and the People's Democracies;
6. humble acknowledgment of the USSR.[12]

Patriotism, for example, is one of the chief motives behind the
mass participation in athletic activities encouraged by the party.
In every major town and even some of the farm villages, blaring
loud speakers broadcast morning exercises which are viewed as
necessary for the "self-assertion of a strong nation." Like the
Soviets the Chinese are training teams for world athletic meets
with the resolve to prove the superiority of the "socialist environment." [13]

A fifth major goal is to apply the experiences and standards of
the Soviet Union. As Liu Shao-ch'i put it, "The pressing task before the Chinese people today is to absorb the new culture of the
Soviet Union and to take it as a guide in building up New
China." [14] This means following the Soviet interpretation of "culture" in such forms of mass participation as state-sponsored dance
groups; accepting Soviet artistic standards for the cinema, literature, and so forth; and following the Soviet lead in the promotion
of international cultural exchange with other "democratic" groups
and countries. For example, taking over Soviet dogma in the
field of science is justified on the basis that "The Soviet Union is
the sole country in the world where the advancement and popularization of science has been carried out in a planned and successful manner." One of the most active scientific organizations
promoted by the Chinese Communists was the Michurin Society,
founded in the spring of 1949 and dedicated to the application
of Lysenko's genetic theories in China. By the end of the first
year its membership was over three thousand.[15] To date there have
been no reports on the fate of the society since the apparent fall
from favor of Lysenko during the Malenkov regime.

The activities and developments which the Mao regime considers "cultural affairs" are too numerous for treatment in a brief survey. Yet a good idea of the extent to which the goal of applying Soviet standards is being realized can be derived from an examination of a few of the major "cultural" problems faced by the Communists and their methods for handling them.

One of the chief of these problems is the matter of minority groups in Chinese territory. The Chinese refer to themselves as Han people, and the non-Han people have been a vexation for Chinese rulers for thousands of years. According to Peking statistics there are more than sixty different minority nationalities with a total population of over 40,000,000.[16] The largest concentration of these non-Han people—almost half of them—is in the southwest part of China. The Communists have classified all of these groups, which range from a few hundred in population to several million, according to their stage of class development. Thus, the Miao people are at the primitive pastoral stage, the Lolos live under the serf system, the Tibetans outside of Tibet live in a well developed feudal stage, and some such as the Mongols in Inner Mongolia are in a semifeudal stage.

Because these people maintain their own languages and customs and in many cases have been hostile to the Han Chinese, handling them has proved a very ticklish matter. Since coming to power the Communists have followed a policy of establishing "autonomous areas" for the minority groups. One of the largest of these areas, for example, occupies almost half of Kwangsi province and contains one-third of the population of the province. This Chuang Autonomous Region has forty-eight different minority groups. Other important minority group areas include the Miao Autonomous Region in Hunan, regions in Kweichow which constitute 40 per cent of that province's population, the Thai area in Yunnan, the Tibetan areas of Ch'inghai, Mohammedan areas of Kansu and Ninghsia, and the Mongolian areas in Inner Mongolia which account for more than half the population there.

Most of the policies adopted by the Chinese Communists toward the minority nationalities are based on the writings of Stalin, especially his two sets of theses on the nationality problem adopted by the Tenth and Twelfth Congresses of the Russian Communist party in 1921 and 1923.[17] *The Common Program* (Articles 50 through 53) laid down the principles of equality, regional autonomy, and freedom to develop national languages, customs, and religious beliefs; these are repeated in the New Constitution of 1954. The Communists have gone all out in their efforts to win the support of the minority nationalities. They have fostered publication of books in the national languages, organized dance and art groups, improved medical care, and developed communications facilities in the areas. The activities of the Commission on Nationalities Affairs under the direction of Li Wei-han are closely integrated with those of the Communist party and the People's Revolutionary Military Council. The commission holds periodic conferences of representatives from the various minority nationality areas; the Third Conference (Enlarged) was held in September 1953.[18] The most important part of the program, however, has been the training of Communist cadres from the minority nationalities, whose duty it is to insure party control in the areas. To date more than 100,000 such cadres have been trained, most of them youths.

Although the Chinese Communists have given more attention than previous regimes to winning over the minority groups, and their propaganda claims great success, there are indications of growing resistance in the form of revolts and sabotage as the minority peoples become aware that their interests are to be subordinated to those of the Han Chinese. The only areas where the Land Reform class struggle has not been completed are those of the minority groups, many of whom have not accepted "liberation from landlord oppression." At the Third Conference of the Commission on Nationalities Affairs the minority groups were told that they "must recognize the advanced experience and leading role of the Han Chinese," and the Communist spokesmen warned the Mongols that Inner Mongolia "must not secede from China because if it does, it cannot preserve its independence." [19] Fei Hsiao-

t'ung, vice-president of the Central Nationalities College in Peking, in commenting on the 1954 Constitution told the minority
groups, "Although ours is a multinational country, it is also a
united one. We are all marching toward the same goal [social-
ism]." [20]

Han Chinese cadres working in minority areas have had an
especially difficult time in trying to follow the policies of Peking.
On the one hand they are urged to bring the minority nationalities
under control and on the other they are publicly, at least, repri-
manded for some of their actions. The Committee on Nationalities
Affairs in Honan, for example, reported that Mohammedan nationality rights were not being respected by Han cadres, who
ignored Mohammedan proposals and suggestions and insisted that
in a "people's state" the "minority must follow the majority
rule." [21] In Kwangsi minority groups were forced to turn in their
jewelry ("To wear jewelry is a sign of feudal backwardness!")
and the Han cadres refused to give payment or issue receipts. [22]
In areas where Han Chinese and minority groups live together,
the People's Banks have practiced discriminatory loan policies. [23]

The *People's Daily* of 9 September 1953 admitted that it was
common practice for the minorities not to be consulted by government organs dealing with their affairs, and that often governments at a higher level ignore the autonomous areas under them.
Most of the minority group officials were found by the organ of
the Central Committee to have empty titles and no power. On
the other hand, the same issue of the newspaper warned representatives of the minority nationalities that "narrow nationalism"
is the same as forming "small cliques." This, they were told, was
"contrary to patriotism and internationalism" and would have to
be abandoned.

In general, then, Communist policy has involved an attempt to
utilize the national cultural forms of the minority groups and at
the same time develop active party leaders who will be able to
bring the minority areas into eventual complete control by Peking. [24]

Probably the most ticklish minority problem for the Communists is the handling of the Mohammedans. The *People's Daily* estimates the nine Islamic "nationalities" in China at about 10,-000,000 persons, but other pro-Communist sources have sometimes put the figure at more than 50,000,000, obviously an exaggeration.[25] Many difficulties have been surmounted temporarily by treating the Mohammedans not only as a religious group but also—following the example of the Nationalists—as a minority nationality. The Communists' stand in principle against any group which demands superior loyalty remains unequivocal, but by treating the Moslem groups as distinct national minorities they have been able to be lenient in practice. The Peking rulers are fully aware that the Moslems in China are an organic part of the Islamic world of Southeast Asia, where Communism has definite political ambitions; and they do not want to offend Moslem nations on the borders of China, Pakistan, and Afghanistan.

Despite the relative restraint with which it has dealt with the Mohammedans in China, Peking has run into difficulty in attempting to impose control upon members of this religious community whose faith and discipline are strong. The Moslem areas have been involved more than any others in reports of rebellion and resistance to Communist rule. Probably the largest open rebellion admitted by the Communists since they seized control of the country was staged by more than 20,000 Mohammedans in Kansu province between April and July of 1952. The insurrectionists, according to Communist sources, killed over 3,000 cadres, including civil and military officers, and seized three districts before the People's Liberation Army was able to put down the revolt. The incident was not reported until October 1952, when the Communists admitted peasant dissatisfaction with the Land Reform and "adventurist tendencies" toward oppression of religion by the cadres.[26]

Other religious groups in China have not fared so well under the Communists. The Chinese Reds accept the orthodox Marxist-Leninist view that religion is an "opiate for the masses" and has no place in a classless society. They are firm in their determination eventually to eradicate all traces of religious devotion and organization from the Chinese scene. Many religious leaders came over to the Communists in 1949 and 1950 under the impression that they could continue as before. Article 5 of *The Common Program* guaranteed them freedom of religious belief.[27] They were soon disabused of any hopes.

Undoubtedly the Buddhist faith has suffered much oppression under the Communists, and it has for the most part been forced to suffer in silence. The loose organization of Buddhism in China has made the Communist attack an easy task and at the same time prevented any sort of organized protest from reaching the outside world. Mention of Buddhism in the Communist press is hard to find.

During the Land Reform the lands of a large percentage of Buddhist monasteries were seized and redistributed, and many monks were classified as landlords. Buddhist temples were often selected for struggle meetings and executions in the countryside. Temples and shrines in both city and country have been converted into workers' "cultural palaces." In the larger cities, the devout Buddhists were found mainly among the older people; the Communists have succeeded in preventing new converts from among the masses.

In November 1952 a Chinese Buddhist Association was formed in Peking with several leading Buddhist scholars in its top leadership. Its role in serving the Communist state was forecast in an article by party Central Committeeman Ch'en Ming-shu which appeared in all the major newspapers in May 1951. Ch'en denounced much of the Buddhist canon and outlined some of the chief tasks for China's Buddhists: 1) participate in Land Reform, 2) struggle against counterrevolutionaries, 3) play a leading role in the Resist America, Aid Korea Movement, and 4) recognize the Buddhist duty to construct a new religion in the new society.[28] Such statements and such organization meant that Buddhism, whose very essence is quiet service and contemplation, was being organized out of existence. In Tibet, the Communists have had to proceed more slowly against a more tightly organized form of Buddhism, Lamaism.

Taoist belief in China has frequently been associated with secret societies, and many of these societies played a role in the overthrow of dynasties in the past. The Taoists' belief in magic, divination, and secret organization made them a natural first target for the Communists. During 1950 and 1951 the campaign against Taoist societies in China was ruthless and merciless. Their members were executed as counterrevolutionaries.[29] At the end of a vicious drive against the Taoists in 1953, P'eng Chen reported to the Government Council that more than "4,000,000 duped members had withdrawn from these reactionary sects and societies," and the battle was essentially won.[30] Yet in 1954 reports of resistance led by "reactionary Taoist sects" continued to appear in the Communist press. Communist figures on the size of the sects being eliminated, however, have grown gradually smaller over the past five years. It is probable that Taoism will soon cease to have any importance in China.

The stories of the Christian refugees pouring into Hong Kong have made the plight of Christians in China well known throughout the world. Christianity has been under attack because in Communist doctrine it represents Western imperialism in China. No aspect of the humanitarian work of devoted Christian missionaries over the past century has been spared attack. Chinese Christian leaders have been forced to write denunciations of their past activities and associations. By April 1952 there were less than 100 Protestant missionaries left in China out of more than 3,000 living there when the Communists came to power.[31] Catholic missionaries in China declined in number from 3,222 in January 1951 to 364 in November 1953. In a majority of cases the missionaries were subjected to some combination of imprisonment, torture, house arrest sometimes lasting for years, and public mass trial.[32]

The campaign against the Christian churches in China started in July 1950 with a movement to sever all foreign connections. The Communists organized a National Christian Council which issued a *Christian Manifesto* in September 1950. All Chinese Christians were required to sign or risk being accused of aiding imperialism. One section of the *Manifesto* stated the future fundamental aims of the church in China:

The Church must teach the evils of past imperialism, purge itself of the influences of imperialism, especially American imperialism which is plotting to use the Church for its own ends. The Church should "oppose war and uphold peace" and support the government's land reform policy.

Through self-criticism, austerity measures, and thorough reform of itself, the Church should instil a "patriotic and democratic" spirit among its members and aim at self-reliance.[33]

One of the many great Christian leaders in China to obey the call to sever all foreign connections was Chao Tsi-chen, dean of the Department of Religion at Yenching University, prolific author, and a recipient of honorary degrees in the United States. In a letter to the *People's Daily* of 16 April 1951 he said:

In July of last year, the World Federation of Christian Associations made an announcement condemning North Korea as an aggressor and impugning the motives of the World Peace Conference's appeal for peace. This announcement placed me in a very embarrassing position, for on the one hand I am one of the chairmen of the World Federation of Christian Associations and on the other a faithful citizen of the Chinese People's Republic. Being a patriot, I cannot but raise my protest against the above announcement, which sounded like the frantic cries of the people of Wall Street. It was probable that, being a chairman, I would be taken as favoring this announcement. I therefore feel obliged to resign from my post as a chairman of the World Federation of Christian Associations. I have also requested that my name be dropped from the list of the various committees of the Federation. In doing so, I should say that I have full freedom in reaffirming my confidence and faith in Jesus Christ.

Chao's letter was evidently unsatisfactory to the Communists, for although he had followed their wishes, he was subsequently arrested and since March 1952 nothing has been heard of him.[34]

A concerted effort has been made to present all mission work of any nation or Christian sect as scheming by "American imperialism." In an important article in the *People's Daily* of 13 April 1951 entitled "How Did Imperialism Use Religion for Aggression in China?" Hsieh Hsing-yao maintained:

In the past hundred years, churches have been the bastion of the aggressors, while the latter have served as the background for the former. Whenever chances occurred for diplomatic negotiations, certain missionaries came to muddle in affairs. For instance, J. Leighton Stuart, former president of Yenching University, had posed as a religious leader and educator for many years. Outwardly he acted as if he really sympathized with China but in fact he was one of the most important secret agents for American aggression on China. Unveiling himself, he became the American ambassador to China in order to carry out America's aggressive policy toward China.[35]

Catholics in China have been the subjects of more bitter persecution than any other sects. The extent to which the Peking regime was willing to go in its attempt to eradicate all sympathy for the West is indicated by the charges leveled against Catholic sisters in China. The Sacred Heart Home for Children in Nanking was labeled "Little Buchenwald," and the sisters were accused of deliberately starving, neglecting, torturing, and selling Chinese children into slavery.[36] The many hospitals established by the medical missionaries in China were charged with practicing on human guinea pigs. According to the Communists medical ethics in mission hospitals were nonexistent.[37]

Mission schools were subjected to bitter attack. They were accused of serving as centers for spying and sabotage activities and for "cultural aggression." Catholic schools were singled out as centers for promoting fascism in China and as espionage organizations for the United States Army.[38] The Vatican is stated by

Peking to be the tool of United States imperialism and Catholic priests constitute the organized spy network.[39]

The campaign against Christianity built up gradually and in many respects followed the other manifestations of the extension of Communist control. Christians were alerted to their fate by execution of many of their number during the violence of 1951. During 1952, the year of regimentation, they were frequently denounced as special targets of the mass drives. In 1953 the final purge to eliminate any remaining influence was launched. By July and August of that year the campaign against the Catholic Church was in full swing. In Canton, for example, the People's Liberation Army issued a proclamation on 5 August banning the Legion of Mary as an "international anti-Communist and anti-people reactionary organization in the guise of religion and manipulated by imperialism." In Shanghai a special exhibition was staged to demonstrate "Catholic espionage activities." [40]

Paragraph 21 of the Election Law of 1 March 1953 indicated that the day of religion was ended in China as far as the Communists were concerned. Under its provisions Christians and Buddhists are denied the franchise unless their organizations are members of government-sponsored bodies and their political good behavior is beyond doubt.[41] The Chinese Communists' systematic attack on religion has followed the dictates of Soviet orthodoxy, and in many respects their compromises have been fewer and their success more marked than was the case in Russia. This may be, of course, because religion is not as deeply rooted in China as it was in Russia.

But religion has not been considered as important a part of China's cultural heritage by many as her wealth of literature, art, music, and scholarship. In his talks on art and literature in Yenan in 1942 Mao stated that "literature and art" must form a "part of our revolutionary machinery." This has meant that since the Communist seizure of power all China's past literature has been examined to determine which items serve the "revolutionary machinery." On this score the Communist press's description of actions by the two largest publishing houses of prewar China is only too eloquent:

Since the conclusion of the First All China Publications Conference, the Commercial Press and the Chung Hua [China] Book Company have successfully carried out the work of examining their inventory of books and periodicals published before liberation, in preparation for embarking on specialization of trade.

In more than 50 years the Commercial Press has published approximately 15,000 titles of books and periodicals. It is estimated that in the summer of 1950 there were in stock approximately 8,800 titles of books, the majority of which were questionable in viewpoint, ideology, terminology, and contents. In order to be responsible to the readers, all these items were examined. At the end of November 1951 the Commercial Press completed its examination of stock and found only 1,234 titles proper for circulation, constituting only 14 per cent of the titles listed. For these books and the new books published after liberation a new catalogue has been compiled. . . .

In respect to the examination of preliberation books and periodicals, the Chung Hua Book Company has used the same disposal and examination methods as the Commercial Press. The catalogue now lists 2,000 odd items instead of the original 13,000. In the Shanghai office alone, from 1 to 23 November, 1951, ¥229,400,000 were gained from the sale of waste paper . . . of more than 80 tons of destroyed books . . . From January to December 1951, in the Shanghai office alone, a total of 237 tons was destroyed for sale as waste paper.

Judging from the above-stated facts, it may be seen that with a view to enabling themselves to serve truly as publishing organs of the people for strengthening their ideological education, the Commercial Press and the Chung Hua Book Company have carried out strong struggles against the business viewpoint of the past. They have demonstrated their will by destroying poisonous books and periodicals and by examining and revising preliberation books and periodicals.[42]

For the libraries which possessed books banned from the publishers' lists a member of the staff of the Kiangsi Library explained "How We Should Dispose of Bad Books." [43] Some of the most famous libraries in China have been consigned to flames. For example, the Hunan provincial government seized Wang Jen-ch'iu's famous collection of masterpieces of literature and art in Hsiangtan, the native home of Tseng Kuo-fan, the great nineteenth century general. Over 17,000 cases of books were burned on the spot.[44] In Swatow more than 300,000 volumes containing the "vestiges of feudal culture" were collected and burned in a bonfire which lasted from 22 to 25 May 1953. In March 1953 the regime even ordered the burning of the matrices of books by the Commercial Press and China Book Company stored in the British Crown Colony of Hong Kong, and dispatched agents to supervise. The attempt was frustrated only after protests by Chinese scholars and supporters of the Nationalist government to the British authorities.[45]

Only a few of the works from China's great literary heritage have been spared. One of the Thirteen Classics, the *Book of Odes,* has been preserved, because it contains "popular" poems and chants of ancient times. A few poets, such as Ch'ü Yüan, have escaped destruction because they supposedly wrote for the masses; and the Chinese vernacular novels and plays are being preserved. But to all of these, new commentaries are being provided which interpret their plots in terms of class struggle. The day may not be far off when but a scattered few Chinese will have any knowledge of the Chinese heritage of literature.

In order to guarantee the production and circulation of ideologically correct works the Peking government has complete control over the press and publishing houses. By 1952 the New China Book Stores had already assumed responsibility for distribution of 80 per cent of the books published.[46] Under the September 1952 Regulations for the Control of Publications, Printing, and Distribution Enterprises, the editorial staffs of all publishing firms are required to register with the government and submit regular reports. Periodicals are now distributed by the Post Office, and the postmen are frequently made responsible for filling subscription quotas. By the fall of 1953 drastic reforms had been carried out in the management of all periodicals in China. The *China Monthly Review*, for example, which had followed every turn in policy line laid down by Peking, suspended publication in July 1953. The *Progressive Daily* and the Shanghai *Ta Kung Pao* were merged in January 1953 to become the Tientsin *Ta Kung Pao*. The only English language daily in Shanghai, the *Shanghai News*, ceased publication in December 1952. Both periodical and book publishers have been organized under Communist party auspices to specialize in their publications. Thus the Commercial Press and the China Book Company publish only works on natural science, physics, engineering, agriculture, medicine, and public health.[47]

All has not been smooth for the Communist control program. Criticism brought forward at the conference of representatives of the New China Book Company in July 1953 indicated that distribution work left much to be desired. The Communist press reported:

The New China Book Company has been inclined to operate blindly in the past. This was most conspicuous in its inability to differentiate between the peculiar needs of the cities and the villages . . . As a result, blind and careless deviations were brought about in rural distribution work. In the spring of 1951 the company arranged for the setting up of large numbers of rural libraries and the distribution of 100,000,000 copies of Resist America, Aid Korea books and magazines. Because this was far in excess of the cultural study needs and the purchasing power of the rural readers, the books had to be distributed by forced allocation.

Expression of this blindness manifested itself not only in a lack of understanding of the number of books needed by the readers but also in a lack of understanding of the types of books actually needed. Books needed by readers were understocked while those not wanted were overstocked. . . . Books about wheat growing in Shantung were sent to Sinkiang and Kwangtung, while books about the cultivation of a vegetable in Szechwan were sent to Kiangsu and Shantung where no such vegetable was grown.[48]

How are the great gaps in the Chinese bookshelves being filled? There is every reason to accept Communist statements that the

196 CHINA UNDER COMMUNISM

printing presses are turning out materials in greater quantities than ever before in Chinese history. Figures released for 1952 indicated that by then more than 760,000,000 copies of books were being printed annually, 365 magazines with a total of 200,000,000 copies, and 276 newspapers at administrative district level and above.[49]

Basically Communist publications can be grouped into four general categories. The first and probably the most important is composed of translations from the Russian. These include the works of Communist leaders, Soviet-approved Russian literature, and Soviet textbooks and technical manuals. Peking's minister of higher education reported in June 1953 that more than 130 different textbooks translated from Russian had been adopted in Chinese institutions of higher learning.[50] By December 1952 the Communists claimed to have translated and published over 3,000 Russian books, and the authorities called for more. Prominent among the Russian materials were Soviet youth publications and the collected works of Stalin.

The second general category of publications in Red China comprises the theoretical works and technical productions of the Chinese Communist leaders. These include, for example, the collected works of Mao—which have been hailed with great fanfare —rewritten school textbooks, and ideological guidebooks.

The third general category, popular level propaganda works, constitutes the bulk of the published material. There is official Communist propaganda for every conceivable group and every conceivable subject within China. But the foremost target of propaganda literature is the Chinese youth, and there are more publications for these than for any other group. Especially important are the comic books produced in pocket size in millions of copies. These tell stories of class heroes, war victories, production records, and other achievements of the new society. They are designed to induce extremes of emotion, and some of the scenes depicted are full of savagery and sadism.[51]

The fourth category of works turned out by the Chinese Communist publishing houses encompasses what the Peking leaders call literature and art. These are the approved works of Communist writers, painters, and musicians. The output has been very thin, and the authorities have admitted difficulties in getting writers to produce satisfactory works in sufficient quantity.

The Communists have been able to draw upon the talents of many distinguished authors. After World War I there was a remarkable flowering of literature in the Chinese vernacular. Most of the works were leftist in slant and represented a strong protest against existing conditions in China. Several of the novels were translated into Western languages and were very successful. The names of such Chinese authors as Lau Shaw, Pa Chin, Lu Hsun, to name but a few, became well known throughout the world. Lu Hsun, who was bitterly attacked by the Communists before his death, is now enshrined as the "Gorky of China." Most of these writers had aided the Communist cause among the literate Chinese and they flocked eagerly to the side of Mao when his armies began to move southward in 1948 and 1949, little realizing that a literature of protest would no longer be possible under Communist rule. The failure of the hundreds of literary lights gathered in Peking and Shanghai to produce a single work of distinction in the course of five years of Communist rule may be an early indication not only that they misunderstood the nature of the Communist cause they helped but also that they have been unable to adjust themselves to Mao's rule.

At his Yenan talks in 1942 Mao laid down a firm line for the writers and artists of the new China. He warned them that "All culture or all present-day literature and art belong to a certain class, to a certain party, or to a certain political line. There is no such thing as art for art's sake, or literature and art that lie above class distinctions or above partisan interests. There is no such thing as literature and art running parallel to politics or being independent of politics. They are in reality nonexistent." [52] Mao set the official canon for all future work; it should "serve the interests of the workers, peasants, and soldiers"; it should draw upon the class struggle in the countryside and cities; it should use the language of the masses, especially of the peasants and the proletariat; and it should avoid the sins of the "bourgeois writers," which he defined as incorrect themes, personal writing and production, imperialist influence, and "isolation from the masses." Mao told the revolutionary writers and artists of China that they "should go into the midst of the masses."

The criticism leveled against Communist writers at the many celebrations held 23 May 1952 on the tenth anniversary of Mao's *Talks at the Yenan Literary Meetings* left no doubt that neither writers nor artists were fulfilling their tasks. They had apparently failed to solve the dilemma posed by Mao's insistence that their products should promote the Communist ideology and at the same time be inspired.[53] In 1953 the rulers in Peking began to force writers to live in rural villages or factories or with the soldiers. Still they have failed to satisfy the demands of the party. In the *Literary Gazette,* Ting Ling, foremost Chinese Communist woman writer, criticized the failure of the comrade writers to create heroic types on the basis of their experience. The characters portrayed in present Chinese fiction, she said, "are created entirely from imagination—which is like a virgin talking about the experiences of childbirth." [54]

Under the Communist procedure works of literature and art are submitted at an early stage to group discussion, and thereafter to constant criticism. A specific number of works must be produced within a fixed period. For example, the Association of Chinese Dramatic Workers met during October and November 1953 and laid down the exact number of operas, plays, and so forth to be written and produced in the coming year.[55] Prior to the conference the *People's Daily* had informed the participants that "writing and art form part of the work of the party; they must be controlled by the party; the party must insure the purity of the political thought in the works of the writers; the directives of the party must be followed strictly." [56]

Mao's teachings have also formed the basis for all music in

about him as a great "people's artist." [58] The Indian journalist
Raja Hutheesing describes the poverty in which Ch'i lives in
Peking and how this distinguished old man is being exploited and
pushed around in order to be presented as new China's greatest
artist.[59] Other Chinese artists are producing posters, cartoons,
block prints, and paintings on such subjects as "Death to the Enemies," "The Execution of Landlord Huang," and "Victory for the
Chinese People's Volunteers."

The literary and artistic productivity of Communist China
under the inspiration of Mao is probably best symbolized by two
items which appeared within a week of each other in Peking in
April 1952. The first was a poem written by Kuo Mo-jo, famous
Chinese leftist scholar and winner of the 1951 Stalin Peace Prize,
who has served as the vice-premier of the cabinet in charge of
cultural and economic affairs. According to the Communists he
symbolizes the glory of the revolutionary literary talent in China
today.[60] The poem appeared in the *Current Affairs Handbook*
and was greeted with acclaim; it does not suffer much in translation.

CRUSH OUT THE GERM WAR

American imperialism—the root of all evil—
It is nearing the edge of death and yet it dares wage a germ war against
    the Chinese and Korean people.
American imperialism—the root of all evil—
We are determined to crush out the vicious germ war to uphold human
    dignity.
Crush it out, crush it out, crush it out,
Crush out the germ war, capture germ war criminals and let Ameri-
    can imperialism be done with it along with its bed bugs, lice, fleas,
    and flies!
Crush it out, crush it out, crush it out,
Crush out the germ war, capture germ war criminals and mobilize
    the peoples of all China and the entire world! [61]

The second item was the announcement in the *People's Daily* of a
new magazine, *Songs,* which represents the new music for the

masses in Communist China. The contents of the first issue were
listed as follows:

1. Exterminate Germ Warfare
2. Repulse the Remnant Attack of the Bourgeoisie
3. Bloody Blows
4. Production Increase for the Sake of the Volunteers
5. Human Determination Overcomes Destiny
6. The Heroic Positions and the Mountain of Steel
7. Add Another Bundle of Firewood On
8. Victory to the Heroic People
9. Song of the Red Scarves
10. We Are Members of the Youth Corps of Tomorrow
11. March Forward Shoulder to Shoulder.[62]

One aspect of life always linked with "culture" is education.
Here the Chinese Communists have given careful attention to the
reorganization and supervision of the schools where the technicians for the "new society" are to be created. The changes in policy
in the educational field are an interesting reflection of the increasing regimentation throughout China.

At the time the Communists came to power, they relied heavily
on the students for support in disrupting Nationalist educational
institutions. Leftist students heckled professors, organized boy-
cotts of classes they did not like, and insisted on having much to
say about the administration of the schools.[63] The party laid down
as one of its basic policies emphasis on quantity rather than quality
in training. Emphasis on quality had prevented the masses from
becoming literate in the "old society"—and education should be
popular and broad. The party also insisted that education should
be scientific, that is, Marxist and materialist, and that much time
at all levels should be devoted to political discussion classes.
Students were urged to take part in as many extracurricular activities as possible, and encouraged to express contempt for the long-
gowned scholars who were unable to follow Stalin and Mao in
combining theory with practice.[64]

The Peking authorities moved slowly at first in attempting to establish centralized control over the educational system. Government policy was finally laid down at a series of educational conferences beginning in 1952, and in that year the whole system of education was subjected to sweeping revision. The Ministry of Education under Ma Hsü-lun had issued a directive for the reorganization of primary schools on 1 October 1951, and this was carried into effect in the course of 1952. Primary school training was reduced from six to five years because it was maintained that the six years worked a hardship on the people. Provisions were made for the admission of spare-time worker and peasant graduates into middle school, which was to last six years as before. In April 1952 Ma decreed a complete reorganization of institutions of higher education.[65] The nation's 201 institutions of higher learning were reduced to 182 under a plan which made most of the schools specialized centers in some discipline. The names of many famous Chinese universities disappeared. Yenching and Tsinghua universities in Peking were fused to form a Polytechnic Institute. Nanking and Chekiang universities are now an Institute of Aeronautical Engineering.[66] By the beginning of the academic year 1953–54 Peking claimed that more than 40 per cent of all students in institutions of higher education were taking some form of technical training in preparation for industrialization of the country.[67] Among the 182 remaining institutions, only 14 universities of a comprehensive type were left, and these were organized after the Soviet pattern. The pattern established throughout the higher educational system of China in general duplicated that in the USSR. The departmental divisions and curricula of many leading institutions were revamped with the assistance of Soviet advisers.[68] Ma Hsü-lun stated that the basic principle to guide all higher education was to copy the "advanced experience of the Soviet Union." For this the study of Russian has become a required subject in most institutions of higher learning. The *People's Daily* of 8 November 1952 declared: "To facilitate our study of the Soviet Union, we must first learn Russian, the important instrument for us to understand the Soviet Union." Obviously the

Communists saw no conflict here with their drive to eliminate the study of English in the universities as a manifestation of "cultural aggression." [69] By the end of 1952 the State Statistical Bureau exultantly declared that the number of college students in China had reached 203,000, secondary school students 3,280,000, and primary school students 55,000,000.[70] The last figure was undoubtedly the result of questionable statistical work, but a trend toward expanding the number of students was obvious.[71] The Nationalist government, for example, had listed only 129,000 in institutions of higher learning in 1946.[72]

The year of retrenchment, 1953, brought many changes in Communist educational policy. In March the *People's Daily* complained that teachers were being indiscriminately drafted into extracurricular activities and current events discussion groups, which interfered with training personnel to industrialize the state.[73] At the Second Educational Conference in June the government announced that lower level education was not to be expanded further. This was followed by a cabinet instruction of 24 November stating that industrialization must take precedence over the broadening of education, and in December 1953 the *People's Daily* stated that the young should be directed toward glorious work in the fields and factories.[74]

At a series of conferences on higher education held during the summer of 1953 high party officials denounced as a deviation the placing of quantity above quality.[75] In September educational reports referred to a campaign which was being conducted to bring about better discipline among the students. One newspaper reported that students had been coming late to class, leaving early, reading novels in class, interrupting the instructor, and even arguing with the teacher in class. It added that such deviations were being overcome in the main through "disciplinary education," and in some cases punishment.[76] The August 1953 issue of *People's Education* denounced the administrative personnel of schools for having launched emulation campaigns among teachers. It accused the administrators of being excitable in temper and not understanding that educational work is different from production work. This language must have sounded odd to people who but two years before had been told that the expansion of education was essentially the same as the expansion of industrial production and that emulation campaigns were one means for success.[77]

In the summer of 1952 the Communist press began to note happily that college graduates were being assigned jobs under government distribution quotas. The New China News Agency reported that in their "heightened political consciousness" the students were one and all eager to accept the tasks assigned to them by their fatherland, no matter how far away these might be. To the outside world the students' attitude was described as "warm, enthusiastic, spontaneous, and happy." [78] A glance at the issues of *China Youth* for the months following graduation in both 1952 and 1953 indicates that all was not quite so smooth. Students were upbraided for complaining and for unwillingness to accept the jobs assigned to them or to go to the frontier areas. In one article entitled "Obey the Government Allocation of Work!" the students were told that it was "quite incorrect" to call the government allocation program "less free" than life under the Nationalists.[79] By 1954 education like agriculture was being geared to the first five-year plan, with the major goal that of serving industrialization.

One item in the educational field which the Communists continued to push even during their year of retrenchment was the mass literacy campaign. They boasted that all the Chinese workers and peasants would be able to read in a very few years. The main reason for this enthusiasm was the success they claimed for the rapid teaching method of Chi Chien-hua by which, it was asserted, more than 2,000 Chinese characters could be taught in 100 hours of study. But in 1954 enthusiasm for the method rapidly faded, and in March Communist authorities were forced to admit that it had no lasting effect. Workers forgot all the characters they had learned within two months, and the reaction of the peasants to the classes they were obliged to attend was a grumbled "I'd need another reincarnation to learn all these characters.[80] Rapid literacy methods are still at the stage of study and discussion.

The Communists recognized from the outset that educational reforms would be valueless unless they could control and reform the minds of China's intellectuals. This story deserves to be told in some detail, for it epitomizes the fate of a once great civilization under Communist rule.

The party of Mao Tse-tung undoubtedly had the support of a large proportion of the Chinese intellectuals and artists when it came to power. This support was a result in part of growing protest against conditions in mainland China during the early postwar years and in part of the persuasive quality of the Red propaganda and Marxist penetration into the intellectual atmosphere.[81] When, for instance, the Reds called the first All China Conference of Writers and Artists in July 1949, three months before the inauguration of their regime, leading novelists, playwrights, artists, and poets of all political shades and from all over China rallied under the Communist banner. During the flush of victory period many of China's teachers and intellectuals appeared to be enthusiastic about life under the Communists, although Mao had warned them that "Ideological reform, first of all the ideological reform of the intellectuals, is one of the important conditions for our country's all-out complete democratic reform and industrialization." [82]

The method used by the Communists to carry out Mao's instructions was the Ideological Remolding Movement which got under way during 1951, the year of violence; it is still being carried on although the intense phase lasted only a year. During this movement psychological control techniques were applied to China's leading intellectuals and artists in a thoroughgoing attempt to guarantee party control over the minds of a group which has played an outstanding role in modern Chinese history. The movement was more than an attempt to force reluctant liberals into step; its goal was to impose a rigid pattern of thought upon the Chinese mind and to define the limits within which it could operate. One scholar who has studied the movement feels that it "is probably one of the most spectacular events in human history. Tens of thousands of intellectuals, indeed the most educated group of a nation with a population of 470 million, have been brought to their knees, accusing themselves relentlessly at tens of thousands of meetings and in tens of millions of written words." [83]

The uncompromising tone in which the Ideological Remolding Movement was to be conducted was set in a preliminary move by the Communists, an attack upon the motion picture, *The Story of Wu Hsun*. Wu Hsun was a popular nineteenth century figure who had risen from poverty to become a leading exponent of popular education under the Manchus. A leftist, but independent, studio in Shanghai produced a film of his life, believing that the Communists would support it. Many Communist leaders had alluded favorably to Wu Hsun in the past. But in May 1951 no less important a body than the Central Committee of the Communist party leveled an attack on the film and demanded that cadres and educationalists throughout the land should hold discussions of the movie and uncover its ideological blunders. The party criticism pointed out that Wu was "entirely feudalistic in ideology," "was not a progressive or a revolutionary," had turned into a "usurious money lender and large landlord," and was a rogue and vagabond, "not a true proletarian worker." The attack upon the film was intended to show the party's determination to eradicate liberalism and establish the Marxist class point of view as the only criterion for judging people and their creations.[84] It also demonstrated that the party and not the artists would henceforth do the judging. Many party cadres as well as leftist critics had made the mistake of applauding the film without waiting for the official party line. This undoubtedly taught them a lesson.

The incident of the Wu Hsun film was scarcely over before Peking began to publish accounts of a Soviet fight against "ideological decadence in literature" then in progress. Chinese writers and critics were alerted to study Soviet methods and Soviet standards and to inaugurate criticism and self-criticism toward their own work.[85]

These incidents, however, were only preliminaries. The Ideological Remolding Movement began 29 September 1951 with a five-hour lecture by Chou En-lai to a group of Peking intellectuals. Chou instructed them to change their thoughts, to use criticism and self-criticism, and even criticized himself before the group. Within a month the chief intellectuals in the Peking-Tientsin area were organized into small discussion groups under Communist leadership, examining their thoughts and criticizing each other. The movement then spread gradually over the whole country. In December many intellectuals turned their attention to Dr. Hu Shih, liberal educator and statesman, whose "poisonous influence" they denounced. On 2 December a symposium on Hu Shih's thought was held in Shanghai. Many of China's grand old scholars and friends of Hu Shih wrote scathing denunciations of him and of his influence in China. A feature article in the 27 December *Progressive Daily* in Tientsin summarized: "Hu Shih is an intellectual who has sold out to the imperialists and the reactionary ruling class, and has helped the enemy as an accomplice. This man, who is guilty of the most heinous crimes against the people, still refuses to repent and is even now taking refuge in America as an imperialist instrument." [86]

With a speech by Chou En-lai on 5 January 1952 the Ideological Remolding Movement was tied in with the other drives of that year as a campaign against the bourgeoisie. Writing for *Study*, Ai Ssu-ch'i insisted that criticism of the ideology of the bourgeois class was the basic program of the Ideological Reform Movement.[87] "Bourgeois standards" in art and literature were denounced as a part of a Literature and Arts Rectification Movement which was incorporated in the Ideological Reform.

By the beginning of 1952 the results of the campaign to reform the intellectuals were beginning to appear in mass quantity in the leading Communist journals, in the form of recantations and confessions which reflected endless hours of discussion meetings, lessons in Communist theory, and the writing of autobiographies and diaries. Practically all the leading scholars in mainland China were involved.[88] Not only are the texts of these confessions a key to understanding the Communist methods and the goals which the rulers intended to achieve through the Ideological Reform, but many of them also bring out the nature of the "thought struggle" involved. A professor of physics at Tsinghua University stated frankly in his confession, "Such thought struggle has caused me great pain. It made me weigh constantly what I had to lose and what I had to gain. I wavered on the fence and did not know what to do." [89]

One early confession dating back to May 1949 had in many respects set the pattern which was to be followed during the Ideological Remolding Campaign—a pattern which testified to Communist ability to squeeze the expression of thousands of fine minds into one mold. The author was Ch'en Yüan, a famous historian in his seventies and president of the now defunct Fu Jen [Catholic] University in Peking. Ch'en's recantation was in the form of an open letter to Hu Shih in the *Progressive Daily,* denouncing him. He stated that on reading Mao Tse-tung's works

a new world has opened before me. I realize for the first time that our whole study of history has been subjective, unscientific. Man's mind is determined by his society. We must study that society in order to understand the individual, and can reform the individual only through reforming the society. All culture follows politics and at the same time leads politics. The realization of this fact is the freedom that the government has brought to me.[90]

An American scholar commented on this statement made during the flush of victory period: "Here is an eloquent and, I believe, sincere expression of the feeling of widened mental horizons and spiritual exhilaration that Marxism has recently brought to not a few traditional Chinese scholars." [91] It is interesting to examine some of the subsequent recantations for signs of this exhilaration and broadening of horizons.

The usual confession or recantation begins with an autobiographical sketch of the author and an analysis of the influences which "distorted" his thinking. These are usually the "feudalistic background" or the bourgeois influence of Europe and America. The next part is a denunciation of all past work. Many of the writers confess that they imagined themselves to be progressive and following Marxist precepts but now see how far behind they have lagged. In the third part the writer usually tells of discovering the great "truth" of Marxism-Leninism-Stalinism and the "thought of Mao Tse-tung." He states that he realizes now that these doctrines are universally applicable and offers thanks to Chairman Mao and to the Communist party for guidance, inspiration, and help in reforming his thought. The fourth part gives the writer's conclusions based upon his "study" and offers his humble promise to continue to follow the great leader Mao and the party.[92]

One recantation or confession is usually not enough. Many of the foremost scholars have made three or sometimes even five published statements. Apparently the Communist leaders are never satisfied. Tsui Shu-chin explains the plight of the intellectual as follows:

When a professor shows what the Communists call progress, he is accused of having made "simulated progress." When he admits too many mistakes, he is accused of confessing imaginary shortcomings in order to conceal the real ones, i.e.,—dissembling. And if he becomes too frank at the confession meetings, the Reds censure him for simulating reform for get-it-over-with purposes. On the other hand, if he refuses to confess, they condemn him as a reactionary. No matter what course he takes—right, left or middle—he is always wrong.[93]

Despite the success which the regime claimed for the Ideological Remolding Movement when it summed up achievements in mid-1952, and despite thousands of confessions extracted, the strict regimentation of so many active minds has been recognized as a long-range problem. During the summer of 1953 more than 6,500 Peking and Tientsin professors and university staff members underwent further ideological training under the direction of Ai Ssu-ch'i.[94] Almost a year later the *People's Daily* still complained about intellectuals who "do not make any effort to adjust their minds, ignore mental transformation, do not want to learn the Russian methods, and kind and polite, do not appreciate the method of mutual accusation and self-criticism." [95]

What were the thoughts which the Communists wished to eliminate from the minds of China's intellectuals? Actually some of the confessions themselves provide the most forceful answers. Ch'ien Tuan-sheng, now dean of the College of Law at Peking National University, for example, in confessing his own sins took occasion to stress the decadent nature of the background at Peking National University under the great liberal scholar Ts'ai Yüan-p'ei. His confession illustrates how the professors were obliged to go into the countryside and participate in the violence of the Agrarian Reform class struggle as a part of Ideological Remolding:

Aside from the mental makeup of the general run of intellectuals hailing from the capitalist class, I am possibly even more handicapped by capitalist education. In my complete apathy, I thought that, having already discarded the old democratic ideals and individualism, I had only to read up on Marxism-Leninism and the thoughts of Mao Tse-tung, and to emulate the Communist style of work in order to improve myself.

But I was mistaken, completely mistaken. While it was impossible to acquire the new before discarding the old, it was also difficult for me to single out the old and the undesirable. Following the comparatively penetrating process I went through in the course of actual participation in the revolutionary process of agrarian reform I realized the mistake of excusing myself on the grounds of such trifling reasons as "through force of circumstances" and out of "good motives," and the danger of overlooking these defects under the false impression that I have made progress. . . .

The undesirable ideology and style of work of the old intellectuals was also exhibited in the part I played in the administration of Peita [Peking National University]. . . .

Ts'ai Yüan-p'ei should be held only partly responsible for Peita's laxity and liberalism, while the greater part of this responsibility should be put to the account of the senior teaching staff, including myself, who managed to retain for a long time in Peita the pedagogical philosophy of "freedom of thought" and "freedom of study" of Ts'ai Yüan-p'ei.[96]

There was real irony in Ch'ien's statement, for Peita had been one of the centers of leftist intellectual activity under Ts'ai Yüan-p'ei; under his "freedom of thought" philosophy Ch'en Tu-hsiu, the founder of the Chinese Communist party, had taught as a respected professor and organizer of student groups, and Mao Tsetung had been influenced in the direction of Communism there as a student.[97]

In the earthy profanity of Chinese coolie talk felt by the Communists to be proper proletarian style, Liang Ssu-ch'eng, China's foremost architect and son of Liang Ch'i-ch'ao, the great nineteenth and early twentieth century reformer, castigated himself and his father. He maintained that his two greatest sins had been his "worship America" thoughts and actions (one of which was having lectured at Yale University) and succumbing to his father's influence.[98] In his confession Liang admitted that he had once been so feudal in his thoughts as to pledge himself to make his father proud of him.[99] Hsia K'ai-ju, a professor of geography confessed to liking periodicals in English, especially the *Geological Survey;* Quentin P'an, a well known sociologist, confessed to being afraid of the brutality of the class struggle and admitted that he could not learn to hate America (he was trained at Columbia) with due vehemence; Li Tsung-en, president of Peking Union Medical College, acknowledged that he had not been sufficiently class-minded or politically conscious in his work; Lo Ch'ang-p'ei, a noted linguist, confessed to having believed in individualism and liberalism and spoke enthusiastically of Stalin's new linguistics, denouncing Marr and other capitalist linguists.[100] Other crimes and mistakes confessed are: "purely technical viewpoint," "accent on professional interest," "bourgeois worship of America and the West," "idealism," "aloofness," "insistence on objectivity," "exclusive concern with technique," "isolation of theory from practice," and so forth.

One of the best known Chinese scholars in academic circles in the United States is Fung Yu-lan, philosopher and author of many famous books. In his *mea culpa* he denounced all of his previous writings in language strange and repetitious for such a clear thinker. It bespoke a very tired mind:

Had I taken flight with Hu Shih, Mei I-chi and their kind at the time of liberation, I would have turned myself into an instrument of American imperialism and a traitor to my fatherland. . . . Now I feel I also have been liberated. Marxism-Leninism and the Thought of Mao Tse-tung as well as practices in the various aspects of the new society have changed my thought, turning me from reaction to revolution, from service to individuals to service to the masses, from abstract things to concrete things, from illusions to realities.

Formerly I felt it strange that in the revolutionary camp a political leader should also be a philosophical and ideological leader, and attributed it to the results of controlled thought. Now I come to understand that a leader capable of leading revolution and leading society too in its forward progress is always able correctly to understand the laws of the world and social development and able to apply it [*sic*] flexibly to concrete revolutionary practice. That he is able to do so is precisely because he establishes and develops, in the revolutionary practice of reforming the world, a revolutionary philosophy for reforming the world. A revolutionary philosophy for reforming the world is entirely different from the philosophy which maintains that it "interprets the world." It is precisely because of its inability to reform the world that it is also unable to interpret the world. I now come to understand that I should make an entirely new start in my study before I can make myself a philosophical worker in the new society. Formerly when I heard some people saying that they wanted to be the pupils of Chairman Mao, it seemed an exaggeration to me. But now I feel that I am even disqualified to be a pupil of Chairman Mao, and that I have to strive hard to be one.[101]

One of the truly ironical touches of history concerns the American scholar who had found evidences of exhilaration and widened mental horizons in the letter from the president of Fu Jen University to the *Progressive Daily*. This scholar has spent more than a decade of devoted labor translating Fung Yu-lan's *History of Chinese Philosophy* into English—a work which Fung, in language remarkably similar to that 1949 letter, has now denounced as completely erroneous and decadent.

The Indian visitor to China, Frank Moraes, was profoundly stirred by the plight of the Chinese intellectuals: "For the first time I realised what for many years I had sensed vaguely but never grasped. To have your body imprisoned behind prison walls is degrading. But to have your mind captive with invisible chains is far more degrading. In the democratic beholder such a spectacle creates pain and nausea difficult to describe or overcome." [102]

There can be little question that the Chinese Communists have moved rapidly toward the goals which they set for "cultural and educational work in the new China": party control, conformity, elimination of "undesirable influences," patriotism, and copying of the Soviet experience. National customs, religion, art, literature, education, the intellectuals: all have succumbed to the combined power of Communist organization and ideology with its new weapons of psychological control. The Westerners familiar with Chinese character might be tempted to hope that the famous Chinese sense of humor would offer some relief from the pressure. But in his confession Lau Shaw, the author of *Rickshaw Boy,* admitted that "Unprincipled humor which encourages people to treat everything in a light-hearted manner is actually harmful to the people in that it encourages inaction and the attempt to get by through compromise." [103] Even humor must obey the dictates of the party and carry a political message.

In five years Chinese culture and the Chinese intellectuals have moved far forward—toward totalitarian orthodoxy.

9. TERROR

In Communist China the regime's dependence upon naked force to carry out its measures has been plain. The armed forces, the security police, the Social Affairs Department of the party all have shown the ability to apply force. One of the first things noted by correspondents accompanying the British Labor party delegation to China in the summer of 1954 was the presence everywhere of soldiers fully armed with automatic weapons and even hand grenades.[1] Methods of psychological coercion in China as in the Soviet Union and its European satellites have been developed to a new level of effectiveness, but behind their success lies the appreciation of armed might and armed violence. The Communist leaders are acutely aware that much of their success in psychological control depends upon the ability to instil fear, and they also know that nothing instils fear more than public proof of the ability and willingness to employ force and violence.

Under Mao's government fear has crept into every soul. In 1951 a capable commentator in Hong Kong noted, "Those who have come out of Communist China with an astonishing unanimity refer to, though they fail in attempting to describe, this constant haunting fear. It follows one wherever he is, regardless of the work he is engaged in. The arms of the Party are far reaching. They extend . . . to each individual, and affect the words and thoughts of all." [2] The manner in which this fear has been inspired and the pattern of the application of force and violence resemble events within the European satellites of the Soviet Union—with one major exception: in China the violence in the form of mass executions has been more open.

Merle Fainsod has observed, "What distinguishes twentieth century totalitarianism from earlier patterns of more primitive dictatorship is not the use of terror and a secret police as instruments of control but rather their high development as an organized

214

system of power." [3] Certainly this applies to the structure of control which Mao and his colleagues have erected in China. Much of the power of the Communist regime in China is based on a terror which is designed to paralyze the will of all its subjects to resist. In their application of terror as a system of power the Chinese Communists have demonstrated that they have learned much from their schooling in the land of the big brother, as well as been able to utilize some aspects of their own traditional despotism.

In many of the rural areas the Communists had applied methods of terror long before 1951, as a part of the Agrarian Reform, but their land program did not reach its peak until that year, and then it was combined with the Campaign against Counterrevolutionaries in both city and country. The result was a calculated year of violence which spread terror over the China mainland, laid the basis for subsequent consolidation of control, and did much to cripple any will which the Chinese people might have to resist.

The year of violence really started with the promulgation by Mao Tse-tung of the Regulations for the Punishment of Counterrevolutionaries on 21 February 1951. This document was unprecedentedly severe. Under its provisions the death penalty was prescribed for a long list of vaguely defined crimes. Penalties were retroactive so that a man could be punished for an act committed twenty or thirty years before. Article 9, for example, read:

Any of the following provocating and instigating acts with counterrevolutionary purposes shall be punished by prison terms of more than three years; serious cases shall be punished by death sentence or life imprisonment:
a) Instigating the masses to resist and sabotage collection of grains and taxes, labor service, military service, or implementation of other administrative decrees of the people's government.
b) Alienating and splitting the solidarity between the Government and the nationalities, democratic classes, democratic parties and groups, and people's bodies.
c) Conducting counterrevolutionary propaganda and agitation, fabricating and spreading rumors. [4]

Under the terms of this article, the Chinese may be sentenced
to death for any utterance which is not in line with the official
views.

The promulgation of the Regulations for the Punishment of
Counterrevolutionaries was evidently a sign that the Communists
were ready to take over the administrative and industrial leadership from the officials of the former government. Many former
Nationalist leaders had been allowed to retain their high positions
with Communist understudies during the flush of victory period.
Although they were undoubtedly aware that they might eventually
be squeezed out, they had probably not anticipated physical annihilation. But in 1951 most who were potential or past leaders of
opposition to Communist control were liquidated.

In March 1951 newspapers began to report mass executions
being carried on throughout the land. In Peking the pattern to be
followed throughout the country was set by a huge and effectively
staged mass trial on 24 March. The *People's Daily* the next day
reported that more than five thousand people had been present in
Central Park to participate in the trial of counterrevolutionaries.
This first big trial was presided over by P'eng Chen, member of the
Central Committee of the Communist party and mayor of Peking.
Instead of the accusations coming from the populace, the pattern
developed later, the mayor and other high government officials
made long speeches denouncing the group of culprits, who were
roped together in public view. According to the newspaper account, "with each speech the bitter hatred was blown more white
hot." After five hours P'eng Chen wound up the drama by saying:
"Comrades, what should we do with all these criminals, bandits,
secret agents, evil landlords, heads and organizers of reactionary
Taoist sects?" "Shoot them," the crowd roared with one voice.
"Should we have mercy on them?" And the crowd answered "No,
no!" "Truly, no mercy for them," P'eng continued. "If we par-
doned them, that would be a great sin on our part." The crowd
responded that the people were right, the culprits wrong; "Long
live Mao Tse-tung!"

"We are here representing the people," concluded the mayor. "It is our duty to do the will of the people. We suppress the counterrevolutionaries. This act we perform according to the law. Those who have to be killed, we kill. In cases where we could kill or not, we do not kill. But when it has to be killing, we kill. . . . Now you all want them suppressed. Tomorrow the Court will pronounce judgment and they will be executed." [5] The following day the executions took place before a big crowd outside the city walls and were broadcast over Peking radio stations. When executions were held in Tientsin three days later the authorities claimed that the people were so organized that the broadcast was heard by half a million and more than fifteen thousand participated in the mass meeting.[6]

By April Communist handbooks were explaining to the cadres the techniques of the "accusation meetings" and urging them to stir the masses to revolutionary vigilance against the enemies of the state through participation in these meetings.[7] The editorial in the *People's Daily* of 3 April stated that although some few persons felt the liquidation process had gone far enough, the inspired masses "warmly welcomed" the executions. It recalled the party's warnings in October 1950 against the deviation of "boundless magnanimity" and warned the people that any softness or lack of decision was a sign "that they have underestimated the righteousness of suppressing counterrevolutionaries."

The Campaign against Counterrevolutionaries reached its climax during the summer months. Almost every newspaper reported daily executions in the name of the people. The *People's Daily* of 12 July reported that one of the largest mass executions in Peking two days before had eliminated 277 counterrevolutionaries. The Shanghai military court carried out a thoroughgoing reign of terror from July through September. Dr. T. F. Tsiang, representative from the Nationalist government of China to the United Nations, presented the Communist figures on this to the United Nations General Assembly in the form of a chronology based on the official court releases. The following is an excerpt:

218 CHINA UNDER COMMUNISM

On 7 July 1951, the military court condemned to death and executed 60 persons, condemned to death, but with sentence postponed for two years, six persons, imposed life imprisonment on 27 and imprisonment for lesser terms on 92, and placed under police supervision or private guarantee 16 persons.

On 9 July, the military court condemned to death and immediately executed 48, condemned to death, with execution postponed, 15, imposed life imprisonment on 115, and placed under police supervision or private guarantee 23.

On 11 July, the military court executed 58, condemned to death, with execution postponed, six, and imprisoned 20.[8]

The Communists issued many sets of figures when it came to summing up the results of their Campaign against Counterrevolutionaries in October 1951. In some areas they gave precise numbers while in others their figures were vague and suggested inadequate statistical work. Hence it is impossible to estimate with any degree of precision the number of people executed. Attempts at estimates are complicated by the combination of the Campaign against Counterrevolutionaries with the Land Reform in the countryside. Figures on executions in the countryside were seldom published, yet all refugees and commentators in Hong Kong agreed that the casualties were much higher there than in the cities.[9] Despite these difficulties, it is worth while to cite a few of the figures given by the Communists in order to point up the intensity of violence involved in this campaign.

In his report on the situation in the Central-South Region on 21 November 1951, Teng Tzu-hui stated that from the winter of 1949–50 until November 1951 more than 1,150,000 "native bandits" had been inactivated and that 28 per cent of these or 322,000 had been executed.[10] These were figures for only one of the six major administrative areas in China. The *Southern Daily* in Canton reported that in the ten months between 10 October 1950 and 10 August 1951, 28,332 "criminals" had been executed in Kwangtung province.[11] The figures published for October 1949 to October 1950, before the drive to eliminate counterrevolutionaries got under way in earnest, are illuminating: a total of 1,176,000 were liquidated in four of the six administrative regions, according to the chairmen of the regions involved.[12] Yet according to statements by Communist officials themselves the campaign did not assume major proportions until 1951. By 1952 Peking no longer reported in such detail on the number of people liquidated; the figures were being used against the Communists on the world propaganda front.

It was on the basis of these incomplete figures and others provided by the Communists that the Free Trade Union Committee of the American Federation of Labor estimated in October 1952 that the Mao regime had been responsible for the deaths of more than 14,000,000 people over the previous five years. This total included more than 5,000,000 executed in rural areas and more than 2,600,000 executed as "bandit agents" or counterrevolutionaries. It is difficult when dealing in figures of millions to keep in mind that these are human beings rather than mere statistics, and the press of much of the world in 1954 indicated that those outside of China had begun to forget the calculated terror which raged under Mao in 1951. But it is unlikely that the people in China will forget, and it was clear that the Communists did not want them to forget. As the *New York Herald Tribune* correspondent pointed out:

It seems strange to inhabitants of liberal democratic countries that the Communists should not only stage these executions but brag of the number of deaths in their newspapers. Our psychology would be to hush up such unpleasantness. Even Hitler, for example, tried to keep the concentration camps quiet. But to the Chinese revolutionists the main point of the executions is not just to punish the accused (they would be more useful in slave labor camps) but to frighten any would-be opposition. Every Chinese must be made to feel that any slip would mean the same fate for him.

This technique of terror was described for me by a French official recently returned from Shanghai. "You would see the prisoners with cords around their necks like dogs. They would be driven by the truckloads to the big Shanghai stadium where the dog races used to be held. Nobody could get away from the impact of the trials. The proceedings were broadcast from morning till night. Powerful loudspeakers at every street corner would blare the shouts of the crowd and the screams of the accused, some of whom were stoned or beaten to death. You could hear the roar 'kill! kill!' all day long." [13]

By the end of 1951 the Communists reported great successes in their drive to eliminate counterrevolutionaries. The Canton Communist newspaper, the *Southern Daily,* for example, claimed that only 809 "bandits" were still at large in the province of Kwangtung.[14] One year later the minister of public security, Lo Jui-ching, reported that during the first three years of the regime fundamental success had been achieved in the suppression of counterrevolutionaries. But he warned that the battle would have to go on as long as United States "imperialism" continued in Asia. The "remnant counterrevolutionaries" in China are, according to him, the determined agents of the United States and Chiang Kai-shek.[15] Thus the basis has been laid for reminding the Chinese people periodically of the consequences of resistance to the decrees of the regime. Brief campaigns against "counterrevolutionary criminals," with public executions, were launched during some of the difficult days of 1953 in Shanghai when people were complaining of lack of food.[16]

The consequences of the mass executions in Communist China have been more far-reaching than the creation of a fear psychosis among the people. Many of those who were executed in both city and country were the stable administrators and literate elite in China who might have made contributions to the future of the country. The Communists indicated, however, that they would prefer to pay the price of inefficiency and loss of trained personnel rather than tolerate those with insufficient enthusiasm or "reactionary" backgrounds.

Most of the "counterrevolutionaries" not executed by the Communists have been required to undergo "reform through labor service" or, more bluntly, slave labor. Article 7 of *The Common*

Program stated: "Feudal landlords, bureaucratic capitalists and reactionary elements in general, after they have been disarmed and have had their special powers abolished, shall, in addition, be deprived of their political rights in accordance with law for a necessary period. But, at the same time, they shall be given some means of livelihood and shall be compelled to reform themselves through labor so as to become new men." [17] The minister of public security elaborated on official policy in an article in the *People's Daily* of 11 October 1951 in which he reviewed the Campaign against Counterrevolutionaries:

The subjection of counterrevolutionaries to forced labor is an indispensable means for the liquidation of the counterrevolutionary class, as well as a basic policy for the thorough reform of the culprits into new human beings. This sort of reform is a combination of punishment and education. In order to turn the culprits into new men, it is necessary on the one hand to eradicate their counterrevolutionary political and ideological stand and point of view, and on the other hand to give them training in production technique so as to turn them into skilled workmen. It is up to all levels of people's governments and various people's public security organs to pay adequate attention to and to make a success of this aspect of work which is possessed of the greatest political and economic significance.[18]

The policy of the government was officially stated again by Teng Tzu-hui the following month in a manner which makes it difficult for anyone to disagree with him. According to Teng, "The policy of reform through labor service is the People's Government's most enlightened policy of dealing with criminals, and only a People's Government could have decided on this new policy." Teng went on to cite figures for the Central-South Region which gave some indication of the numbers involved in the forced labor program: "Among the criminals arrested in the Central-South Region, only 28 per cent were executed, about 2 per cent had their death sentences stayed for two years, 50 per cent were made to undergo reform through labor while serving their sentences . . ." [19] Coupled with Teng's statement that between 1949 and 1951 1,150,000 native bandits had been inactivated, this statement would indicate that in November 1951 there were a minimum of 575,000 slave laborers in the Central-South Region.

Actually the slave labor program of the Chinese Communists did not go into full operation until 1952, the year of regimentation. The formal regulations under which counterrevolutionaries were subjected to forced labor were passed by the cabinet 27 June 1952. Under these Measures for the Control of Counterrevolutionaries the period of forced labor "may be fixed at 3 years or less, but may be extended if necessary." [20] A subsequent set of Measures for the Control and Reform of Landlords in the Central-South Region issued 18 August 1952 provided for standard terms of five years of labor service.[21]

By the end of 1952 observers in the outside world were beginning to put together figures on forced labor in Communist China. Once again published Communist statistics were of help in making estimates. For example, in the report on the work of his Ministry of Water Conservancy in October 1952 Fu Tso-yi stated that "in the past two years, 10,370,000 conscripted workers participated in water conservancy work throughout China under the supervision of 320,000 armed police." [22] By 1953 the Free China Labor League, a nongovernment organization in Taiwan, estimated that there were more than 18,000,000 slave laborers in over 5,000 labor camps in China.[23] On 23 April 1954 a United States spokesman at the United Nations stated that forced labor had grown to "dragon proportions" in Communist countries since the end of World War II and singled out China especially. He was sustained by Dr. C. L. Hsia of the Chinese Nationalist delegation, who provided statements and documents from Communist sources to support his estimate of more than 24,000,000 slave laborers in China.[24]

In handling their slave laborers the Communists have been quite serious about their talk of "reform." By this they mean, of course, that they view the period of forced labor as an opportunity to convince the victims of the necessity for supporting the party dictates with enthusiasm in the future. Thus the slave labor camps have a number of the characteristics of political training centers, with small group discussions and the process of mutual criticism. One escaped slave laborer who had worked on underground hangars at an airfield in south China stated:

We got up at 6 in the morning. We had 15 minutes for our toilet. From 6:15 to 6:45 we were briefed about the day's task. Then break-fast followed, and work started at 7 sharp. There was a one-hour break for lunch from 12 noon until 1 PM, and work was resumed from 1 till 6 PM. Supper was at 6. We washed ourselves from 6:20 to 6:30. From 6:30 to 7 we discussed our day's work in groups. A political lesson came at 7 and lasted until 8, and from 8:10 to 8:30 we again had group discussion. There was a large group general meet-ing from 8:30 to 9. From 9 to 10 there was an hour of "cultural activi-ties." The roll call came at 10:10, and at 10:30 we went to bed. The most harrowing ordeal was the "review of work," during which you were expected to criticize yourself for any fault or shortcoming.[25]

As in the case of so many other subjects, however, the most revealing descriptions of slave labor conditions and of the close regimentation and supervision involved come from the official Communist press. The official organ of the Communist party in Kwangsi province reported on the progress of "reform" in two of the provincial labor reform corps at Nanning:

When the labor reform corps were established, the culprits in gen-eral had the ideology of fearing labor, pretending to be ill, and work-ing wearily and clumsily. They tried to muddle on until their release. Some criminals even tried to cheat and deceive the superintending cadres. For instance, Huang Tuan-liang, a culprit of the 16th squad of the First Reform Corps under the jurisdiction of the Labor Reform Office of the Public Security Department of the provincial people's government, carried two baskets, which were only half loaded with mud. On hearing that the overseers were on the way, he immediately turned his back and had his baskets fully loaded with mud. Having dug two or three baskets of mud, culprit Yang Ping-tun went to have a smoke. Having enjoyed his smoke, he pretended that his bowels were loose and that he should be excused to go to the latrine. It was

224 CHINA UNDER COMMUNISM

later found out, however, that his defecation was normal. Five culprits of the labor reform corps of the Public Security Bureau of Nanning have escaped.

In view of such circumstances, the reform corps of the Public Security Bureau of Nanning has adopted the following measures for reform of culprits:

(1) To strengthen the political, ideological education of the culprits and to explain repeatedly the current situation and the significance of reform through labor. . . .

(2) It is necessary to mobilize the culprits to criticize and supervise each other, and to draw up work plans. . . .

(3) All culprits should be forced to work. Those who have shown up well in the course of labor reform should be eulogized, encouraged, and passed for lightening of punishment. Those who have shown up badly should be criticized and punished heavily.[26]

By admission of the Communist authorities slave labor has, as in the Soviet Union, become an important part of the Chinese economy. There are few statistics available from the Communist press on the number of deaths among the slave laborers, but according to reports of escapees and refugees casualties on some of the vast labor projects are very high. The Free Trade Union Committee of the American Federation of Labor, working from figures published by the Communists and statements by refugees, estimated in October 1952 that more than two million Chinese had died under the abuses of the slave labor system.[27] By the end of the fifth year of Communist rule this was surely a conservative figure.

There is an irony in the fact that the projects in Communist China usually given most uncritical and favorable treatment in the outside press are commonly those which have involved the use of forced labor. Two of the best known works from China's past history, the Great Wall and the Grand Canal, similarly involved the forced labor and death of countless millions. A Chinese tradition of forced labor combined with its development in the Soviet Union provided the Mao regime with ample background experience for embarking upon some of its most ambitious projects. Modern propaganda techniques have enabled the Commu-

nists to talk of the activities of slave laborers in terms of "engineering corps" or "conservancy commands" and to do so in a manner
which has concealed the real nature of the system from much of
the outside world.

Undoubtedly one of the major uses for forced labor has been in
the construction of military installations and in logistical support
of troops. Here information and statistics are inadequate for any
real assessment. The Chinese Federation of Labor in Taiwan
estimated that more than 2,500,000 prisoners and their dependents were engaged in defense work along the Chinese coast in the
spring of 1954.[28] While the Chinese consider railroad and road
construction as vital military construction too, their figures on
these have been more open.

From the Communist accounts of China's railroads today one
would gather that nothing had been achieved before they came
to power. They would lead readers to believe that the Soviet
experts are the only people in the world with any railroad knowledge and that the Communist leaders in China and the Soviet are
solely responsible for the new lines which have been opened.[29]
The two lines which have received most publicity are the 314 mile
Chungking-Chengtu railroad in Szechwan and the 215 mile
extension of the old Lunghai railroad from T'ienshui to Lanchow,
the former opened to traffic 1 July 1952 and the latter 1 October
1952. Actually most of the material used had been supplied by
UNRRA, and according to reports of the Chinese Nationalist
government 39 per cent of the work on the Chungking-Chengtu
line and 27 per cent of that on the line to Lanchow had been
completed before the end of 1947.[30] According to the report of
the minister of railways a total of 904.7 miles of new railways was
opened during the first four years of Communist rule, a figure
which hardly justified the sweeping claims of "unprecedented
accomplishment" advanced by the Peking press.[31] The Nationalist
government, for example, had increased China's railway mileage
by 2,090 miles in the nine years from 1926 to 1935.[32] In fact,
with one major exception the plans for railroad development under

the Communists follow closely the plans developed under the Nationalist government. The exception is the heavy accent on establishing connections with the Soviet Union along China's northern border.[33]

The Peking regime has admitted the use of more than 2,000,000 conscript laborers on the Chungking-Chengtu line, 70 per cent prisoners from Szechwan, 20 per cent "landlords" and their dependents.[34] One escaped slave laborer from this project whom I interviewed in Hong Kong during the summer of 1952 stated that more than half the laborers in his company died from exposure, undernourishment, disease, and overwork. Over half of the estimated 200 who died had been former intellectuals who collapsed under the strain of heavy labor to which they were unaccustomed. The thirteen-hour working day was usually followed by endless political meetings. Little was provided in the way of shelter, and there were but two scant meals a day.

Yet despite the unprecedented mobilization of vast reserves of manpower for railroad building in China, the minister of railways in his report to the cabinet in November 1953 noted serious shortcomings. His figures do not compare favorably with achievements under the Nationalist government between 1931 and 1935 despite the fact that the latter faced an armed Communist insurrection and damage by sabotage.[35]

Another important use for forced labor has been in road construction. Here one of the most extensive projects has been the construction of a series of roads into Tibet.[36] The Chinese Communist press reported that on one of these roads elevations reached as high as 5,000 meters, but that despite intense cold and rarified air the first half of the "all weather" Chengtu to Lhasa road had been opened by January 1953. This first stretch, which reached as far as Changtu in Sikang province, was built under the direction of the armed forces.[37] The Communists have also laid emphasis on building roads into the minority areas and military supply routes connecting north and northwest China with the Soviet Union.

Other projects for slave laborers have included large schemes for afforestation and the opening of new land to cultivation. The regime has reported plans for planting more than 7,000,000 acres of shelter belts of trees to protect north China from the dust storms coming out of the loessal highlands. Although small sprouts were first planted in 1951, only two years later Peking authorities were claiming impressive results in curbing dust storms from more than 400,000 acres of trees planted.[38]

The major publicity from Peking, however, has been reserved for the vast water conservancy works under the direction of former Nationalist general Fu Tso-yi and the Ministry of Public Security. The moving of masses of earth and the great excavations necessary for flood control have traditionally involved intensive labor in China by millions of men using primitive methods. With their ability to mobilize and control the masses, the Communists could be expected to show achievements in this field. By September 1952, following three rather fortunate years from the point of view of weather conditions, the reports of Fu Tso-yi exuded confidence and optimism. The "danger of disastrous floods which was a scourge to the Chinese people for thousands of years has been basically removed, and normal agricultural production and the security of the people's livelihood are now assured in a major part of China." [39] There have been several major projects which have received much publicity inside China and out.

First in importance among these has been the Huai River project. According to the Communists, "The project to harness the Huai River is one of the greatest epics of modern times. In the first and second phases of the project (1951–1952), a total of 4,600,000 workers and peasants threw themselves into the struggle against their old enemy. They were assisted in this gigantic campaign by 40,000 non-technical government employees and 16,000 engineers." [40] These "enthusiastic volunteers" had by the end of 1952 equaled the digging of two Panama Canals and one Suez Canal, the Peking authorities stated.[41]

A second important project was the creation of a flood detention basin for the Yangtze River. Claiming this to be a great victory over the Yangtze, when it was finished in the summer of 1952, the Communist authorities stated:

> This newest achievement is unprecedented in scale in China, closely rivals the Huai river project, and is one of the great engineering works of the world. By removing a four-centuries-old menace of flood, it will bring security to the 3 million people who live on the Kianghan plain in Hupeh province—a rich rice and cotton-growing area. It will protect 533,000 hectares of land producing a normal annual harvest of 1,500,000 tons of rice, and a large quantity of cotton.[42]

According to reports by the Communists more than 200,000 laborers had worked on the Yangtze detention basin at one time.[43]

Other important water conservancy works carried on by forced labor under the Communists included over 82,000,000 cubic meters of earthworks on the Yellow River, work on the Yi and Shu Rivers in east China, and control projects for five rivers in north China.[44] One of these last was the creation of the Kuanting reservoir by the erection of a dam across the Yungting River outside of Peking. This dam, 45 meters high and 290 meters long, was completed in May 1954.[45]

The Communist claims of unprecedented success in the water works in China became a major feature of the propaganda concerning the superiority of the Marxist system for foreign visitors to Mao's domain in 1952. Although the slave labor aspect was played down, the Indian cultural delegation that year was taken to view the Huai River project. Both Raja Hutheesing and Frank Moraes of that delegation expressed disappointment in what they saw and some surprise that so much of the work seemed to be only in the talking stage.[46] Hutheesing described his reactions after a long and disappointing trip to see one of the featured works of the Huai project, the Junghochi dam.

> I looked at the sight with baffled surprise. So much had been said about this project and its completion in three months' time last year through "the strength and the intelligence of the masses of people." We saw before us not a dam but a simple three-part *anicut* or obstruc-

tion built across the river to control the water's flow. . . . Despite
the formidable statistics of men and material used, here was something so simple that I felt I did not want to look at it. Our guide and
host, the Deputy Chief Engineer, saw the obvious disappointment on
my face. There were no enthusiastic millions of rural workers, nor
any evidence that they could once have been housed here for three
months. . . . Work was now going on further upstream at Futzling
. . . and if I were interested in seeing China at work I should have
gone there. As is usual in Communist countries, what is of interest
is generally out of one's reach. One must instead be content with what
is offered in innumerable official statements and handouts.[47]

In 1953 Fu Tso-yi was far less optimistic than he had seemed
before. Many natural disasters struck mainland China, and reports
in the Communist press admitted floods in those very areas which
Fu had claimed would never again be bothered by such calamities.
The Huai River and Yellow River areas were given "disaster
relief" by the Communists. The famines resulting from the floods
were serious, but the press gave no indication of the number of
victims, and indeed, as one observer points out, seemed interested
only in material damage.[48] The disastrous nature of the floods and
consequent food shortage in 1953 prompted the calling of a Water
Conservancy Conference in Peking at the end of the year. As the
China News Analysis noted:

Its disappointing and disturbing report is not likely to make its way
into propaganda publications. The judgment on past efforts is stern,
the heaviest censure falling on ill-considered insistence on huge monu-
mental works, to the neglect of the more simple works carried on under local, provincial and county direction. The directives for future
action are aimed primarily at the correction of past errors; they also
reflect the past financial difficulties of the government.[49]

At the conference Fu Tso-yi made no such optimistic statements
as in 1952.

A climax came in the summer of 1954. In July the water of the
Yangtze reached the highest level in the history of many cities
along its banks. The floods were termed the worst in Chinese

history. By the beginning of August more than 100,000 people were working day and night on the embankments of one small segment of the river's course.[50] Railway communications were severed between north and south China. Finally, Minister of Interior Hsieh Chüeh-tsai in a report to the National People's Congress in Peking on 26 September revealed the scope of the floods. More than 42,000 square miles (chiefly in the Yangtze and Huai River valleys) were inundated and more than 10,000,000 people had to be evacuated. The area involved was far greater than the record of 34,000 square miles set by the disastrous floods of 1931. The Nationalist government on Taiwan estimated that 12 provinces and more than 210,000,000 people had been directly or indirectly affected by the 1954 floods and stated that planes had dropped food to stricken areas in four provinces at great risk to the crews.[51]

The disaster was too great to be kept secret, yet Peking did not admit the difficulties until after the Geneva conference on Indo-China ended on 23 July, apparently feeling that official acknowledgment of the crisis would be an admission of weakness and endanger its bargaining power at the conference tables. By the time the announcement was made two basic principles had been stated for coping with the problem: 1) "Relief workers in calamity-stricken areas should keep in mind not only their duty to the people on the spot but also their duty to the whole country," and 2) the people must be taught to help themselves. "These principles sound hard," commented the *China News Analysis*. "They are meant to be hard; for they express the government's determination, indicated in the texts, that economic reconstruction of the country shall come before all things else,—or, to put it more bluntly, that the government's program of industrialization must not be imperilled for the sake of a few million lives." [52]

It might have been expected that the disasters of 1954 would lead the party to reconsider some of its basic attitudes, but the reactions have been strictly in line with policies enunciated earlier. Food exports to the Soviet Union have continued. In August when the International Red Cross offered flood relief the Communists refused it.[53] The refusal reflected not only the determination to have no dealings with the West which might involve the presence of Westerners in China but also Mao's willingness to assign the inhabitants of whole sections of the country to oblivion in order to save face and uphold the principles of Communist infallibility and Stalinist autarchy.

Although floods in themselves are tragic events in China, the suffering from the famines which follow is always far greater. Both of these may cause some changes in the schedules for the first five-year plan, but it is not impossible that the Communists view the disasters of 1954 as an opportunity to demonstrate their powers of control and ability to impose their will on the people. The party's policy has always been to turn defeat to advantage. The *People's Daily* has frequently pointed out that natural calamities provide "education in socialism" by forcing people to work together. Such work it is believed highlights the need for vigorous leadership which only the Communists can provide.[54] The regime has also never failed to claim that its performance in the face of natural disasters far surpasses that of any previous government.

In effect, the floods of 1954 offered one more opportunity for instilling terror. The people have come to know that the regime will not subordinate any of its goals to humanitarian considerations. Thus there is built up the feeling of uncertainty so necessary to a terror strategy. Individuals never know when the rulers will find it expedient to eliminate them for the sake of the plans of the regime. Only those who make themselves vital cogs in the party machinery by enthusiastic support are likely to be spared, and even they can never be sure. The combined threat of slave labor on the great projects aimed at preventing natural disasters and of suffering and starvation if those projects fail aids the Communists to create the fear psychosis they deem so necessary for effective rule.

The disasters of 1954 coincided with the close of the first five years of the Communist application of terror. By that year Mao's government had succeeded in a terror strategy which involved the shift from mass liquidations and hysteria to the more subtle methods of "enlightened terror." There are always a few public executions taking place, to remind people what the regime is capable of. For example, in order to demonstrate the government's determination to establish a food monopoly great publicity was given in January 1954 to the execution of some residents of Shanghai who had dared to sell cooking oil privately.[55] But the major aspect of Communist terror is the fear created in each individual by the knowledge that the instruments of force are always in the background, combined with ignorance of when or how they will be used against him.

In China everyone knows of the conditions of slave labor either at first hand or from the lips of friends; everyone is aware of the regime's ability to liquidate people, remembering the year of violence; and everyone has heard of the methods of torture and punishment in Communist prisons.[56] Little wonder that a correspondent with the British Labor party delegation to China in August 1954 should speak of the "drab, dull apathy" that has "settled over everyone" and lament that a "horrible uniformity is the order of the day." [57] Such a uniformity is one of the inevitable consequences of the terror of a police state where the individual fears to express himself.

10. THE CONDUCT OF FOREIGN RELATIONS

Because of the complexities and scope of the foreign relations of the Chinese Communist regime it might be argued that this subject should be reserved for a separate volume. Yet Peking's foreign policy is such an integral part of the whole Communist program for China that some attempt must be made to outline the main features. Although the discussion which follows is of necessity spotty and incomplete, it does attempt to bring into focus some of the major aspects of Red China's foreign policy over the past five years and highlight them with examples.

In discussing the foreign policy of Red China it is important to point out three general background features which are frequently forgotten or overlooked by statesmen and commentators in the West. In the first place, for a regime which like that of Mao monopolizes the outward expression of all aspects of life within its area, there are no unofficial relations. Every contact with the outside world is official. This means that except on the surface the conduct of foreign policy in many respects bears little resemblance to traditional Western diplomatic practices now standard throughout the world. From this fact certain distinct advantages accrue to the Peking leaders. There is small chance that different sectors of the society will work at cross purposes abroad as happens so frequently elsewhere in the world. During the Crimean War, for example, a Russian loan was floated on the London market with the permission of the British government.[1] There is little likelihood that Mao's government would allow such a thing to happen.

The fact that the Peking rulers control all phases of relations abroad offers them an opportunity to make the most of differences within and between other countries. By exploiting relations which for the non-Communist areas of the world are unofficial, Peking can frequently develop support for its policies at the official level. When, furthermore, all those who are permitted to go abroad from Communist China present a current policy as if with one voice, the impression is fostered of complete accord and conviction in China, whereas on specific aspects of policy nationals of the democracies abroad—businessmen, reporters, diplomats, artists, military, tourists—are likely to express widely divergent views and give the impression of weakness and division not only within their countries but between them. For example, the Peace Committee for Asia and the Pacific Area which met in Peking from 3 to 6 May 1954, the Asiatic labor representatives (including delegates from India, Ceylon, Siam, Indonesia, Viet Minh, Korea, Mongolia, and Russia) who met there from 5 to 8 May, and Chou En-lai negotiating a truce for Indo-China at Geneva at the same time all gave an identical diagnosis of the problems of peace for Asia and advanced the same solutions. The Peace Committee included representatives (fellow travelers) from countries which, like the Philippines, supported the United States position; the presence of some labor delegates also represented a split within these countries, a sign of lack of unity on opposition to the policies of Communist China; and Chou En-lai took advantage of splits not only within the individual countries but also between nations.[2]

A second feature of Peking's conduct of foreign relations which must be kept in mind is that these relations never fail to be viewed within the framework of conflict and struggle. External relations like internal affairs are presented and carried on in terms of battles, campaigns, attacks, advances, and retreats. Here, in consonance with the whole Marxist-Leninist philosophy, there can be no neutrality. Mao Tse-tung asks rhetorically:

Has not the history of the past thirty-one years of Soviet power proved how completely false and bankrupt is the so-called "middle way," the so-called "third path" which, to deceive the working people is so loudly proclaimed by all those who do not like Marxism and who hate the Soviet Union—the socialist fatherland of the working people of the world—by all those who are trying to maintain some kind of intermediate position between the counterrevolutionary front of the imperialists and the revolutionary front against imperialism and its lackeys in all countries? [3]

The Peking government soft-pedals its contempt for neutrals when their policies seem to serve the Communist cause, but at other times the contempt is expressed forcefully.

The struggle in which there can be no neutrality from the Communist point of view is, of course, the Marxist worldwide class struggle. Here the Chinese Communists follow the Stalinist revision of Marx's doctrine which transferred the "final battle" from a worldwide class basis to a struggle between the socialist and capitalist nations; that is, to a territorial basis. To the Soviet Union as the "great bulwark" for the spread of Communism to the industrial nations of the world there has now been added the bulwark of Communist China, which together with the Soviet Union can lead the campaign in the underdeveloped areas of the world. The key for the application of Marxism to these areas which have no proletariat strictly speaking is Lenin's theory of imperialism (borrowed in large measure from the English liberal Hobson). Because these "colonial and semicolonial" areas have suffered capitalist oppression in the form of imperialism, their people are viewed as reliable allies who can proceed to socialist industrialization without having to suffer further capitalist exploitation. Thus by the simple expedient of definition the life-death struggle between the "proletarian nationalism" of the Soviet camp and the "bourgeois nationalism" of the capitalist camp is extended to all areas of the world in terms of the struggle between the camps of imperialism and anti-imperialism. By the same imposed definition, of course, the Communist camp can never be imperialist. It hardly needs to be added that the colonial records and attitudes of most of the Western powers have aided the Communists in their appeal to the people in such areas.

This doctrinal core is hard and final and, according to spokesmen in both Peking and Moscow, is the basis for the conduct of all foreign relations. The overriding goal of Communist world victory makes possible the adoption of policies based entirely on expediency. Thus while changes in policy, including the abrogation of treaties immediately after they are signed, may seem irrational or even wrong-headed from the point of view of other nations, they are usually quite consistent when viewed in the perspective of Communist doctrine. Such Machiavellian expediency is naturally not unusual in the relations of sovereign states. In the case of China, however, it is especially effective because it embraces all aspects of foreign contact, including many which lie beyond the control of governments in the West.

The hard core of Communist doctrine also underlies the third general feature in the background of Communist China's foreign policy. The Chinese Communists do not separate internal and external affairs. All events in and outside China are viewed within the framework of the class struggle. Therefore the external enemy is also the internal enemy and vice versa. This is why, for example, all who resist the measures of the regime inside China are immediately viewed as agents and tools of the imperialists. This inclusion of all events within the over-all Communist world interpretation makes possible not only the very close coordination of internal and external policy but also a deep involvement in events all over the world. Thus Mao Tse-tung in his interview with Clement Attlee in August 1954 echoed Moscow's demand that the West abandon its plans to rearm Germany and stated that it was one of the major demands of Chinese Communist foreign policy.

Probably no event demonstrates the extent to which Chinese Communist foreign policy is linked to domestic policy and to the strategy of the world Communist camp than the Korean War. In retrospect it is easy to see that the war was utilized as one of the major tools to enable the Peking rulers to consolidate their hold on the mainland. Actually the Communists have themselves admitted the relationship between the Korean War and the consolidation of power. The *People's Daily* of 25 December 1952 stated that the experience of the previous two years had proved that the struggle in resisting America and aiding Korea had been "a great dynamic power which drove forward national construction programs in all aspects." In other words, war was actually necessary to the revolutionary regime.[4] The creation and promotion of an external threat in order to justify internal dictatorship has been a common phenomenon in the history of many peoples.

With these three background factors in mind let us turn to an analysis of the foreign policy of the Peking regime and give first attention to the various methods and techniques by which it is conducted. The fact that all Communist China's relations with the outside world are official relations means that Peking has many more media for carrying on diplomacy than are available to some of the countries whose actions the Communists attempt to influence. In the actual conduct of relations the Chinese Reds have followed closely the pattern set by the Soviet Union.

There are first of all formal diplomatic relations. Article 56 of *The Common Program* stated: "The Central People's Government of the People's Republic of China may negotiate and establish diplomatic relations on the basis of equality, mutual benefit and mutual respect for territory and sovereignty with foreign governments which sever relations with the KMT reactionaries and adopt a friendly attitude towards the People's Republic of China."[5] This was in essence the content of the message which the new foreign minister Chou En-lai proclaimed to the world on 1 October 1949. Peking claimed that

the Central People's Government elected by the Chinese People's PPC is the sole government that can represent the Chinese people and that the delegates sent to the United Nations General Assembly by the bogus government of the remnant reactionary forces . . . are unqualified to represent the Chinese people. This is the solemn declaration of the Chinese people to the whole world as the master of the country. This completely conforms to the actual conditions of the

Chinese political situation which has undergone a fundamental change, and reflects the common will and wish of the people throughout the country. KMT reactionaries, the running dogs of American imperialism, have been cast aside by the people throughout the country because of their policy of national betrayal, civil war and dictatorship.[6]

On 2 October 1949 the USSR extended recognition to Mao's government. The Soviet satellites followed suit quickly. Burma was the first non-Communist country to extend recognition, on 9 December 1949, and it was followed by the other members of the South Asia "neutral bloc." In January 1950 a few European countries, led by Great Britain's Labor government, recognized the Chinese Communist government. By October 1953 Peking claimed to have established formal diplomatic relations with nineteen countries (including Ho Chi-minh's Communist government in Viet Nam, North Korea, the East German Communist regime, and Mongolia). Actually it was not until August 1954 that Mao's government got around to sending an ambassador to Communist Indo-China.[7] And although the Communists claimed to have established formal relations with Albania, there had been no news of an exchange of ambassadors after more than four years. Peking never bothered to acknowledge the recognition which Yugoslavia extended four days after the Communist government of China was proclaimed.[8]

In addition to the nineteen countries with which Peking claimed to have established formal diplomatic relations, six other countries were described as "having recognized the People's Republic of China": Great Britain, Ceylon, Norway, Israel, Afghanistan, and the Netherlands.[9] Although Great Britain led the way among countries in the West in recognizing Mao's government and London went more than halfway in an attempt to set up formal relations, negotiations were still in progress on the fifth anniversary of the Peking regime; and the British had suffered many humiliations at the hands of the Chinese Reds.

In the conduct of diplomacy at the official level the Chinese Communists have usually been very punctilious about all matters of protocol. When, for example, the new Bulgarian ambassador, Dimitr Dimov, arrived in Peking on 1 September 1954, the NCNA reported fully on his reception, his formal presentation of credentials, the banquets in his honor, and so forth.[10] The notes from Peking to foreign governments, as well as the many notes sent to the United Nations demanding admission, have always been framed according to the requirements of traditional diplomacy in the West. The attention the Chinese Communists give to the formalities tends to obscure the other means they rely upon to implement their policy and present their views abroad.

There are, to be sure, other aspects of Peking's diplomacy which are common practice in international relations, such as the negotiation of treaties and agreements and high-level official visits. The Chinese Reds have signed treaties of "friendship, alliance and cultural exchange" with most members of the Soviet bloc. Meanwhile, however, they have abrogated all former treaties signed by past Chinese governments with Western powers. This means that in the first five years of Communist rule Western residents in China have had no treaty protection for their private rights and interests. Western businessmen have been persecuted and imprisoned without recourse to the courts; missionaries have been subjected to suffering and indignities; assets have been seized without compensation. Interestingly enough, despite Britain's lead in extending recognition, British citizens have in many respects suffered more heavily than those of any other Western power. The Communists have seized hundreds of millions of dollars worth of British assets in China without compensation and have even forced the British to continue to send cash reserves into China to keep going their establishments which were not allowed to close their doors.[11]

Practically all of Peking's international trade relations are managed under government agreements signed with either private interests or the executives of other countries. Here the Communists negotiate from a monopoly position and are only too ready to exploit agreements signed with private business establishments in foreign countries for political advantage. When in 1953 a Japanese trade delegation concluded a goods exchange agreement with the Chinese Reds following a relaxation of restrictions by the Japanese government, the results were presented to the world as proof that the whole Japanese people desired close relations with Communist China.[12] Such barter agreements have been concluded with many Asian countries as well as with Britain, France, and other Western powers. In almost every case both government and private trade delegations are given special welcome and presented to the Chinese people as representing the demands of their "people" for close ties with the new "People's Government." By the end of October 1952 the Chinese Communists had sold the Indian government 660,000 tons of rice under such agreements. A trade pact signed with Ceylon on 4 October 1953 supplemented the five-year trade pact of 18 December 1952 under which Peking had already agreed to take more than 60 per cent of Ceylon's rubber production in exchange for rice. By October 1954 Ceylon was experiencing difficulties over the price the Communists were willing to pay and was beginning to appreciate the strong bargaining position which Peking had achieved, a position aided incidentally by American policies of subsidizing increased synthetic rubber production in the USA.[13]

Almost all of Peking's barter agreements during the first five years involved shipping food from China.[14] The Chinese people were told in the midst of their 1953 famine that food shipments to "brother countries" could not be curtailed; and again in 1954, despite disastrous floods, the export of foodstuffs was stepped up. In part because of the blockade of strategic goods during the Korean War, but largely as a result of deliberate Communist policy, trade agreements with members of the Communist bloc have involved an ever increasing part of China's foreign trade. By 1954 trade with Communist countries accounted for about 80 per cent of the total. Official figures on the Soviet Union's share were 26 per cent for 1950, 61 per cent for 1951, and 70 per cent for 1952. This trade has of course been publicized as "glowing proof" of the solidarity of the Communist world front.

Stalin's classic remark when Roosevelt proposed the inclusion of the Pope in a conference—"How many divisions has he?"—has come to symbolize Communist appreciation of raw military power in being. As in the Soviet Union the use and display of such power has become one of the important factors in Peking's conduct of foreign affairs. The Reds are obviously firm believers in Machiavelli's dictum that it is better to be feared than loved. Beginning with the parade of 1 October 1949, the day the Communist government was proclaimed, the People's Liberation Army has staged parades of military might lasting for many hours on several occasions each year. On the fourth anniversary of the regime in 1953, for example, more than 400,000 troops were reported to have passed in review in Peking before visitors from more than twenty foreign countries, including eight members of a British trade union delegation and some British business leaders. Jet planes zoomed overhead, and the display of Soviet artillery and other equipment left no doubt in the minds of observers that the Chinese Communists had organized for the Korean War one of the largest modern land armies in history.[15]

To date Peking has backed up its parades of military power with concrete action demonstrating a willingness, in fact an eagerness, to use it. These demonstrations have ranged from the shooting down of a British commercial airliner off Hainan island on 23 July 1954 (only three days after the signing of the Indo-China truce agreement) to full-scale participation in a war against the United Nations in Korea. They have served to convince many of the world's leaders that peace in Asia can be achieved only on the basis of terms laid down by the rulers in Peking. Some, such as Britain's Clement Attlee, who had played vital roles in containing Communist expansion elsewhere in the world, have manifested a willingness to accept some of those terms.

Undoubtedly a very important instrument in the conduct of foreign policy is Mao's propaganda machine, and here the technique of the "iron curtain" is an important tool. Peking exercises great care to make sure that derogatory information does not get out of China, that news from China is in complete accord with the current Communist line. Here again the pattern is that with which the Soviet Union has familiarized the world. Some examples of what is involved will point up the effectiveness of the propaganda machine as an instrument of foreign policy, but in such limited space it is impossible to explain fully the efficient manner in which all the parts work together. Here the advantages of the Communist state over the democracies, where controlling statistics and information are available to outsiders and where news services and the press are independent, are only too obvious.

There is first of all the dissemination of news abroad. With minor exceptions the only news coming from mainland China on a regular basis is that released by the official New China News Agency or contained in the publications of the Foreign Languages Press in Peking. In 1951 the Chinese Communists began to extend careful control over publications leaving the mainland. The methods of control included limiting the areas of circulation of local Chinese newspapers and preparing a list of a few papers and magazines which alone would be allowed to leave China. Anyone caught taking prohibited publications from the country was subject to severe punishment, especially after the campaigns of 1952. By December 1953 local newspapers and many of the important journals were available to the outside world only through smuggling operations, and agents in Hong Kong who undertook to procure mainland publications charged extremely high fees.[16]

The dispatches and publications distributed outside China (all official) show careful editing. Frequently when NCNA releases texts of important articles, editorials, or reports printed in the *People's Daily*, the self-criticism sections are omitted entirely. On 7 May 1953, for instance, NCNA issued a dispatch to the world purporting to be a translation of a report on the results of the economic plan in Manchuria for 1952 as printed in the *People's*

Daily the day before. Examination of the *People's Daily* for 6 May, however, reveals that the whole section on "problems and defects" in the work was omitted. The full article left the over-all impression of failure. Peking's claims to the world were in terms of glowing success.[17] This type of control of news proved so thorough by the summer of 1954 that the outside world was able to get few facts and figures on the disastrous floods in China despite their unprecedented severity.

For its releases abroad the Peking government does not hesitate to employ outright fabrication of figures and documents. An important journal that does this is *People's China,* an English language magazine published twice a month by the Foreign Languages Press in Peking (there is also a Japanese edition). This journal is widely distributed on a subsidized basis and has probably proved a great aid to the worldwide propaganda effort of the Communists. In distributing it abroad Peking takes advantage of the fact that there are few people who have actual facts for checking and even fewer who could read the Chinese sources if they were available. Because *People's China* is an official publication of the Red government, there is likely to be a tendency to believe its figures are at least to some extent accurate—and yet many of its articles are thoroughly unreliable. A reader who did not or could not check might quickly come to believe that Mao's government has solved all its problems, that everyone in China is contented and happy, that the millennium has indeed arrived in the Middle Kingdom. The magazine is in many ways reminiscent of the journals which came from the Soviet Union in the decade 1928–38.[18]

Some idea of the effectiveness of *People's China* can be gathered from passages in two books which like the magazine itself have had wide circulation in India. In a volume entitled *China Today,* Sundarlal, leader of the Indian Goodwill Mission to China in 1952, states: "To those who may desire to know more about New China, her aspirations, her achievements and her trends, I especially recommend the informative and thought provoking

writings of Mao Tse-tung and Liu Shao-ch'i, and also that remarkable magazine, the 'People's China,' including all its back
volumes, since its start in January 1950, which are a mine of
useful information about New China." [19] In a somewhat more
perceptive report on Communist China another Indian, K. T.
Shah, states: "Magazine articles by leading Chinese writers in
such publications as *People's China* or *China Reconstructs,* have
been taken factually, as authoritative, even though their views
may be one sided." [20]

Peking also takes great care to ensure that foreign visitors get
only the information and the impressions the Communists want
them to. The iron curtain technique of the guided tour is now
the hallmark of Mao's government as well as of the Soviet Union.
Visiting dignitaries are provided with official guides who are
responsible for their every action. They visit model farms, model
schools, and model factories; they talk with labor heroes; they
visit new housing projects and other large projects and listen to
speeches giving official statistics for their benefit. U Kiaw Min, a
discerning member of a Burmese delegation to Communist China
and the Soviet Union in 1952, states that supervision was even
more thorough in China than in the Soviet.[21]

Control over foreign residents in China, including for instance the British chargé d'affaires and the Indian ambassador, is
thorough. Until 1954 the British representative was virtually a
prisoner in his compound.[22] The Communists have also used a
system of Chinese guarantors for those foreigners who have been
permitted to leave China. During the first three years of the
regime many expelled missionaries did not dare to talk freely of
their persecution for fear of reprisals against their guarantors.
Here is another reason why Communist outpourings are not balanced by the story of the other side in such places as India or,
for that matter, Great Britain.[23]

Most of the visitors who enter Mao's domain are either Communists or fellow travelers, many of whom, like the Indian Sundarlal, return home to write glowing accounts of Communist

achievement. Frequently these accounts are taken directly from NCNA handouts, with quotation marks omitted. Usually these visitors go to China in connection with one of the many conventions, conferences, meetings, festivals, or cultural delegations which the Communists sponsor. The use of these international conferences and delegations is not only part of the propaganda mechanism of the Red government, it is also an instrument of international diplomacy which the Communists have shown a marked ability to exploit. The conferences and cultural delegations, as well as the great international campaigns and drives, offer a field of diplomacy where the Communists possess a distinct advantage over the rest of the world. In the free areas of the world neither the themes of such conferences nor the personnel fall within the purview of government interest or control.

The following items are a small but typical sample of the international news stories released by NCNA between 15 and 21 August 1952:

Communist party organizations send greetings to Korea on Korean Liberation Day
Tremendous ovation greets premier performance by Czech Ensemble in Peking
Indonesian and Costa Rican peace delegates visit Shanghai
Farewell dinner for Polish Basketball Delegation
Indonesia's Independence Day marked in Peking
Agreement on one-year program of Sino-Hungarian cultural cooperation reached
Rumanian Song and Dance Ensemble warmly welcomed in Peking
Exhibition about Hungary opened in Peking
Hungarian Cinema Week held in Peking
Chinese Students' Delegation leaves for Bucharest
Chinese acrobats group warmly welcomed in Finland

The activities represented by these headlines constitute an effective method for promoting solidarity within the Communist bloc while promoting division elsewhere in the world. Chinese

newspaper readers are kept constantly aware of international relations in terms of good and evil: the warm solidarity of all those
who sympathize with their government, the bitter division within
and hatred for the camp of the enemy. So important is this part
of Red diplomacy that international agreements are negotiated
(as indicated in the sixth headline above) about the exact amount
of effort which will be devoted to international cultural exchange.
International conferences and delegations consider every conceivable field of human endeavor.

The participation of Chinese Communists in the international
conferences was on a firm postwar footing before Mao's government was proclaimed. In the spring of 1949, for example, a
delegation of outstanding Chinese Communist professors, writers,
and artists headed by Kuo Mo-jo attended the World Peace Conference in Paris, stopping first in Moscow for consultation with
Soviet leaders.[24] From that time forward Chinese delegations to
conferences and congresses sponsored by the international Communist movement were usually accorded a position second only
to that of the Soviet delegates. As soon as the Peking government
was proclaimed, the Chinese joined in playing hosts for the international propaganda conferences.

Undoubtedly one of the most important conferences staged by
Peking during the first five years of Communist rule, because of its
size, scope, and the propaganda effort devoted to it, was the
Peace Conference of the Asian and Pacific Peoples held from 2
to 12 October 1952. Most of the 429 delegates and the specially
invited guests from over forty countries who participated arrived
in time to witness the mammoth display of military and organizational power which the Communists staged on the third anniversary of their regime. The conference was given the widest
possible publicity abroad by the leftist press, and Peking turned
out special posters, booklets, and reports on the proceedings. The
results of the conference, an "Appeal to the Peoples of the
World," an "Address to the United Nations," and nine resolutions, could have been forecast with almost word for word ac-

curacy by anyone familiar with the current Communist world line, long before the delegates met. Needless to say, all of these items were passed unanimously by the delegates.[25] The speakers, who ranged from Kuo Mo-jo to Louis W. Wheaton, leader of the United States "delegation," lauded the achievements of Mao's regime and joined in common vituperation against the United States. Comments by delegates from some of the smaller nations of Southeast Asia attested that the 1 October display of military power had had the desired effect.

Most of the conferences and the delegations which carry on Peking's "cultural exchange" with the Communist bloc as well as with the outside world operate under the auspices of a front organization within China officially sponsored by the regime and in which Communists occupy key positions. The China Peace Committee, for example, was official sponsor of the 1952 Peace Conference of the Asian and Pacific Peoples. One of the most important as well as commonest forms of international exchange organization is the "friendship association." For the countries outside the iron curtain these associations are organized under the Chinese People's Association for Cultural Relations with Foreign Countries. This central body ensures that cultural relations serve the current policy of the regime and that no contradictions appear. Under it, for example, comes the Sino-Indian Friendship Association which since its formation on 16 May 1952 has sponsored numerous exchange visits and exhibitions. Under the auspices of the Sino-British Friendship Association a seven-member trade union delegation arrived in Peking from Britain on 16 September 1954 and was given the grand tour.[26]

By the end of its fifth year in power Mao's regime had organized or was organizing such associations for most of the major countries outside the Communist bloc. Their members aid in distributing Peking's publications and in exploiting differences in foreign policy views within these countries. For example, the Tokyo branch of the Sino-Japanese Friendship Association undertook to distribute more than 30,000 copies of *People's China*

and *China Pictorial* during its Japan-China Friendship Month
from 15 September to 15 October 1954.[27] The unofficial status
of the non-Chinese half of these organizations is usually passed
over by Peking spokesmen or else treated as a temporary manifestation of imperialist and fascist control which will end as soon
as the particular country is "liberated."

As in the internal rule of the country, the Communists use movements and drives at the international level as a means of linking all
the cultural organizations and exchanges and solidifying the
Communist world camp. Just before the Korean War and almost
immediately after Mao's return from his talks with Stalin, the
Chinese Communists joined in the signature campaign for the
Stockholm Peace Appeal. According to the official press the Chinese peasants affixed their signatures with "enthusiasm and fervor"
—though whether most of them could write was an open question—to the many peace appeals which were circulated in the
name of the World Peace Congress, including Moscow's demand
for a five-power peace pact. For some of their efforts the authorities claimed more than 300,000,000 signatures in China.[28]
When a new worldwide Communist peace offensive got under
way in April 1953 following Stalin's death, China's Chou En-lai
played a key role in helping to bring the Korean War to a close
and, in the eyes of many of the Asian neutrals, easing world tension. The peace campaign at that time helped not only to maintain
the solidarity of the Communist bloc but also to obscure from
the nondiscerning the fact that the United Nations side had been
trying every conceivable method to persuade the Communists
to make peace.[29] Other drives in which China under Mao joined
with other Communist states include the Soviet drive to expand
trade with the non-Communist world, commemorative drives for
Communist leaders such as Marx, and campaigns against the rearming of Germany and Japan.

The Communist propagandists have shown marked ability to
use foreign visitors and foreign publications in their efforts at
home and abroad. Citizens inside the iron curtain are subjected

to a barrage of material indicating that most of the "good" people of the world are backing the Mao government. Because all foreign guests are official guests of the government, their thanks for any courtesies extended can easily be interpreted as approval and support of the government itself. This was probably never more apparent than during the visit of the British Labor party delegation headed by former Prime Minister Clement Attlee in August and September 1954. Many of Attlee's speeches of thanks were made to sound like all-out endorsements of the Mao regime.[30]

The London *Economist* gave an excellent description in advance of the use to which Chinese Reds would put the Attlee visit:

The Labour delegates have presumably reconciled themselves to the fact that during their tour they will be photographed, filmed, recorded for radio, and exhaustively written up by the worldwide "disinformation" network; that their simplest expressions of thanks to their hosts will be represented as prostrations before the might and glory of Mao Tse-tung's regime; and that if they venture to comment unfavorably on anything they see, no breath of that criticism will reach the millions behind the iron curtain. They presumably think this a price worth paying in order to see Peking's peepshow.[31]

Peking also employs the services of foreign visitors to add an air of authenticity to its publications abroad. For example, the Indian ambassador K. M. Panikkar wrote an article for the 1 October 1951 issue of *People's China*. This was at a high point in the Communist year of violence when such support was needed to calm apprehensions in the outside world.[32] Speeches by delegates to conferences and trade representatives are also presented abroad as articles in various publications.[33] In a similar manner the official Chinese Communist press pulls together and quotes all major foreign newspapers and magazines whose position can in any way be construed to support the position of Mao's regime. In September 1954, for example, the Peking propaganda machine quoted spokesmen everywhere from Calcutta to London as supporting their demand to "liberate" Taiwan.[34] It hardly needs to be added that nations outside the Communist bloc would be hard pressed to find such easily utilized opinion supporting their side in the China mainland press.

Another technique which the Chinese Reds have learned well from their Soviet teachers for the conduct of foreign relations is the use of vituperation. In face to face negotiations the Reds employ language so vitriolic when they meet with opposition that the other side tends to make small concessions in order to avoid the unpleasant atmosphere which usually develops. The Chinese who negotiated the truce in the Korean War, Chou En-lai at the 1954 Geneva conference, and the late Andrei Vyshinsky at the United Nations have all manifested the same ability to express vicious hatred for anyone who opposes them. The Indian members of the Neutral Nations Repatriation Commission in Korea were shocked at the charges which were leveled against them, such as being in the pay of the American imperialists. The Chinese press of course echoes the official spokesmen. A typical instance of how far the Reds will go was an article widely circulated on the mainland in February 1951 entitled "The Vatican—Tool of Imperialism," which accused the Vatican authorities including the Pope of every conceivable political crime.[35] In most cases where the Communists employ this form of intimidation they are obviously unconcerned whether the language or the argumentation possesses either logic or honesty.[36]

Peking has shown on many occasions that no considerations of morality, manners, or international law will be allowed to interfere with its determination to conduct its policy as it sees fit. As a part of a program for demonstrating its firm hold on the mainland, for intimidating the overseas Chinese, and for getting scarce foreign exchange, for example, the Reds embarked in 1951 on a campaign of blackmailing Chinese abroad for remittances to save their relatives on the mainland from persecution and possible execution. Millions of dollars poured into Red China from all over the world, including United Nations members whose soldiers were at that time engaged in fighting Chinese Reds in Korea. Over 60 per cent of the Chinese living in the large cities of the

United States, for instance, received letters and follow-up cablegrams from relatives begging for money to avert death or torture.[37] Similar letters received all over the world indicated that the mainland authorities had been very efficient in gathering data on Chinese residing abroad. That same year Peking secured large amounts of foreign exchange by selling about five hundred tons of opium illegally on the world market. The Permanent Central Opium Board in Geneva, which released this figure, stated that it was about half of the world's legal consumption for one year.[38] This violation of a world-recognized narcotics code was also undoubtedly viewed by the Communists as an aid in their goal of encouraging moral degeneration in the capitalist camp. They might indeed have thought of it as a justifiable turning of the tables, remembering that in the 19th century China's efforts to prohibit the importation and use of opium were thwarted by Western traders.

Shortly after the Peking government was established in 1949, Professor H. A. Steiner of the University of California at Los Angeles reviewed the basis on which the world could anticipate its conduct of foreign relations. After five years his analysis remains as valid as when it was written, a tribute not only to his scholarship but to the single-minded determination of the Communist masters of China. Steiner concluded his study by pointing out:

Communist China typifies a new *kind* of state, organized and motivated by a revolutionary ethic thoroughly incompatible with the existing structure of international law and relations. It struggles to attain unbridled freedom of action for the implementation of doctrines which can no longer be exposed to objective scrutiny and evaluation. If it accepts restraint, it does so from political and tactical considerations alone and not from any sense of legal obligation under international law. International law does not even receive its lip-service.[39]

What then are the major policies to which the Chinese Communist regime applies its diverse techniques in the international arena?

All policies of the Peking government during its first five years have been consistently subordinated to the Communist two-camp world view. The camp led by the USSR is unified, strong, and solid. Within it there can never be any attitude other than friendship and unanimous support. This is the camp of the future world order for which all Communists must work with enthusiasm, vigor, and a militant aggressive spirit. The other camp is led by the United States, the most advanced capitalist country. This camp is divided not only by the contradictions and rivalries among the capitalist powers but also by the class struggles within those countries and by the hatred for them of the colonial and semicolonial peoples under their control. The Communist goal is complete victory in this divided world, and the two main pillars of this foreign policy are support for the Soviet Union and enmity for the United States. On this score there has not been the slightest deviation in five years of Red rule on the mainland. A detailed examination of these two main aspects of over-all foreign policy is reserved for the next two chapters. Here, however, let us outline six other leading policy goals which fit into this world view of Mao's government and which have played a significant role in its conduct of foreign relations since 1949.[40]

A first important policy of the Chinese Communist leaders has been to establish Peking's position as one of the five great world powers and *the* major power in Asia. Peking has from the outset demanded that it be consulted on all matters of international importance and insisted that it alone has the right to occupy China's seat in the United Nations. One of the first items usually mentioned in claims to great-power status is the tremendous population of China. An official spokesman writing in the 7 August 1954 *People's Daily,* for example, stated:

the ancient Chinese saying goes, "Veiled by one leaf the eye could not see Tai mountain."

Yet it is impossible "not to see," because Tai mountain exists objectively and those who deny objective existence will certainly know the cost of knocking their heads against walls. Truman, who did not believe these words, forced his way to the Chinese frontier with his

eyes shut and, true enough, ran his head against Tai mountain, bleed-
ing and disgraced.

The lesson Truman received is probably not lost on Dulles. But
the latter does not resign himself to his fate. Though he was compelled
to attend the Geneva conference, to sit in one room with Premier
Chou, he still exhausted all ways and means to ignore the Big Power
status of China. . . .

Imperialists, beware of knocking your heads against the "wall" built
by 600,000,000 people! [41]

Chou En-lai has repeatedly warned the world that peace in Asia
depends upon the recognition of Communist China's great-power
status and admission to the United Nations.[42]

These claims to great-power status are echoed by Moscow and
by the Communist leaders throughout the world. In February
1951 the international Communist organization issued a manifesto calling for a five-power peace pact, Communist China of
course being one of the five powers mentioned. The Reds claimed
to have enlisted more than 600,000,000 signatures throughout
the world.[43] The Communists never fail to remind the world of
Red China's armed might when demanding admission to the
United Nations and recognition as a great power. An important
result of the war in Korea has been to establish Red China's repu-
tation as a great military power. As one of the top leaders in
Peking said when reporting the results of the war to the meeting of
the Government Council on 12 September 1953, "This victory
has further strengthened our national defence, and it has also
raised our status in the community of nations." [44] Thus, although
leaders in the Communist camp may hail Red China as a "pillar of
peace in Asia," it is usually on the basis of military power that this
appraisal is made.[45]

In many respects this goal of obtaining status as a great power
had been realized by Mao's government after only five years. The
fact that China had stalemated a coalition of the great powers of
the West who were fighting for the United Nations in Korea
proved, at least to many of her neighbors, that Communism had

brought the power and status which Peking claimed. And many non-Communist statesmen in the West contended that it was un-realistic not to recognize a regime which ruled 600,000,000 people effectively.

A second major policy of the Peking regime in foreign affairs has been to assume the role of leader in Asia. This policy has been pursued with especial emphasis on Red China as 1) head of an anti-imperialist bloc, 2) leader of the "liberation" movement in the colonial and semicolonial areas of Asia, 3) teacher of the successful method for Communist seizure of power, 4) a model of success in establishing political authority, 5) the proof for left-wing and liberal leaders in Asia of the validity of the Com-munist solution for their problems, and 6) leader of the "peace" movement in Asia.

From the outset the Soviet Union gave Peking full support and aid for this leadership role. On 30 April 1953 *Pravda* pointed out for the world Communist leaders that the "Chinese people's vic-tory over the imperialists and the Kuomintang clique, their bulwark within their country, and the creation and strengthen-ing of the Chinese People's Republic . . . revolutionized the East . . . and made possible a growth in the liberation struggle of the colonial and semi-colonial peoples." [46] In a special article which *Pravda* printed with its stamp of ap-proval, Lin Po-chu, a member of the Central Committee of the Chinese Communist party, pointed out that only those who rec-ognized the validity of Communist doctrine could be truly anti-imperialist, only the Communists could offer true liberation, and that Communist China was leading the way toward liberation in Asia. "The banner of Lenin is the banner of the struggle for na-tional liberation in Asia," he said. "People of Asian nations, for-ward under the banner of Lenin!" [47] At the Peace Conference of Asian and Pacific Peoples in Peking in October 1952, Communist leaders from all over Asia stated their faith in Peking's leadership, guidance, and assistance to their liberation movements. The dele-gate from Cambodia, for instance, stated: "The Chinese people, under the leadership of Chairman Mao Tse-tung, are a great bulwark of world peace, the close friend of all people struggling for liberation. Inspired by the great example of the Chinese people the Khmer people will strengthen their fight against aggression until their own independence and world peace are secured." [48]

As of 1 October 1949 the Chinese Communists regarded themselves as an "advanced nation" and therefore obligated to extend assistance to "liberation movements" in other countries, just as the Soviets assisted their cause. As early as December 1949 Liu Shao-ch'i called for "moral and material support to the fighters of the national liberation wars in Malaya, Burma, Indo-China, Indonesia, and the Philippines." [49] Central Committeeman Yeh Chien-ying stated: "All oppressed peoples of the world demand liberation. But if the nations which want liberation do not get help from the advanced nations, they will not achieve victory. This has been the case with the liberation war in China, and is likewise the case with the liberation war in Korea." [50]

Chinese Communist leaders believe that their revolution has become the "classical type" for the liberation of colonial and semi-colonial areas.[51] Perhaps the significance of this attitude is best illustrated with reference to Viet Nam, where this "classical type" of revolution in 1954 achieved another success—aided over the preceding years, it should be added, by French colonial policies. Early in 1954 Ton Duc Thang, president of the National Committee of the Viet Minh National United Front, spelled out very clearly the essentials for successful seizure of power as learned from the Chinese Communists:

the Viet Nam people learn precious lessons from the Chinese revolution and people. These are the thoughts of Mao Tse-tung—an ingenious application of Marx-Engels-Lenin-Stalin ideology to practice in China. These are the three lessons on national united front, armed struggle and the building of the vanguard party, which have led the Chinese revolution to success and which President Ho Chi Minh and the Viet Nam Lao Dong Party have ingeniously applied to the concrete conditions of Viet Nam in leading our people to fight and score important victories in the past and certainly to win complete victory. The unity between the Soviet Union and China further strengthens the world camp of peace and democracy. We are happy to strengthen our ties with the two great countries of the world.[52]

This statement of the ingredients of success in China by the Viet Minh leader constitutes a realistic appraisal of Communism as an organizational weapon for seizing power rather than an ideology. To date the technique of organized subversion, guerrilla warfare, and sabotage, together with the political propaganda that can be based on having a united front (usually against Western imperialism), an organized military force, and aid from the outside, has been an almost unbeatable combination in economically underdeveloped areas. It pushes the established government into a defensive military pose, promotes corruption and defeatism, and prevents the expenditure of limited resources on necessary reforms. The established authorities gradually lose the support of the liberals and the intellectuals as they are forced to rely more and more upon costly military measures to cope with the problem of armed insurrection; and for the liberals and intellectuals the united front propaganda gains ever greater appeal. All of this has the advantage of appearing as a native movement of protest against military dictatorship and oppression. It is all the more effective when the territory involved is a colony where there is bitter and usually justified hatred for the West, such as Malaya or Indo-China, or a country where there are close ties with the Western powers, such as the Philippines or Thailand. The insurgents frequently get the moral support of those countries where anti-Westernism is still a major force.[53] This hidden aggression by subversion is at the present time probably the most powerful weapon in the arsenal of post-World War II Communist imperialism. It was undoubtedly to this that Prince Wan Waithayakon, foreign minister of Thailand, referred when speaking before the United Nations General Assembly 28 September 1954: "The question of aggression already has the attention of the United Nations but not yet the question of subversion, which constitutes the real danger for my country as also for other countries. The question of subversion in all its aspects should, therefore, be studied so that it may be considered by the General Assembly at a later session." [54]

By 1950 Red China was not merely aiding the Communists in Viet Nam with arms; Chinese Communist cadres were training Ho Chi-minh's troops and teaching them methods for psychological control of the masses. In 1952 Russian-made arms as well as Chinese arms were reaching the Viet Minh in sizable quantities.[55] Despite increasing evidence of Chinese intervention in Indo-China, especially after the Korean truce in 1953, Peking spokesmen denied giving any but moral support to the Communists there. At the Geneva conference the official spokesman of the Chinese Communist delegation stated that Red China had "made no intervention of any kind" in the Indo-China war and that the Viet Minh rebels had obtained all their arms by capturing them from the French. This, he said, had been true in the Chinese civil war where the armies of Mao Tse-tung, unaided by the Soviet Union, obtained all their arms from Chiang's forces.[56] In June 1954 Chou assured Nehru that Communist China followed a policy of noninterference in Indo-China as elsewhere.[57] Yet when the victorious Viet Minh armies moved into their new capital at Hanoi on 10 October 1954, they rode in Molotov trucks and carried the latest Russian and Chinese weapons.[58] Following the truce arranged at Geneva, Viet Minh leaders gave profuse thanks to the Chinese Reds for being unstinting in material as well as moral aid.[59]

Meanwhile the government set up by Ho Chi-minh in Viet Minh-controlled areas parallels Mao's dictatorship down to the last detail. There is the same use of "democratic parties and groups" within a united front controlled by the Communists, the same criticism and self-criticism sessions, small group and large group meetings, confessions, "agrarian reform" conducted in terms of class struggle, labor emulation, and so forth.[60] The French prisoners released by the Communists in Indo-China even told tales of brain-washing and camp routine which were parallel to the experiences of UN prisoners of the Chinese Communists in Korea.[61] Mao's China is indeed the pattern for future Communist states in Asia. But the structure bears a marked resemblance to that of North Korea and the European satellites of Soviet Russia as well.

Red China's bid for leadership in Asia has meant a rivalry with India, whose Nehru has established his own claim to leadership, especially in the "neutral bloc." The Communist themes of racialism, Western imperialism, peace, and coexistence strike a particularly responsive chord in India, and of course in its propaganda directed toward India Peking plays down its contempt for the neutral position. India's attempt to be completely neutral means that she must appear to give the same credence to Red statements as to those coming from the West, and Peking can take advantage of this fact.

Actually the Indian government has been in the position of courting the favor of Red China during most of the first five years of Mao's regime.[62] China's position was expressed by Mao in 1949 at the time that Nehru's government extended recognition: "I firmly believe that relying on the brave Communist party of India and the unity and struggle of all Indian patriots, India will certainly not long remain under the yoke of imperialism and its collaborators. [India had, of course, already attained its sovereignty.] Like Free China, a free India will one day emerge in the Socialist and People's Democratic family; that day will end the imperialist reactionary era in the history of mankind." [63] Since Peking justifies its leadership in Asia on the grounds that only a Communist state can be anti-imperialist, whenever Nehru's government disagrees with Chinese Reds the latter maintain that Indian policy is being determined by outside powers and therefore India is not truly independent. They then adduce this as proof that China, not India, is qualified to be the true leader of Asians against Western imperialism.

In July 1949, for instance, when Tibetan local authorities expelled Chinese Nationalist officials and other Chinese in order to forestall Communist "liberation," the Chinese Communists claimed that the action was inspired by British and American imperialists and their "stooge, the Indian Nehru government." [64] Again in October 1950, in an exchange of notes regarding Tibet, Chou En-lai charged that the Indian government was submitting to "outside obstruction." [65] The Indian authorities protested indignantly, but the Chinese refused to back down on their charges. Whenever their opinions favored the United Nations side, the Indian members of the Neutral Nations Repatriation Commission in Korea were accused of having given in to pressures of the American imperialists and KMT agents. One Indian general was said to have been "stuck with tent poles and compelled to sign three demands by KMT agents." [66] The Indians experienced the real problems involved for neutrals, for somewhat similar charges were leveled in the American press and especially by South Korean spokesmen when their decisions tended to favor the Communist side of a dispute.

The Chinese Communists have professed great sympathy for the "Indian people"; accusations are not directed against them, but against the Indian government. At the official level Chinese Communist representatives in India are frequently contemptuous in their behavior toward Indian civil servants. At the propaganda level they push Sino-Indian friendship and support the activities of the Indian Communist party. [67]

Throughout its first five years in power Mao's government lost no opportunity to demonstrate its capacity as a leader in all fields. In 1951 when India was suffering an acute food shortage, Peking dramatically offered to send one million tons of grain. This was intended as proof that the Reds had already solved China's pressing food problem and was made as a gesture of "unselfish and sincere friendship." Actually only 507,720 tons of grain reached India from China during all of 1951 and the first four months of 1952 and these were the result of four intergovernment sales agreements made by hard bargaining. In the same period the United States shipped 3,800,000 tons of grain to India at prices appreciably below those of the Reds. Yet the Communist propaganda network was able to take advantage of the Chinese offer which was never fulfilled to present Communist China as the true friend of the Indian people and the United States as the imperialist power attempting to take political advantage of India's dire situation. On this issue the Peking machine was extremely effective.[68] It might be added that the openly publicized debate within the United States prior to the decision to send grain was of commeasurable assistance.

By 1954 China's premier Chou En-lai had seized much of the initiative from Nehru. In his position as chief Asian spokesman at the Geneva conference he made several bids for leadership in Asia. During a break in the conference he flew dramatically to New Delhi where he and Nehru issued a statement concerning their respective countries' faith in "Five Principles" which now became the new Communist propaganda line in Asia: 1) mutual respect for each other's territorial integrity and sovereignty, 2) nonaggression, 3) noninterference in each other's internal affairs, 4) equality and mutual benefit, and 5) peaceful coexistence.[69] But it was Chou who received credit for the initiative, since Nehru's faith in such principles was already a matter of record. Nehru immediately communicated his belief in China's good faith to the rest of the world. A truly ironical testimony to the success of Peking's propaganda efforts and Red China's bid to become the leader and model for Asia followed on 8 September 1954 when an NCNA dispatch quoted Nehru as advocating using China's flood control methods in India.[70] This came at a time when the Communists were finally having to admit that the 1954 floods were the worst in Chinese history.

The third general policy of the Peking rulers has been to maintain a state of continual tension which seemingly can be eased only by making concessions to Communist demands. This policy is based upon the belief that because of its inherent contradictions the capitalist world is incapable of bearing up during a sustained period of crisis. In 1949 relations between Peking and New Delhi were strained over the occupation of Tibet. In 1950 while still mopping up resistance on the mainland the Chinese Communists entered the Korean War and began their campaign against any interference with their "liberation" of Taiwan. In 1952 Peking began to step up demands for recognition of the Communists in Indo-China. That spring the Reds launched a violent campaign against the British in Kwangtung province which borders on the British Crown Colony of Hong Kong.[71] In short, there has not been a moment since the establishment of Mao's government when its relations with several outside countries, especially the Western powers, have not been strained or openly hostile.

The strange logic of the Communist position which at the same time claims to work for peace and harmony yet by its expansion-ist and conspiratorial nature creates tension and violence was expressed in an article on Communist China's foreign policy written in commemoration of the second anniversary of the re-gime in 1951:

the Chinese people know from their own experience the truth of the slogan: "We definitely cannot wait for peace; we must go and fight for peace." The Chinese people are fully aware that the imperialists are beasts thirsting for war. In dealing with these beasts, peace cannot be achieved by entreaties and sorrowful supplications, or through non-resistance. The Chinese people sincerely concur with Chairman Mao's perspicacious observation: "The threat of war from the strongholds of imperialism still exists; the possibility of a third world war is still there. However, the forces guarding against the dangers of war, and the outbreak of World War III, are growing very rapidly. The vigilance of the vast majority of the people of the world is increasing. Only if the Communist parties throughout the world unite all the forces of democracy and peace and help them expand on a large scale, can a new world war be held in check.[72]

A good example of the policy of a sustained state of tension would be Peking's relations with Thailand, which has been active in the fight against Communism and which the Reds claim is a colony of "American imperialism." Even before the truce in

Korea, Communist China was warning the Thai government to "stop undermining the interests of the Chinese in Thailand immediately" or suffer "grave consequences." [73] Not only has Peking used Thailand's colony of more than three million overseas Chinese for pressuring the Thai government but it has taken advantage of a large Thai minority in Yunnan province for training Thai cadres. In January 1953 the Chinese Communists set up a Thai autonomous area in Yunnan, and the outside world began to hear about a "Free Thai" movement which was being propagandized there. On 30 July 1954, just one month and two days after Chou En-lai had given Nehru his solemn word that Communist China's policy was noninterference in the affairs of other people, the Peking *People's Daily* printed an article by Pridi Phanamyong, former premier of Thailand, whose whereabouts had been clothed in mystery since 1947. Now linked with the Free Thai movement and officially sponsored by the Chinese Communists, Pridi called upon the Thai people to wage a struggle to overthrow their rulers, whom he identified as "American imperialism and its puppets." He stated that only by hard struggle "can the obstacles standing in the way of peace, independence and self-determination of the Thai people be removed." His article was broadcast in China and abroad by the Chinese Communist radio with Peking's full endorsement.[74] By September 1954, following the truce in Indo-China, Peking spokesmen began to accuse the Thai government of preparations for war "under U.S. instructions." [75] In view of the Communist state established in Viet Nam, the organizational activities of the Chinese Communists among the Thai peoples in south China and Viet Nam, the Communist sabotage organizations uncovered among the overseas Chinese in Thailand, and the increasingly hostile attitude of Peking, it is not to be wondered that the Thai foreign minister took his plea for a United Nations study of aggression by subversion to the General Assembly after the Soviet delegate had vetoed such a proposed study by the Security Council.[76] The whole pattern was only too familiar to him.

Only six days before Thailand's Prince Wan Waithayakon made his proposal at the United Nations, the delegate of the Khmer "Resistance Forces" in Cambodia, another group officially backed by Peking, had refused to surrender arms to the legitimate Cambodian government under the terms of the Geneva settlement. His stand was also supported by Peking spokesmen.[77] By October 1954 Burma too was seriously worried about renewed Communist organization of resistance forces. Meanwhile Peking had maintained a state of tension in both Indo-China and Korea by division of both countries and by truce agreements which not only were unstable but offered many opportunities for violations and charges of violations. Mao's government had succeeded to an admirable degree in maintaining a high state of international tension during its first five years in power.

A fourth general policy of the Mao government has been to extend control over the more than twelve million overseas Chinese, but here so far it has met with failure. These Chinese residents abroad constitute a sizable proportion of the population of many of the countries of Southeast Asia. In Malaya, for example, there are almost as many Chinese as Malays. The overseas Chinese have traditionally given first loyalty to the government on mainland China; this has tended to intensify discrimination against them by nationalists in these areas and in turn makes them ideal tools for aggression by subversion. By the end of 1952, however, as a result of the extortion campaign, the year of violence, the 5-anti Movement, the general nature of Mao's rule, and contact with the refugees who streamed from the mainland, Mao's government had lost the support of most of the overseas Chinese; they pledged their loyalty to the Nationalist government on Taiwan. In October 1953 and again in October 1954 the contrast in the celebrations of the Communist holiday on the first of the month and the Nationalist holiday on the tenth in the major overseas Chinese centers indicated that probably 80 per cent or more of the Chinese residents abroad were profoundly anti-Communist. From the high levels of 1949 and 1950—around U.S. $25,000,000 per month—the remittances from the overseas Chinese to the mainland dropped to less than $700,000 a month in 1954.[78]

The Peking regime began in 1953, however, to try to win back the sympathies of this group. Relying on its strong power position and the pride which Chinese naturally take in the new world status of their country, the Communists have undertaken to champion the rights of the overseas Chinese against the established governments where they reside. The Reds have recruited young students whom they have then sent back to Southeast Asia as organizers; they have given "relief" to "victimized overseas Chinese"; they even allotted the Chinese abroad thirty seats in the National Assembly which met in Peking on 15 September 1954.[79] Peking's attitude toward Chinese residing abroad is more than faintly reminiscent of Hitler's handling of his nationals outside the borders of the German fatherland. In a special article written in connection with the participation of overseas Chinese representatives in the National Assembly, a high-ranking Communist stated:

The overseas Chinese are endeared children of the Chinese nation. They are also good children. Most of them love their fatherland dearly. . . . After the establishment of the People's Republic of China, the overseas Chinese felt for the first time the close concern of the government in the fatherland. Their proper rights and interests are now protected by their country. Some people are of the opinion that since the overseas Chinese reside in foreign lands, they should not be given part in politics. . . . The freedom of an individual to love his fatherland is a right that should not be usurped.[80]

As a part of its general program of tension in foreign relations and use of vituperation, the Communist regime in Peking has accused the authorities throughout most of Southeast Asia of "horrendous acts" against the Chinese and has threatened reprisals and just punishment. In November 1952, for example, British authorities were charged with torturing and maltreating more than fourteen thousand Chinese whom they deported from Malaya.[81] The Philippine and Thai governments have been accused of barbarous deeds against the Chinese, and the British in Hong Kong of purposely setting fire to squatter settlements there. Such charges are aired at conferences on overseas Chinese affairs like that held in Peking from 1 to 5 November 1953 and attended by 412 delegates.[82] Only a few months after Chou En-lai's visit to New Delhi in 1954, even Nehru expressed some apprehension about the "vast" Chinese communities in Thailand, Indonesia, Malaya, and Burma and the fact that Peking's policy did not allow the overseas Chinese to divest themselves of their nationality.[83]

At the end of its fifth year Mao's regime had failed to revive the enthusiasm the overseas Chinese had shown during the flush of victory period. Most of these Chinese are businessmen, traders, and private industrialists, and they showed fear of Peking's statist policies. Further, they were still able to pledge their support to an alternative government, the Nationalist government on Taiwan. The Communists, however, were able to evoke some enthusiasm among the overseas Chinese youth. Given the discrimination against the Chinese caused by the growing nationalism in the areas where they reside and their failure to assimilate, they continue to present Mao's government with an excuse for strained relations, retaliation, or invasion in Southeast Asia.[84] The collapse of the Nationalist government would by default offer Peking the unified support of the overseas Chinese and present the Communists with ample excuse and support for any moves they planned in Southeast Asia. Thus the Communist policy of extending control over the overseas Chinese is vitally connected with the policy of "liberating" Taiwan.

Here we come to a fifth major policy which the Mao regime pursued during its first five years in power: the expansion of its area of influence and control. In 1949 Communist authorities declared that they would not permit "a single inch of Chinese territory to remain outside the rule of the Chinese People's Republic." [85] At that time they included Taiwan and Tibet as inviolable parts of Chinese territory, stating with regard to the latter that "the Tibetan people is an indivisible part of the Chinese people." This of course raises many questions. Although the Chinese claim to suzerainty over Tibet has been acknowledged by international agreements in the past decades, former Chinese emperors advanced claims to all of Korea and most of Southeast Asia, whose rulers acknowledged Chinese suzerainty while Tibet was still independent. Even the ruler of Ceylon acknowledged Chinese overlordship as late as the fifteenth century. Are areas where Chinese outnumber natives, such as Malaya and sections of Thailand, to be considered Chinese territory, especially if there is a past history of Chinese suzerainty? Is Hong Kong to be included in that "every inch of Chinese territory"? At the end of its fifth year the Red regime had limited itself to the extension of full control over Tibet and demanded "liberation" of Taiwan, but no precise definition of just what was Chinese territory had been given. Peking had maintained an ominous silence on its intentions toward such places as Hong Kong and Macao.

The "political mobilization directive" for the invasion of Tibet was announced on 24 October 1950, the day before Chinese troops entered the fighting in Korea. The following September troops of the People's Liberation Army took over Lhasa. In succeeding years intense efforts were devoted to consolidating control over the whole Tibetan area. On 1 July 1952 telegraphic communication was opened between Lhasa and Chungking, and on 1 May 1953 the Reds started their Tsinghai-Tibet military highway. Early in 1955 the first convoy of trucks rolled into Lhasa over the completed road. By 1954 reports were reaching the outside world on the stepped-up construction of military roads and airfields.[86] The occupation of Tibet led to several exchanges of notes with India. Peking told Nehru's government to mind its own business, that the liberation of Tibet was purely a domestic matter. India acceded, and on 29 April 1954 the two governments signed a pact regarding Tibet under which India agreed to withdraw all troops stationed along Tibetan trade routes and hand over Indian-owned facilities "at a reasonable price." [87]

Meanwhile, reports reaching Kalimpong, the Indian terminus of the main route to Lhasa, indicated that all was not smooth in the land of Shangri-la. Clashes with Chinese troops were reported in the fall of 1951.[88] In the spring of 1952 food was scarce and because of the size of the Chinese garrisons and the animosity of the local people the Communists called off their policy of fraternization and required their troops to stay within limited areas.[89] In November of that year Mao Tse-tung stated his intention to raise the population of Tibet from three to ten million, a statement which some people took as implying the need for Chinese migration to control the Tibetans.[90] While the young Dalai Lama gave profuse thanks to Chairman Mao and the Communist party of China at the National Assembly in Peking in September 1954, and there was talk of unbounded gratitude for the Red regime which had "done so much for Tibet," refugee monks and priests pouring into India in October told a different tale, one of oppression, religious persecution, exploitation, and bloodshed. By 1954 Tibet, like China, was separated from the Western world by an iron curtain.[91] Meanwhile there have been frequent and disturbing reports of Red pressure and organizational activity in the small neighboring kingdom of Nepal.

Communist China's expansion into Korea has been of a different nature. Here Mao's government has limited itself to creating a condition of military and economic dependency. Between the time when the Chinese troops entered the Korean War on 25 October 1950 and the conclusion of the armistice agreement on 27 July 1953, Red China assumed the role of directing the Korean military forces, a role that some people believed Russia had exercised from the beginning. The Sino-Korean Agreement on Economic and Cultural Cooperation signed on 23 November 1953 by Kim Il Sung and Chou En-lai with the aid of a Soviet adviser guaranteed Communist China a decisive role in Korea's future. The wording of this agreement, which the Chinese Communists stated had been "forged in blood," also indicated that there could be no hope for a unified Korea except under Communist rule or as a result of a resumption of hostilities.[92] Perhaps a symptom of the close cooperation of the Peking and Moscow authorities in their relations with North Korea was the fact that *Pravda* hailed the establishment of through train service between Peking and Pyongyang on 3 June 1954 as a further cementing of the solid front in the Far East.[93]

Mao's regime also relied on the existence of armed conflict to extend its influence in Indo-China, and a trade agreement in July 1954 cemented relations.[94] After the truce arranged by Chou En-lai at Geneva there was a marked increase in the exchange of personnel between Communist China and Viet Minh areas. Elsewhere in Asia Peking had extended its activities as leader and inspirer of Communist insurrection movements. Evidence continued to pile up, for instance, indicating closer ties between Red China and the Malayan Communist insurgents.[95] Peking had also shown a marked ability to utilize its government foreign trade monopoly to expand its areas of influence and control. At the end of only five years of Communist rule China's area of influence and control was greater than it had been for more than two centuries.

The sixth major foreign policy goal of the Mao regime has been to convince the outside world, and especially other Asians, that it has indeed achieved complete independence. China's whole role as a model and leader for the "liberation" of other peoples depends upon her ability to prove to them that a Communist-led revolution brings full sovereignty and that anything less than full membership in the Soviet bloc constitutes a curtailment of independence. This is no small task, for China's new "independence" has involved an undeviating acceptance of the party line dictated from Moscow.

By October 1954, however, the Chinese Reds could claim relative success in this goal. Peking's assertion that it has complete independence has been backed up by concrete actions against the Western powers. Western rights and properties in China have been eliminated, the "foreign devils" have been expelled from China and humiliated in the process, and Chinese military prowess has brought many of the Western powers in Asia into an apparent attitude of supplication. This has been especially impressive to the many leaders in Asia whose memories of the colonial era remain bitter. China's new unification, power, initiative, and vigor are enough to justify Peking's claims of independence among her neighbors, for whom these remain unrealized goals.

This claim to complete independence and sovereignty has been accepted by many foreign observers who are still prone to analyze China's relationship with the USSR in terms of nineteenth century Western diplomacy and have not studied the strength of the international Communist organization. Other observers have studied subtle theoretical differences between Peking and Moscow stemming from the time when Mao represented a heresy in the Chinese Communist movement, and have failed to appreciate Communism's major role in China as a system of control and organization of the masses rather than an ideology. Still other observers in the West have constantly looked for and talked of possible signs of Chinese "Titoism" on the part of Mao. This speculation also has helped the Chinese Reds in their campaign to convince the world that independence can be truly achieved under Communism.[96]

Actually the determination of China's degree of independence hinges on an analysis of the Sino-Soviet tie, to which we turn in the next chapter. But with regard to her neighbors Red China's foreign policy had been firmly established by 1954. The demands of industrialization, the need for an external threat to justify continued internal repression, the emphasis on increased military power, the pledges of aid to "liberation" movements, Peking's claim to leadership in Asia, the revolutionary goals of world Communism: all of these point toward continued expansion, pressure, threats, and crises around China's borders. This was made only too clear when on the fifth anniversary of Mao's rule the acting Chinese Communist chief of staff called for a great increase in all China's armed forces, despite the conclusion of truces in Korea and Indo-China.[97]

The significance of Red China's first five years for the rest of the world has been spelled out by Joseph E. Starobin, foreign correspondent of the New York *Daily Worker,* who spent a year in China under Mao's government. "What has happened in China makes a big impression on half of the world's population which is 'semi-feudal and semi-colonial,'" he said. "This half of the world faces the same changes China did. China is the model for what is going to happen in these areas; first Southeast Asia, then India and South Asia, then Africa, then South America. The process will not stop until these areas have been 'liberated.'" [98]

11. CHINA AND THE SOVIET UNION[1]

Since the Communist victory on the China mainland probably no subject concerning the Communist bloc has caused more speculation in the outside world than the exact nature of the relations of the new Red state with the Soviet fatherland. The relationship is unquestionably unique in the history of the Soviet Union. For the first time the Soviet has recognized that it is dealing with a partner—although a junior partner—and has had to accord to Mao Tse-tung and his party not only some degree of political initiative but also recognition of a right to interpret matters of ideology.

There has, however, been no doubt about the stand of the Chinese Communist party and its leaders. In their first five years in power there was not a single major instance discernible to the outside world when the Mao regime failed to extend support and allegiance to the USSR. This incredibly smooth outer appearance of Sino-Soviet relations was one of the chief stimulants to speculation. Many were inclined to believe that no partnership could work quite that well.

Since the founding of the Chinese Communist party in 1921 there have been many dramatic struggles for power and conflicts over ideology and strategy in the top leadership, and the Soviet leaders have been deeply involved in them. During most of this thirty-three year period Stalin dominated the international Communist movement. He managed to maintain a firm hold on the Chinese party and to exercise discipline almost at will. For example, he successfully purged the top ranks of the Chinese party many times, forcing leaders such as Chou En-lai and Li Li-san to recant for mistakes which had been his own. In the 1920's the fate of the infant Chinese Communist party was subordinated to the exigencies of his struggle with Trotsky, and Stalin reluctantly accepted Mao's rise to leadership and Mao's adaptation and application in China of the Lenin formula of relying on the peasants for seizing power. Mao's emergence as the top Communist leader in China was probably the outstanding exception to Stalin's ability to call the turn within the Chinese Communist party.[2]

Yet Mao, who had for a long time represented a heresy within the ranks of the Chinese Red party, has been absolutely unwavering in his allegiance to the Soviet fatherland and loyalty to its leader Stalin. In 1926 he wrote:

The present situation is a situation where the two forces, the revolutionary and the anti-revolutionary, are engaged in their final struggle. These two forces unfold two big banners: on one side is the big red revolutionary banner raised high by the Third International and signaling all the oppressed classes of the world to assemble thereunder; on the other side is the big white anti-revolutionary banner raised high by the League of Nations and signaling all the anti-revolutionary elements of the world to assemble thereunder. Those classes in between must undergo rapid disintegration, scampering perhaps to the left to join the revolutionary faction or perhaps to the right to join the anti-revolutionary faction. There is no "independent" ground for them.

Again in 1940 Mao wrote:

The moment the contest between the socialist state of Soviet Russia and the imperialist states of England and America becomes further sharpened, China must stand either on one side or on the other. This is the inevitable tendency. Cannot China be neutral without leaning to either side? This is dream talk. The whole globe will get embroiled in these two battle lines. In the world from now on, "neutrality" is only a term for deceiving people.[3]

Certainly one of the major ties between the Chinese Communists and the Soviet Union was the recognition and great personal attachment accorded Stalin as the symbolic embodiment of world Communist leadership. On the occasion of Stalin's sixtieth birthday in 1939, for example, at a time when the Kremlin was giving large amounts of aid to Mao's archenemy Chiang Kai-shek, Mao spoke to the leaders of the Chinese Communist party in terms which left no doubt about the position which they were to accord to the Soviet leader: "It is a great event that mankind has Stalin. Since we have him, things can go well. . . . Had there been no Stalin, who would there be to give directions?" [4]

Stalin's death on 5 March 1953 gave rise to speculation on the Sino-Soviet relationship in every major capital outside the iron curtain. There was naturally some question as to whether the chief cement of the alliance had been his leadership or the Leninist party structure which he manipulated. By the end of the fifth year of Communist rule in China it was obvious that the death of Stalin had made little difference, and it was possible to discern relatively clearly, at least in broad outline, the general pattern of Sino-Soviet relations. [5]

The basis for the formal attitude of the Mao regime was laid down in Article 11 of *The Common Program* which embodied Mao's principle of "leaning to one side" in the world struggle and placed mainland China firmly in the camp headed by the USSR. Shortly after the inauguration of his government Mao and a delegation of high-ranking Chinese Communists went to Moscow, arriving 16 December 1949. Mao stayed several months talking with Stalin and other Soviet leaders. During this visit a basic Treaty of Friendship, Alliance, and Mutual Assistance and several other agreements were negotiated. The key sentence in the treaty reads: "In the event of one of the contracting parties being attacked by Japan or any state allied with it and thus being involved in a state of war, the other contracting party shall immediately render military and other assistance by all means at its disposal." The agreements included a promise by the Soviet to hand over the Chinese Changchun Railway by the end of 1952, the extension of economic assistance to the extent of $300,000,-000 at 1 per cent interest over a period of five years, a promise by the Soviet to withdraw its forces from Port Arthur and Dairen by the end of 1952, and provisions for setting up joint Sino-Soviet companies for prospecting, producing, and refining petroleum, coal gas, and nonferrous metals in Sinkiang. In addition trade and barter agreements were signed as a result of the Moscow talks.[6] As I have noted elsewhere, it may have been during these Moscow talks that Mao and Stalin decided upon launching the Korean War. The Moscow meetings and their results constituted the formalization before the world of a firm Sino-Soviet alliance.

But, as the preceding chapter has pointed out, such formalities are a minor part of Peking's foreign relations. This is especially true in the case of the Sino-Soviet tie, which involves a more intensive use of Communist techniques of diplomacy—cultural delegations, congresses, conventions, campaigns, educational exchange, propaganda control at all levels—than either country employs in any other relation. The result is an infinitely complex official relationship. At the lowest level of Chinese society the people are impressed with the necessity and importance of the Sino-Soviet alliance and told that they are to participate in it actively. Throughout China practically every activity is in some manner linked to the alliance. It is important, therefore, to analyze in some detail the nature of some of these less formal bonds linking Communist China and the USSR, for their alliance is in many respects a new page in the history of international politics. The Sino-Soviet tie also constitutes Communism's greatest challenge to the world beyond the iron curtain.

Most significant is the ideological bond of revolutionary leadership. Both countries and their leaders are pledged to the creation of a Communist world and apparently are little concerned that, strictly speaking, their basic philosophy—Marxism—has undergone what Benjamin Schwartz of Harvard calls a steady process of "decomposition" through time and expansion.[7] The writings of Liu Shao-ch'i, Ai Ssu-ch'i, and even Mao himself, which are used for the intensive indoctrination of cadres, as well as the documents of the various party reforms of the last decade, indicate clearly that the ideology in China has become more and more an organizational ideology accenting control of the masses. In this field the teachings of the Soviet Union have been followed with the utmost vigor and determination. Beginning with the party reform in China during the second World War, there was no question that *the party* came first, and the Communist world demanded abject obedience to the dictates of this great impersonal organization. Mao himself made this clear in an article entitled "The Greatest Friendship" written a few days after Stalin's death: "The Communist party of the Soviet Union is a party personally reared by Lenin and Stalin; it is the most advanced, the most experienced and the most theoretically cultivated party in the world. This party has been and is our model both in the past and at present and will still be our model in the future." [8]

In the years following the Mao-Stalin meetings there was a continuous effort on both sides to strengthen the bonds between the two countries. This extended first of all to the tremendous organization which runs Communist China, and it is important to understand that this structure in itself constitutes one of the strongest bonds. Not only is the whole Chinese party and government structure patterned after the Soviet Union, but a large proportion of the top leaders are Moscow trained. In fact, more than 57 per cent of the Central Committee of the Chinese Communist party received their training in the USSR.[9] This new leadership which has replaced the traditional Chinese "gentry" has developed a vested interest in maintaining the present relationship with the Soviet Union as a source of strength and as a justification for rule. Their high positions and prestige, their investment of time and effort, their language training, their jargon, their past crimes against their fellow Chinese: all these are to a great extent bound up with the maintenance of the Soviet tie. Each highly placed official facing the new problems involved in the central direction of all phases of life in China probably draws comfort and assurance from the idea that there is in the Soviet Union his counterpart on whom he can rely for direction and aid.

Another important element in the bond is the matter of Soviet assistance. The Soviet Union is the only state willing to back the spread of Communist revolt in Asia, and the Chinese Communists look to the USSR to help them build a power structure comparable to that of the Soviet Union. There has been a large influx of Soviet advisers into China, and although we have no direct figures on their numbers the Mao regime openly admits that they "have played an outstanding role in all fields." [10] One usually reliable journal states that the Soviet advisers "outnumber the total foreign population of China during the boom between the wars." [11] Their numbers have also shown a steady increase with each passing year.[12] These Soviet advisers constitute a widespread reporting network, and given the nature of the Communist party structure they may constitute a supervision and control network with relatively great power.

Following Stalin's death, Moscow publicized promises of additional assistance to Communist China over and above the $300,000,000 which the Soviet Union agreed to lend at the time of the signing of the Sino-Soviet pact in 1950. On 15 September 1953 Li Fu-ch'un, vice-chairman of the Committee on Finance and Economics, reported back from negotiations in Moscow that the Kremlin had agreed to render "systematic economic and technical assistance in the renovation and construction of 141 projects of enormous scale by 1959." [13] Again in October 1953 there was talk in Moscow of another big loan to China, and in October 1954 on the occasion of the fifth anniversary of the regime a joint announcement hailed a loan of another $130,000,000 by the Soviet.[14] Although these figures are small in comparison with the amount of aid extended to China by the United States in the past, they are large enough to guarantee the presence of Russian experts at all the key industrial centers in China.

The Chinese Reds look forward to this assistance as offering improvements in every phase of life in China, even in fields where the Chinese have had no small amount of experience in the past themselves. With regard to the bridge across the Yangtze at the

Wuhan cities, the faith of the Chinese comrades was expressed in a dispatch to the world: "The work of the Yangtze River Bridge may be fraught with difficulties but will certainly result in victory, not to mention that the Soviet experts will help us solve all difficulties in the technical aspects." [15]

Beginning in 1952 the Chinese launched a drive for study of the new Soviet method of "painless childbirth." Chinese mothers expressed themselves as grateful to the Sino-Soviet alliance for bringing them this new blessing. The method, which the Chinese claimed as another proof of the superior development of Soviet science, was said to be "based on Pavlov's theory of conditioned reflexes, as applied to obstetrics by the Soviet specialist Dr. I. Z. Velvovsky." [16] That it bore a remarkable resemblance to the Read method developed in Britain and the United States a few years before was of course not mentioned. This was just one of the minor aspects of learning from the Soviet Union which fell under the general heading of "cultural work." By 1954 the *People's Daily* was able to claim that in all fields "Advanced Soviet culture is helping China's cultural work to make progress." [17]

"Cultural work" as defined in both China and the USSR involves the careful control of all artistic and literary activities, and as pointed out in Chapter 8 has brought the destruction of much of China's cultural heritage. In its place has come the culture of the "big brother." (Interestingly enough, the Mao regime sponsors the term *lao-ta-ko* or "big brother" for referring to Soviet personnel in China.) Chinese delegations go to the USSR and to the "people's democracies" of eastern Europe in order to study "cultural work" there and report on it.[18] The Ministry of Education boasts that a high percentage of textbooks now used in Chinese schools are translations of Soviet textbooks. Works of the Soviet theoreticians are pouring from Chinese presses. The *People's Daily* reported on the first anniversary of Stalin's death: "From 1949, the year of liberation, to the end of last year over 10,000,000 copies of Stalin's works were published. . . . During the same period, some 3,900,000 copies of Chinese translations of Stalin's works, published by the Foreign Languages Publishing House in Moscow, were imported from the Soviet Union." [19] The publication of the works of Soviet comrades in all fields, combined with the destruction of the Chinese traditional literature, is another method for cementing the relations between the two countries. Given the high birth and death rates in China, it may be but a few more years before those in power will have only a Soviet Communist background of learning and will be unwilling to allow any prestige to be attached to a knowledge of China's traditional culture.[20]

Of course this whole complex of ties is reinforced by the mass support organizations within both countries. The major organization is the Sino-Soviet Friendship Association with its claimed membership of more than fifty-eight million in China. The officers of this and other organizations draw the benefits of prestige and travel by their participation in the delegations and conferences promoted on an almost daily basis. Young Chinese cadres who have never before been outside their country draw inspiration from their visits to the Soviet fatherland to see what their tomorrow will be like.[21] These like many others find themselves committed to the goal of identifying Chinese interests with those of the land of the big brother in a manner which makes retreat difficult. They also know the price which will be paid for any words or actions unfavorable to the USSR.

Again, China and the Soviet Union have effected a great increase in transportation and communication facilities across their border, which is the longest international boundary in the world. Long distance telephone service to Moscow was opened in November 1953.[22] In February 1954 the world was surprised to hear that through trains had started regular service between Peking and Moscow. Symbolically, the Moscow to Peking train arrived two days before the Peking to Moscow train.[23] The outside world found it difficult to believe that the whole Chinese railway system involved had been changed to the Soviet wide gauge, and was prone to discount the claim of through service until one of the Chinese Communist publications for schoolchildren offered the explanation:

Advanced Soviet science and technique has solved this difficulty [that is, the differences in the gauge of Chinese and Russian railways]. The wheels of the train are changed and other wheels are put on when it reaches the border. The wheels are changed at Otpor, the first railway station on the Soviet border.

At the Otpor railway station there is a section of railway, 2 to 3 *li* [one *li* is one-third of an English mile] long, specially for this purpose. The gauge of this railway track is slightly wider than that of the Chinese railways but narrow enough to hold the Chinese trains, while it is slightly narrower than the Soviet track but wide enough to allow the Soviet trains to get on it, though a little tight. . . .

Are the wheels taken off one by one and replaced by Soviet wheels?

No, the wheels are fixed to the chassis of the car. When the change is made, the car is lifted and the chassis and wheels are removed and replaced by Soviet ones.

As the car is large and heavy, how could it be lifted?

This is accomplished by electric power. Four electric cranes hold the four corners of the car. When a button is pushed, the 4 cranes lift the car. As the cranes work slowly and smoothly, the passengers in the car do not even feel it being lifted. . . .

The chassis with wheels fixed on is first placed on the empty track. A crane capable of lifting 15 tons takes away the Chinese chassis, and the Soviet chassis is then pulled up under the car. The cranes then slowly lower the car and place it snugly on the chassis.

It takes 18 minutes to change one car and a little over 40 minutes to complete a train of 6 cars . . . Then the cars are connected together and the train runs direct to Moscow.[24]

By the end of 1954 the Chinese section of another railroad link through Mongolia had been completed. Another important development in the field of communications came in September 1954 when the Central People's Broadcasting Station in Peking began the rebroadcasting of Chinese language programs originating in Moscow.[25]

In the matter of trade, too, the pattern has been one of making each country dependent upon the other. Most of the trade is carried out on a barter basis between the two countries, and it is of more than passing interest to note that despite difficulties in both 1953 and 1954 in Chinese agriculture the agreements called for increases in food exports from China, notably rice, meat, fruit, tea, vegetable oils, soya beans and grain.[26]

In the matter of foreign and military policy there was a parallel strengthening of Sino-Soviet ties during the first five years. Soviet advisers are closely associated with the major units of all Chinese armed forces. The Chinese Communist armies are increasingly dependent on Soviet aid because of their switch to heavy and complicated equipment; and there has been no indication of anything but complete agreement on the conduct of affairs in Korea, Indo-China, and on the world front. The Soviet played a key role in enabling Chou En-lai to participate in the Geneva conference in the spring of 1954, and Moscow has continued the pressure started immediately after the formation of the Red regime to have Communist China represented at the United Nations. On 30 September 1954 N. S. Khrushchev, first secretary of the Communist party of the Soviet Union, told a large gathering in Peking that the Soviet would support the efforts of Mao's forces to "liberate" Taiwan.[27] On all major issues the Peking government has committed itself internally and in its external propaganda to the position advanced by Moscow. There is also an identity of purpose established by the fact that in its guided tours, severe restrictions upon communications even for the representatives of friendly powers, and techniques of the iron curtain the Chinese Communists follow the model established by the Soviet big brother.

It is perhaps in this last fact that the strength of the Sino-Soviet tie really lies. The Soviet Union does indeed constitute a *model* for the Chinese leaders who have achieved power, just as Red China constitutes a model for the Communist comrades in the colonial areas of the world who are attempting to seize power. With their party in power the Chinese Communist leaders firmly believe that the conditions exist for the rapid realization in China of Soviet society with all its ramifications. This attitude extends to every conceivable field. In science, for example, the *Kuangming Daily* hailed the eighteenth anniversary of the death of Pavlov by stating, "The brilliant revolutionary victories won by the Chinese people under the leadership of the Chinese Communist party have provided the ideological and material prerequisites for Chinese scientists and other people to study advanced Soviet science." [28] At the National Higher Medical Education Conference in Peking in August 1954 the authorities put forward the claim that "advanced theories and experiences of Soviet medicine" already permeate all Chinese medicine.[29]

Obviously their adoption of the Soviet Union as a model has its greatest importance for the Chinese in connection with their determination to industrialize the country rapidly at all costs. All materials used for cadre training in connection with the first five-year plan show that the Chinese comrades have, for the most part, accepted as valid Soviet claims of phenomenal success in industrialization and of rapid progress that could only have been made under a Soviet system. The cadres are urged to devote the utmost concentration to studying the experiences of the big brother. Thus, Mao was not speaking merely for the benefit of external observers when at the beginning of the first year of the plan he called for a "tidal wave of learning from the Soviet Union." [30] The faith of the Chinese was expressed by one writer:

The Soviet people began their industrialization after repairing the ravages of two wars—the World War of 1914–18 and the Civil War of 1918–22. More recently, they restored and expanded their economy in record time after the grievous damage of World War II. Their experts are familiar not only with the problems of rapidly changing an agricultural country into an industrial one but also with the quick healing of war wounds.[31]

With regard to the first five-year plan the Chinese Communists admit their great dependence for guidance upon the Soviet big brother and the advisers sent to China. This was pointed out by

Chu Teh in a special article written for *Pravda* in which he told the Soviet readers that "The plan for building socialism in our country was drawn up according to the theory of socialist industrialization of V. I. Lenin and the great successor to his immortal cause, J. V. Stalin." [32] The Chinese are told that Soviet experience and the advice of Soviet "experts" should be the deciding factor in making decisions. Of course the Chinese emphasis on heavy industry at the expense of all other segments of the economy, in line with the Soviet pattern, makes Peking all the more dependent on Moscow for economic aid. [33]

But learning the Soviet system of the five-year plan involves many complications which are not easily translated into the Chinese language. This is one of the important reasons behind the fact that the Russian language has now become the second language of the China mainland. Russian has been introduced into the lower grades of the Chinese schools, and Russian language classes are sponsored in the army, in factories, and in radio courses by the Sino-Soviet Friendship Association. Vysokov, a Soviet correspondent in Peking during the 1 May 1953 festivities, described the May Day parade there: "Young men and girls carried a huge model of a Russian-Chinese dictionary. The study of the Russian language more and more becomes a mass-movement; the knowledge of the Russian language aids in the study of the advanced Soviet experience." [34] Here again the investment of time in language training helps to reinforce the determination of some of China's younger cadres to maintain the Soviet tie.

These then are some of the major ties which in a positive manner bind the Mao regime to Moscow. Of course there are many other reasons for Mao's determination to lean to one side. They include the patterns of international relations and the power structure in eastern Asia, as well as past history. The Chinese Communist leaders share Soviet apprehensions concerning a revival of Japanese power, and they are also very much impressed with the power position they have obtained in eastern Asia through Soviet military aid. To the steady reader of the Chinese mainland press, however, these factors shrink compared to the intense determination to fit China into the organizational pattern imposed upon the Soviet people under Stalin. As the Communist leaders have become more hated in China they have had to lean more and more upon Soviet methods developed for coping with the same type of hatred in Russia. Thus it is possible the very nature of the Communist system and the resultant oppression of the Chinese people, more than any other factors, drive the Chinese comrades into the arms of the Soviet leaders of world Communism and cement the ties of the great impersonal organization which binds them together.

The Chinese Reds apparently accepted the proclamation of the "collective leadership" principle within the Soviet Union after Stalin's death as indicating that their mentors had moved just that much farther along the path toward the "eventual bright day of Communism." Collective leadership is, of course, not a strange sounding principle to those who have experienced the intense cadre training. They probably view Mao Tse-tung as the leader for the important transition period in China, just as Stalin is credited with leading the way in the transition from socialism to Communism in the USSR.

But what about the leaders in the Kremlin? How do they regard Mao and his regime, especially since the death of Stalin? Apparently the ban on the "cult of the leader" has not been extended to Mao. The new Soviet leaders have accepted Mao as one of the leading theorists in the Communist hierarchy. Four volumes of the selected works of Mao Tse-tung were published in Russian before the end of 1953, and each was hailed with detailed articles and with enthusiasm by the Soviet press. In reviewing Volume 3 N. Fedorenko stated:

An important contribution of Mao Tse-tung to Marxist-Leninist theory is his creative development of the theses of V. I. Lenin and J. V. Stalin on the change in the nature of the revolution in colonial and dependent countries in the era of the downfall of imperialism and the triumph of socialism and his working out of the problems concerning the content of the revolutionary rule and political system born in the course of this revolution.[35]

Another review of Mao's works referred to the Chinese leader as "a great Marxist theoretician of the world liberation movement."[36] Volume 26 of the *Soviet Encyclopedia* which was published in August 1954 gives full credit to Mao as one of the leaders of the revolutionary movement in colonial and semicolonial areas.[37]

Not only has Mao been recognized as a leader in the revolutionary movements in "colonial and semicolonial areas," but his country has been accorded a position of equality with the Soviet people in many respects, a tendency that has been more pronounced since the death of Stalin. For example, the Chinese are the only people besides the Soviets who are referred to as "great" in the Russian press.[38] The 14 November 1952 issue of *Pravda* advised its Russian readers what time and on what frequency to tune in daily broadcasts from Peking. So far as I have been able to find out this is the only example on record of Soviet citizens being encouraged to listen to broadcasts emanating from outside the borders of their land.[39] It indicated not only a special position for the Chinese comrades but also a confidence that their programs would be in strict accord with the party line. The Moscow lead has been followed by the leaders of east Asian Communist movements who accept Peking's unique position and leadership.

On the other hand, during the first five years Peking has in turn shown its firm determination to follow the lead of the Soviet teacher in its relations with the outside world. Mao's government has waited for Moscow to take the lead on most major questions, and whenever the Chinese Reds have taken the initiative, prior coordination was clear. For example, just four days after Chou En-lai returned from Stalin's funeral he made fresh proposals for ending the deadlock in negotiations for a truce in Korea. In handling President Eisenhower's proposal for a pool for the peaceful development of atomic power, the Chinese press waited for the Kremlin to take a stand, which they then supported "enthusiastically." [40]

The Korean War, which has been hailed as a great victory in Communist China, probably served the joint purposes of China and the Soviet Union. Like the victory of the Viet Minh Communists in 1954, it demonstrated the division in the outside world and offered convincing proof of the power and weight of Soviet assistance and the necessity for maintaining a solid world front. Although both conflicts made the Peking regime increasingly dependent upon Soviet-style military equipment and involved expenditure of China's meager resources, the Chinese Reds were obviously willing to pay the price for the increased control at home and prestige in Asia which they achieved.[41]

Mao's *Problems of Art and Literature,* which was studied intensely in 1951 and 1952, showed the impact of the Soviet Stalinist approach in these fields. There have been widespread translations of approved Soviet literature into Chinese. Time and time again high Chinese officials have accepted Soviet opinions. An interesting example occurred in January 1954. A Chinese movie, *Red Flag over Tsuikang,* which had been directed by an American-trained drama student, had been denounced for not "manifesting satisfactorily the heroic struggle of the people" and for having a hero who was not a "positive character." After the film had been awarded honorable mention in a Communist film festival in Eastern Europe, the Peking critics made a hasty reappraisal.[42] China's Communist spokesmen show far more of austere and dedicated vigor in matters of ideology than do those of the Soviet, and it is possible that after five years of association with the big brothers in China some of the leaders feel a disappointment at what would seem to be laxity on the part of their Soviet friends.

This then is a brief appraisal of the structural relationship between Communist China and the Soviet Union after five years of close association. On the surface all has been smooth, and certainly an imposing structure has been built. Some of its foundations have grown steadily stronger. On the other hand there are some weaknesses and tensions in the relationship which though not apparent at first glance deserve mention for the sake of a balanced presentation.

Most significant is the fact that the Soviet is dealing with a country over which it cannot exercise immediate military control as in the European satellites, and this simple fact means that Moscow is confronted with the problem of accommodating its internal and external policies to those of an ally. It is improbable that there can always be a complete identity of interests without complete subordination. Let us therefore turn to some of the aspects of this relationship which are probably not quite so smooth as the propaganda to the rest of the world would indicate.

After the death of Stalin, certain weaknesses in the Soviet homeland under the Malenkov regime came to light, and some of these have undoubtedly proved disturbing to the Chinese comrades. Of these, probably none has been more disquieting than Khrushchev's revelation in his speech of 3 September to the Central Committee that twenty-five years of collectivization of agriculture have proved a dismal failure. These admissions were embodied in a resolution of the Central Committee published in *Pravda* 12 and 13 September 1953, and Khrushchev's speech was published on 15 September.[43] The timing is important here, because on the very day that the Khrushchev speech was issued in the Soviet Union, twelve days after its delivery, the Chinese Communists released the text of Li Fu-ch'un's report on his negotiations in Moscow for Soviet aid to the Chinese five-year plan. The Chinese Communists featured Moscow's rather imprecise promises of aid, but there was no word of the *big* news from Moscow in the controlled Chinese press.[44]

What Khrushchev had revealed, in short, was that the food situation in the land of the big brother was critical. Grain production had risen less than 10 per cent since 1940, fertilizers were in short supply and, most serious, there had been an actual decline in the number of livestock below pre-Revolution (1917) figures —this despite the tremendous growth in Soviet population. The Soviet Union was in need of foodstuffs and especially meat, and would obviously be interested in getting all it could from China. Khrushchev's figures demonstrated what scholars in the West had known for a long time: collectivization was a measure designed for totalitarian control, not to improve the lot of the people.[45] Revelations of an even more sweeping nature followed in February 1955 at the time of Malenkov's fall.

For a country like China, which would have to rely upon the agricultural sector of its economy to provide the necessary surplus for industrial expansion, this was serious news indeed. All the official propaganda organs had been instructing the cadres in China to inform the peasants how socialized agriculture would improve their lot.[46] In view of the figures from the Soviet Union, a decision to collectivize in China would be a cynical admission by the Mao regime of its exclusive concern for power over the people and not for their welfare. This disquieting news reached the Chinese Communist leaders, some of whom are possibly still idealistic in their faith that Soviet Communist methods will in all ways prove superior, at the very time when Communist China was facing a critical food problem at home because of unfavorable climatic conditions in the year of retrenchment.

There was some hesitation. A firm decision to collectivize would mean a terrible cost in human lives, given the small margin of subsistence in China and the fact that much of Chinese agriculture is of a labor intensive type and not suited for collective methods. We do not know what discussions took place among the top Chinese Communist leaders following the Khrushchev report, but it would seem that the decision was a difficult one. Finally, four months later, on 9 January 1954, the Central Committee of the Chinese Communist party published its 16 December 1950 Decision on the Development of Agricultural Producers' Cooperatives. The goal was 800,000 of these producers' cooperatives by

1957.[47] The decision had been reached. Khrushchev's revelations remained suppressed in China. Peking had determined to go inexorably ahead with collectivization.

The Malenkov promises of more consumer goods in the Soviet Union were also probably somewhat disturbing in China. Throughout 1953 and 1954 the Chinese were being told to tighten their belts and make further sacrifices. These sacrifices made possible the shipment of increased quantities of food to "brother countries." Surely even some of the most devoted adherents of the Mao regime must have detected inconsistency in the demands to send more food to a land where, according to the propaganda, there was supposed to be an abundance of everything.[48] Peking boasted the construction of many new refrigerator cars, but these could hardly help China's economy when they were intended to facilitate meat shipments to the Soviet Union, which was now absorbing more than 2 per cent of China's total yearly pork production.[49]

The news which Peking published instead of the Khrushchev report on 15 September 1953 gave some impression that all had not been smooth in the negotiations which Li Fu-ch'un had carried on in Moscow regarding aid for China's industrial construction. In the first place, there was no specific sum mentioned—merely the statement that the Soviet was going to extend "systematic economic and technical aid in the construction and renovation of ninety-one new enterprises in China and the fifty enterprises now being built or renovated." Secondly, Li indicated something of the nature of the negotiations when he stated in his report that the Soviet had "agreed to satisfy the demands" of the Chinese government. Theretofore, Peking had never indicated that it had to *demand* anything from the Soviet Union. Finally, the fact that the Kremlin had not satisfied the demands of Peking was borne out two days later when Finance Minister Po I-po, who had drawn up the budget for the first year of the five-year plan, was dismissed.[50] The Chinese subsequently reduced the goals of their five-year plan twice.[51] One of the big goals for the first year became the mobilizing and organizing of the people to make further sacrifices.[52]

While the Chinese Communists had not been completely starry-eyed about their hopes for industrial construction, they had counted heavily on Soviet assistance to make it rapid.[53] One writer had stated just prior to Li Fu-ch'un's report that "China is able to set high goals for her first five-year plan because she knows she can obtain assistance from the flourishing and expanding economy of her great socialist neighbor and ally." [54] Now Stalin's successors had indicated that the Soviet economy was not so flourishing, and Chinese goals were reduced.

Events in the Soviet bloc were probably disturbing to the Peking leaders on other counts. The purge and execution of Beria may have indicated to some that the collective leadership principle was not so solid and, once again, that the major concerns of the Soviet leaders were not with idealistic goals but with power struggles. Thus, while the Peking *People's Daily* stated that "the criminal conduct of the traitor Beria and his traitorous group has evoked the deep indignation of the Chinese people," there was some possible truth to the subsequent statement that "From the incident . . . the Chinese people will draw a valuable political lesson." [55] In China, as in the Soviet Union, Beria's greatness had been hailed at the time of Stalin's death. Again, the East German riots, which were finally put down by Soviet armed might, may have been of some concern to Mao and his colleagues. Even the seemingly unbeatable Soviet methods of persuasion and control were showing some weaknesses.

Another important aspect of the Moscow-Peking relationship, which may well prove decisive, involves the internal Chinese situation itself. The Kremlin, as the great "socialist tutor," is now responsible for the success or failure of the Mao regime, which is determined to industrialize a country that in many respects is not suited to be either an industrial power or a great power.[56] A failure in China will in many ways spell the end of Soviet attraction for other areas in the world. The cost of success in China in terms of assistance will be tremendous, yet the Soviet faces the problem of reconciling this cost with the demands of its own people. A crucial question then is whether the Soviet Union is able or willing to assume the burden of China's large-scale industrial development. As one journal put it, "Clearly the Soviet Union cannot or will not grant Malenkov aid on the Marshall Plan scale, and intends to share whatever profits are going by channeling Chinese trade in the Communist world through Moscow and Soviet Russia." [57]

In traditional China there has always been a pronounced xenophobia, probably as strong as in any major culture of the world. In the last few years the Communists have been systematically expelling foreigners from China. The net result, of course, is that the cumulative forces of dissatisfaction will, by elimination, have only Soviet representatives as a focus for expression. Further, Russians have over the past century been among the most disliked foreigners in China. Yet the Chinese Communist cadres have pushed the flattery and imitation of the Soviet with great energy. Soviet advisers in China have frequently behaved with arrogance, and it is clear from the reports of the Chinese press and of refugees coming from the mainland that many of these visitors are persuaded they are the first to bring any kind of modern science to China and share the party's conviction that their job is to bring "culture" to the land of their "little brothers." [58] The Chinese might, however, be justified in feeling that the achievements of their country on this score have not been inconsequential. There are already many indications of popular antipathy toward the big brothers. Soviet guests now live apart from the Chinese and frequently travel in curtained automobiles in the streets. According to some refugees Chinese are cleared from stores before Soviet representatives enter to do their shopping, and not infrequently the comrade shoppers arrive at the stores in ambulances to conceal their movements from Chinese eyes. According to one source, the Chinese public was bitter about the show put on during Sino-Soviet Friendship Month at the end of 1952—"revolted by a display of fatuous and obsequious flattery of a foreign power un-precedented in the annals of the race." [59]

There are traditional areas of conflict between China and Russia, and some of these may develop as sources of increased friction. The Chinese resent Russian expansion at the expense of their land. During the first five years of Mao's rule the Soviet extended its influence into Chinese Turkestan (Sinkiang) through the joint Sino-Soviet companies set up by the agreements nego-tiated by Mao and Stalin in 1950. Mao's regime has extended full diplomatic recognition to the Communist state of Mongolia, with which it signed a ten-year agreement on economic and cul-tural cooperation on 4 October 1952.[60] The Russians have main-tained their traditional interest in Manchuria, and at the end of the fifth year of the Mao regime were the only foreigners still retaining extraterritorial rights in China, at Port Arthur and Dairen. On these questions the Chinese Communist leaders have seemed to accept the Leninist view that by definition the Soviet Union can never be imperialistic.

As a result of negotiations conducted by high-ranking Soviet authorities following the 1 October 1954 celebration of the Chinese Communists' fifth year in power, the two governments announced that all Soviet armed forces would be withdrawn from Port Arthur before 1 April 1955 and that installations in the area would be transferred to Communist China without compensation. Another communiqué stated that Soviet interests in the joint Sino-Soviet companies in Sinkiang, the joint enterprise for build-ing and repairing ships in Dairen, and the joint civil airline com-pany would be transferred to China on 1 January 1955. It con-tinued: "The value of the Soviet share shall be repaid to the Soviet Union over the course of several years by supplies of goods which are usual export commodities" from China. At the same time the two regimes also issued declarations on their view of the international situation, on relations with Japan and on the con-struction of two new railroad links between them.[61] While some of these statements to the world could be taken as evidence that

Mao's regime was bargaining hard for Chinese national interests, it is also possible to view them as evidence that the Soviet has faith and confidence in Peking's political allegiance. In any case the actions tended to relieve tension and indicated that Stalin's successors were aware they could not be insensitive to Chinese feelings. The actual extent of the Soviet withdrawal from Sinkiang and Manchuria has yet to be determined.

Given the present Communist habit of claiming for Russia the credit for most inventions of importance, one may well wonder whether there exists any possibility of friction between Russia and China over the latter's claim to have invented in ancient times such instruments as the compass, the seismoscope, the world's first mileage meter, and an armillary sphere. This claim is virtually asserted in the four new postage stamps issued by Peking on 1 December 1953 in commemoration of these Chinese inventions. Is it possible that China is deviating from the "correct position" which holds that the Soviet Union has made every important invention and discovery in history?

Undoubtedly disillusioning to some of the Chinese comrades who visit the Soviet fatherland are the intemperance and moral degeneration which have become more and more evident everywhere. The Chinese Communists through their first five years showed a restraint and frugality in personal habits and a dedication to principle no longer evident in the Soviet.[62]

The crucial issue making for tension in Peking-Moscow relations, however, is whether the Soviet system can help solve China's problems. On this score, as we have seen, Stalin's successors revealed briefly but dramatically to the world that the Soviet system has failed in the field which for China is most important: agriculture. As a method for organizing and controlling human beings, the Communist apparatus of compulsion proved a signal success in its first five years in China. But in its extension to the agricultural scene, in the form of collectivization, it may fail at the critical moment.

With this background in mind, let us try to see the over-all pattern of Sino-Soviet relations, to balance the ties against the tensions. This can probably best be done by examining the question most frequently raised on the subject in Western capitals: what are the chances for Chinese Titoism?

Some of the general bases for the expectation of a "Titoism" on the part of Peking deserve first examination. To begin with, such an expectation frequently involves a questionable interpretation of Chinese history and usually carries the convictions expressed in the United States 1949 *White Paper* on China: 1) that traditional "democratic individualism" will reassert itself in China, and 2) that the Chinese will "absorb" their invaders as they have always done in the past.[63] Despite its humanistic Confucian philosophy, however, the traditional Chinese political system was extremely authoritarian, and its despotic institutions provided antecedents for many Communist practices—for example, conscript labor, banishment, a system for maintaining doctrinal purity within the officialdom, fear of contamination from the outside, and even the guided tour. The roots of democratic political institutions have had little time or opportunity for growth in China, although scholars and statesmen in the first half of the twentieth century made many contributions.[64] The authoritarian structure of China facilitated the control of the country by her invaders. Since the fall of the Han dynasty in A.D. 220, the Chinese in north China have been controlled more years by unabsorbed invaders—most of whom were later expelled as foreigners—than they have ruled themselves.[65] Many Chinese leaders served the interests of the foreign invaders faithfully under the conquest dynasties. These are historical facts frequently overlooked by those who insist that the Chinese Communists will be more Chinese than Communist.

On the other hand, Chinese nationalism cannot be ignored. It has grown to be a powerful force in recent years, and part of the Communists' success lies in their ability to address themselves to the aspirations of Chinese nationalists. The strength of Chinese nationalism has prompted speculation concerning the existence of a nationalist clique as opposed to an internationalist clique within the high ranks of the Communist party, and indeed it is not improbable that there are high-ranking Communists who think in terms of China as their first loyalty. It is frequently pointed out that hostile relations with the West constitute the chief basis for reconciling nationalism with Soviet internationalism within Mao's domain. Some observers have even suggested that the USSR is aware of this and that the Soviet really does not want Peking representatives seated at the United Nations, that the very timing and manner of its support for Red China's admission to the United Nations have been designed to guarantee opposition.

Yet within China the "two camp" view of the world has been making steady headway. In the press, in schoolbooks, in cadre training, throughout the society, the philosophy and the language of "proletarian internationalism" have been supplanting those of the "bad" (i.e. bourgeois) nationalism of the past.[66] Party leaders have probably had relative success in convincing many Chinese that former goals of nationalism—power, unity, prestige, equality, and expulsion of the "imperialists"—have been realized and that the time has come to turn to an uncompromising allegiance to the Soviet camp. Further, it must be remembered that since Yenan days during World War II there has been no overt instance in which the Chinese Communist leaders challenged Moscow policies even when they were definitely detrimental to Chinese national interests. For example, the only Communist known to have spoken out openly against the Soviet looting and destruction in Manchuria following the war—Hsiao Chun, a well known journalist—was purged from the party.[67]

In the second place, talk of "Titoism" in China in terms of Mao's breaking with Moscow is usually based upon a misreading of the Tito incident itself. The important point to be kept in mind is that although the two sides took different stands, an intolerable situation within the Communist framework, the initiative in the break came from Moscow, which expelled Tito. Tito repeatedly pleaded that he had been misunderstood and pledged loyalty. Mos-

cow had evidently anticipated that it would be able to seize control
within Yugoslavia and oust Tito, an expectation which backfired.
The failure of the action against Tito constitutes in itself one of
the strongest reasons for the Soviet not to commit the same blunder
again.[68] Some of those who talk of Mao as a prospective Tito in
terms of Tito's "breaking" with Stalin frequently point out that
Chiang Kai-shek, an ardent Chinese nationalist who turned against
the Communists in 1927, was a "Tito before Titoism existed."
It must be remembered, however, that Chiang took the initiative
in expelling the Reds from the coalition he led, and that he never
made any pretense of accepting the party line as dictated from
Moscow. During the first five years of Communist power in China
there was every indication that Moscow had profited by the Tito
experience; since 1949 the Kremlin has manifested "an unprecedented caution and forbearance toward Communist China." [69]

A third general basis on which the expectation of "Titoism" is
raised involves the propaganda of the Communist world organization. To make the choice of Communism attractive in the colonial and former colonial areas of the world, Moscow has joined
Peking in stressing China's independence and sovereignty (see
Chapter 10). At the Geneva conference in 1954, for example,
the Soviet delegates made a point of taking careful notes when
the Chinese comrades spoke though they paid little attention to
the speeches of the other Communist delegates. Molotov is reported to have told Anthony Eden that if the British would only
restrain the Americans the Soviet would try to restrain the Chinese.[70]

A fourth basis is the symbol of Mao himself, who has been
built up in the eyes of the world as an independent and highly nationalistic leader. Most of the studies of Mao published in the
West concern themselves with his relatively idealistic and early
period as a Communist when his activities marked him as a deviationist from the policies then laid down by the Comintern.[71] There
is no extant close study of Mao since his intensive concentration
on Leninist-Stalinist principles of organization in Yenan. While

Mao's actions and those of his party mark him as dedicated to power, position, and prestige, he has never given any indication of being other than an "internationalist" faithful to the line as laid down by Moscow. Yet he is still presented before the world in terms which for the most part portray him as basically interested in the welfare of the Chinese peasants and the Chinese nation. There is, of course, the possibility of a power struggle in the event of Mao's death, and Chinese nationalism versus "proletarian internationalism" could conceivably become the central issue among his successors. It is likely, however, that most of the other factors operative in the Sino-Soviet relationship would continue to carry weight even without Mao.

Yet another basis on which the expectation of a Titoist heresy rests is the unconscious projection by Westerners of their own past pattern and methods of diplomacy into their consideration of the relations between these two great Communist states. Some observers still fail to appreciate that the Soviet has developed new dimensions in its conduct of international diplomacy, and they still prefer to think about and analyze the pattern of Sino-Soviet relations in terms of their own present overriding concern for national interest. The Sino-Soviet alliance—as I think the foregoing pages have in some measure indicated—has been made a living part of the work of every organization within a China where today it is well nigh impossible to draw a line between governmental and nongovernmental activities.

A final possible basis behind the talk of Titoism could be the existence of wishful thinking among those who would prefer not to face up to the implications of a solid alliance dedicated to the expansion of this version of Communism throughout the world.

On balance, at the end of the first five years of Red rule in China chances of Titoism there seem very slim. But there are other aspects of the question which deserve mention and which argue even more forcefully against the possibility of the split for which many in the West have hoped.

The addition of China to the Communist bloc has been a tremendous gain for Moscow-led Communism on the world scene. Stalin's successors dare not lose this area. The blow would be fatal to the aspirations of world Communism. The Soviet leaders have shown an eagerness to eliminate whatever tensions may develop. For example, following the open resentment against the Soviet personnel who were buying up luxury goods in vast quantities in China during the first three years of the Mao regime, Moscow enforced a strict order for more austere living on the part of its personnel.[72]

Certainly the top leaders in Red China consider discussion of heresy on their part to be ridiculous. It is as a result of their allegiance to the Soviet Union that they have achieved positions of power in their own country and abroad far beyond their probable expectations. China's military might and the firm hold which the Communist party maintains over all the people are, according to their own statements, the result of the Soviet tie. Why, they would argue, should they give them up?

Their whole rule has been bound up with a commitment to the Soviet pattern of life. This is especially true with regard to the many crimes which they have committed against their fellow Chinese. They have destroyed fellow humans as well as literary and art products in the name of the superior culture of the big brother. They are now in the same position in which they placed the poor peasants who participated in the mass executions of landlords. Their deeds committed in the name of the superior "Soviet culture" have set them on a course where retreat is well nigh impossible; repudiation of the Soviet would mean discarding the only basis they have had for justifying deeds which under any other system would deserve the harshest penalties.

Again, the increasing isolation of Mao and his colleagues from the people, the economic and military dependence upon the Soviet fatherland which they have accepted during their first five years in power, the many organizations whose officers and very existence are dependent upon the tie, and especially the vested interest of millions of people who have now devoted a great amount of time to activities connected with the alliance: all these are factors weighing in favor of continuing the Soviet tie.

The Mao regime is in a position which for several reasons is likely to encourage expansionist policies. The economic dictates of the five-year plan make the addition of the rice surplus areas of Southeast Asia important for China; and as failures and shortcomings of the Communist system, especially under collectivization, become evident, expansion may well be the obvious solution for maintaining prestige abroad. Extension of the area of Chinese control is an ideal method for the Communists to suppress dissatisfaction at home and to create the tension which they firmly believe will lead to the division and eventual collapse of the West. Further, the Peking regime will continue to feel insecure as long as sizable colonies of Chinese remain free to plan for the overthrow of the Communist system. Expansionist activities also constitute and justify keeping the large People's Liberation Army in training. For its expansion program and its aid in "liberating" other areas in Asia, Peking is in large measure dependent upon the USSR for material as well as moral support. So long as a world war can be avoided, Moscow is likely to encourage Peking's role of spreading Communism in Asia and to view this as one good method for ensuring that Chinese nationalism continues to work in favor of the alliance.

Further, any attempt on the part of Chinese Red leaders to split with the Soviet Union would probably involve a struggle within the ranks of the Chinese Communist party. The Chinese leaders know from their own practices what would be their fate if they failed. In the case of success, they would be thrown into the camp of the West where sympathy would be far from universal and where their need for aid would involve the loosening of the very control structure by which they maintain their power.

Again, since the Soviet Union attaches so much importance to its alliance with the Chinese Communist regime, it is not to be anticipated that the USSR would give it up without a struggle. The Soviet advisers in China, the children of high-ranking Chinese comrades in Soviet schools who are in effect hostages, the armed might of the Soviet Union and her possession of the hydrogen bomb are just a few reasons for fearing Soviet reprisals in case of a break.

Certainly the tensions which underlie the alliance are serious, and perhaps in the long run the weight of the Chinese cultural tradition, Chinese xenophobia, or the inability of the Soviet system to answer China's agrarian problem may prove more decisive than the present structure of the relationship seems to indicate. Yet it must be remembered that most of the tensions are at the level of popular resentment and would hardly seem to be a matter of major concern to the present group of leaders whose actions have shown that they are not overly concerned about popular opinion as a factor against them. They obviously feel sure that they can control it.

A major argument advanced by competent statesmen in some Western countries for the world-wide recognition of the Mao regime is that it would facilitate the promotion of division between the two Communist collossi. These men argue that the contacts with the outside world resulting from diplomatic recognition and admission to the United Nations would offer the West opportunities to demonstrate to the Chinese Reds that their doctrines are invalid. It is to be wondered whether experience with the European satellites of the USSR or even with the Soviet Union itself bears out such hopes. The action would be more likely to be interpreted in both Peking and Moscow as proof of weakness and capitulation and of the historic inevitability of Communist victory.

Although there are many imponderables and unknown factors in the alliance between Communist China and the Soviet Union, close study of the relationship over its first five years has convinced me that the opposition of the West has not been the major factor which has thrust the Mao regime into the arms of the Soviet, but rather the weaknesses of the West and the organization, doctrines, and ruthlessness of the Communist system. Given the Communist ideology and convictions and the facts of the first five years of

China under Communism, I believe that the unity, strength, and determined opposition of the world outside the iron curtain will prove the most effective method to make Chinese Communist leaders reconsider the validity of their doctrine and the dubious advantages of a future under a Soviet alliance.

12. CHINA AND THE UNITED STATES

The counterpart of the "permanent and unbreakable" friendship between China and the Soviet Union is the deep and intense hatred for the United States which has been promoted by the Mao regime at home and abroad. Both of these policies have been written into the new Soviet-type constitution adopted on 20 September 1954.

It is impossible to convey the full intensity and viciousness of the Hate America Drive which the Chinese Communists have waged almost without letup since the early 1930's.[1] After the close of World War II the campaign moved to new heights of intensity from which it has never receded. No holds have been barred in the effort to picture the United States as the major enemy. Much of the purposes of the campaign and of its impact throughout the world remains unappreciated, however, even in America.

Although many examples in earlier pages have spelled out some of the implications of the Hate America Drive, it is essential to show in more detail what an important element enmity for the United States constitutes in the whole Chinese Communist approach to internal as well as external affairs. Internally the enemy is made so execrated that any and all sacrifices appear justified for the sake of solidarity against him. Externally, as Steiner says, "This enmity is so vibrant and controlling that the isolation and defeat of the United States becomes the most pressing urgency in the field of Chinese Communist foreign policy."[2]

The general internal goals of Peking's campaign against the United States involve much more than the creation of hatred to sustain Chinese Communist military ventures. The drive is used to distract attention from shortcomings and oppression at home and to direct blame away from the regime, which is always pictured as trying to save the Chinese people from difficulties created by United States imperialism. It serves as excuse and means for eradicating Western influence in China and destroying all respect for Western civilization. It promotes simultaneously contempt of Western power and fear of having anything to do with the West, especially with Americans. Its vehemence is calculated to throw the Chinese willingly into the embrace of world Communism and the Soviet alliance.

The first task of the regime in pushing this drive was to break down the good will and respect built up in the thousands of Chinese who came to the United States for schooling and in the millions who benefited from American philanthropic enterprises in China. The means chosen was to picture the United States and its way of life in the blackest possible terms. The Canton *Southern Daily* gives an idea of the extremes to which this has been carried:

Every Chinese citizen who is willing to recognize facts may discern . . . what kind of a country the United States is. This is a country which is thoroughly reactionary, thoroughly dark, thoroughly corrupt, thoroughly cruel. This is the Eden of a pinch of millionaires, the hell of countless millions of poor people. This is the paradise of gangsters, swindlers, rascals, special agents, fascist germs, speculators, debauchers, and all the dregs of mankind. This is the world's manufactory and source of all such crimes as reaction, darkness, cruelty, decadence, corruption, debauchery, oppression of man by man, and cannibalism. This is the exhibition ground of all the crimes which can possibly be committed by mankind. This is a living hell ten times, one hundred times, one thousand times worse than any hell that can possibly be depicted by the most sanguinary of writers. Here the criminal phenomena that issue forth defy the imagination of human brains. Conscientious persons can only wonder how the spiritual civilization of mankind can be depraved to such an extent! Here is the graveyard of truth, righteousness, reason, progressiveness, science and culture. Here all the phenomena that issue forth constitute the most shameless chapter in the history of mankind. Everyone who is conscientious, rational, truth-worshipping, willing to uphold the dignity and morality of mankind and unwilling to see mankind degraded to a lower level than animals, cannot help arising in righteous indignation to condemn the cursed phenomena of this cursed place. Everyone who does not want the people of his beloved fatherland contaminated by these criminal phenomena is charged with the responsibility of arising to condemn her, curse her, hate her, and despise her.[3]

Examples are supplied in abundance to support these charges. They illustrate mainly two topics: the "American way of life," which is pictured as increasing oppression of the proletariat by a diminishing number of ever richer monopoly capitalists, and America's "imperialism" against China throughout the whole history of their relations. Communists have vied with each other since the inauguration of their regime in attempts to prove that, "in the eyes of the world, Americans are veritable devils and cannibals," as Mao Tun, minister of cultural affairs and noted writer, put it.[4] This, they maintain of course, is all the result of the decadent capitalist system. In the same article Mao Tun went on to assert that there were over fifteen million unemployed in the United States while countless other millions were on the verge of starvation. "Mad craze for speed, extravagant absurdity, aimless existence, and yearning for excitement have turned one out of every thirteen Americans into psychopathic cases."

Chinese writers have turned to the writings of their Soviet big brothers and to those of American Communists for much of their information about life in the United States. Every recantation by a student or professor returned from America includes a denunciation of the bestiality and oppressive conditions he observed in the United States. "As for the 'American way of life' I witnessed," one such student wrote, "my main impressions are of jobless young men sitting on park benches, weary-looking workers reading comic strips in subways, drunks inside a bar hovering around a television set watching some stupid or corrupting program, and schoolboys gossiping to each other about Superman and western cowboys." [5]

Charges of cannibalism are supported by stories such as one about an unemployed laborer supposedly living in a railway station in New York:

Acting upon the advice of other unemployed persons, Meyer sold his blood to a "blood bank" three times in one week. One month later, new disaster awaited him: the "bank" no longer wanted him because he was suffering from serious anemia.

The proprietor of the "blood bank" is . . . a doctor rich in professional ambition. He pays little money to the blood sellers—the unemployed laborers of New York—and reaps a net profit of $500,000 annually.

The merchants of the gold dollar country are thus sucking the blood of the unemployed in name as well as in fact.[6]

Thus the Chinese are led to believe that blood has become a medium of exchange and a standard of value in the United States. To prove the moral decadence of Americans, one Peking magazine carried an account of a boisterous American institution which its readers were ill prepared to understand and which could lend itself admirably to the purposes of the regime. Under the title "Lying Is Wonderful" it stated:

The American Liars Club is twenty years old. In order to celebrate the twentieth anniversary, a lying competition was held to determine the world champion liar. At the beginning of the contest . . . the chairman of the club said: "Lying is a great art, a great movement. We hope to discover many new talents this year." Although the results of the competition have not yet been announced, one thing is certain: the winner of the contest will be assured of finding work with the publishers of the yellow press in the United States.[7]

All of this might be funny if it were not for the purpose of backing up a policy of international hatred. And of course the Communists do not have to rely only on evidence supplied by American humor to paint a black picture of the United States. Statistics on crime or demonstrations of racial intolerance, freely and properly discussed in an uncontrolled press, provide ample material, regrettably supplemented on occasion by intemperate statements urging "massive retaliation" or "unleashing Chiang Kai-shek" or by ill-judged acts such as the inadequately controlled experiments with the hydrogen bomb at Bikini.

The general theme of all the mass hate America literature is that the United States has taken over the mantle of Hitler, Mussolini, and Tojo and is now the world center of fascism. The official comment of the *People's Daily* on the 1952 presidential election was "Wall Street has put Eisenhower, a blood-thirsty warmonger, into the White House as next President." [8] The Chinese people are told about "slave labor" Taft-Hartley Law, the Ku Klux Klan, and that the FBI is far worse than Hitler's Gestapo. Of the law outlawing the Communist party in the United States in 1954, Peking stated officially: "This fascist measure is the darkest and most reactionary one in United States history." [9] Mao's party never fails to congratulate William Z. Foster on his birthday and to express confidence that under his leadership the Communist party of America will win the victory against internal fascism and external aggression.

The hate campaign and the attempt to erase all favorable impressions of America were prosecuted with amazing thoroughness throughout the first five years of Red rule. American educational, medical, and missionary activities were described as expressions of cultural aggression and imperialism. The Chinese president of St. John's University in Shanghai, before the Reds abolished it, was quoted as saying in a recantation that "American cultural aggression not only ruined the missionary colleges but also spoiled all the educational work throughout the country." [10] Any relief or assistance extended in the economic field is, by the Marxist interpretation, economic aggression; and when it comes from the United States it is pictured as especially disgusting. According to Mao Tun, "American imperialist products, dumped into the world for the spiritual destruction of man, consist in the main of American motion pictures in praise of the dollar, naked women, killers, masked bandits, adventurers; Coca-Cola; nylon stockings; plastic brassières, etc." [11]

The speech of 18 September 1947 to the United Nations in which Vyshinsky blamed the United States for world tension because of its warmongering has become a main source on the subject. An example of propaganda linking the two was the campaign which the Chinese Communists conducted along with the rest of the world's Communist parties in 1953 for saving the Rosenbergs, convicted atom spies, from death. The couple were pictured as innocent young people whose only crime had been to want peace and object to the United States "war policy." Said the *People's Daily:*

> It is clear that in the United States people with a genuine desire for peace are confronted with the threat of death cells and electrocution while war-mad senators and generals stalk the halls of Congress and the United States government. These people keep up a loud clamor for war. Their latest war cry is the demand for the United States to "go it alone" in Korea and take atom bombs over the Soviet Union. In fact, the criminal attempt to kill the Rosenbergs at a time when people throughout the world, including the American people, are raising their voices for peace, reflects the fear and hatred of the American ruling groups of peace.[12]

Perhaps the most eloquent and convincing spokesman of the Hate America Campaign throughout the first five years of Communist rule in mainland China was Chou En-lai. A section of his 1953 "Political Report to the Chinese People's Political Consultative Conference" sums up the Chinese Communist point of view as propagandized to the world. It deserves quoting in full:

> The present U.S. imperialist policy of war and aggression is a universal menace that threatens the peaceful life of all the peoples of the world. The American imperialists have occupied and are building a large number of military bases in many countries in Europe, Africa, Asia and the Americas. They are ruthlessly interfering in the domestic affairs of these countries, enslaving their people and forcing them to

germs

supply manpower and material for the unjust war of aggression in
Korea. The U.S. government is tightening its control over the already
weakened British and French colonialists and spurring them on in the
wars they are waging in Malaya and Viet-Nam where they are mas-
sacring the people. Under the pretence of "aid," it is actually trying
to control and seize all the British and French colonies in Asia and
Africa. The U.S. imperialists are attempting to attain their sinister
end of extending aggression by means of intrigues to make "Asians
fight Asians." They are trying by every means to gather a handful of
reactionaries throughout Asia, above all to rearm the militarist forces
of Japan and organize an aggressive Pacific bloc, seriously threatening
the security of the Asian nations. The barbaric U.S. imperialists have
the habit of using the people of Asia for "testing" their "new weapons."
Their first two atomic bombs were dropped in Asia; their first germ
bombs were dropped in Asia. Korean and Chinese prisoners of war
have been constantly sent to secret places and used as victims in such
"tests." Obviously, American imperialism has become the biggest
menace to peace in Asia and the whole Far East. Only by checking
and throwing back this threat can the people of Asia achieve peace
and security. This is the common task of the peoples of all Asian countries.[13]

Certainly the Chinese Communists used the Korean War with
great effectiveness to promote their Hate America Campaign,
and vice versa. The people were told that the moral depravity
of the capitalistic environment was the main reason for the "bestial
conduct" of American troops throughout the world. The propagandists and cadres were advised how to depict American behavior
in Korea:

The methods the American murderers employed in their slaughter
were most cruel. Some victims were axed or bayoneted, some were
electrocuted or burned and some were hanged or buried alive. The
Americans cut away ears, noses, tongues and breasts of victims, gouged
out eyes, ripped open bellies and dissected limbs. In Seoul the American murderers scalped Korean patriots alive and kept the scalps as
souvenirs. The frantic massacre by American aggressive forces cost
Korea nearly a million of its population in a year.[14]

As Chou En-lai indicated in his report, one of the major themes of the campaign against the United States is racialism, an accusation especially effective in Asia. The Chinese Reds charge that the United States has taken over Hitler's attempt to exterminate the "inferior races." This argument was epitomized in the germ warfare charges which Chou leveled against the United States in connection with the Korean War. He asserted that on 28 January 1952 United States planes launched bacteriological warfare in Korea. The accusations were supported by the world-wide Communist network. Madame Sun Yat-sen told the Peace Conference of the Asian and Pacific Peoples in Peking that, "not content with outdoing Hitler in the matter of senseless destruction, the United States armed forces are intent upon surpassing him in the matter of destroying whole peoples." The peoples of Asia, she warned, would never forget the "germ warfare, indiscriminate destruction and bestial slaughter." [15]

The campaign of international hatred embodied in the germ warfare charges, which were continued even after the Korean truce had been signed, constituted perhaps as extensive and intensive a use of the "big lie" as the world has ever seen. Supporters were enlisted from among leaders in every major country. Britain's dean of Canterbury, Hewlett Johnson, and noted scientist Joseph Needham lent support to Peking's propaganda effort. Probably no campaign officially conducted by a formally established government has reached a greater intensity of abuse or more eloquently revealed the nature and intentions of its authors. Chinese spokesmen and publications screamed for the punishment of "American war criminals" and the total annihilation of the great threat to world peace, "American imperialism." Members of the United Nations with forces in Korea were warned that they too bore responsibility because they were supporting the war efforts of "germ war criminals." [16]

Although the Chinese Communists frequently charged the United Nations with aggression in Korea, they usually insisted that they were fighting the United States and a handful of its "satellites."

The germ war charges were leveled exclusively against the United States. According to Kuo Mo-jo "The American imperialists desecrate the United Nations. Thus by their criminal aggressive actions in Korea they have made the United Nations flag a rag to hide their shame. This is indeed a monstrous insult to 1,850 million people." [17] Together with the rest of the Soviet bloc Peking has never abandoned its position that both the United States and the United Nations were guilty of aggression in Korea. In blustering language Chou branded every United Nations resolution "illegal" and throughout the war warned all countries supporting "American imperialism" that they would have to bear the consequences of their actions. The Peace Conference of the Asian and Pacific Peoples in its 12 October 1952 "Address to the United Nations" charged that organization with violating its own charter and called upon it to mend its ways.[18]

The Korean War also served Peking's purpose of convincing some of the Chinese people that the United States is "a 'paper tiger' which can easily be defeated." [19] Chou En-lai maintained that the great power of the new China had humbled and isolated the United States, compelling it to admit defeat in Korea and stop obstructing a settlement in Indo-China.[20] During the campaign to convince the Chinese people that there was no reason to fear the power of the United States, the Communist leaders promised that "after the liberation of Western Europe" the industrial and resource potential of the Communist bloc would make the defeat of the United States a simple matter.[21]

With regard to its internal goals, the Mao regime could claim great success for the Hate America Campaign by 1954. American institutions and assets had all been confiscated, many Americans had been expelled from China after public humiliation, and a large proportion of the few Americans remaining were isolated from the Chinese by prison walls.[22] Correspondents as well as businessmen returning from Mao's domain have reported that all of the Chinese youth are dominated by the desire to "kill Americans" and that no one dares to utter a favorable word about the

United States.[23] The Communists have gone far toward convincing their people that world peace can be assured only by the destruction of "American imperialism." It should be noted that under the Communist regime the term *Mei-kuo,* meaning America, seldom appears. Most Communist publications use *Mei-ti,* an abbreviation standing for American imperialism, when referring to the United States. Thus in their language the destruction of America and "American imperialism" are one and the same thing.

The purposes served in the rest of the world by the Hate America Campaign have sometimes been less obvious, though in many respects no less important. The over-all goal is of course the isolation and defeat of the United States; and unfortunately a combination of the campaign with the "peaceful coexistence" propaganda and not a few American blunders has already given Peking some victories.

One of the first purposes served by the drive is the intimidation of countries which are or might become allies of the United States. Here the Chinese operate with all the advantages of the aggressor. Because the United States is openly declared to be the hated enemy of the "Chinese people," anyone having dealings with it can be accused of harboring unfriendly intentions toward China. Charges and interpretations publicized by Peking to the rest of the world are frequently worded so as to prompt others to take an exceedingly cautious attitude toward the United States. Signers of proposed treaties with America, for example, are warned that the signing will be considered by Peking authorities as "provocation." Whenever a foreign delegation supports the United States at the United Nations, it is likely to be accused of giving in to bribery or else demonstrating that it is an American satellite.

Not only is the United States represented as China's major enemy; it is also portrayed as the greatest threat to world peace. Here Peking is aided not alone by inflammatory statements of American generals and legislators but also by the leftist press the world over, which usually expresses alarm when the United States takes a strong stand against Communism. The propaganda is also designed to destroy the prestige the United States has enjoyed throughout the world. For example, there is a general belief in America's humanitarianism; but in some areas of Asia the germ war charges did much to undermine that belief and to weaken American support among Asiatics. The Hate America Campaign served to blackmail "neutrals" and furthered the attempt to isolate the United States from its allies and to encourage conflict among them.

A good example of the working of the anti-United States policy of the Peking regime occurred in connection with the signing of the Japanese Peace Treaty in San Francisco on 18 September 1951. Some of the signatories were highly critical of the unilateral way it was negotiated, but the Chinese Reds indicated well in advance their unalterable opposition. They told the world that any nation participating in the treaty would be helping the United States enslave the Japanese people, aiding the revival of Japanese militarism, abetting a United States plot of aggression in Asia, and showing an unfriendly attitude toward China. Pakistan and Indonesia were criticized for submitting to American intimidation by signing the treaty. Interestingly enough, although we cannot assess the weight which Peking's propaganda had, both India and Burma refused to sign, and desire not to be unfriendly to Communist China was one of the official reasons given, while the Indian press echoed most of the arguments advanced by the Chinese.[24]

Mao has sought to break up the negotiation of agreements between the United States and its allies by arguing that the latter were permitting their sovereignty to be infringed by the Americans. Efforts of the United States to prohibit or restrict trade with Communist China were interpreted by Chou En-lai as part of an American plan to wreck the economics and take over the colonies of Britain, France, and the Netherlands.

Peking also charges that the United Nations has failed to admit Communist China into its membership because the United States is able to dictate the foreign policies of other governments. While some countries share the views of the United States on the issue of

China's admission, it is natural to suppose that the strongly voiced
opposition of the Americans has carried great weight. When
Great Britain voted with the United States against seating the
representatives of Peking or even abstained from voting on the
issue in the United Nations, the act was proclaimed to be "unfriendly" and "following the dictates of Washington." [25] American
troops in Britain were said to constitute a military occupation
which dictated such policies. [26]

The effectiveness of the Chinese—and international—Communist propaganda campaign to isolate the United States is probably best demonstrated in the relations between the two great
English-speaking allies, Britain and the United States. Aware of
Britain's dependence on trade, Mao has made good use of the
commercial argument to sabotage Anglo-American unity. He
has attributed many of Britain's economic difficulties during the
past four years to the "illegal embargo" of the United Nations, an
American plot to narrow the market for British goods for the ultimate purpose of aggravating Britain's economic crisis and taking control of Britain's sphere of influence in Asia. [27] British traders
in China have been told that the United States has depressed tin
and rubber prices in order to have a reason for eventually invading
and occupying Malaya. [28]

All of the Communist propaganda organs throughout the world
—as well as other leftist spokesmen—have played up Peking's
arguments. By 1954 results of the campaign were appearing in
Great Britain (where fear of an atomic war is particularly acute),
in the ranks of the British Labor party; some left-wing leaders
apparently still nourished a belief that Communism has much to
commend it to the world. Harold Wilson, who had been president
of the Board of Trade when the Labor party was in power, argued
along with the others that the danger to peace in Asia came from
the "lunatic fringe of the American Senate." He urged, "we must
not in this country join, form or in any way encourage the formation of an anti-Communist alliance in Asia." [29] The statement
partially reflects Peking's 1954 campaign against the pact of the

Southeast Asia Treaty Organization, a campaign which warned that such an organization would represent a threat to peace in Asia and that those countries which joined it would be committing unfriendly and provocative acts against the Chinese Communist government. Despite the fact that the Chinese Nationalists were excluded, Chou En-lai termed British participation in the signing of the SEATO pact in Manila in September 1954 an "obstacle" to the establishment of formal diplomatic relations, although five years had already passed since Britain extended recognition.[30] Peking had sent a chargé d'affaires to London to match the mission which London had managed to maintain in Peking, but evidently the appointment of an ambassador was to be held out as a reward for a more acceptable British policy.

It is interesting to reflect on the state of relations between Communist China and Great Britain in August–September 1954 when the British Labor party delegation paid a formal visit on Peking under the lead of Clement Attlee who, by virtue of his position as head of the party, may once again be prime minister. Communist China still held British subjects in Chinese prisons on trumped-up charges or no charges at all, denied British citizens exit visas, extorted regular monthly sums from Britain for the support of British enterprises which were not permitted to shut their doors, had confiscated hundreds of millions of dollars' worth of British assets without indicating any desire or intention to reimburse, still maintained that Britain along with the United States and the United Nations was guilty of aggression in Korea, was itself condemned by the UN for aggression in Korea, had not yet acknowledged the recognition which Attlee's government had extended almost five years before, regularly charged Britain with accepting the dictates of Washington, actively backed terrorism against British rule in Malaya and repeatedly demanded the withdrawal of British troops there which it maintained were a threat to world peace, charged the British with torturing and killing thousands of Chinese in Malaya, failed to keep the truce agreements signed in Korea, exported opium illegally on the world market, had pushed a charge of germ warfare to extremes which implicated Britain, was openly dedicated to the destruction of British democratic institutions, and had as yet shown few intentions of living in peace except in its propaganda talk.

Attlee and some of his colleagues have since been highly critical of the Communist regime (a fact which Peking not unexpectedly interpreted as a sign of ingratitude). And yet some of their statements, such as Attlee's proposal that Taiwan be handed over to the Communists, reflected the wishes of the Mao government, and by the logic of British politics were forcing the Conservative government into opposition to the United States. So convincing had been the propaganda from Communist China—aided to be sure by bellicose outbursts from America—that leading statesmen of a proud and powerful nation expressed more apprehension concerning the firm stand of a proven ally than about the aggression of a regime openly dedicated to their destruction and whose every action had contravened their highest principles.

Peking's charges of "American imperialism" have proven especially effective in Asia, where several newly independent states have been trying to maintain the position of neutrality which Mao denounced as impossible. In contending that American economic aid and capital were turning Indonesia into a United States colony and supplanting British and Dutch influence,[31] Peking hoped at the same time to promote friction between the Western powers and influence the policy of Indonesia. The accusation that American aid was a tool used to undermine their independence may have played some role in the decisions of Burma and Indonesia to refuse further assistance. The Indonesian foreign minister who advocated accepting aid from the United States was promptly replaced. NCNA reported with obvious satisfaction that Lucknow University in India had declined an offer of aid from the United States on the ground that it would interfere with the freedom of the university. This was cited as proof of the growing awareness of "United States imperialistic ambitions." [32]

The Chinese Communist position has been the same with regard to Japan. Mao's government refuses to recognize Japan as a sovereign state because of her mutual defense treaty and economic agreements with the United States and because she has granted the Americans military bases. Chinese Communist propaganda may have played its part in producing the disapproval some Japanese evince of the American about-face in regard to rearming Japan. Despite nonrecognition, the Chinese Communists try to convince the Japanese of their friendly interest. In September 1954 Chou En-lai stated, "The Chinese people deeply sympathize with the plight of the Japanese people under the military occupation of the United States." [33] An editorial in the *People's Daily* that same month announced that the time had come for the Japanese people to choose between continued servitude to the United States and the path of peace. It warned the Japanese government that it was still technically at war with China and the Soviet Union, and if it were "trapped" into joining a northeast Asian defense organization (which has been discussed in some American circles) "Japan will inevitably be plunged into a new U. S. military adventure in Asia." [34] It is interesting to speculate how many Chinese readers wondered at the contradiction between Peking's position that Japan was not a sovereign state and the warning to Tokyo which implied that the Japanese had some choice in the matter of foreign affairs after all.

The Chinese Communists made especially effective use of the trade argument in approaching Japan. The proof of their failure to achieve sovereignty, the Japanese people are told, is their inability to trade freely with the "People's China." The embargo imposed upon China at the "instigation of United States imperialism" is cited as the major cause of all Japanese economic ills. This argument was getting increasingly sympathetic attention in Japan after more than four years of endless repetition and in the face of continued restrictive tariff policies on the part of the United States. Some Japanese questioned whether Communist China had much to offer in the way of trade, and openly resented the condescending attitude with which the Chinese approached their country.[35] Nevertheless, the growing demand for increased trade with Communist China and the failure of Japanese Premier Yoshida to win the support he sought in America led to the installation of a new Japanese premier more favorably inclined to do business with the Mao regime not long after it celebrated its fifth anniversary in power.

In the Asian countries which have identified themselves with the United States' opposition to Communism the Chinese Reds are counting upon "liberation" movements to bring about a change in policy. The governments of these countries—Thailand, South Korea, the Philippines, Japan, Pakistan—are accused of fascism, national betrayal, serving imperialism, and increasing the threat of war. Their attempts to curb armed Communist revolt are termed aggression against "the people," who can, of course, only be truly represented by the Communist party. Interestingly enough, Peking has allowed Moscow to level such charges against Nehru, who has taken harsh measures against the Communists in India. In general, however, the abusive language reserved for Asian leaders who oppose Communism and its wide dissemination by the world Communist propaganda machine is in itself almost enough to discourage all but the staunchest in their stand.

After five years of Communist pressure, the United States remained firmly committed to a policy of opposition to the Peking regime despite the obvious risks involved. With the conclusion of temporary truces in Korea and Indo-China the Communists were in a position to present the United States' support of the Taiwan government as the major obstacle to peace in Asia. "So long as Taiwan is not liberated," stated Chou En-lai, "China's territory is not intact, China cannot have a tranquil environment for peaceful construction and peace in the Far East and throughout the world is not secure." [36]

The United States was accused of "occupying Taiwan." Said Chou, "Directed and assisted by the United States aggressive group, the traitorous Chiang K'ai-shek group . . . is stepping up its extortion in Taiwan, stripping the people of their wealth, reorganizing its military forces, clamoring to attack the mainland and is bent upon provoking world war. Therefore, this group is the public enemy not only of the Chinese people, but also of all peace-loving peoples in Asia and the world." [37] The liberation of Taiwan was a strictly internal affair, Chou warned, and no interference would be tolerated. The warlike language from Peking and the call on Communist armed forces to mobilize for this liberation were convincing enough to many people throughout the world to make them see what Chou wanted them to see: that opposition by the United States offered the very real possibility for another major war. Once again the Chinese Communists were aided by a background of incautious statements emanating from America and the use of such unfortunate phrases as "Let Asians fight Asians." The reaction was what Chou desired. Many world leaders, such as Nehru, and Attlee following his visit to China, called for the removal of the United States forces protecting Taiwan. But the United States replied by signing a mutual defense treaty with the Chinese Nationalist government on 2 December 1954, in which it pledged to support Taiwan and the Pescadores in case they were subjected to armed attack.

What is implied for the future in the strange logic behind the condemnation of Chiang Kai-shek as a traitor has received little notice. According to the Chinese Communists, the United States had maneuvered Chiang into initiating the civil war in 1945 and dooming the Chinese people to four more years of suffering following World War II. Chiang was a war criminal, a "traitor," because he tried to preserve his government against an armed Communist insurrection and had accepted help from the United States. Given the weight and power of Mao's propaganda machine, it was possible that few Chinese would remember General George C. Marshall's efforts to prevent the Chinese civil war and to effect a coalition government back in the days when American policy was based in part on the assumption that the Chinese Communists would behave like a normal and legitimate political party.[38] Certainly no one on the mainland dared to point out that

the Communists were themselves in large measure responsible for
the shattered morale, corruption, and ineptitude of the last years
of Nationalist rule on the mainland, conditions which were of
great help to them in depicting Chiang as the "enemy of the Chinese people."

The implications for the rest of Asia of this Communist condemnation of Chiang were that all who resisted armed Communist insurrection—in Thailand, Malaya, the Philippines, Laos,
Cambodia, and even Burma and Indonesia—were guilty of aggression against their "people" and were to be condemned as
traitors and war criminals. Those who accepted United States
aid became "public enemies" and "tools of imperialism."

There is no question that the United States position has been a
difficult one. Because it supports the Nationalist government
which is dedicated to the overthrow of the Mao regime it is
charged with threatening peace and stability in Asia. American
military bases in the western Pacific, and large naval forces there
far from their own shores, can easily be depicted in an unfavorable light by a power which resents their presence. Strongly anti-
Communist governments which the Americans support in Asia
are frequently subjected to severe criticism in the world's liberal
press (besides being denounced outright by the Communist and
pro-Communist press) for their measures to repress internal
threats and their reliance upon military strength. Further, in the
realization that military strength and a strong alliance are essential for coping with Communist subversion and the armed
might of Red China, the United States has frequently insisted
on linking economic with military assistance, feeling justified in
this course since aid to economic development is worse than fu-
tile if through military weakness the economic improvements fall
into Communist hands. The dilemma thus posed has frequently
enabled critics of America to portray it as backing "reaction"
and militarism in Asia. Such beliefs have naturally been of great
assistance to Mao and his colleagues.

After the truce in Indo-China in the summer of 1954, Peking

went all out in its propaganda offensive against the United States' protection of the Chinese Nationalist government, in the effort to depict this as the major threat to world peace. The Communists warned in August: "The liberation of Taiwan is not a purely military job. Work must be intensified in the fields of diplomacy, economy, politics and publicity to coordinate with this action before all the difficulties can be overcome and final victory won." [39] Propaganda about living conditions in Taiwan was stepped up. NCNA claimed that Taiwan is a concentration camp with disease rampant and with brutal oppression evident everywhere.[40] The lead article in the *People's Daily* of 5 September 1954 proclaimed: "Taiwan compatriots! We have every confidence that Taiwan will be liberated. Your distress will be over. Your days of freedom and happiness will arrive. Final victory is ours!" [41]

All over the world the Communist propaganda machine swung into action, and the results were evident in the activities of other left-wing organizations. On 30 September N. S. Khrushchev stated in Peking that the Soviet Union would support Communist China's effort to liberate Taiwan. The London *Daily Worker* accused the United States of turning Taiwan into a powder keg that would set off a new world war, and demanded the withdrawal of American protection.[42] A British trade union delegation in Peking for the fifth anniversary celebration of the Mao regime telegraphed London: "It is evident there is the greatest desire for peace and friendship [in Communist China]. The Delegation is convinced that American protection is a threat to world peace. We urge the British people to demand that Formosa be united with the mainland." [43]

The military and propaganda preparations for the liberation of Taiwan came as a logical climax to many years' production of international hatred and enmity for the United States. They revealed how successful the campaign had been, how powerful was the world-wide Communist propaganda network, and what some of the weaknesses of the American position in Asia were. The strange combination of aggressive military threats and talk of peaceful coexistence by a solid Communist bloc seemed to have the desired effect in a world increasingly aware of the meaning of war in an atomic age. Divided from many of its allies, the United States stood almost alone in its determination to defend Taiwan. The Communist build-up of the Taiwan issue as a major threat to international peace carried weight in both Asia and Europe. One result was that in many cases pressure for a change in policy was put upon the Americans rather than upon the Mao regime. Some British leaders stated that the China issue was one on which the United Kingdom should assert its "independence" from the United States and refuse to be led down the path to war.

The paradox for the British was an interesting one. According to the Communist position, on one hand the defense of the legitimately constituted government of Malaya against guerrilla insurgents was a threat to world peace and a matter of international concern, while on the other the armed invasion of Taiwan with international Communist support in no way involved the rest of the world. But still there were highly placed Britishers who managed to take both views at once.

What was in store if Taiwan were "liberated" was only too obvious. According to the *People's Daily,* "For five years now the remnants of the Chiang Kai-shek clique, squatting on the island of Taiwan, and preserved from the wrath of the Chinese people by their American masters, have continued their career of treason." [44] How great the "wrath of the Chinese people" under the regime of Mao Tse-tung could be had been demonstrated only too effectively on the mainland. One of the effects of American withdrawal of support from Taiwan would be to sign a death warrant for thousands of Chinese who would be killed in the resultant battle and to condone the mass executions of thousands of "traitors" following the victory made inevitable by the promised Soviet support. Chinese in Hong Kong and on Taiwan recall that more than fourteen thousand Chinese soldiers demonstrated dramatically in Korea that they would prefer death to a forced return to their own homes under Communist rule; their choice represented probably the greatest blow to the prestige of Mao's China in its first five years. The war in Korea was greatly prolonged and additional thousands of United Nations casualties were incurred in order to maintain their right not to be forcibly repatriated. Now the United States was being urged to condone the forcible repatriation not only of those men but of more than a million mainland Chinese as well as other millions of Chinese residents of Taiwan.[45]

The American defense of Taiwan has not been entirely altruistic. Taiwan is supported for strategic military reasons and because of the important role it plays in countering Communist designs on Southeast Asia as well as on Japan. Nevertheless, having recognized the Nationalist government as the sovereign government of China, the United States is living up to its obligations under the Cairo Declaration that Taiwan should be turned over to the Chinese government.[46] Behind United States support of the Nationalist government lies the conviction that the development of free institutions and economic prosperity there can play an important role in proving the emptiness of the Communist claims that the future is theirs.

13. THE CHALLENGE OF COMMUNIST CHINA

Although five years are but a moment in the long course of Chinese history, the first five years of Communist rule probably constitute one of the most portentous moments in that history. While we cannot discern the future with precision and thus place the moment in proper perspective, neither can we afford not to attempt assessing the significance of events in China today.

The initial accomplishments of the Mao regime—power, prestige, control, organization—have in many respects been unmatched in modern Chinese history. Yet, these achievements, which have tended to obscure the nature of the new Communist state, represent in large measure a utilization of assets already available on the Chinese scene. It is the performance from here on which will be the crucial long-run test of Chinese Communism in the eyes of those who have been initially impressed. The character of the Communist rule is not likely to remain long concealed from them. Future achievements will be measured against the price which, on the basis of facts now available, we know the Chinese people are paying.

How then shall we characterize the regime to which China is subjected? What is its significance for the Chinese, for the United States, and for the world?

In the first place, it is a regime based upon war, not peace. According to the statements of the top Chinese Communist leaders, warfare—class, civil, and international—has been a key factor in all of the major achievements to date. This is one characteristic of Communist China which is unlikely to change, for war and violence pervade what is rapidly becoming the everyday language, the new education, and the whole philosophy of the nation. Thus, while Peking may continue to talk persuasively about peaceful coexistence, this is still, as Lenin said it should be for good Communists, only a tactic. The implacable struggle between the Communist and the non-Communist world remains the basic creed underlying the whole structure of the state and society in China today.

The thesis advanced by the Communist leaders in Peking that China needs peace for construction sounds enticing to a world which longs for peace. Yet the instances in history which argue to the contrary should be remembered; war has frequently served as a method to tap additional reserves of energy. Peking talked earnestly of the need for peace immediately after the establishment of the Communist dictatorship, yet in less than a year the outbreak of war in Korea was being utilized with surprising effectiveness to serve those very purposes for which the Reds had claimed to need peace. And we should not forget that the remaking of China is planned in terms of building the strength necessary for the eventual victory of Communist forces. The internal makeup of Mao's China will probably continue to give the lie to its external propaganda of peaceful coexistence.

Secondly, despite an almost religious dedication to a doctrine, and in part because of that doctrine, the Red regime has grown corrupt in proportion as its power has increased. This is not to be wondered at when Mao himself has insisted that there is no such thing as abstract truth apart from the class struggle.[1] Communist rule has been based upon deceit and dishonesty. The deceit is probably most eloquently portrayed in the story of the fate of the peasants, the workers, and the intellectuals since 1949. Dishonesty has been evident throughout the daily press, as in the charges that the United Nations was guilty of aggression in Korea, that the United States carried on germ warfare, that Catholic orphanages in China practiced genocide. The result has been a suppression and inversion of many of the values which have been intimately associated with Chinese traditional culture.[2]

Thirdly, I believe it may be safely asserted that the Commu-

nist regime in China will fail to provide room for many aspects
of human life—for the individual's aspirations, devotion to family, and imaginative and aesthetic development. Visitors have
remarked on the somber expressions which have replaced the
cheerfulness long associated with the Chinese. Mao's dictum that
there is no love except class love is seen at work in the denunciations of parents by children, of husbands by wives. As has been
noted of Soviet Russia, the shallow nature of dialectical material-
ism may be showing up in the fact that not a single literary or
artistic work of note has been produced since the Mao regime
came to power.[3] One observer has said, "The deepest battle of
Communism in China is being fought not in Korea, nor in the
mass meetings, nor at the grand parades before Tien An Men,
but in the hearts of the people. It is the battle for the soul of
China." [4] Here, in the deliberate disregard of the right of the individual to be and to express himself, the Chinese Communists
may have made their greatest long-run miscalculation.

Finally, only five years after coming to power the Communists
have laid the foundations for a great new type of oriental despotism approaching "general slavery." [5] It is an apparatus of total
compulsion in the hands of a "monopoly bureaucracy." Among
the essential features are complete centralization of control over
the economy, slave labor, massive military and police organizations, and ability to mobilize and control the whole population.
To the coercive structure of an oriental despotism the Chinese
Communists have added the gadgets of modern communications
and new techniques of psychological control.

It is comforting for many people to believe that such a patently
unpopular and oppressive form of state cannot last. But as Karl
Wittfogel has pointed out, oriental despotisms have manifested
great staying power long after their initial vigor has died away.
Bureaucracy tends to perpetuate itself; patterns are established
which are difficult to break. In many respects popular government
might be viewed as the exception in the recorded history of man-

kind. The stories of many civilizations—the Egyptian, Babylonian, Byzantine, Indian, Aztec, to name but a few—are written for the most part in terms of long-enduring oppression. To those who argue that the Communist leaders cannot remain in power because they cannot retain the support of the people, the recorded history of mankind—or for that matter the history of the Soviet fatherland to which Mao's China is firmly bound—is perhaps the most eloquent answer. Given the structure and nature of the Mao regime, it is difficult to envisage its early collapse from internal causes. Short of all-out war, it will prove hard to break the power of this great bureaucratic despotism which Communism has erected in China.

Indeed, it is altogether probable that the Mao regime will accomplish further impressive feats. Despite bureaucratic inefficiency, oppression which may increase passive resistance, and a population problem which grows more acute, it has the power to mobilize its great human resources for undertaking vast projects: irrigation, flood control, road building, defense works. Such large-scale public works have been a distinguishing characteristic of oriental despotisms—the Grand Canal, the Great Wall, and the pyramids come immediately to mind. This fact will in itself make Communist China a continuing challenge to the outside world.

But the long-range over-all Communist achievement in China will be measured against what is accomplished with the aid of the West in economically underdeveloped areas outside the iron curtain. This poses a particularly grave problem because most of the world's underdeveloped lands lie outside Communist control and many of them are still subjected to an outworn colonial system. The inhabitants of these regions will compare their progress with that of China under Communism. It will be only as the basic features of the new Chinese despotism become clear, and as the political and economic conditions in other areas improve, that the alternative systems of the West will be recognized as more desirable.

In general Communist China constitutes a challenge to all the non-Communist world, and here lies the real significance of the first five years of Mao's regime.

There is first of all a challenge to face up to the threat posed, not to take our eyes off the fundamental structure and doctrine of this Communist state when its leaders attempt to distract our attention with gaudy banners and displays proclaiming peace. It is vital to remember that the goals and the conflicts remain unchanged. Communist China will, whenever expedient, continue to promote revolution, violence, and intrigue abroad and to apply in surrounding areas the strategy which has brought success thus far.

It has become clear in these last years that Western policy must oppose the further spread of Communism. This is a task to tax the wisest minds. It involves creating unity and determination among sovereign states with free institutions, some of which are in disagreement as to the nature of the threat. It necessitates coping with totalitarian techniques of propaganda and hidden aggression against which few defenses have so far been markedly effective. It calls for analysis, understanding, sacrifice, and hard work. Such efforts are unlikely to be made unless the threat is understood and the struggle seen to be what the Communists say it is: implacable.

There is a need for dedication to the cause of breaking the power of this tyranny. But up to now we have seemed able to think in terms of only one method: war. This possibility is naturally in the minds of many Chinese, both in and outside Communist China. After one year of the Mao regime a British missionary reported: "The Chinese can see no hope for the future—no hope except the third world war. While the rest of the world talks of it with fear and anxiety, the Chinese eagerly await it . . ." [6] But the costs of war today make this an almost impossible choice. There is therefore heavy obligation placed upon statesmen, scholars, and thoughtful citizens to comprehend the nature of the new Communist despotism and to discover if possible those weaknesses which can make its power disintegrate internally, as the Communists expect institutions outside their areas of control to disintegrate.

As the greatest power outside the iron curtain, the United States is perforce a leader against the Communist forces pledged to its destruction. Our position, as we are becoming increasingly aware, requires a fine balance between restraint and patience on the one hand and firmness and determination on the other. We are challenged to match our power with our statesmanship. But perhaps in the long run the challenge goes even deeper. It reaches into the whole philosophy and educational system of America today. Leadership involves training civil servants and a people equipped to understand their obligations. Our global role demands that we no longer instruct our children about our Western civilization alone and send out into the world representatives and travelers with a haughty Western ethnocentrism which has already cost us much respect in many areas of the world. We will fail in our role of bringing about a coalition of free nations unless we can educate our people to be capable of appreciating other cultures and approaching them with a degree of humility. If our faith is to be in humanity as opposed to despotism, it is imperative for us to understand that neither the West nor the United States has a monopoly of human values or achievements.

In the non-Communist areas of Asia as well as other economically underdeveloped areas of the world the United States has the opportunity to aid in creating alternatives which the people will choose instead of Communism. This will require imaginative action as well as cooperation with our allies in the resolve to eliminate colonialism. It may involve, for example, a cooperative plan for economic development dwarfing even the Marshall Plan. It may mean guaranteeing against aggression both the results of economic assistance and the security of the people involved. However great the cost of such creative responses to the Communist challenge it will be insignificant compared to the cost of failure to take up the challenge.

Communist China's threat to the United States also means, I believe, that we must maintain the strength to oppose it. But a determination not to allow this new Communist colossus to score further victories demands vigilance as well as strength. The Communist leaders must not be allowed to win tactical victories of propaganda or to split us from our allies. I believe that such vigilance involves also a continued refusal to recognize Communist China. Recognition cannot but be interpreted as acquiescence in the subjection of a great people and a rich culture to oppression. And in the global battle which according to Mao Tse-tung is so all-embracing that " 'neutrality' is only a term for deceiving people" it is vital that the Chinese people retain in Taiwan a symbol which will keep alive the hopes of those within the iron curtain and serve as a rallying point for those outside it.

The Communist despotism which has been erected in their land constitutes a grave challenge for all those Chinese who remain free, and especially for the government on Taiwan. There is an injunction placed upon the leadership and people there to learn from their past, to reassess the values and the meaning of their traditional civilization in today's complicated world, and to help make this symbol one to which free Chinese can with hope pledge their faith and future. The way in which the world outside the Iron Curtain reacts to the challenge of Communist China may well determine whether the recrudescence of oriental despotism in an even more oppressive form is a passing moment in China's long history or the fate of the whole world.

Bibliographic Note

Documentary Material

In writing this book I have had the advantage of a unique collection of Chinese Communist sources in the Yale University Library. The basis for this collection was laid with the acquisition in 1951 of one copy of everything that was contained in a Dairen bookstore. This included the files of more than 30 Chinese language periodicals and more than 1,300 books and pamphlets in Chinese published in Manchuria and in the Soviet Union between 1946 and 1950. For a review of the contents of this collection see my article " 'Literature' from Communist China," *Yale University Library Gazette, 25,* No. 4 (April 1951), 139–145. During a trip to the Far East in 1952 I was able to supplement this collection with the back files of more than 80 Chinese Communist periodicals published since the establishment of the Red regime in October 1949. Since then the Yale University Library has continued to receive the major publications of the Chinese Communists, so that the collection is one of the most complete sources on Mao's China in the United States. Following and studying these publications over the past four years have provided the general background knowledge for planning this volume, besides giving rise to the original conviction that such a survey was needed.

It must be remembered that under Communist regimes, where all publishing is a state monopoly, every book, article, or newspaper is official. All publications are supervised closely and few deviate from the official party line. The major source for that line in China is the official organ of the Central Committee of the Communist party, the *Jen-min Jih-pao (People's Daily)*, which I have tried to study closely day by day. It publishes signed articles by Communist leaders, and its editorials are statements of government policy on all phases of life. Two other newspapers deserving mention are the Tientsin *Ta Kung Pao,* which features economic and financial news, and the Peking *Kuang-ming Jih-pao (Kuang-ming Daily)*, which is in the main concerned with educational and cultural matters and is the organ of the "democratic" parties of the united front.

There are many important Chinese Communist magazines, but a few which I have utilized in the Yale collection deserve special mention. *Hsüeh-hsi* (*Study*) is the chief theoretical organ of the Chinese Communist party. It contains (especially in the issues for 1953 and 1954) articles on the application of Soviet experience and policies to the Chinese scene. The *Hsin-hua Yüeh-pao* (*New China Monthly*) is a large and comprehensive journal covering all walks of life. It frequently selects and reprints significant editorials from the *People's Daily* as well as texts of regulations and policy statements by the high Communist leaders. The *Shih-shih Shou-ts'e* (*Current Affairs Handbook*) is a widely distributed handbook published twice a month to help propagandists spread the official views among the masses in as simple a manner as possible. Two other useful sources are the organs of the All China Democratic Women's Federation, *Hsin Chung-kuo Fu-nü* (*New China Women*), and of the New Democratic Youth League, *Chung-kuo Ch'ing-nien* (*China Youth*).

Chinese Communist English language publications are of lesser value. The fortnightly *People's China* contains some official statements, but its articles must be compared carefully with the Chinese originals where they exist. Because it is published for overseas consumption, its statistics are frequently unreliable and it usually omits the Communist self-criticism contained in the Chinese texts. *People's China* succeeded *China Digest,* which was published in Hong Kong from late 1946 until 1950. The slick pictorials *China Reconstructs* and *China Pictorial* issued by the Peking government are of even smaller value. These three English language journals are supplemented by a stream of pamphlets containing Communist documents and pronouncements as well as the works of such theorists as Mao Tse-tung and Liu Shao-ch'i.

By far the best documentary sources on Communist China are the mimeographed serial publications of the United States Consulate General in Hong Kong. These sets of English language documents have been distributed to major libraries and to individual scholars in the United States and abroad by the External Research Staff of the Department of State. To date the material exceeds 45,000 pages in volume. The purpose is to present documentary source materials on the Mao regime for scholarly use, and the work is remarkably free of political bias. There are four basic series:

1. The *Current Background* (CB) series reproduces important Chinese Communist documents and statements, usually in topically organized issues, with valuable introductory comments which are often of an analytical nature. This series, which runs to over 300 numbers, has been for the most part the work of Howard L. Boorman, who deserves the profound thanks of all students of contemporary China for his pioneering effort to bring together the outstanding documents from the huge Communist output and arrange them in understandable form. I have compared the documents and analysis with the Chinese originals in many cases and have found them to be consistently reliable. Where Peking's English language releases are reproduced, the fact is indicated.

2. The *Survey of the China Mainland Press* (SCMP) series, published about five times a week, reproduces the English language news releases of the New China News Agency (NCNA) and translates a considerable proportion of the more important Chinese language releases, as well as significant articles from the major Chinese mainland newspapers. As a result of spot checking, discrepancies between NCNA releases for consumption abroad and the original texts are occasionally pointed out. By January 1955 almost a thousand numbers had appeared.

3. The *Review of the Hong Kong Chinese Press* (HKCP) series, which contains in the main summaries of news items and editorial opinion reflecting various shades of the Hong Kong political spectrum, is of somewhat lesser value. It has, however, occasional worthwhile translations from reputable non-Communist journals in Hong Kong. Like the SCMP, it is issued five to six times a week.

4. The *Chinese Communist Propaganda Review* (CCPR) series, which was the work of Richard M. McCarthy, A. Doak Barnett, Robert Burton, and Charles T. Cross, contained 46 issues during its publication from August 1951 to August 1953. It produced many translations from Chinese Communist magazines which have been difficult to procure in the United States. Especially valuable are its translations from *Hsüeh-hsi*.

Soviet Press Translations, which were published by the University of Washington at Seattle from 1946 until March 1953, contained translations of some Chinese Communist documents not to be found elsewhere. Documents and articles by the leaders of the Peking government are frequently translated from Russian into English in the *Current Digest of the Soviet Press,* published weekly in New York since 1949 by the Joint Committee on Slavic Studies of the American Council of Learned Societies and the Social Science Research Council. This is a valuable source for official Soviet statements and articles dealing with Sino-Soviet relations. Official documents on Peking's relations with the international Communist movement also appear frequently in the English language weekly of the Cominform, *For a Lasting Peace, for a People's Democracy!,* published in Bucharest.

Periodicals Dealing with Communist China

Chinese language periodicals published in Hong Kong and Taiwan are numerous. Many of them contain articles on mainland conditions documented from Communist sources. In addition they constitute a source for information from refugees who have escaped from Communist areas. Outstanding among the Hong Kong journals is *Tsu-kuo Chou-k'an (China Weekly),* published by a talented group of young Chinese refugees and containing documented analysis of mainland material. Although this magazine is strongly anti-Communist, it is not in any way sensational and is very circumspect in substantiating its statements with references to Communist sources. Also important among the anti-Communist magazines in Hong Kong are *Tzu-yu Chen-hsien (Freedom Front), Hsin-wen T'ien-ti (Newsdom),* and *Chung-kuo-chih Sheng (China's Voice).* Hong Kong's pro-Communist magazines are little more than reproductions of mainland material with some Communist interpretations of events on the Hong Kong scene. Journals published in Taiwan include *Min-chu Chung-kuo (Democratic China)* and *Chung-kuo I-chou (China Newsweek),* both of which reflect Nationalist views and research on mainland conditions, and *Tzu-yu Chung-kuo (Free China),* an independent and strongly anti-Communist fortnightly.

Outstanding among English language periodicals dealing with Communist China is the *Far Eastern Economic Review,* issued in Hong Kong by Eric Halpern, a former Shanghai publisher. Though sometimes uneven in quality, this is nevertheless an indispensable and objective weekly with a refreshing style. It provides trade and exchange statistics and many valuable articles on all phases of life in Communist China. The *China Missionary Bulletin,* which began publication in

1948 and changed its title to *Mission Bulletin* in September 1953, is issued ten times a year by the headquarters of the Catholic Missions in Hong Kong and contains useful translations, articles, and reports on mainland conditions.

One of the editors of the *Mission Bulletin* began independent publication of the *China News Analysis,* a weekly newsletter, on 25 August 1953. This periodical, which is produced almost singlehandedly by Jesuit Father L. LaDany, appears 48 times a year and promises to become one of the most valuable sources on Communist China. Its issues display admirable analytical ability and command of Chinese sources, and are thoroughly documented.

Articles dealing with Communist China in the London *Economist* and the *Manchester Guardian Weekly* are frequent and usually worth careful attention. For day to day coverage of main events the dispatches of Henry R. Lieberman in the *New York Times* are consistently high quality reporting.

Books and Monographs

Although most of the information on the first five years of Communist rule in China must be gleaned from the sources listed above, some valuable monographic studies have begun to appear. *Prospects for Communist China* by W. W. Rostow and associates (Technology Press of MIT and John Wiley, 1954) fills an important gap in the literature. I had the opportunity of seeing the preliminary mimeographed edition and the benefit of consultation with the group of scholars at the Center for International Studies, MIT, Cambridge, Massachusetts, who worked on it. The exhaustive bibliography of Western language materials dealing with Communist China (pp. 327–373) includes all major works up through the summer of 1954, and I recommend it as first recourse for anyone seeking further material on any of the topics covered in this volume. Professor Rostow and his associates also brought out a series of specialized monographs for limited distribution in multilithed form.

The three series of Studies in Chinese Communism produced from 1951 to 1953 at the University of Southern California under the direction of Theodore H. E. Chen contain some good monographs on special topics such as religion, mass movements, and propaganda strategy, and I benefited greatly from reading them. The *Papers on*

China from the Regional Studies Seminar at Harvard University, prepared under the direction of John K. Fairbank, Edwin O. Reischauer, and Benjamin I. Schwartz, include scholarly treatments of specialized aspects of Chinese Communist history.

Chinese Communism in Action by H. Arthur Steiner (University of California at Los Angeles, 3 parts, 1953) is a carefully organized collection of documentary excerpts taken for the most part from the publications of the United States Consulate General in Hong Kong. Professor Steiner, a capable political scientist, has provided valuable analytical introductions. He was editor of the symposium *Report on China* issued as Volume 277 of the *Annals of the American Academy of Political and Social Science,* September 1951. This collection of articles by recognized experts is dated but still of value.

Personal accounts of Communist China are numerous, but many of them are by uncritical visitors invited by the Peking government. Relatively balanced accounts which have aided me in selecting and appraising Chinese Communist documents and claims include Raja Hutheesing's *The Great Peace* (New York, Harper, 1953) and Frank Moraes' *Report on Mao's China* (New York, Macmillan, 1953). In addition to these two accounts by Indian visitors, a Burmese, U Kiaw Min, has provided further impressions which reflect critical capacity in *Through the Iron Curtain via the Back Door* (Rangoon, Burmese Advertising Press, 1952). Surely deserving of mention is the series of articles by Leonard Constantine in the *Manchester Guardian Weekly* from 23 November 1950 to 8 February 1951. *Out of Red China* by Liu Shaw-tong (New York, Duell, Sloan and Pearce; Boston, Little, Brown, 1953) is a free translation of the personal experiences of a Chinese Communist trainee who fled to Hong Kong. *The Umbrella Garden* by Maria Yen and Richard M. McCarthy (New York, Macmillan, 1954) is a reworking of the Chinese volume *Hung-ch'i-hsia-ti Ta-hsüeh Sheng-huo* (*College Life under the Red Flag*), published by the Union Press, Hong Kong, 1952. It covers the early honeymoon period and helps to explain how so many Western observers were misled by the Communists. Its author, Yen Kuei-lai (pseudonym), lived under the Red rule for nineteen months.

Monographs and books in Chinese are too numerous for an exhaustive listing. Three series, however, have been of great assistance to me and deserve particular mention. Two are published by the

Union Research Institute in Hong Kong: the Communist China Problem Research Series, and the Questions and Answers on Chinese Communist Problems Series. Individual studies in the former are being made available in English by this group of relatively young and enthusiastically industrious refugee scholars. The third is the Know Your Enemy Series, produced in Taiwan by a group known until 1953 as the Sixth Section of the Central Reform Committee of the Kuomintang. These studies are based upon documents in the possession of the Chinese Nationalist government and are for the most part scholarly and measured in tone. Many of the books published by the Freedom Press in Hong Kong make valuable contributions to an understanding of Communist China.

In addition to the sources listed above, I should add that I have had the benefit of interviewing many Chinese refugees from the mainland. Their accounts were a necessary supplement to the sometimes deadening effect of reading the Peking publications. Without such contacts with people who have lived under the Communist rule, one tends to forget the significance of the laws, decrees, drives, and statistics published daily.

I have indicated in the footnotes, which are arranged by chapters in the pages that follow, additional major sources and studies for the more specialized topics. As the notes show, I have for the most part used documentary material provided by the Communists themselves, rather than secondary sources, for study and analysis.

Abbreviations Used in Notes

CB: *Current Background,* United States Consulate General, Hong Kong
CCPR: *Chinese Communist Propaganda Review,* United States Consulate General, Hong Kong
CDSP: *Current Digest of the Soviet Press,* New York
CNA: *China News Analysis,* Hong Kong
FEER: *Far Eastern Economic Review,* Hong Kong
HH: *Hsüeh-hsi (Study),* Peking
HKCP: *Review of the Hong Kong Chinese Press,* United States Consulate General, Hong Kong
JMJP: *Jen-min Jih-pao (People's Daily),* Peking
MB: *Mission Bulletin,* Hong Kong
NCNA: *New China News Agency*
PC: *People's China,* Peking
SCMP: *Survey of the China Mainland Press,* United States Consulate General, Hong Kong
SPT: *Soviet Press Translations,* Seattle, Washington
TKCK: *Tsu-kuo Chou-k'an (China Weekly),* Hong Kong

Notes

CHAPTER 1. Five Years of Communism in China

1. For a good summary of China's economic position and the changes in it see "Economic Development in Mainland China, 1949–53," *Economic Bulletin for Asia and the Far East,* publication of the United Nations Economic Commission for Asia and the Far East, *4,* No. 3 (Bangkok, Nov. 1953), 17–31. The Communist version of problems and achievements is given in *New China's Economic Achievements, 1949–1952* (Peking, China Committee for the Promotion of International Trade, 1952), 285 pp.

2. The Communists undoubtedly have the support of many of the Chinese youth as well as of a devoted group of intellectuals who threw in

their lot with Mao at an early date. But the tales of refugees, the admissions of resistance by the regime (discussed later in the book), and especially the evidence furnished by the prisoners of war in Korea all confirm the existence of widespread hatred and fear of the Communists. A good summary of the attitudes of the former POW's from Korea is given by Professor Allen S. Whiting, "They Hit Red China Where It Hurt," *Saturday Evening Post*, 21 August 1954, pp. 25ff. Whiting interviewed more than 200 former prisoners.

3. The first story is told by Leonard Constantine, "Communist China: a New Sense of Purpose," *Manchester Guardian Weekly*, 23 Nov. 1950, p. 5. The second story is told as a personal experience by Liu Shaw-tong, *Out of Red China* (New York, Duell, Sloan and Pearce; Boston, Little, Brown, 1953), pp. 115–117.

4. Mao Tse-tung (3d ed. Peking, Foreign Languages Press, 1950; in English), p. 25.

5. Mao Tse-tung, *On New Democracy*, quoted in *The Strategy and Tactics of World Communism: Supplement III, Communism in China*, U.S. House of Representatives, Committee on Foreign Affairs (Washington, D.C., 1948), p. 78.

6. *The Common Program and Other Documents of the First Plenary Session of the Chinese People's Consultative Conference* (Peking, Foreign Languages Press, 1950), p. 1.

7. For a discussion of the position of the other "democratic" political parties see the article by H. Arthur Steiner, "Mao's Charlie McCarthys," *The New Leader*, 10 Sept. 1951.

8. For fuller elaboration of the implications of the "period of transition to socialism" see Chapter 5.

9. The summary which follows is for the most part based on Mao's *On People's Democratic Dictatorship* and his report to the Third Plenary Session of the Seventh Party Congress of the Chinese Communist party on 6 June 1950, in *New China's Economic Achievements*, pp. 1–9, and *The Common Program and Other Documents*.

10. *On People's Democratic Dictatorship*, pp. 24–25.

11. *Ibid.*, p. 22.

12. Many of the passages of *On People's Democratic Dictatorship* are almost direct quotations from Lenin's *State and Revolution* and his earlier *Two Tactics*. See V. I. Lenin, *Selected Works* (2-vol. ed. Moscow, Foreign Languages Publishing House, 1951), *2*, Pt. 1, 233–234, 288–294, 302–306. On the important influence of Lenin and Stalin on Mao's thinking see K. A. Wittfogel, "The Influence of Leninism-Stalinism on China," *Annals of the American Academy of Political and Social Science, 277* (Sept. 1951), 22–34.

13. Here again the Mao regime has taken a leaf from the book of Stalin

in handling the more than 40,000,000 members of minority nationality groups in China. This volume discusses the nationalities problem and the Communist treatment of it only briefly, in Chapter 8. The problem is currently the subject of an intensive piece of research by Charles Chu of Yale University. A definitive policy article on national minority problems and Communist official policy appears in the Chinese Communist cadres' journal *Hsüeh-hsi* (*Study*), No. 7 (1 Oct. 1952), and another article translated from *Ti-li Chih-shih* (*Geographical Knowledge*) appears in SCMP #718. Some very interesting points are raised by Liu Yü-lüeh in one of the Union Press Series, Questions and Answers on Chinese Communist Problems, *How Do the Chinese Communists Treat the Minority Nationalities?* (*Chung-kung Tsen-yang Tui-tai Shao-shu Min-tsu?*), Hong Kong, Union Press, Jan. 1953.

14. In its 1 Jan. 1951 editorial.

15. A brilliant analysis of this aspect of Chinese Communist strength is given by E. Stuart Kirby in his *Introduction to the Economic History of China* (New York, Macmillan, 1954), esp. ch. 3.

16. The Manchurian experience between 1945 and 1949 has yet to be examined carefully by Western students of Communist China, although one study fills in many details of progress during the pre-1949 period: K. C. Chao, *Northeast China* (*Manchuria*) *Today*, Center for International Studies, MIT, Cambridge, Mass., March 1953, 131 pp. On the propaganda experience see my " 'Literature' from Communist China," *Yale University Library Gazette, 25*, No. 4 (April 1951), 139–145. An effective operation carried on in Hong Kong was the publication of *China Digest*, an English language fortnightly running from 31 Dec. 1946 until 1 Feb. 1950. The files of this periodical are full of official CCP documents and statements of policy and progress.

17. *New China's Economic Achievements*, p. 6.

18. A Chinese Research Team, "System of Exploitation of Chinese Communists," FEER, 16 April 1953, pp. 499–502, argues that there was actually a three-year economic reconstruction plan for China which was never made public by the Communists.

19. For a good discussion of the antecedents of the policy which the regime applied when it came to power see W. W. Rostow et al., *The Prospects for Communist China*, Center for International Studies, MIT, Cambridge, Mass. (Technology Press of MIT and John Wiley, 1954), pp. 3–57.

20. The text of Mao's proclamation can be found in *China Digest, 7*, No. 1 (5 Oct. 1949), 2.

21. *Compendium of the Central People's Government Laws and Regulations, 1949–50* (*Chung-yang Jen-min Cheng-fu Fa-ling Hui-pien*), Peking, People's Press, Sept. 1952.

22. One item of interest in connection with Mao's visit to Moscow is

the question whether he had ever made the trip before. Three different sources have reported seeing him there, and there is the additional fact that on his arrival in Moscow Mao did not refer to this visit as being his first. See Eudocio Ravines, *The Yenan Way* (New York, 1951) pp. 88, 122–125, 146, 148–149, 315 and 318; Ypsilon, *Pattern for World Revolution* (New York, 1947), pp. 423–426; and a letter by Victor Serge to *Politics* magazine, 2, No. 2 (Feb. 1945), 62. An interesting exchange on the Ravines book took place between Ravines and Professor Derk Bodde in the *New York Times Book Review*, 9 Dec. 1951. During the summer of 1952 I discussed this question with several people in Taiwan and Hong Kong, including Chang Kuo-t'ao, a former member of the Chinese Communist Politburo, and several Kuomintang generals who had had close contact with Mao's forces during the times when he was supposed to have been in Moscow. There seemed to be general agreement that the 1949–50 trip was Mao's first, and that the person seen in Moscow was Mao's brother Mao Tse-min, whose facial features and name greatly resembled Mao's and who could easily be mistaken by Westerners for his brother. Mao Tse-min died in Sinkiang on his way back from Moscow in 1941.

23. Chou's speech of 30 Sept. 1950 is reproduced in *The First Year of Victory,* a collection of anniversary reports issued by the Foreign Languages Press, Peking, 1951.

24. A barometer of this change is the "Mission Chronicle" section of the *China Missionary Bulletin,* Hong Kong. Note the contrast between the March 1950 issue, pp. 290–318, and the summer issue, pp. 583–598.

25. On this point see CNA #6, p. 2.

26. For bibliography and background on how early observers were fooled by outer appearances see two review articles by the author: "How to Misunderstand China," *Yale Review,* Spring 1951, pp. 537–541, and "A Rebel from Red China," *Problems of Communism, 2,* No. 6 (1953), 61–63. A good brief description of Communist China as a tight police state at the end of 1951 is Henry R. Lieberman's dispatch in the *New York Times* of 16 Dec. 1951.

27. *New York Times,* 13 Nov. 1951. The figures are discussed in more detail in Chapter 9.

28. A discussion of this drive is found in MB, March 1951, pp. 252–253.

29. See for example Ku Ling, " 'Philanthropic' Orphanages," PC, 16 April 1951, pp. 19–20.

30. *New York Times,* 3 Dec. 1951. A strangely light sentence in view of the seriousness with which the charges were made.

31. The full text of P'eng's report is reproduced in CB #91.

32. "Two Years of the People's Republic of China," PC, 1 Oct. 1951, pp. 10–13.

33. See, for example, *New York Times,* 14 Nov. 1951.

34. See first reference cited in note 1 above.

35. Henry R. Lieberman, *New York Times,* 5 Nov. 1951.

36. Fourteen of the statements made on the thirtieth anniversary are reproduced in CB #89 and 100, and a general summary history by Hu Ch'iao-mu is reproduced in CB #102.

37. For a more detailed summary of the events of 1952 see the author's article "Communist China" in *1953 Collier's Yearbook Covering the Year 1952* (New York, 1953), pp. 137–141.

38. PC, 16 Oct. 1952, p. 10.

39. PC, 1 Oct. 1951, pp. 10–13.

40. See *New China's Economic Achievements.*

41. On the new regional organization set up see CB #245. CNA #43, 9 July 1954, contains a particularly acute analysis of the history of the regional administration system.

42. The germ warfare charges are currently the subject of book length study by Robert D. Barendsen at Yale University.

43. A more detailed account of the events of 1953 can be found in the author's article "Communist China" in *1954 Collier's Yearbook Covering the Year 1953* (New York, 1954), pp. 96–100.

44. *New York Times,* 12 June 1953.

45. The Huang Yi-feng case is the subject of CB #244.

46. NCNA, Peiping, 10 Dec. 1953.

47. See H. Arthur Steiner, *Chinese Communism in Action* (University of California at Los Angeles, 1953), Pt. 2, pp. 125–137.

48. For an excellent report on the Marriage Law and resistance to it see CNA #5, p. 3, and #15, p. 6. The Marriage Law is discussed in more detail in Chapter 4.

49. JMJP, 7 March 1954; SCMP #774.

50. This decision is translated in CB #278. The full issue of CNA #23 is devoted to an analysis of the significance and historical background of this move.

51. See CNA #34.

52. JMJP, 20 June 1954.

53. J. L. Buck, *Land Utilization in China,* Chicago, 1937.

54. HH, No. 3, 2 March 1954, p. 6.

55. For an analysis of the draft constitution see CNA #41. The official Communist press had equated New Democracy and People's Democracy before, for example in the 1 Jan. 1953 editorial of the Tientsin *Ta Kung*

Pao. On the various actions of the People's Congress and for the text of the New Constitution see CB #294–298.

56. Text in the *New York Times,* 29 June 1954.

57. The whole of the Stalinist power structure is brilliantly summarized and analyzed by Merle Fainsod, *How Russia Is Ruled* (Cambridge, Harvard University Press, 1953), especially in Chapter 4, "The Dynamics of Power," and the section there entitled "Stalin's Totalitarian Formula," pp. 109–117. A comparison of Fainsod's analysis with the pattern described in the subsequent chapters of the present volume will, I believe, show that Mao and his colleagues have followed "Stalin's totalitarian formula" faithfully in evolving their own power structure in China. This does not mean that the Chinese Communist leaders are not capable and powerful politicians, but merely that they have found most of the Stalinist totalitarian structure admirably well developed, well designed, and well suited to their own ends in China. As might be expected, they make few of the distinctions that scholars do in the West between Leninist and Stalinist Communism. Any version of Communism which is not orthodox in the Soviet view is simply not Communism to them. Yet there is a possibility, as Benjamin Schwartz points out ("China and the Soviet Theory of People's Domocracy," *Problems of Communism, 3,* No. 5, Sept.–Oct. 1954), that they are maintaining an interpretation of Communist doctrine for such underdeveloped areas as China which is itself not strictly in accord with Soviet theory. (See Ch. 11, note 36.)

CHAPTER 2. How China Is Ruled

1. This point was developed by Lucian W. Pye in a paper delivered before the Far Eastern Association in Boston, 2 April 1952.

2. Very good biographies of key Communist leaders are contained in Robert S. Elegant, *China's Red Masters,* New York, Twayne, 1951. For statistical analysis of the background and nature of the leadership, see R. C. North, *Kuomintang and Chinese Communist Elites,* Stanford, July 1952. Max Perleberg, *Who's Who in Modern China* (Hong Kong, 1954), lists the names of Central Committee members and provides biographical sketches.

3. North, *Kuomintang and Chinese Communist Elites,* p. 44.

4. On Mao see B. I. Schwartz, *Chinese Communism and the Rise of Mao,* Harvard University Press, 1951, and R. C. North, *Moscow and Chinese Communists,* Stanford, 1953. Robert Payne's *Mao Tse-tung* (N.Y., Schuman, 1951) is popular but highly inaccurate. Most Chinese, including refugees, with whom I have talked make this point about Mao's

popularity as a national symbol and his dissociation from unpopular measures of the regime in the eyes of the Chinese.

5. HH, No. 3, 2 March 1954, pp. 6–8.

6. On the party structure and the meaning of democratic centralism see Liu Shao-ch'i, *On the Party*, Peking, Foreign Languages Press, 1951. The constitution of the party is included as Pt. 2.

7. CNA #8, p. 3. A detailed discussion of local government is to be found in S. B. Thomas, *Government and Administration*, pp. 83–94 and 131–134; Steiner, *Chinese Communism in Action*, pp. 114–137; and Hsiang Li, *Chung-kung-ti Cheng-fu Tsu-chih* (*Governmental Organization of Communist China*), pp. 48–70.

8. One of the best analyses of the role of the regional governments can be found in CNA #43, pp. 1–7. See also K. C. Chao, *Northeast China* (*Manchuria*) *Today*.

9. Steiner, *Chinese Communism in Action*, pp. 156–159. See also CB #208.

10. Thomas, *Government and Administration*, p. 41.

11. JMJP, 18 Feb. 1954.

12. For a good account of developments in the party see the two-part article entitled "The Development of the Party," in CNA #12 and 13, and Fang Shu, *Campaign of Party-Expansion of the Chinese Communist Party in 1953*, Hong Kong, Union Research Institute, Nov. 1953.

13. CCPR #39, p. 15.

14. For example, An Tzu-wen in an article in HH, 5 March 1953; translated in CCPR #39, pp. 39–46.

15. CNA #6, p. 2.

16. Quoted in Frederick T. C. Yu, *The Propaganda Machine in Communist China*, University of Southern California, 15 Feb. 1952. See also Chang Shih-sheng, "The Chinese Communist Propaganda Magic," *Annual of Communist-occupied Mainland of China* (Taipei, Taiwan, China News Press, 1953; in Chinese), pp. 148–158.

17. HH, 16 Aug. 1951; translation appears in CCPR #3, pp. 2–6; italics added.

18. For a detailed discussion of three of these organizations and their policies and a listing of others see K. C. Chao, *Mass Organizations in Communist China*, Center for International Studies, MIT, Cambridge, Mass., Nov. 1953.

19. *Ibid.*, p. 130.

20. NCNA, 4 July 1953.

21. One of the chief ones is *China Youth* (*Chung-kuo Ch'ing-nien*), with a circulation of over 600,000.

22. Speech of Hu Yao-pang before the Second Congress, 24 June 1953, CB #252.

23. NCNA, Peking, 28 May 1953; SCMP #580, pp. 12–13.

24. NCNA, 30 May 1954.

25. Frank Moraes, *Report on Mao's China* (New York, Macmillan, 1953), pp. 28–29.

26. CB #252, p. 2.

27. *Ibid.*, pp. 5–12.

28. Chao, *Mass Organizations*, pp. 120–123.

29. *Ibid.*, p. 123.

30. *Ibid.*, pp. 123–214.

31. SCMP #555, pp. 14–15.

32. CNA #25, p. 6.

33. This organization was known as the All China Federation of Labor until at its Second Congress the official translation was changed to accord with the Moscow-led World Federation of Trade Unions of which it is a member. The former translation was a more accurate rendering of the Chinese. On this organization see CB #248; Chao, *Mass Organizations*, pp. 4–61; and Richard L. G. Deverall, *People's China, Sweatshop Arsenal*, chs. 3–9.

34. NCNA, Peking, 2 May 1954.

35. CB #248.

36. CNA #25, pp. 2–4.

37. NCNA, Peking, 25 Dec. 1953.

38. SCMP #687, pp. 40–43.

39. See Chao, *Mass Organizations*, pp. 116–128, for a list.

40. Chou En-lai gave this figure in his speech before the National Committee of the CPPCC on 4 Feb. 1953, CB #228. But the JMJP of 23 Sept. 1953 used the figure 106,000,000, indicating a bit of disagreement in the party line on statistics.

41. Thomas, *Government and Administration*, p. 61, quotes Chou En-lai's October 1951 figure for four of the six regions as 88,000,000.

42. JMJP, 21 May 1954.

43. FEER, 1 April 1954, pp. 385–387; CB #279.

44. On party control stopping at the gates of the village see an Associated Press dispatch in the *Christian Science Monitor*, 11 Jan. 1954.

45. JMJP, 23 Dec. 1953.

46. "Strangulating Security Controls in China," FEER, 25 Sept. 1952, p. 387.

47. Leon Trotsky, *The Revolution Betrayed* (Garden City, New York, 1937), p. 51.

48. "The Special Service Organization of the Chinese Communist Party," *China's Voice* (*Chung-kuo-chih Sheng*), 17 July 1952.

49. Steiner, *Chinese Communism in Action*, p. 151.

50. The regulations governing the people's tribunals created in connection with the Communist Land Reform campaign are given in CB #44 and #151.

51. JMJP editorial 25 March 1952, quoted in Steiner, *Chinese Communism in Action*, p. 138.

52. Henry Wei, *Courts and Police in Communist China* (University of Southern California, 15 Feb. 1952), pp. 20–25.

53. *Ibid.*, pp. 78ff.

54. For a summary of these conditions see the dispatch of Henry R. Lieberman in the *New York Times*, 16 Dec. 1951. Such regulations for city dwellers, passed on 16 July 1951, were published in the Shanghai *Liberation Daily*, 18 July 1951.

55. All the details of these committees are spelled out in the regulations published 10 Aug. 1952 and issued by NCNA that day. They are reproduced in CB #216, pp. 11–13.

56. On the provisions of the Election Law see CB #233 and 234. Details of the census regulations are given in CB #241.

57. CNA #19, p. 3, and #30, p. 6.

58. For an analysis of the election technique and the results of the elections see CNA #30, p. 6, and #42, p. 6.

59. NCNA, Peking, 19 June 1954.

60. See my article, "The Control System of the Chinese Government," *Far Eastern Quarterly*, Nov. 1947, pp. 2–22.

61. Yü Heng, "Supervision Organs of the Chinese Communist Government," TKCK, 12 Oct. 1953.

62. CNA #2, p. 1.

CHAPTER 3. Psychological Control

1. *On the Party*, p. 101.

2. These figures, with the exception of the last, are given by Yü Heng in "The Chinese Communist Party in 1953," TKCK, 4 Jan. 1954. The figure for 1954 is given in JMJP, 18 Feb. 1954.

3. W. E. Gourlay, *Chinese Communist Cadre: Key to Political Power*, Russian Research Center, Harvard University, Feb. 1952, 122 pp.

4. For a discussion of cadre training in Romania strikingly similar to that in China see *News from Behind the Iron Curtain*, 3, No. 6 (June 1954), 22–26.

5. New York, Vanguard Press, 1951.

6. For an excellent article on converting enemies see Léon Trivière, "La rééducation des prisonniers en Chine Communiste," MB, Sept. 1953, pp. 639–645.

7. *People's China,* 16 April 1950, p. 17.

8. Yueh Fung, "Ke Ta—'A Furnace of Revolution,'" *People's China,* 16 April 1950, pp. 17–19. Further information on the number of cadres trained and the schools is given in an NCNA dispatch from Peking, 24 July 1953, SCMP #624.

9. "Achievements in Work Connected with Cadres during the Past Three Years," NCNA, Peking, 30 Sept. 1952, CB #218, p. 26.

10. Information on the Moscow schools in published sources is limited. One Japanese, Kazama Jokichi, has written of his experiences in them. My information comes from talks with him and some Chinese graduates of these schools.

11. Boyd Compton, *Mao's China, Party Reform Documents, 1942–1944* (Seattle, University of Washington Press, 1952), p. xxxix.

12. *Ibid.*

13. *Ibid.,* p. xlix.

14. Liu Shao-ch'i, *How to Be a Good Communist,* Peking, 1951.

15. Alan M. G. Little, "Pavlov and Propaganda," *Problems of Communism, 2,* No. 2 (1953), 17–21, gives an excellent discussion of some of the ramifications of the application of Pavlov's theories to propaganda in China.

16. Mao, p. 23.

17. Yueh Fung, "Ke Ta—'A Furnace of Revolution,'" *People's China,* 16 April 1950, p. 19.

18. CNA #9, p. 6.

19. The description of the cadre training process which follows is based upon 1) interviews with 17 refugees who had personally been through the process (conducted in Hong Kong during the summer of 1952), 2) a general survey of Western and Chinese literature dealing with the topic, and 3) study of Chinese Communist material such as recantations, etc. For the Communist description of another aspect of cadre training see An Tzu-wen, "Training the People's Civil Servants," PC, 1 Jan. 1953, pp. 8–11.

20. Interview with refugee from Huai-yang in Kuang-tung province, Hong Kong, 21 July 1952.

21. Yen Kuei-lai (pseud.), *Hung-ch'i-hsia-ti Ta-hsüeh Sheng-huo (College Life under the Red Flag)* (Hong Kong, 1952), p. 37. For a review article covering this volume as well as Liu Shaw-tong's *Out of Red China* and other similar works, see my "A Rebel from Red China," *Problems of Communism, 2,* No. 6, (1953), 61ff.

22. A similar scene is described by an informant interviewed by Edward Hunter. See *Brain-washing in Red China*, pp. 30–33.

23. Liu Shaw-tong, *Out of Red China*, p. 11.

24. Tokyo *Evening News*, 15 April 1953.

25. "The Study Magazine," PC, 16 Sept. 1950, p. 25. Latest circulation figures given in SCMP #732, p. 25, are over 500,000.

26. Gourlay, *Chinese Communist Cadre*, p. 47. Gourlay's study presents an excellent summary of Ai's doctrines and his position in Chinese Communist ideology.

27. PC, 16 Sept. 1950, p. 25.

28. Gourlay, p. 52.

29. Liu Shaw-tong, *Out of Red China*, p. 97.

30. Hunter, *Brain-washing*.

31. Liu Shaw-tong, p. 40.

32. Chang Chih-min, "I Began to Realize My Erroneous Ideology," *Chiao-shih Yüeh-pao (Teachers' Monthly)*, Dec. 1951.

33. *Hsin-chung-kuo Fu-nü (New China Women)*, 1 March 1952.

34. This point is developed by Yü Heng in his "Supervisory Organs of the Chinese Communist Government," TKCK, 12 Oct. 1953 (in Chinese).

35. Lin Han-ta, "The Drive against Illiteracy," PC, 1 Feb. 1953, p. 7.

36. Raja Hutheesing, *The Great Peace* (New York, Harper, 1953), p. 174.

CHAPTER 4. The Role of the Drive

1. Moraes, *Report on Mao's China*, p. 36.

2. Few studies have been completed up to now on the role of the drives in Communist China. A notable exception is Wen-hui C. Chen, *Mass Movements in Communist China*, University of Southern California, Studies in Chinese Communism, Series 2, No. 4, 15 Oct. 1953.

3. Chao, *Northeast China (Manchuria) Today*, p. 1.

4. MB, Nov. 1951, p. 787.

5. NCNA, Peking, 24 April 1951.

6. This is in part because of the relatively later "liberation" of the south, but it is also traceable to such factors as the more intransigent nature of the southerners, the existence of many national minority areas, and the disappearance of illusions about the Communists before the regime was fully in power there. For some examples of what is involved, see "Agrarian Reform in Kwangtung Enters Critical Stage," CB #211, and "Immediate Communist Tasks in Kwangtung," CB #226.

7. HKCP, 1953, #31.

8. NCNA, Peking, 24 Oct. 1951.

9. The major documents in connection with the Huang Yi-feng case are reproduced in CB #244. The Campaign against Bureaucratism, Commandism, and Violation of Laws and Discipline is handled in documentary form in CCPR #39.

10. SCMP #514, CCPR #39.

11. CCPR #39, p. 18.

12. CCPR #39, p. 19.

13. JMJP, 13 Feb. 1953.

14. NCNA, Peking, 25 March 1953.

15. Tientsin *Ta Kung Pao,* 19 March 1953.

16. *Ibid.,* 31 March 1953; SCMP #547, p. 20.

17. NCNA, Peking, 15 April 1953.

18. SCMP #520 and 524.

19. *Daily Worker,* Peking, 26 Feb. 1953; SCMP #522, pp. 19–20.

20. *Chung-kuo Ch'ing-nien,* No. 3, 1 Feb. 1953; CCPR #39, p. 25.

21. *Ibid.,* No. 5, 1 March 1953; CCPR #39, pp. 27–29.

22. *People's Daily,* 27 Feb. 1953; a report by the Second Secretary of the Shantung Subbureau of the Central Committee of the Communist party; CCPR #39, pp. 30–38.

23. JMJP, 28 Feb. 1953.

24. JMJP, 12 April 1953.

25. JMJP, 15 July 1953.

26. The Land Reform is discussed in more detail in Chapter 6. The implications discussed here are spelled out clearly in several places; for an example, C. M. Chang, "Mao's Stratagem of Land Reform," *Foreign Affairs,* July 1951, pp. 550–563.

27. CB #218.

28. Chou En-lai's "Report" is produced as a supplement to PC, 16 Feb. 1953; see p. 3.

29. See the 18 Aug. 1952 "Provisional Measures for the Control and Reform of Landlords in the Central-South Region," CB #216.

30. *The Marriage Law of the People's Republic of China* (Peking, Foreign Languages Press, 1950), gives the text as well as two articles discussing the law. That the Communists view the results as thus far unsatisfactory is borne out by the steady series of campaigns for realizing the goals of the law.

31. *Ibid.,* pp. 1–3.

32. JMJP, 29 Sept. 1951.

33. CNA #5, pp. 2–4. This is a good summary of the problem. This very important Chinese Communist attack on the family is documented in numerous publications of the United States Hong Kong Consulate

General. See especially CB #136, 236, 243, and 273 as well as CCPR #36. Also of value is C. K. Yang, *The Chinese Family in the Communist Revolution,* Center for International Studies, MIT, Cambridge, Mass., May 1953, 373 pp.

34. NCNA, Peking, 22 Jan. 1953, describing the results of the 1951 investigations.

35. CNA #5, p. 3; this is carefully documented.

36. *Hsin-hua Yüeh-pao (New China Monthly),* Feb. 1953, p. 48, cited in CNA #5, p. 4.

37. 6 May 1953; cf. CB #243.

38. JMJP, 19 Nov. 1953, issued as CB #273.

39. For some details of the early part of this movement, which still continues in Communist China, see Wen-hui C. Chen, *The Resist-America Aid-Korea Campaign in Communist China,* University of Southern California, Studies in Chinese Communism, Series 2, No. 4, 15 Feb. 1952.

40. *People's China,* 16 Feb. 1953, Supplement, p. 9.

41. *Shih-shih Shou-ts'e (Current Affairs Handbook),* No. 17, Sept. 1952.

42. The one million figure is given in CNA #1, p. 3. More details are given on this aspect of the movement in Chapter 9; see also CB #101.

43. "Great Success in the Suppression of Counterrevolutionaries during the Past Three Years," NCNA, Peking, 27 Sept. 1952.

44. See the 1951 issues of the FEER and MB for some accounts.

45. "Comment," CB #156, p. 4.

46. "The Campaign against Hu Shih," CB #167.

47. "Recognize Clearly the Reactionary Nature of the Ideology of the Bourgeois Class," HH, 16 March 1952.

48. FEER, 30 July 1953, p. 135.

49. There have been many studies of this movement and its results. By far the best to date is the concise summary of A. Doak Barnett distributed privately by the Institute of Current World Affairs. In addition, a clear summary is given by Sherwin Montell, "The San-fan Wu-fan Movement in Communist China," *Papers on China,* Regional Studies Seminar, Harvard University, 8 (Feb. 1954), 136–196. There is an extensive monograph on the movement by James T. C. Liu produced for the Center for International Studies, MIT, Cambridge, Mass.; and there are of course many articles, most of which are cited in these other sources. Most of these sources discuss the alienation of the overseas Chinese mentioned below.

50. PC, 16 Oct. 1952, p. 10.

51. On the suicides and the different estimates of their number, see

Montell, "The San-fan Wu-fan Movement," note 31. The various issues of the FEER during the first half of 1952 give an excellent account of the development of the movement; see especially the issue of 24 April 1952.

52. Montell, pp. 164–165 and A. Doak Barnett, work cited in note 49.

53. Cited by Montell, p. 162.

54. On this "general line of the state" see CB #285.

55. The JMJP called for the increase of production and revenue, economy, retrenchment in expenditures, and overfulfilling of national plans. Editorial of 6 Sept. 1953. By mid-September the drive was in full swing.

56. Tientsin *Ta Kung Pao,* 29 June 1953.

57. Quoted in T. C. Mendenhall et al., *The Quest for a Principle of Authority in Europe, 1715–Present* (New York, Henry Holt, 1948), p. 73.

CHAPTER 5. Economic Control

1. Several significant studies of the Chinese economy under the present regime have been undertaken, some of which have already been published. The section of W. W. Rostow's *Prospects for Communist China* dealing with "Communist Power and the Chinese Economy" is one of the highlights of the volume. It is in large measure the work of the very talented Alexander Eckstein. I have been aided greatly by this work and by personal contact with Professor Rostow and his colleagues. Ronald Hsia's *Economic Planning in Communist China,* Center for International Studies, MIT, Cambridge, Mass., Nov. 1953, is also of great value. There are numerous articles, including those of Douglas Paauw and K. C. Chao, which contribute to an understanding of economic problems in China. The volumes of the FEER are indispensable on this score. In addition, numerous publications of the Union Research Institute in Hong Kong contribute documented appraisals. Several of these have been published in English: Cheng Cho-yuan, *Monetary Affairs in Communist China;* Hsin Ying, *The Foreign Trade of Communist China;* Hsiao Chi-jung, *Revenue and Disbursement of Communist China;* Hsin Ying, *The Price Problems of Communist China.*

2. *Hsin-hua Yüeh-pao (New China Monthly),* No. 2, Feb. 1952.

3. For example, an article in the 2 March 1954 issue of *Study* by Ai Ssu-ch'i is entitled "Study Stalin's Theories in Our Struggle to Build Socialist Society." It should be noted that since Stalin's death there has been some effort in the USSR to disavow his authorship of the *History of the Communist Party of the Soviet Union (Bolshevik).*

4. Quoted from the government's official decision by Li Wei-han in

his 27 Oct. 1953 speech to the Federation of Industry and Commerce. Two days after Chou had announced the plan the *People's Daily* stated that the first purpose was national defense, and the following day, 27 Dec. 1952, it announced that the focus would be on "the development of heavy industry, machines, fuel, and electric power."

5. Chi Yün, "How China Proceeds with the Task of Industrialization," JMJP, 22 May 1953, translated in CB #272, pp. 10–15. Chi goes into great detail about the possibility of "imperialist attack" and quotes the warnings of Stalin.

6. The statements were published in *New China's Economic Achievements.*

7. Hsia, pp. 9–11.

8. Rostow, ch. 13.

9. *Bulletin* of the Commission, Bangkok, Nov. 1953, pp. 17–31; figures extrapolated by Rostow, p. 238. It should be pointed out that many of the statistics one gives for Communist achievements must of necessity rely on the published figures of the Peking government.

10. This is the figure given by Edwin W. Pauley, *Report on Japanese Assets in Manchuria to the President of the United States,* Nov. 1945, p. 37. A much higher figure was arrived at by a group of Japanese industrialists, and it is broken down in detail in the publication of the Chinese Association for the United Nations, "A Report on Russian Destruction of Our Industries in the Northeastern Provinces," Taipei, April 1952.

11. Report by Po I-po in *New China's Economic Achievements,* p. 159.

12. JMJP, Peking, 22 Sept. 1953.

13. Po I-po, p. 156.

14. See FEER, 21 Aug. 1952, pp. 226–227, and Eckstein's analysis in Rostow, ch. 13.

15. Moraes, *Report on Mao's China,* pp. 138–139, and Hutheesing, *The Great Peace,* pp. 145–147.

16. As summarized by the *Economic Bulletin for Asia and the Far East,* Nov. 1953, p. 19.

17. See, for example, accounts in the Tientsin *Ta Kung Pao,* 1 June 1954.

18. Quoted in CNA #40, pp. 5–7. This gives an excellent account of the Communist methods for controlling private industry. See also the account of controls in FEER, 29 April 1954, pp. 522–523, entitled "Chinese Private Factories' Fate." Another account with good statistical support can be found in TKCK, 4 Jan. 1954, entitled "Private Enterprise on the Chinese Mainland."

19. CNA #15, p. 3.

20. Tientsin *Ta Kung Pao*, 4 Jan. 1954.

21. Li's address to the congress was released by NCNA 10 Nov. 1953 and is reproduced as CB #267.

22. *Kuang-ming Jih-pao*, Peking, 31 Jan. 1954; see also the article in TKCK, 4 Jan. 1954, cited above. The Tientsin *Ta Kung Pao* of 11 May 1954 headlined: "Private Industrialists and Merchants Should Correct Their Mistake of Withdrawing Funds from Their Enterprises."

23. Tientsin *Ta Kung Pao*, 30 July 1953, cited by CNA #2, p. 5. On the fate of the handicrafts see CNA #5, p. 6.

24. See CNA #18, p. 2. The matter of the change of ambassadors is somewhat overstressed by Deverall in *People's China*, pp. 201–204, but he provides some interesting suggestions on this score.

25. Quoted by Ronald Hsia, p. 22. Hsia gives an excellent description of the remaking of the educational system. A much more detailed study and one that is very important for understanding what has happened in Chinese institutions of higher learning is Chuang Shih, *Higher Education in Communist China*, Communist China Problem Research Series, Union Research Institute, Hong Kong, Dec. 1953, 97 pp.

26. Kiyoshi Morikawa, "Industrial Recovery in Red China," *Oriental Economist*, Tokyo, Feb. 1954, pp. 85–90; quoted by Deverall, p. 210.

27. The three sets of targets are given in the *Economic Bulletin for Asia and the Far East*, Nov. 1953, p. 30.

28. See Ronald Hsia's discussion of the program for training 650,000 to 700,000 technical managerial personnel under the plan, and its shortcomings, in *Economic Planning*.

29. It was sharply criticized by Po's successor Teng Hsiao-p'ing who presented the 1954 budget in mid-1954. NCNA, Peking, 6 July 1954.

30. "Pravda on Sino-Soviet Economic Relations," NCNA, Peking, 2 Oct. 1953; SCMP #662.

31. To my knowledge no economist has yet been able to develop even the basic principles on which to build a theory and formula for coping with the problem posed by overpopulation in economically underdeveloped countries. An excellent analysis of the problem is provided in Eugene Staley, *The Future of Underdeveloped Countries*, New York, Harper, 1954.

32. NCNA, Peking, 19 June 1954.

33. NCNA, Peking, 11 June 1954; SCMP #828, p. 3; 29 according to the Chinese method for calculating ages.

34. FEER, 29 April 1954, pp. 528–529.

35. Reproduced from Rostow, *Prospects*, p. 239.

36. "Communiqué on Rehabilitation and Development of National Economy, Culture and Education during 1952," NCNA, Peking, 29 Sept. 1953. This communiqué, which was issued by the State Statistical Bureau one day earlier, is reproduced as CB #262.

37. For an excellent statement of this whole problem see Franklin L. Ho's "The Land Problem of China," *Annals of the American Academy of Political and Social Science, 276* (July 1951), 6–11. Though latest Communist figures make it somewhat dated, the conclusions remain valid.

38. *Economic Bulletin for Asia and the Far East,* Nov. 1953, p. 27.

39. CNA #11, p. 6.

40. JMJP, 18 Aug. 1953.

41. See "Food Quality," CNA #11, p. 6.

42. Tientsin *Ta Kung Pao,* 21 June 1954. Italics added.

43. *Ibid.,* 11 Oct. 1953; quoted by CNA #16, p. 7.

44. Chang Wei-chi and Hu Ming, "The Relationship between Export of Native and Special Products and Industrialization of the Country," JMJP, 7 Feb. 1954.

45. F. L. Ho, article cited in note 37.

46. The problem of application of increased amounts of chemical fertilizers to Chinese soil is discussed in greater detail in Rostow, pp. 264ff.

47. Numerous cases are cited in the Tientsin *Ta Kung Pao* of 24 March 1953.

48. TKCK, 4 Jan. 1954.

49. On taxation see A. S. Chang and T. K. Ho, "China's Agricultural Tax," FEER, 23 July 1953, pp. 109–110, and "New Taxation in China," FEER, 29 Jan. 1953, pp. 134–136. The Chinese "Commodity Circulation Tax," similar to that of the Soviet Union, is described in a translation of a Chinese Communist article in SCMP #509.

50. The regimentation of the workers is discussed in Chapter 7.

51. Soviet relations to the five-year plan are discussed in Chapter 11.

52. *Chieh-fang Jih-pao (Liberation Daily),* Shanghai, 6 Feb. 1953.

53. On Russia's railways see W. H. Chamberlin, *Russia's Iron Age* (Boston, Little, Brown, 1934), p. 59. For a complete listing of China's railways as well as discussion of their condition by Communist leaders, see CB #274.

54. JMJP, 17 Oct. 1952.

55. These data are contained in documented form in CNA #35, pp. 1–5.

56. This was the title of an article in *Chung-kuo Ch'ing-nien (China Youth),* No. 15, 1952.

57. CNA #35, p. 5. Pages 1–5 of this issue contain a first-rate summary

of the state of Chinese Communist statistical work as of 14 May 1954. A summary of the results of the congress, as well as the JMJP editorial, can be found in SCMP #784, pp. 16–20.

58. NCNA, Peking, 25 April 1953; SCMP #559.

59. *Economic Bulletin for Asia and the Far East*, Nov. 1953, pp. 30–31.

60. Hsia, p. 28.

61. Po's report on the 1953 budget is reproduced as CB #230. The figures are quoted in this form in Rostow, p. 279.

62. See for example, JMJP, 10 Nov. 1953; SCMP #693, p. 27.

63. NCNA, Peking, 18 July 1953.

64. On the Soviet style "space planning" see Edward Szczepanik, "On the Economic Theory of Maoism," FEER, 17 Dec. 1953, pp. 183–185.

65. NCNA, Peking, 25 Dec. 1952; SCMP #488.

66. On the establishment of thoroughgoing economic control by the courts see the NCNA dispatch on the subject dated 17 March 1954.

67. CNA #2, p. 6.

68. Quoted by Deverall, *People's China*, p. 214. Further implications of Soviet economic ties are discussed in Chapter 11.

69. FEER, 8 Oct. 1953, pp. 459–460.

70. See Hsia, p. 63.

71. *Chung-kuo Ch'ing Kung-yeh* (*Chinese Light Industry*), Peking, Sept. 1953.

72. JMJP, 17 Jan. 1954; SCMP #737, pp. 17–18.

73. "The Case of the Canton Organic Fertilizer Plant," CB #250.

74. Tientsin *Ta Kung Pao*, 5 Aug. 1953.

75. JMJP, Peking, 25 Nov. 1953.

76. Tientsin *Ta Kung Pao*, 5 March 1953.

77. Tokyo *Yomiuri Shimbun*, 19 Oct. 1953, summarizing report by Huang Ching released by NCNA.

78. NCNA, Anshan, 26 Dec. 1953; SCMP #715, pp. 3–4.

79. *Yomiuri Shimbun*, 19 Oct. 1953, Hong Kong dispatch.

80. Ronald Hsia, "The Chinese Economy under Communist Planning," *Pacific Affairs*, 27, No. 2 (June 1954), 112–123. The 23 per cent figure represents the final goal for 1953 after the two reductions referred to above.

81. At the 32d meeting of the Government Council of 19 June 1954, reported by NCNA, 25 June 1954.

82. Tientsin *Ta Kung Pao*, 4 March 1954, quoted by CNA #44, p. 2.

83. Rostow, p. 278.

84. On the Communist versus the democratic methods for economic

development see Staley, *The Future of Underdeveloped Countries,* Pts. 2 and 3.

CHAPTER 6. The Peasants

1. Boston, Houghton Mifflin, 1950, p. 498.

2. Mao Tse-tung, published under the title *Turning Point in China* (New York, New Century Publishers, 1948), p. 12.

3. *The Agrarian Reform Law of the People's Republic of China* (2d ed. Peking, Foreign Languages Press, 1951), pp. 75–76.

4. Both Frank Moraes and Raja Hutheesing, for the most part critical observers of the "new China," accept all three of the fallacies discussed below. Moraes, *Report on Mao's China,* pp. 42–58; Hutheesing, *The Great Peace,* pp. 79–90.

5. The acceptance of the terms "feudal" or "semifeudal" by Western scholars as applicable to China is frequently a clue to either political bias or naïveté.

6. R. H. Tawney, *Land and Labour in China* (New York, Harcourt, Brace, 1932), pp. 34 and 63.

7. S. T. Tung, "Land Reform, Red Style," *Freeman,* 25 Aug. 1952. Tung Shih-tsin, long-time editor and publisher of the *Chinese Farmer* and a Ph.D. in agriculture from Cornell University, has published first-hand accounts of the Chinese Communist land policies. Two of these books contain excellent material in very readable form: *Kung-ch'ü Hui-yi* (*Remembrances of Communist China*) and *Lun Kung-chan-tang-ti T'u-ti Kai-ko* (*On Chinese Communist Land Reform*), Hong Kong, Freedom Press, 1951. Tung explains how some of the minor tensions and inter-family quarrels in the villages were exploited by the Communists to create a "class struggle" which had not previously existed. He also explains from firsthand experience the effectiveness of the propaganda techniques among the peasants. Most of the peasants had latent grievances which the Communists were able to direct against the village elders and landlords with great skill. Tung is a Chinese agrarian expert who has devoted much of his life to research on the possibilities for peaceful and rational land distribution as a partial answer to the pressing problems of the Chinese peasant.

8. Tung, "Land Reform, Red Style."

9. J. L. Buck, *Land Utilization in China.* See also his "Fact and Theory about China's Land," *Foreign Affairs,* Oct. 1949.

10. If farmers who owned their own households but rented crop land were classified as tenants, the figures would be 54.2 per cent owners,

28.9 per cent part owners, and 16.9 per cent tenants; Buck, *Land Utilization in China,* statistics, p. 57.

11. G. F. Winfield, *China: the Land and the People* (New York, W. Sloane Associates, rev. ed., 1950), p. 280.

12. Winfield, p. 281. Winfield's volume is especially effective in explaining that the pauperization of the Chinese peasant has been the result of other forces than an inequitable land distribution; see pp. 279–282, 301–303, and 394–396.

13. Tung Shih-tsin, *On Chinese Communist Land Reform,* pp. 19–33.

14. This figure is now given in most Communist sources; for example, see Teng Tzu-hui's address to the Youth League 2 July 1953, CB #255, which also contains the expression "basically completed." One wonders just what is meant by this term which is so frequently found in Communist statements about the success of their various movements.

15. CB #262.

16. Wu Yi, "Achievements in the Economic Development of Kwangtung," *Economic Weekly,* Hong Kong, 13 Oct. 1953 (in Chinese); summary in HKCP #191, 1953.

17. "The Chinese Communists and the Peasants," *Problems of Communism, 1,* No. 2 (1952), 1–2.

18. For the 20 July 1950 General Regulations Governing the Organization of People's Tribunals, see CB #44.

19. For an analysis which strangely enough steers clear of the violent aspects but shows the thoroughness of the work of the cadres and the methods used, see K. C. Chao, "Land Reform Methods in Communist China," *Papers on China,* Regional Studies Seminar, Harvard University, 5, 107–174.

20. Hsiao Ch'ien, *How The Tillers Win Back Their Soil* (Peking, Foreign Languages Press, 1951), pp. 74–80.

21. "The Chinese Communists and the Peasants," *Problems of Communism, 1,* No. 2 (1952), 2.

22. The Chinese Communist press as quoted in the Hong Kong *Standard,* 19 Feb. 1951.

23. CNA #7, pp. 2–4. This is a very well organized analysis of the role of the cooperatives. A further discussion of rural cooperatives is to be found in CB #106, "Cooperatives in the Central-South Region." The "introductory comment" by the United States Consulate General staff highlights the role played by these organizations as well as the importance which the Communists attach to that role.

24. With regard to this fact the testimony of refugees, of former POW's in Korea, and of Communist self-criticism is consistent. For good discus-

sions see CNA #7, 21, 27, esp. 36 and 38. There are two good articles in FEER, 29 Jan. 1953, pp. 134–136, and 23 July 1953, pp. 109–110. See also notes 53 and 67 below.

25. This point as well as most of the others in this paragraph is very forcefully made and well documented from Communist sources by C. M. Chang in "Mao's Stratagem of Land Reform," *Foreign Affairs*, July 1951, pp. 550–563. This article stands today as the most penetrating and prescient analysis of the motives for the Communist Land Reform in China.

26. Stalin, "Problems of Agrarian Policy in the USSR," *Problems of Leninism* (Moscow, 1940), p. 311.

27. HH, Vol. 4, No. 11, 16 Sept. 1951.

28. *Ch'ang-chiang Jih-pao* (*Yangtze Daily*), 2 Sept. 1951.

29. HH, Vol. 5, No. 1, 1 Nov. 1951.

30. In a very interesting article entitled "Ideological Problems among Village Cadres," HH, Vol. 4, No. 12, 1 Oct. 1951.

31. This is the gist of the general statement to the high-ranking party cadres by Kao Kang on 10 Jan. 1952, reported by the JMJP, 24 Jan. 1952. Interestingly enough, in quoting the article from *The Common Program* dealing with the subject, "The People's Government shall also guide the peasants step by step in the organization of various forms of mutual aid in labor and cooperation in production," he omitted the rest of the sentence, "according to the principles of willingness and mutual benefit." For an analysis of the import of the speech by Kao see "The Chinese Communists and the Peasants," *Problems of Communism*, *1*, No. 2 (1952), 3–6.

32. A good discussion of agricultural developments in the European satellites appears in a series of three articles in *News from Behind the Iron Curtain*, Vol. 3, Nos. 2–4, Feb.–April 1954.

33. On the development of the various forms of "socialized" agriculture see A. Doak Barnett, "China's Road to Collectivization," *Journal of Farm Economics*, *35*, No. 2 (May 1953), 188–203.

34. Stalin, "Dizziness with Success," *Problems of Leninism* (Moscow, 1940), pp. 333–338.

35. For example, an NCNA dispatch from Foochow dated 10 Nov. 1952 described a collective farm which had been set up for the settlement of returned overseas Chinese.

36. See, for example, the NCNA release from Mukden of 3 July 1952, "A Successful Collective Farm in the Northeast: the 'Spark' Farm."

37. NCNA, Peking, 7 Feb. 1953. On 27 Feb. that year the JMJP editorial was entitled "False Peasant Models Must Not Be Tolerated."

38. For example, the *Jen-min Shou-ts'e* (*People's Handbook*) of 1

July 1952 featured an article entitled "The Happy Life of the Soviet Farmers Is Our Example."

39. An NCNA dispatch from Peking dated 18 March 1953 entitled "Women in Agricultural Production" claimed that 80 per cent of the women in some areas were taking part in organized farming. Such NCNA Peking dispatches are as a matter of course usually reprinted in all major newspapers throughout the country.

40. NCNA, Mukden, 25 June 1952: Kao's summary of the 3-anti 5-anti Movement.

41. An interesting example of the contrast in propaganda between the first two phases of Communist policy is seen in the two major publications turned out in English by the Foreign Languages Press in Peking. The first, which was quoted extensively above, is Hsiao's *How the Tillers Win Back Their Soil,* 1951. The second, entitled *Agriculture in New China,* 1953, is devoted almost entirely to a discussion of "mutual aid and cooperation in agriculture."

42. PC, 16 Feb. 1953, "Supplement," p. 4.

43. NCNA, Peking, 22 March 1953; italics added.

44. *Ibid.*

45. Stalin, "Dizziness with Success," *Problems of Leninism,* pp. 333–338; "Reply to Collective Farm Comrades," *op. cit.,* pp. 339–358.

46. "Rural Work: Its Basic Mission and Policy," CB #255.

47. A. A. Andreev, Speech at the Eighteenth Party Congress, *Stenographic Report* (Moscow, 1939), pp. 109–110. I am indebted to Professor Frederick C. Barghoorn for calling this speech to my attention and for the translation.

48. Stalin, "The Results of the First Five-Year Plan," *Problems of Leninism,* p. 435.

49. NCNA, Peking, 19 July 1953; SCMP #621.

50. NCNA, Chungking, 26 July 1953; SCMP #626.

51. "Failure of State Farms in China," FEER, 17 Sept. 1953, pp. 358–359.

52. See CCPR #42, p. 1.

53. JMJP, 17 April 1953.

54. JMJP editorial of 20 April 1953; SCMP #555, pp. 23–24. Cf. also "Grain Problem of China," FEER, 30 April 1953, p. 565.

55. *Nan-fang Jih-pao (Southern Daily),* Canton, 29 June 1953.

56. JMJP, 12 Sept. 1953, quoted by CNA #7, p. 5.

57. JMJP, 23 Sept. 1953.

58. For a good summary, see Henry R. Lieberman's dispatch to the *New York Times* dated 31 Aug. 1953.

59. CNA #9, p. 7, quoting JMJP 5 Oct. 1953. Part of the directive by the Ministry of the Interior was issued by NCNA, Peking, on 11 Dec. 1953.

60. The significance and implications of the Khrushchev report are discussed in Chapter 11.

61. NCNA, Peking, 24 Dec. 1953.

62. The decision is reproduced as CB #278.

63. Harry Schwartz, *New York Times*, 3 Aug. 1954. Liao's article is reproduced in CDSP, 6, No. 27, pp. 14 and 35.

64. NCNA, Peking, 24 Sept. 1954.

65. CNA #35, pp. 6-7.

66. NCNA, Peking, 23 Mar. 1954.

67. CNA #23 gives an excellent background and analysis of the decision on collectivization.

68. *Ibid.*

69. NCNA, Loyang, 23 July 1953.

70. JMJP, 26 May 1954; Chou's statement was released by NCNA on 24 Sept. 1954.

71. SCMP #278, p. 4.

72. Hong Kong *Ta Kung Pao*, 4 Dec. 1952; HKCP #222, 1952.

73. CB #278, p. 4.

74. JMJP, Peking, 16 Jan. 1954 editorial; SCMP #735, pp. 11-14.

75. See note 1. According to Harry Schwartz (*Russia's Soviet Economy*, New York, Prentice-Hall, 1950, p. 322), "By the middle of 1932, however, the struggle over collectivization and the confusion reigning on the hastily organized *kolkhozy* had resulted in the loss of roughly 40 per cent of all horses, over 40 per cent of all cattle, over half of all hogs, and almost two thirds of all sheep and goats, an agricultural catastrophe without parallel in peacetime." Schwartz also states (p. 110) that "Perhaps as many as five million *kulak* families may have been deported to Siberia and the Far North for their resistance." Stalin himself disclosed some of these results in 1934; cf. Isaac Deutscher, *Stalin: a Political Biography* (New York and London, Oxford University Press, 1949), p. 325. For an account of the deaths attendant upon Stalin's policy of liquidating the kulaks see William Henry Chamberlin, *Russia's Iron Age*, Little, Brown, 1934; for example: "famine stalked through great areas . . . levying a 10 per cent death toll on a population of fifty or sixty millions" p. 67.

76. A good discussion of the neglect of agriculture in planning is given by Rostow, *Prospects*, pp. 264ff. See also Chapter 5 *supra*.

77. Edward Szczepanik, "On the Economic Theory of Maoism," FEER, 17 Dec. 1953, pp. 783-785.

78. For figures on the failure of Soviet production under collectivization see the references cited in the discussion of the Khrushchev revelations in Chapter 11.

CHAPTER 7. The Workers

1. This chapter originally appeared in somewhat different form as an article entitled "The 'Working Class' in Communist China," *Problems of Communism*, Vol. 2, Nos. 3/4, 1953.

2. The full text is given in CB #287.

3. Liu Shao-ch'i, *On the Party*, p. 14.

4. This figure for the industrial workers which is still cited and accepted by most officials of the Communist regime is given in the *Short History of the Chinese Labor Movement* by Chang Shao-wen, published serially in the Shanghai *Ta Kung Pao*, Nov. 1950–Feb. 1951. It is translated as CB #108.

5. NCNA, Peking, 24 April 1953. Chang Shao-wen in the work cited above gives the figure 13,000,000.

6. An official Communist survey of the past history of this organization and its first six congresses appeared in the *Daily Worker*, Peking, 7 April 1953; SCMP #556, pp. 28–31.

7. *The Trade Union Law of the People's Republic of China*, Peking, Foreign Languages Press, 1951. Prior to the Seventh Congress of the ACFTU in 1953, the organization was known as the All China Federation of Labor in its English translation. The ACFTU is now the official rendering approved at that congress.

8. For a more detailed discussion of the organization and recent changes in the ACFTU see Chao, *Mass Organizations in Communist China*, pp. 4–61.

9. Cf. William Ayers, "Labor Policy and Factory Management in Communist China," *Annals of the American Academy of Political and Social Science*, Vol. 277, Sept. 1951. This article gives the first good sketch of labor under the Communists to appear in the English language. It is still valid for reference on basic points. TKCK, 4 Jan. 1954, estimates that one ACFTU member in 14 is a member of either the Communist party or the Youth League.

10. On 10 July 1953; NCNA, Peking, 11 July 1953.

11. An interesting example of the attention given to the workers is the amount of space devoted to them in the *Compendium of the Central People's Government Laws and Regulations, 1949–50 (Chung-yang Jen-min Cheng-fu Fa-ling Hui-pien)*, 660 pp. The largest single section, 75

pages, contains 30 decrees on the workers. This is more space than is given to trade, land reform, etc.

12. The job of supporting the "non-productive military and administrative personnel" is stressed by Po I-po, "Report on the Compilation of the Draft National Budget for 1950," Document #14, Research Project on Chinese Communist Economic Policy, Russian Research Center, Harvard University, Cambridge, Mass., 16 Oct. 1951. Of more than passing interest is the fact that by 1952 the bureaucratic apparatus already comprised 2 per cent of the population—almost as large a group as labor itself.

13. "Deviation toward Principle of Punishment Must Be Stopped in the Strengthening of Labor Discipline," *Daily Worker,* Peking, 12 Aug. 1953; SCMP #647, p. 17.

14. Lai Jo-yu, "The Chinese Working Class Today," PC, 16 Nov. 1952.

15. Hsia, *Economic Planning in Communist China,* p. 22.

16. JMJP, 17 Aug. 1952.

17. NCNA, Peking, 12 May 1954; SCMP #807; the exaggeration of such claims is pointed out in Chapter 8.

18. *New York Times,* 16 Aug. 1954, p. 2 (Reuters dispatch from London). For figures on Soviet technicians see Rostow, *Prospects,* p. 208.

19. NCNA, Peking, 13 Aug. 1952.

20. See A Chinese Research Team, "The Wage Policy of Communist China," FEER, 14 May 1953, pp. 644–646. The Central-South Regulations were published in the *Yangtze Daily,* Hankow, 17 Aug. 1952.

21. This wage differentiation and the parallel with the Soviet experience was noted by Ayers; see note 9 above.

22. MB, May 1950, p. 481.

23. NCNA, Peking, 13 Aug. 1952. Interestingly enough, these were the same figures cited by Lai Jo-yu for 1953 at the Third Congress of the World Federation of Trade Unions in Vienna in October 1953.

24. CNA #46, 6 Aug. 1954, p. 7.

25. "The Labour Situation in Free China (Taiwan) and in Communist China," FEER, 30 Oct. 1952, pp. 571–572.

26. Quoted from a 1952 issue of the JMJP by the FEER.

27. "Labor Conditions in Red China," *Information Bulletin,* No. 1, Far Eastern Cultural Service, Hong Kong.

28. JMJP, 15 Oct. 1953.

29. JMJP, editorial of 21 Nov. 1953; JMJP, 11 April 1954.

30. JMJP, 20 Sept. 1953.

31. Quoted by Hsia, *Economic Planning,* p. 63.

32. JMJP, 1 Sept. 1953.

33. "Labor Conditions in Red China," as *supra,* note 27.

34. Quoted by the FEER, 30 Oct. 1952, pp. 571–572.

35. *Ibid.*, p. 572.

36. NCNA, Peking, 17 Sept. 1952.

37. NCNA, Peking, 5 Aug. 1952.

38. JMJP, Peking, 6 Oct. 1951.

39. NCNA, 3 Aug. 1952.

40. NCNA, Peking, 28 April 1954.

41. The JMJP editorial is cited along with other evidence in CNA #31, p. 6.

42. *Ibid.*

43. NCNA, Peking, 11 Jan. 1953. The revised regulations are issued as CB #225.

44. For further documentation and analysis see CNA #31, pp. 2–6.

45. NCNA, Peking, 19 March 1954; SCMP #774, pp. 9–10.

46. This article from the Shanghai *Liberation Daily* is ably summarized by Tillman Durdin in his dispatch from Hong Kong of 26 July 1951 which appeared in the *New York Times* 27 July 1951.

47. *Ch'ang-chiang Jih-pao* (*Yangtze Daily*), Hankow, 16 March 1952.

48. Liu Lan-t'ao, chairman of the North China Administrative Committee, in the JMJP, Peking, 26 Aug. 1952.

49. FEER, 6 Aug. 1953, pp. 162–163.

50. This dispatch as well as many others on the problem of labor discipline is reproduced in SCMP #631. Various aspects of this problem which the regime regards as of grave consequence are gathered in translations and dispatches in SCMP from #605 through #647.

51. *For a Lasting Peace, for a People's Democracy!* Bucharest, Friday, 30 April 1954.

52. JMJP, 18 Feb. 1954, "Explaining the Workers' Court in Production Enterprises"; SCMP #754, pp. 9–11.

53. JMJP, 5 June 1954; SCMP #836, p. 17.

54. JMJP, editorial of 6 June 1954.

55. Peking *Daily Worker*, 12 Aug. 1953.

56. Teng Ying-chao, "China's Women Advance," PC, 1 Dec. 1952.

57. *Lao-tung Pao-huo Kung-tso* (*Work on Protective Labor*), Shanghai, Labor Publishing House, 1952.

58. For an analysis of this point see CNA #31.

CHAPTER 8. Culture and the Intellectuals

1. Published under the title *Problems of Art and Literature* (New York, International Publishers, 1950), p. 13. This pamphlet contains Mao's two talks to the conference of literary and art workers summoned at

Yenan in May 1942. The first talk, on 2 May, laid down the tasks for the small discussion groups; the second, on 23 May, summarized the results of the conference and laid down the policies to be followed.

2. *United States Relations with China* (Washington, Government Printing Office, 1949), Annex 47.

3. Compton, *Mao's China, Party Reform Documents, 1942–1944.* Compton's Introduction, which deals with the tremendous impact of Stalin on Mao during this period, is basic reading for all students of modern China.

4. This discussion draws much from "The Fate of Science in Communist China," *Far Eastern Notes*, No. 4, 14 May 1953, distributed by the External Research Staff, Department of State, Washington, D.C.

5. In the spring of 1954 the Soviets reversed their position on the genetics question, causing further recantation.

6. See p. 4 of work cited in note 4.

7. Ch'en Po-ta, *Mao Tse-tung on the Chinese Revolution* (Peking, Foreign Languages Press, 1953), pp. 2–4.

8. The text is given in Yao Hua, "Songs of New China," PC, 1 May 1952, p. 23. On the cult of Mao see Hutheesing, *The Great Peace,* ch. 3. More recent observation is in the dispatch of John Ridley to the London *Daily Telegraph* dated 20 Aug. 1954. Ridley accompanied the delegation of the British Labor party to China. His story was reprinted in the *New York Times* of 21 Aug.

9. It will be recalled that this is one of the major divisions of governmental functions made by the Communists in their cabinet, where several ministries are grouped under the Committee of Cultural and Educational Affairs.

10. See for example Mao, *On New Democracy, passim.*

11. JMJP, 21 Oct. 1952.

12. *Hsüeh-hsiao-chung-ti Ai-kuo-chu-yi Chiao-yü (Patriotic Education in the Schools)*, Shanghai, Publishing Bureau of Educational Source Material, March 1953. This book is reviewed and summarized by CNA #10, p. 7, which is the source of the quoted summary.

13. CNA #37, pp. 5–7.

14. Liu Shao-ch'i, "Inviolable Sino-Soviet Friendship," speech delivered on 5 Oct. 1949 at the ceremony marking the founding of the Sino-Soviet Friendship Association. Reprinted in *700 Millions for Peace and Democracy* (Peking, Foreign Languages Press, 1950), pp. 9–21.

15. *Far Eastern Notes,* No. 4.

16. Fei Hsiao-t'ung, *Brother Nationalities in Kweichow (Hsiung-ti Min-tso Tsai Kuei-chou)* (Peking, San Lien Book Company, 1951), p. 2.

I am indebted for this reference and for most of the material on the minority groups which follows to Charles Chu of the Institute of Far Eastern Languages at Yale University.

17. Stalin, *Works, 5* (Moscow, Foreign Languages Publishing House, 1953), 33–44 and 184–196.

18. JMJP, 9 Sept. 1953.

19. *Ibid.*

20. JMJP, 20 June 1954.

21. JMJP, 14 Oct. 1953.

22. JMJP, 11 Oct. 1953.

23. *Ibid.*

24. There are very few good studies available in English on the problem of the minorities. Bibliographical notes and a summary treatment are given by John De Francis, "National and Minority Policies," *Annals of the American Academy of Political and Social Science, 277* (Sept. 1951), 146–155. Several studies by the Union Research Institute, Hong Kong (in Chinese), give up to date information gleaned from Communist sources.

25. For these figures, as well as a good general discussion of the Moslem problem, see "Communism and Islam: the Chinese Aspects," CB #195.

26. *Ch'un-chung Jih-pao* (*Masses Daily*), Sian, 21 Oct. 1952.

27. A documented discussion of religion under Red rule is contained in Li I-che, *Chung-kung Tsen-yang Tui-tai Tsung-chiao* (*How Do the Chinese Communists Treat Religion?*), Questions and Answers on Chinese Communist Problems Series, Hong Kong, Union Press, Jan. 1953.

28. *Ibid.*, p. 17.

29. For a good summary of the campaign against the Taoist societies see MB, March 1951, pp. 252–253.

30. P'eng Chen's speech to the Central People's Government Council was released 18 Sept. 1953 by NCNA.

31. MB, April 1952, p. 323.

32. MB, Jan. 1954, p. 56. The various issues of the *Mission Bulletin* tell a story of fanatically directed persecution.

33. A summary of the first two years of the attack upon the church, from which this text is taken, is given by "Barnabas," *Christian Witness in Communist China* (New York, Morehouse-Gorham Company, 1951), p. 37.

34. Chinese Association for the United Nations, *Red China Today* (Taipei, Sept. 1953), pp. 6–7.

35. Hsieh's historical survey of mission work in China is translated as CB #68.

36. Hsiao Ch'ien, " 'Little Buchenwald' Is No More," PC, 16 Jan. 1952, pp. 19–23.

37. "The Crime of the Medical Missions," PC, 1 Feb. 1952, pp. 18–21.

38. "A Catholic University Transformed," PC, 16 Feb. 1952, pp. 21–24.

39. Hsin-hua Yüeh-pao (New China Monthly), Aug. 1953.

40. JMJP, 16 July 1953.

41. The Election Law is reproduced in CB #233; cf. CNA #1, p. 5.

42. Shanghai Ta Kung Pao, 6 Jan. 1952; SCMP #265.

43. Shanghai Ta Kung Pao, 26 May 1952.

44. Although this is reported by the conservative Hua-ch'iao Jih-pao in Hong Kong (7 Oct. 1953), it is based upon quotations from Communist papers and fits into the general pattern of behavior.

45. Accounts of the incident were carried by most Hong Kong and Western newspapers; cf. HKCP, March 1953.

46. NCNA, Peking, 26 July 1953.

47. Chin Ta-k'ai, "Chinese Communist Control of Publications," TKCK, 25 Jan. 1954. This article is a well documented summary of the state of the printed word in China.

48. NCNA, Peking, 26 July 1953; HKCP #45, 1953.

49. Communiqué of State Statistical Bureau, NCNA, Peking, 29 Sept. 1953; CB #262.

50. Hua ch'iao Jih-pao, Hong Kong, 7 Oct. 1953.

51. I made a collection of several hundred of these juvenile propaganda publications and comic books while in Hong Kong in 1952. Of the comic books over 60 per cent contained themes of violence. Less than 3 per cent showed any "deviation" toward family affection.

52. Mao, Problems of Art and Literature, p. 23.

53. T.T., "The Intellectual in the New China," Problems of Communism, 2, No. 2 (1953), 1–7, is a first-rate analysis of this problem, based for the most part on CB #156, which contains many recantations of leftist writers.

54. Chao Ts'ung, "Extraordinary Phenomena in Chinese Communist Art and Literary Circles," TKCK, 7 Dec. 1953.

55. Kuang-ming Jih-pao, Peking, 13 Dec. 1953.

56. JMJP, 6 Oct. 1953.

57. "Music and Politics in Communist China," CB #222.

58. See Wu Tsu-kuang, "Chi Pai-shih—Distinguished People's Artist," PC, 1 Feb. 1953, p. 16.

59. Hutheesing, The Great Peace, pp. 55–62.

60. See Yang Yu, "Kuo Mo-jo—Fighter for Peace," PC, 16 Jan. 1952, pp. 10–12.

61. *Current Affairs Handbook* (*Shih-shih Shou-ts'e*), No. 7, 10 April 1952. The translation is given in CCPR #21, p. 10.

62. JMJP, 17 April 1952. *Songs* (*Ko-ch'ü*) sells for ¥800 per copy.

63. Maria Yen and R. M. McCarthy, *The Umbrella Garden*, New York, Macmillan, 1954.

64. A good analysis of the initial principles of education in Communist China is given in *Far Eastern Notes*, No. 3, 15 April 1953, pp. 2–3.

65. The best summary on higher education in Communist China to date is Chuang Shih, *Higher Education in Communist China.*

66. "Reorganization of Institutes of Higher Learning in China Basically Completed," NCNA, Peking, 16 Dec. 1953; *Far Eastern Notes*, No. 4, p. 5, gives a list of some of the most important name changes.

67. NCNA, Peking, 25 July 1953; SCMP #622.

68. Chuang Shih, *Higher Education in Communist China.*

69. Cf. "The Fierce Face of American Imperialism in 'Founding Schools,'" Shanghai, *Liberation Daily*, 25 July 1952.

70. NCNA, Peking, 29 Sept. 1953; CB #262.

71. For an analysis of the inaccuracy see CNA #8, p. 6. CNA #46, pp. 1–4, gives a comprehensive summary of primary education in Communist China through July 1954.

72. Chuang Shih, *Higher Education in Communist China*, p. 7.

73. JMJP, 17 March 1953.

74. The summary of this general retrenchment in education is given in CNA #46, pp. 1–4.

75. Cf. for example, SCMP #646, pp. 29ff.

76. *Kuang-ming Jih-pao*, 27 Sept. 1953.

77. *Jen-min Chiao-yu* (*People's Education*), Aug. 1953.

78. Cf. for example the NCNA dispatch of 25 Aug. 1953 from Peking entitled "13,000 College Graduates Proceed to Construction Posts According to Government Distribution of Jobs."

79. *Chung-kuo Ch'ing-nien* (*China Youth*), No. 13, 1 Aug. 1952.

80. A "Language Reform" supplement to the *Kuang-ming Jih-pao*, Peking, 17 March 1954. It admitted the failure of the Chi Chien-hua method and that to date no successful method for reforming the Chinese system of writing has been devised. A historical survey of the problem constitutes the whole issue of CNA #33.

81. Cf. E. S. Kirby, *Introduction to the Economic History of China*, chs. 2–5.

82. Quoted by Ch'ien Chun-jui, "The Key to the Reform of Higher Education," HH, Vol. 5, No. 1 (1 Nov. 1951); CB #169.

83. Chuang Shih, *Higher Education in Communist China*, p. 36. The materials on the Thought Reform or Ideological Remolding Movement are abundant. Outstanding are the translated texts of official documents with careful introductions by Howard L. Boorman in the Current Background Series. These include "The Communists and the Intellectuals: Stage One," CB #169; "Stage Two," CB #182; and "Stage Three," CB #213; "Mobilization of the Scientists in Communist China," Pt. 1, CB #153; Pt. 2, CB #257; "The Campaign against Hu Shih," CB #167; "The Case of Liang Shu-ming," CB #185; "The New Orthodoxy in Literature," CB #203; "The Party Line in Literature and the Arts," CB #156; "The Case of Wu Hsun," CB #113; and "New Realities and New Tasks," CB #282. A concise summary of the movement is given by Tsui Shu-chin, *From Academic Freedom to Brainwashing*, Taipei, China Culture Publishing Foundation, 1953. Chin Ta-k'ai, *The Ideological Reform of the Chinese Communists (Chung-kung-ti Ssu-hsiang Kai-tsao)*, Communist China Problem Research Series (Hong Kong, Union Press, 1953; in Chinese), gives an excellent analysis of the whole movement, linking it to the party reform in Yenan during the second World War. T.T., "The Intellectual in the New China," *Problems of Communism*, 2, No. 2, (1953), 1–7, discusses the relation of ideological reform to writers and artists. Most eloquent is the collection of confessions published by the Communists themselves in four volumes, *Thought Reform Documents (Ssu-hsiang Kai-tsao Wen-hsüan)*, Peking, *Kuang-ming Jih-pao*, 1952.

84. "The Case of Wu Hsun," CB #113.

85. Cf. HH, 16 Aug. and 1 Sept. 1951.

86. "The Campaign against Hu Shih," CB #167.

87. HH, 16 March 1952; CB #179.

88. Tsui Shu-chin, *From Academic Freedom to Brainwashing*, pp. 5–10, lists some of the outstanding professors who confessed their "sins."

89. *Ibid.*, p. 5.

90. Derk Bodde, *Peking Diary* (New York, Henry Schuman, 1950), p. 184.

91. *Ibid.*

92. For further discussion of the stereotyped character of the confessions, see CB #169, p. 2; and Tsui Shu-chin, *From Academic Freedom to Brainwashing*, p. 14.

93. Tsui, p. 20.

94. Cf. FEER, 30 July 1953, p. 135.

95. JMJP, 25 March 1954.

96. Ch'ien Tuan-sheng, "To Study for Self-Reform So As Better to

Serve the Fatherland," JMJP, 6 Nov. 1951; translated in CB #169. Recantations frequently carry such suggestions of double talk as appear in Ch'ien's last paragraph.

97. An excellent description of the intellectual climate at Peita is provided by B. I. Schwartz, *Chinese Communism and the Rise of Mao,* chs. 1 and 2.

98. I had the privilege of studying Chinese art and architecture with Liang Ssu-ch'eng when he was at Yale. The bitter tragedy of people in his position did not really hit me until I had read his confession.

99. Liang Ssu-ch'eng, "Whom Have I Served for the Past Twenty Years?" ("Wo Wei Shui Fu-wu-le Erh-shih-yü Nien"), *Thought Reform Documents, 2,* 31–39.

100. I also had the pleasure of studying with Professor Lo Ch'ang-p'ei, whose calligraphy hangs framed over my desk. He has made soul-baring confessions and denunciations of his pleasant hours with us at Yale.

101. FEER, 18 Dec. 1952, p. 777. The summary and excerpted translation of Fung Yu-lan's recantation is concluded with the very apt comment by the editors of the FEER: "This is so far the finest essay that has been published on the art of turning oneself inside out."

102. Moraes, *Report on Mao's China,* p. 34.

103. T.T., "The Intellectual in the New China," *Problems of Communism, 2,* No. 2 (1953), p. 3.

CHAPTER 9. Terror

1. John Ridley, "China Revisited: Changes of Eight Years," *New York Times Magazine,* 29 Aug. 1954, pp. 5ff.

2. A.R., "Jottings on the Communist Press," MB, March 1951, p. 246.

3. On "the role of terror in Stalin's formula of government" Fainsod's *How Russia Is Ruled,* ch. 13, "Terror as a System of Power," is excellent. It is useful for comparing the material discussed in the present chapter with the experiences of the Soviet Union under Stalin.

4. The text of the regulations is given in CB #101. There is a summary of their application and implications in a dispatch filed by Marguerite Higgins from Hong Kong, *New York Herald Tribune,* 1 Oct. 1951.

5. JMJP, 25 March 1951.

6. JMJP, 3 April 1951; cf. MB, May 1951, pp. 427–428.

7. For example, a detailed outline was presented by Liao K'ai-lung in an article entitled "How to Hold an Accusation Meeting," *Current Affairs Handbook (Shih-shih Shou-ts'e),* No. 12, 5 April 1951.

8. "Speech made by H. E. Dr. Tingfu F. Tsiang, Chairman of the

Chinese Delegation, in the General Debate of the Sixth Session of the United Nations General Assembly 12 November 1951," English translation, mimeographed by the Chinese Delegation to the United Nations.

9. See Tillman Durdin's dispatch in the *New York Times*, 30 July 1951.

10. *Yangtze Daily*, Hankow, 13 Dec. 1951; CB #157.

11. *Nan-fang Jih-pao* (*Southern Daily*), 18 Sept. 1951; CB #124.

12. The progress reports for the first year of the regime which contain these figures are given in CB #39.

13. Marguerite Higgins, *New York Herald Tribune*, 1 Oct. 1951.

14. *Nan-fang Jih-pao* (*Southern Daily*), 18 Sept. 1951.

15. NCNA, Peking, 27 Sept. 1952; CB #218.

16. Shanghai *Liberation Daily*, 25–28 April 1953, for example, reported on the rounding up and execution of "remnant counterrevolutionaries."

17. *The Common Program and Other Documents*, p. 4.

18. Lo Jui-ching, "The Mighty Movement for the Suppression of Counterrevolutionaries," JMJP, 11 Oct. 1951; CB #171.

19. Teng Tzu-hui, "The Initiation of the Policy of Reform through Labor in the Central-South Region," *Ch'ang-chiang Jih-pao* (*Yangtze Daily*), Hankow, 13 Dec. 1951; CB #157.

20. NCNA, Peking, 17 July 1952. For the text of the measures see my *China and the West, Cultural Collision* (New Haven, Far Eastern Publications, 1954), pp. 202–203.

21. For text and comments on these measures see CB #216.

22. FEER, 30 Oct. 1952, p. 572. Interestingly enough, this passage from Fu's speech was not released in the NCNA dispatch to the outside world; cf. CB #219.

23. *New York Times*, 26 Nov. 1953.

24. *Ibid.*, 24 April 1954.

25. "I Was a Slave Laborer at the Fatshan Airfield," *Chung-nan Jih-pao* (*Central-South Daily*), Hong Kong, 28 March 1954; HKCP #60, 1954.

26. *Kwangsi Jih-pao* (*Kwangsi Daily*), 9 Jan. 1952. The full article is translated and reproduced in CB #171 along with other accounts of forced labor from the Communist press.

27. *New York Times*, 22 Oct. 1952.

28. "Slave Labor on China Mainland," compiled and published by the Chinese Federation of Labor, Taipei, Taiwan, spring 1954; mimeographed.

29. See, for example, *China's Railways*, Peking, Foreign Languages Press, 1952.

30. *China Handbook* (New York, Rockport Press, 1950), p. 617.

31. The report of Minister of Railways T'eng Tai-yüan was printed in the JMJP, 15 Nov. 1953; cf. CB #274.

32. Chang Kia-ngau, *China's Struggle for Railroad Development* (New York, John Day, 1943), p. 76.

33. For an excellent summary of railroad development under the Communists and documented appraisal see CNA #32, pp. 2–5.

34. "Slave Labor on China Mainland," p. 2.

35. CB #274; compare D. N. Rowe, *China among the Powers* (New York, Harcourt, Brace, 1945), pp. 112–116.

36. Cf. a Reuters dispatch from New Delhi in the *New York Times* of 3 Feb. 1953.

37. PC, 16 Jan. 1953, p. 31.

38. FEER, 15 Oct. 1953, pp. 488–489.

39. Fu Tso-yi, "Successes in China's Water Conservancy Work," PC, 1 Oct. 1952, p. 19.

40. Kao Shih-shan, "The Third Stage of the Huai River Project," PC, 1 Feb. 1953, pp. 13–15.

41. *Ibid.*

42. Su Ming, "A Victory on the Yangtze River," PC, 1 July 1952, pp. 28–29.

43. *New York Times,* 23 April 1952.

44. Fu Tso-yi, "Successes in China's Water Conservancy Work."

45. NCNA, Peking, 15 May 1954; SCMP #810, p. 29.

46. Hutheesing, *The Great Peace,* Pt. 2, ch. 3; Moraes, *Report on Mao's China,* ch. 7.

47. Hutheesing, pp. 112–113.

48. CNA #48. This whole issue is devoted to the study of floods, droughts, and locusts in China since the Communists came to power.

49. CNA #26, p. 6. Pages 6 and 7 of this issue of CNA contain a full analysis of the reports on the Water Conservancy Conference.

50. NCNA, Wuhan, 12 Aug. 1954.

51. "This Week in Free China," weekly bulletin of the Chinese News Service, New York, 31 Aug. 1954. On Minister Hsieh's figures see *New York Times,* 30 Sept. 1954.

52. CNA #48, pp. 6–7.

53. Associated Press, Geneva, 17 Aug. 1954; *New York Times,* 18 Aug. 1954.

54. See, for example, the editorial in the JMJP of 6 Jan. 1954.

55. Tientsin *Ta Kung Pao,* 6 Feb. 1954; SCMP #751.

56. The matter of treatment in Communist prisons has not been taken

up here because there is a voluminous literature in English on the subject. Items worthy of mention are R. T. Bryan, "I Came Back from a Red Death Cell," *Saturday Evening Post,* 17, 24, 31 Jan. and 7 Feb. 1953; J. D. Hayes, "China under the Communists," *The American Oxonian, 41,* No. 2 (April 1954), 85–89; and "Prison and the New Man," CNA #25, p. 7.

57. John Ridley, "China Revisited: Changes of Eight Years," *New York Times Magazine,* 29 Aug. 1954.

CHAPTER 10. The Conduct of Foreign Relations

1. Robert C. Binkley, *Realism and Nationalism, 1852–1871* (New York, Harper, 1935), p. 176.

2. For Chou's diagnosis and examples of Red China's "one voice" see CNA #37, pp. 2–3.

3. Mao Tse-tung, "Revolutionary Forces of the World Rally to Combat Imperialist Aggression," *For a Lasting Peace, for a People's Democracy!* 1 Nov. 1948; quoted by H. Arthur Steiner, "Mainsprings of Chinese Communist Foreign Policy," *American Journal of International Law, 44,* No. 1 (Jan. 1950), 89. Steiner's analysis is first rate. It is to be regretted that it did not have wider circulation than that offered by a learned journal.

4. FEER, 8 Jan. 1953, p. 36. The implication of the statement is pointed out by the editor of the FEER.

5. *The Common Program and Other Documents.*

6. *China Digest, 7,* No. 1 (Oct. 1949), Supplement, p. 12.

7. NCNA, Peking, 30 Aug. 1954; SCMP #880.

8. For a listing of the countries which have recognized Peking and of their representatives in Mao's capital see CB #266. This listing is official as of 1 Oct. 1953.

9. *Ibid.*

10. SCMP #881, pp. 12–13; #882, pp. 13–15.

11. For more detailed descriptions of the problems involved for the British see the issues of the FEER, especially those of the summer of 1952 when they began to realize the fate of their Chinese investments. Probably the size of the British investment in China had most to do with the fact that they suffered most. Actually violence against American representatives in China was much more intense.

12. The Sino-Japanese trade agreement involving more than £60,000,-000 sterling was signed in Peking, 29 Oct. 1953; NCNA, Peking, 30 Oct. 1953. On the relaxation of Japanese trade restrictions with Communist China see the *New York Times,* 31 Jan. 1953.

13. United Press report from Colombo, 2 Oct. 1954.

14. For a detailed listing of Peking's trade agreements and an analysis of developments up to October 1953 see Yen Yi, "Chinese Communist Foreign Trade in the Last Four Years," TKCK, 2 Oct. 1953. Yen calls the agreements "hunger export" agreements and gives ample justification. On the trade with Ceylon see E. S. Kirby, FEER, 2 July 1953. A good analysis of the political overtones of the barter agreement for rice to India is given in CB #80.

15. See the 1 Oct. 1953 Reuters dispatch in *New York Times*, 2 Oct. 1953.

16. When I visited Hong Kong in the summer of 1952, the blockade of information from the mainland was already fairly effective. I had great difficulty in procuring copies of many of the more important Chinese Communist journals. A good summary of the effectiveness of the information blockade and the problems faced in trying to procure mainland publications is given by Tillman Durdin in his dispatch published in the *New York Times* 13 Dec. 1953.

17. For the original dispatch see SCMP #571, pp. 31–35; for the full text SCMP #580, pp. 23–24.

18. The charges of germ warfare, and those of murdering Chinese children lodged against the Catholic sisters, are only samples of the Communist kind of fiction employed in *People's China*. As in the news releases of NCNA, self-criticism is omitted. For a more detailed description of how the Reds manage to write stories about the enthusiasm of the various sectors of the society for Communist rule see Liu Shaw-tong, *Out of Red China*.

19. Sundarlal, *China Today* (Allahabad, India, Hindustani Cultural Society, July 1952), p. vii.

20. K. T. Shah, *The Promise That Is New China* (Bombay, Vora and Co., 1953), Bibliographic Note.

21. U Kiaw Min, *Through the Iron Curtain via the Back Door*.

22. Raja Hutheesing, *The Great Peace*. See also U Kiaw Min, *Through the Iron Curtain*.

23. On the blackmail of the missionaries the issues of MB from 1950 forward are eloquent.

24. For a listing and description of the makeup of the delegation and their treatment in Moscow as given by *Pravda*, 13 April 1949, see SPT, 15 May 1949, p. 316.

25. The texts of the documents as well as the texts of reports and speeches were reproduced as special supplements to *People's China*, 16 Oct. and 1 Nov. 1952. For the Communists' appraisal of the importance of this conference, see SCMP #429.

26. An account is given in SCMP #890.

27. NCNA, Peking, 21 Sept. 1954.

28. See "Figures That Will Make the Warmongers Tremble," CCPR #2, for a list of the various petitions and the Communist claims as to the number of signatures collected.

29. Communist China's part in the 1953 peace offensive is documented in CCPR #45, pp. 2–26.

30. For accounts of the use which Red China made of the visit see SCMP #875ff.

31. The *Economist* article was reprinted in full in the FEER, 19 Aug. 1954, pp. 230–231. The releases of NCNA throughout and following the Attlee visit bore out the *Economist's* predictions in almost every detail. These releases are published in SCMP beginning with #875.

32. K. M. Panikkar, "Yenan—Cradle of the Revolution," PC, 1 Oct. 1951, pp. 16–18.

33. An excellent survey of this technique of utilizing foreigners to add authenticity to the various publications and propaganda claims of the regime is given in CCPR #35(a), "How Foreigners Were Made to Serve the Chinese Communists in the Field of Foreign Propaganda," pp. 3–40. See also CB #207, "Some American Views of Chinese Communism."

34. See SCMP #883 through #890.

35. A full translation is given in the *Mission Bulletin*, March 1951, pp. 242–245.

36. General W. K. Harrison and some of the other United Nations negotiators at Panmunjom have reported to the press in detail on the Chinese Communist and North Korean techniques of negotiation.

37. A survey of the situation was carried by the *New York Times* on 14 Nov. 1951. An editorial in the same paper on 20 July 1951 is also eminently worth reading.

38. *New York Times*, 13 Jan. 1953.

39. Steiner, "Mainsprings," p. 99.

40. *Ibid.*, pp. 77ff. Steiner boils Chinese Communist foreign policy as of late 1949 down to six major theses. Although, as indicated above, most of his analysis is still valid, certain theses have since been added by the Mao regime.

41. Jo Shui, "Six Hundred Million," JMJP, 7 Aug. 1954; SCMP #890, pp. 31–33.

42. For example, see the report of Chou's speech of 8 Oct. 1953 in the *New York Times*, 9 Oct. 1953.

43. CCPR #45, p. 2.

44. Chang Chih-chung in his report to the 24th meeting of the CPGC; NCNA, Peking, 12 Sept. 1953.

45. Welcoming Peking's first ambassador on 30 Aug. 1954, the Viet Minh vice-premier stated, "The People's Republic of China is a major power in the world and a pillar of peace in Asia." He then went on to emphasize Red China's great military strength. SCMP #880.

46. CDSP, 5, No. 17, p. 26. Benjamin Schwartz maintains ("China and the Soviet Theory of People's Democracy," *Problems of Communism, 3,* No. 5, pp. 8–15) that while the Soviet accords to Peking a recognition of leadership in methods of seizing power Moscow insists it alone is to play the leader in determining the method for achieving socialism.

47. Lin Po-chu, "Leninism Has Lit Up the Road of Struggle for National Liberation in Asia," JMJP, 21 Jan. 1953.

48. NCNA, Peking, 9 Dec. 1952. For the Chinese Reds "peace," "liberation," and "democracy" come only under Communist rule.

49. In a speech to the meeting of the World Federation of Trade Unions in Peking; translated in the *Mission Bulletin,* Jan. 1950, p. 85.

50. Yeh Chien-ying, "The International Situation Today," 6 Oct. 1950; CB #41. The United Nations command in Korea could hardly have asked for a clearer statement of Red China's intention to enter the Korean War.

51. Lu Ting-i, for example, made this point in a speech on 1 July 1951; CB #89.

52. Ton Duc Thang, 21 Jan. 1954 as reported by NCNA; SCMP #734.

53. For further detail on this strategy as applied in China see my article "Communism—the New Imperialism," *Institute of Social Studies Bulletin, 1,* No. 4 (Jan. 1952), 37ff. To date there has been little research on the role Communist insurrection played in fostering the corruption which became a major cause of the fall of the Nationalist government in China. The Communist strategy for seizure of power in economically underdeveloped areas involves not only an appreciation of the usually unstable and unpopular base of their political institutions but also an awareness of the ease with which corruption can be promoted in a situation of military crisis. Red guerrillas in the areas of Asia work on the principle of "twenty times mobilization"; that is, it takes a minimum of twenty formally organized and equipped troops to protect the countryside against one armed guerrilla. This is, of course, usually too high a price for an independent government to pay, and as the British have found out in Malaya, it turns a colony into a great liability.

54. *New York Times,* 29 Sept. 1954.

55. For an account of Russian arms in Indo-China see the AP dispatch

in the *New York Times* of 25 Nov. 1952 from Washington based on State and Defense Department releases.

56. *New York Times,* 5 May 1954. The Chinese Reds following their victory on the mainland, however, gave much credit to the "unselfish material assistance" of the Soviet Union.

57. Nehru, apparently taking Chou at his word, passed along Chou's statement to Sir John Kotelawala, prime minister of Ceylon, stressing his faith in Chou's sincerity; special dispatch from Colombo published in the *New York Times* of 30 June 1954.

58. See the eyewitness UP dispatch of Louis Guilbert from Hanoi of that date.

59. Many of these statements are reproduced in SCMP #870 through #890.

60. Henry R. Lieberman's dispatch from Hanoi in the *New York Times* of 26 May 1954 describes these many parallels to Peking's dictatorship. With the setting up of a new Communist state in northern Viet Nam in the fall of 1954 it became only a matter of time until a campaign against "counterrevolutionaries" and those who had colluded with "French imperialism" would lead to mass executions. In October hundreds of thousands of refugees were streaming south from "liberated Viet Nam."

61. See Lieberman's dispatches in the *New York Times* in July and August 1954.

62. For an analysis of this see CCPR #37.

63. This statement attributed to Mao is quoted by K. P. Karunakarun, *India in World Affairs* (New York, Oxford University Press, 1952), p. 101.

64. NCNA editorial, *China Digest,* 16 Sept. 1949, p. 3.

65. PC, 1 Dec. 1950, Supplement, p. 9, "Sino-Indian Exchange of Notes on Tibet."

66. NCNA, Peking, 20 Oct. 1953.

67. Chester Bowles, *Ambassador's Report* (New York, Harper, 1954), *passim.*

68. See *Far Eastern Notes,* No. 2, "Food for India: US Shipments and Communist Claims"; also CCPR #37, pp. 2–7, and the article in *Shih-chieh Chih-shih (World Knowledge),* "Who Is the Real Friend of the Indian People?" Vol. *23,* No. 17, 5 May 1951.

69. The text of the joint statement issued in New Delhi 28 June 1954 is printed in the *New York Times,* 29 June 1954, p. 4. The "Five Principles" were first embodied in the Sino-Indian treaty of April 1954 regarding Tibet. A penetrating analysis of how meaningless these principles are as far as the Chinese Reds are concerned is given by Hou Sheng, "A Critique of the So-called Five Principles," TKCK, 4 Oct. 1954, pp. 24–25.

70. SCMP #885, p. 41.

71. For an account see CB #186. The Reds curtailed their Hate America Campaign in the one province but continued it throughout the rest of China.

72. Huan Hsin-yi, "The Foreign Policy of the People's Republic of China during the Last Two Years," translated in SPT, 15 Dec. 1951, pp. 667–677. Again for "forces of democracy and peace," read "Communists."

73. *New York Times,* 9 Dec. 1952. AP dispatch from London quoting Radio Peking as monitored there.

74. *New York Times,* Tokyo dispatch of 30 July 1954 quoting Radio Peking.

75. NCNA, Peking, 19 Sept. 1954; SCMP #892, p. 25.

76. See the account of the United Nations proceedings in the *New York Times* of 29 Sept. 1954.

77. NCNA, Peking, 23 Sept. 1954; SCMP #895.

78. FEER, 26 Aug. 1954, p. 262.

79. For a survey of this attempt to win back the overseas Chinese see TKCK, 30 Nov. 1953.

80. Hu yü-chih, "Overseas Chinese Gloriously Take Part in Management of State Affairs," NCNA, 6 Sept. 1954; SCMP #885.

81. NCNA, Canton, 21 Nov. 1952.

82. SCMP #693.

83. *New York Times,* 30 Sept. 1954. Nehru's brother-in-law shows a realistic appreciation of Peking's intention to use the overseas Chinese for its expansionist policies; see *The Great Peace,* pp. 63–75.

84. On the plight of the overseas Chinese who do not want to support the Mao regime the editorial in the FEER of 5 Aug. 1954 entitled "Peking's Constitution and Overseas Chinese" is especially good.

85. *China Digest,* 16 Sept. 1949, p. 4.

86. FEER, 22 April 1954, p. 516.

87. See the AP dispatch from New Delhi of 29 April 1954 published in the *New York Times* the following day, which gives most of the details. Further details were released by NCNA throughout the first two weeks of May.

88. A lengthy special dispatch from Kalimpong, India, the terminus of the road into Tibet, published in the *New York Times* of 23 Oct. 1951 gives details as reported by refugee lamas.

89. See the dispatch from Kalimpong, India, published in the *New York Times* of 24 April 1952.

90. *New York Times,* 26 Nov. 1952; special dispatch from Kalimpong.

91. Materials on Tibet under Communist rule are rather meager. There

are of course the glowing reports of the happy life under Communism in the official Communist publications, and these offer a bit of information; for example, "Documents and Speeches on the Peaceful Liberation of Tibet," PC, Vol. 3, No. 12, 16 June 1951. Important documents including the Sino-Tibetan treaties and agreements are contained in CB #31 and #76. See also Werner Levi, "Tibet under Chinese Communist Rule," *Far Eastern Survey,* Vol. 23, No. 1.

92. On the Sino-Korean agreement see SCMP #694 and the *New York Times* of 25 Nov. 1953. S. B. Thomas, "The Chinese Communists' Economic and Cultural Agreement with North Korea," *Pacific Affairs,* 27, No. 1, pp. 61–65, stresses the Communist intention to turn North Korea into a showplace but fails to spell out the implications of the agreement for the future of a united Korea.

93. CDSP, 6, No. 23, p. 34; *Pravda,* 5 June 1954.

94. NCNA, Peking, 8 July 1954.

95. The relationship of the Chinese Reds to the Communist movement in Malaya is discussed by Edward Hunter in *Brainwashing in Red China,* as well as in the various issues of the FEER over the past four years. For a recent account see a Singapore dispatch in the *New York Times* of 3 Oct. 1954.

96. Even the *New York Times,* usually objective in its reporting of the news, has assisted the cause of presenting Communist China as independent. It frequently headlines, as front page news, stories of the opinions of other people who forecast a split or see a difference. For example, 29 Oct. 1951, 8 Aug. 1951, or 7 March 1953.

97. SCMP #890.

98. Mr. Starobin spoke at Yale University 4 May 1954 at his own request. The major purpose of his appearance was to champion recognition of Red China by the United States. "The United States cannot stand in the way of history," he warned.

CHAPTER 11. China and the Soviet Union

1. This chapter originally appeared in somewhat different form as an article entitled "Pattern of Sino-Soviet Relations" in *Problems of Communism,* 3, No. 3, pp. 5–13.

2. Some of the struggles between Stalin and the Chinese Communist leaders in the realm of ideology are discussed in detail by Benjamin I. Schwartz, *Chinese Communism and the Rise of Mao.* Harold Isaacs, *The Tragedy of the Chinese Revolution* (London, Jonathan Cape, 1937), provides a better understanding of the manner in which the struggle in China was subordinated to the Stalin-Trotsky feud. Those who have con-

centrated their attention on the internal history of the Chinese Communist party have frequently failed to appreciate the extent to which developments, especially those of 1927, were subordinated to what Stalin considered the major struggle. The China issue was not the central one so far as he was concerned. Again, those who have concentrated exclusively on the Chinese scene have tended to give too much credit to Mao on the score of originality. His formulae for utilizing the peasants had been spelled out by Lenin. On this see K. A. Wittfogel, "The Influence of Leninism-Stalinism on China," *Annals of the American Academy of Political and Social Science, 277* (Sept. 1951), 22–34. In the opinion of Wittfogel, which I share, Mao and Maoism have been given far too much build-up on the score of originality; and this has contributed to the "Titoist" speculation and the failure to devote sufficient attention to the Communist organizational structure.

3. These two selections are given by Henry C. Wei, *Mao Tse-tung's "Lean-to-one-side" Policy,* Studies in Chinese Communism, Series 2, No. 1, University of Southern California, 1952, pp. 4–10. This monograph deserves wider circulation than its limited edition made possible.

4. *China Digest,* Hong Kong, 1 Jan. 1950, p. 4.

5. For an extensive analysis of Sino-Soviet relations see Rostow, *Prospects,* chs. 10 through 12. I have benefited much from talks with Rostow and his associates on this topic.

6. For texts of the Moscow documents see CB #62. The pamphlet *The Sino-Soviet Treaty and Agreements* (Peking, Foreign Languages Press, 1951) interestingly enough did not contain the agreements on Sinkiang.

7. Schwartz, *Chinese Communism and the Rise of Mao,* p. 4.

8. This article by Mao which appeared in the JMJP on 9 March 1953 was subsequently reprinted in all the major Chinese Communist journals as an epoch-making pronouncement on the death of Stalin. For example, this excerpt can be found in *Chung-kuo Ch'ing-nien (China Youth),* No. 6, 1953, p. 6.

9. R. C. North, *Kuomintang and Chinese Communist Elites,* p. 72.

10. JMJP, editorial, 15 Sept. 1953.

11. FEER, 15 April 1954, p. 459.

12. G. K. Reddy, Peking correspondent of the *Times of India,* reported on 1 Oct. 1954 that there were far more Soviet experts then in China than the year before. See the UP dispatch from New Delhi of that date.

13. NCNA, Peking, 15 Sept. 1953.

14. FEER, 10 Dec. 1953, p. 747, and UP dispatch from Tokyo 13 Oct. 1954.

15. NCNA, Peking, 5 Feb. 1954.

16. "Painless Childbirth," *China Reconstructs,* May–June 1953, pp. 45–47. For more details see SCMP #383.

17. JMJP, editorial, 14 Feb. 1954.

18. The high importance attached to this by the central government was indicated in an NCNA report from Peking on 24 April 1953 stating that the 176th meeting of the cabinet that day was devoted to hearing a report on cultural study in the "People's Democracies" by the head of the Chinese Cultural and Educational Delegation.

19. JMJP, 5 March 1954. On the changes in the educational system see Chuang Shih, *Higher Education in Communist China.*

20. The Communists have not hesitated to make this point themselves. For example, it was embodied in an English language broadcast from Peking of 2 Oct. 1953.

21. For a documented study of the promotion of Sino-Soviet friendship and cultural relations see CCPR #32.

22. The great importance attached to this "unprecedented achievement" was indicated in the NCNA dispatch broadcast by Peking radio 25 Nov. 1953.

23. NCNA, Peking, 9 March and Moscow, 11 March 1954.

24. "The Peking-Moscow Through Train," *Chung Hsüeh-sheng (Middle School Student),* April 1954; SCMP #795.

25. NCNA, Peking, 23 Sept. 1954; SCMP #895.

26. Commodities traded in 1953 are listed in the FEER, 3 Sept. 1953, p. 319. Commodities for 1954 were given in an NCNA dispatch from Moscow of 24 Jan. 1954 covering the commodity agreement signed there the day before.

27. NCNA, English language broadcast from Peking, 1 Oct. 1954.

28. Peking, *Kuang-ming Jih-pao,* 27 Feb. 1954.

29. *Ibid.,* 13 Aug. 1954.

30. See H. L. Boorman, "Chronology of Sino-Soviet Relations," *Problems of Communism, 3,* No. 3, p. 16.

31. Li Po-ti, "Soviet Experts Help China Build," *China Reconstructs,* July–August, 1953, p. 11.

32. *Pravda,* 21 Jan. 1954, p. 3; CDSP, *6,* No. 3, p. 7.

33. Two articles appearing in the *People's Daily* in May 1953 left no doubt about whose advice the Chinese comrades were to follow. The first, on 21 May, by Wang Ching-yü, was entitled "Why the Old China Could Not Be Industrialized"; the second, on 22 May, by Chi Yün, entitled "How China Proceeds with the Task of Industrialization," explains

the sacrifices that must be made for the sake of heavy industry. These are, of course, in line with the "general line of the state" laid down by the Central Committee of the party later in 1953.

34. *Pravda*, 2 May 1953. I am indebted to Professor Frederick C. Barghoorn of Yale University for this translation and for the reference.

35. *Pravda*, 10 Oct. 1953; CDSP, *5*, No. 43, p. 8.

36. CDSP, *5*, No. 51, p. 10. Benjamin Schwartz ("China and the Soviet Theory of People's Democracy," *Problems of Communism, 3*, No. 5, pp. 8–15) believes that the Kremlin and Peking have reserved what appear to be contradictory positions on the nature of a "people's democracy" for China, and that the Soviet has been trying to force its own interpretation of the term as well as the term itself upon the unwilling Chinese comrades, who prefer the term "new democracy." The manipulation of such formulae, Schwartz feels, furnishes us with an index (he does not indicate its nature), admittedly unsatisfactory, to political intent and tensions in the Communist world. In arguing that there is tension between Mao and Moscow Schwartz ignores most of the strong ties in the realm of practical politics discussed in this chapter, or discusses them in terms of "due obeisance." He states that Mao's "claims to have introduced theoretical innovations have not been conceded" by Moscow, a point which is somewhat open to question merely on the basis of the reviews of Mao's works in the Soviet press such as that listed above. It is to be wondered whether Mao himself or some of his interpreters have advanced such claims. Schwartz nevertheless raises interesting points in the realm of ideology concerning the Sino-Soviet tie, and since this is a field in which he is eminently qualified, his observations command attention.

37. NCNA, Moscow, 28 Aug. 1954; SCMP #881.

38. Professor Barghoorn also called my attention to this fact. See, for example, Slogan No. 5 for May Day 1953 in the Soviet Union: "Fraternal greetings to the great Chinese people, etc.," CDSP, *5*, No. 15, p. 5.

39. *Pravda*, 14 Nov. 1952, p. 4. Professor Barghoorn again.

40. JMJP, 26 Dec. 1953.

41. Statements hailing the "victory" in Korea were made at the 24th meeting of the Government Council on 12 Sept. 1953. The representative of the overseas Chinese stated: "This victory is inseparable from the support of our great neighbor the Soviet Union." NCNA, Peking, 12 Sept. 1953.

42. *Kuang-ming Jih-pao*, Peking, 22 Jan. 1954.

43. CDSP, *5*, Nos. 37–39.

44. NCNA, Peking, 15 Sept. 1953.

45. CDSP, *5*, No. 39. On collectivized agriculture as an organized

method of control rather than a method to increase production see Naum Jasny, *The Socialized Agriculture of the U.S.S.R.*, Stanford University Press, 1939.

46. For example, a glowing account of Soviet collective agriculture was published in the *Jen-min Shou-ts'e* (*People's Handbook*), Shanghai, 1 July 1952. It was entitled "The Happy Life of the Soviet Farmers Is Our Example."

47. For a good account of the decision see CNA #23. More details are given in Chapter 6.

48. On Chinese trade agreements and food shipments see FEER, 3 Sept. 1953, p. 319; NCNA, Moscow dispatch 24 Jan. 1954.

49. NCNA, Wuhan, 28 Jan. 1954 dispatch talks of 110 refrigerator cars produced there in 1953 and sets higher goals for 1954. For trade statistics in meat products see Chapter 6.

50. *New York Times,* Hong Kong dispatches of 20 and 21 Sept. 1953.

51. See the United Nations dispatch to the *New York Times,* 19 Jan. 1954, and NCNA dispatches of 16–20 Sept. 1953.

52. NCNA, Peking, 15 Sept. 1953.

53. In the article cited in note 33 above, Chi Yün admitted that at the time of the Soviet Revolution 42.1 per cent of Russia's economy was industrial, while at the time of China's Communist revolution only 10 per cent was industrial. He goes on to point out that although India has developed some industry it does not produce capital goods and therefore still has a colonial rather than an industrialized economy.

54. Li Po-ti, *op. cit.,* note 31 above.

55. JMJP, Peking, 27 Dec. 1953.

56. For an appraisal of China's potential as a world power see D. N. Rowe, *China among the Powers.*

57. FEER, 10 Dec. 1953, p. 747.

58. For a good analysis of the developing hostility toward the Soviet see CNA #14, pp. 5–6.

59. FEER, 21 Aug. 1953.

60. See "Soviet Imperialism along China's Borders: I. Outer Mongolia," *Far Eastern Notes,* No. 6, 5 Aug. 1953.

61. The texts of the joint Sino-Soviet communiqués as released by NCNA on 12 Nov. 1954 are given in SCMP #906. Chinese editorial and propaganda interpretations are given in SCMP #907 through #912.

62. On the recent disintegration of social conditions and especially on the increasing drunkenness and juvenile delinquency, see the series of articles by Harrison E. Salisbury in the *New York Times* beginning 19 Sept. 1954, especially the article of 1 Oct. 1954.

63. Dean Acheson, "Letter of Transmittal," *United States Relations with China,* Washington, United States Government Printing Office, 1949.

64. John K. Fairbank devotes a chapter of his *United States and China* (Cambridge, Harvard University Press, 1948) to "The Authoritarian Tradition." For a more extensive treatment of the Chinese despotism see Max Weber, *The Religion of China* (Glencoe, Ill., Free Press, 1951), translated by Hans H. Gerth.

65. On the matter of the conquest dynasties see the definitive "General Introduction" to Karl A. Wittfogel and Feng Chia-sheng, *History of Chinese Society (Liao),* New York, Macmillan, 1949.

66. For a discussion of "good" versus "bad" nationalism as interpreted by the Chinese Reds see H. A. Steiner, "Mainsprings of Chinese Communist Foreign Policy," *American Journal of International Law, 44,* No. 1 (Jan. 1950), 74–77.

67. For an account of the impact of the Russian destruction in Manchuria in terms of its effect upon Hsiao Chun, who was "shocked by what he saw there—Russian arrogance, the raping of Chinese women, the looting of industrial establishments, and the general disregard for Chinese interests by Soviet soldiers and bureaucrats," see C. D. Chang, "Communism and Nationalism in China," FEER, 9 March 1950, pp. 298–299.

68. The Tito-Moscow correspondence was published by the Royal Institute of International Affairs, London, 1949. In two of his letters to Stalin Tito sounds as if he just cannot believe that Stalin really means to expel him from the Cominform. For a definitive treatment see Adam B. Ulam, *Titoism and the Cominform,* Cambridge, Harvard University Press, 1952.

69. This is pointed out by Benjamin Schwartz in "China and the Soviet Theory of People's Democracy."

70. This was told to me personally by one of the participants in the Geneva conference in whom I have implicit faith.

71. A good example is Schwartz, *Chinese Communism and the Rise of Mao.* This excellent study of the early period and the tensions between Peking and Moscow stops, however, at a point in Mao's life before the impact of Stalin's writings had been felt. Schwartz gives an exhaustive bibliography of other works on the same period.

72. See note 12.

CHAPTER 12. China and the United States

1. For some early documents on the Chinese Communist hatred for the United States see the files of *China Today* published in New York by the "Friends of the Chinese People," beginning in 1933. For a more ex-

tensive treatment of the Hate America Campaign including the years 1945–50 see my article "Communist China Looks at the United States," *Yale Review,* Autumn 1951. I have made extensive use of the article in this chapter.

2. H. A. Steiner, "Mainsprings of Chinese Communist Foreign Policy," *American Journal of International Law, 44,* No. 1 (Jan. 1950), 80. Steiner's 1949 observation proved only too accurate in the first five years of Communist rule. In his article he also gives some examples of the Hate America policy between the end of World War II and the founding of the Communist regime.

3. This was the introductory paragraph of a series of three articles entitled "Look, This Is the American Way of Life," printed in the *Nan-fang Jih-pao (Southern Daily),* official organ of the CCP in Canton. A full translation is printed as *Current Background* #55 and constitutes a primer for the study of the Hate America Campaign.

4. Mao Tun, "The 'Masked Bandit' Unmasked," NCNA, Peking, 5 Dec. 1950.

5. PC, 1 May 1951.

6. CB #55, pp. 5–6.

7. CB #55, p. 20.

8. JMJP, 11 Nov. 1952. For a survey of some of the vindictive articles on the United States presidential election see CCPR, No. 34, pp. 3–25.

9. JMJP, 30 Aug. 1954.

10. For more details see my article cited in note 1. The files of *People's China* are full of stories on United States "cultural aggression."

11. Mao Tun, "The 'Masked Bandit' Unmasked."

12. JMJP, editorial of 2 June 1953. A good survey of the propaganda campaign on the Rosenberg case is given in CCPR #43, pp. 2–23.

13. Chou En-lai, "Political Report to the Fourth Session of the First National Committee of the Chinese People's Political Consultative Conference, 4 February 1953," PC, Supplement, 16 Feb. 1953, pp. 7–8.

14. *Shih-shih Shou-ts'e (Current Affairs Handbook),* No. 25, 20 Oct. 1951.

15. Soong Ching-ling, "Mobilize for Peace in Asia, the Pacific Regions and the World," PC, Supplement, 16 Oct. 1952, p. 7.

16. The whole of the germ warfare campaign, as I have indicated earlier, is the subject of an intensive piece of research by R. D. Barendsen. For a good example of how Hewlett Johnson served in this campaign of hate see PC, 1 Aug. 1952, pp. 5–9.

17. Kuo Mo-jo in a speech to the Second World Peace Congress, 18 Nov. 1950; PC, Supplement, 16 Jan. 1951, p. 10.

18. "Documents of the Peace Conference of the Asian and Pacific Regions," PC, Supplement, 1 Nov. 1952.

19. The theme of the "paper tiger" was played up throughout the Korean War. Much of the argumentation involved is given in an article entitled "How to Understand the United States," in the *Shih-shih Shou-ts'e* (*Current Affairs Handbook*), Vol. *1*, No. 2, 5 Nov. 1950. This was issued as CB #32.

20. Chou En-lai, "Report on Government Work," 23 Sept. 1954; CB #296.

21. See reference cited in note 19.

22. As of 15 June 1954, United States government officials reported 122 American civilian and military personnel in China, of whom 61 were reported to be in prison. See Tillman Durdin's dispatch in the 16 June 1954 *New York Times*.

23. See, for example, the AP dispatch from Bonn, Germany, of 24 Jan. 1953, describing the report of a prominent German businessman who maintained that the plight of Americans under Mao is worse than that of the Jews under Hitler.

24. See C. K. Cheng, "Why the San Francisco Treaty Will Fail," PC, 16 Sept. 1951, pp. 9–10, for Chinese Communist elation over the failure of India and Burma to participate. Pakistan's delegate to the Peace Conference of the Asian and Pacific Peoples in 1952, Tahira Mazhar, expressed herself "ashamed to admit that the Pakistan government is a signatory." PC, Supplement, 16 Oct. 1952, p. 35.

25. For example, see PC, 1 June 1950, p. 4, which charges the British with duplicity and states that "the British government, following the dictates of Washington, has persistently abstained from voting on the proposal to oust the KMT representatives from the United Nations." Chou En-lai made the same point in his September 1954 review of the first five years of Communist power; CB #296.

26. See "Chinese Communist Propaganda Efforts to Sabotage the Unity of the United States and Great Britain," CCPR #42, pp. 2–23.

27. "Economic Contradictions of American and Anglo-Dutch Imperialism in Indonesia," *Shih-chieh Chih-shih* (*World Knowledge*), No. 2, 20 Jan. 1950; CCPR #42, p. 11.

28. "New Developments in Anglo-American Contradictions," *Shih-chieh Chih-shih*, No. 44, 8 Nov. 1952; CCPR #42, p. 15.

29. As reported in a London dispatch to the *New York Times*, 3 May 1954.

30. Chou En-lai, "Report on Government Work," CB #296, p. 19.

31. CCPR #42, pp. 11–13.

32. NCNA, Peking, 14 June 1953.
33. Chou En-lai, "Report on Government Work."
34. Tientsin *Ta Kung Pao,* NCNA, 3 Sept. 1954.
35. An excellent survey of the Chinese Communist propaganda line on Japan is given with reproductions of important statements and documents in CCPR #40, pp. 2–40.
36. Chou En-lai, "Report on Government Work."
37. *Ibid.*
38. The story of the Marshall Mission is told in documented form in *United States Relations with China,* Washington, U.S. Government Printing Office, 1949. An excellent account of the complications involved in United States policy toward China in the years preceding the mission is given by Herbert L. Feis, *The China Tangle,* Princeton University Press, 1954. Although the statement on the underlying assumption of the Marshall Mission may be questioned, I believe that it is in general a fair presentation.
39. NCNA, Peking, 28 Aug. 1954; SCMP #881.
40. On Chinese Communist accounts of conditions on Taiwan see SCMP beginning with #880. An NCNA dispatch of 12 Sept. 1954, for example, describing the epidemic proportions of disease is given in #886. The description of Taiwan as a "concentration camp" is given in #889, pp. 14–15. Such accounts can be assessed by reference to the reports of organizations like the World Health Organization, the Joint Commission on Rural Reconstruction, or the Foreign Operations Administration. A strong argument can be made that despite the cost of maintaining a large military establishment Taiwan has become a showplace for social and economic progress in Southeast Asia. Political developments are also encouraging, despite a crisis situation. For more detailed summaries see my articles on "Formosa" in *Collier's Yearbook* covering the years 1952 through 1954.
41. JMJP, 5 Sept. 1954; SCMP #883. The relatively carefree and happy lives of the students at National Taiwan University (despite crowded conditions) are a striking contrast, for example, with the situation described by Maria Yen in *The Umbrella Garden* which deals with student life under the Communists.
42. As quoted by an NCNA Berlin dispatch of 16 Sept. 1954.
43. NCNA, Peking, 3 Oct. 1954; SCMP #901.
44. PC, 1 Sept. 1954.
45. These points were made in conversation by Chinese refugees in Hong Kong as well as by scholars on Taiwan. Their view is, of course, bitter; but they were appreciably disturbed by Attlee's remarks and afraid of the weight of British views in determining the course of United States

foreign policy. They point out that the abandonment of Taiwan in the face of threats of force would undoubtedly undermine the determination of many Asian leaders who are fighting Communism today.

46. The Chinese Communists argue that United States protection of the Nationalist government is in direct contradiction to American promises at Cairo and at Potsdam to turn Taiwan over to the Chinese government. The Communist case rests in large measure on demonstrating that the United States is "occupying" Taiwan, a point which they argue vociferously. Both the Communists and the Nationalists passionately reject suggestions of "internationalization" or United Nations trusteeship of the island; and United States advocacy of such schemes would constitute abrogation of commitments made at Potsdam and Cairo.

CHAPTER 13. The Challenge of Communist China

1. See the quotation at the beginning of Chapter 8.

2. A good discussion of the inversion of Chinese traditional values is given by Maria Yen and Richard McCarthy in *The Umbrella Garden,* Liu Shaw-tong in *Out of Red China,* and Leonard Constantine, "Communist China: the Inversion of Values," *Manchester Guardian Weekly,* 8 Feb. 1951, p. 13.

3. The Communists themselves admit this failure. It is discussed in T.T., "The Intellectual in the New China," *Problems of Communism,* 2, No. 2 (1953), 1–7, and in CNA #20. R. M. McCarthy of the Hong Kong Consulate General staff has followed literary production in Communist China very closely and in conversations with me has stressed this point as being of great significance.

4. A.R., "Notes," MB, March 1952, p. 216.

5. See Karl A. Wittfogel, "The Historical Position of Communist China: Doctrine and Reality," *Review of Politics,* 16, No. 4 (Oct. 1954), 463–474. Oriental despotism, the most autocratic of all the varieties of social and political organization, has been the subject of life-long study by Wittfogel, and his analysis constitutes probably the best framework for understanding the character of Communist power in China. According to him the Communists in China, as in the Soviet Union, have created a completely managerial state, instead of a semimanagerial despotism as of old (which did not control all aspects of the people's life, and permitted a small peasant economy). Wittfogel points out that the term "general slavery" was formulated by Marx, and that Marx and Engels as well as Lenin until 1917 all feared the resurrection of "oriental despotism" in Russia, or as Lenin put it, "an Asiatic restoration."

Wittfogel's study, *Oriental Society and Oriental Despotism,* is scheduled for early publication. A bibliography of some of his earlier discussions of the problem of oriental societies is given in E. Stuart Kirby, *Introduction to the Economic History of China* (London, Allen and Unwin, 1954), as well as in the footnotes of the article listed above.

6. Leonard Constantine, "Communist China: the Price in Human Terms," *Manchester Guardian Weekly,* 30 Nov. 1950, p. 5.

Index

Accusation. *See* Struggle meetings

Activists, 20, 27, 49, 51, 165, 174. *See also* Cadres

Acton, Lord, 100

Administrations: Customs, 18; East China Regional, 80–1; Northeast Regional, 16; Publications, 78. *See also* United Nations

Agrarian Reform. *See* Land, Land Reform program, Laws (Agrarian Reform)

Agriculture: as determining factor in China's ability to industrialize, 113; statistics on cultivated land, 113; nationalization, 114; prospects for increasing food production, 115; use of fertilizers, 115; basic problem, 132–3. *See also* Collectivization, Land, Land Reform program, Laws (Agrarian Reform), Peasants

Ai Ssu-ch'i, 61, 95, 207, 210, 274

All China Democratic Women's Federation, 174; membership, 39; ostensible purpose, 40; type of work engaged in by women, 40; true purpose, 40

An Tzu-wen, 33, 54, 81, 85, 167

Andreev, A. A., 146

Anshan Iron and Steel Works, 41, 118, 125

Armed forces, 18, 81, 214; as chain of command, 31–2; extramilitary role, 32

Associations: Chinese Buddhist, 188; Chinese Dramatic Workers, 198; Cultural Relations with Foreign Countries, 247; Sino-British Friendship, 247; Sino-Indian Friendship, 247; Sino-Japanese Friendship, 247; Sino-Soviet Friendship, 28 f., 39, 143, 278, 282

Attlee, Clement, 236, 241, 249, 313 f., 317

Beria, L. P., 289

Book of Odes, 194

Bourgeois (bourgeoisie), 4, 24, 49, 53, 71

Brain-washing: most thorough aspect of psychological mass coercion, 52; four separate purposes, 52; creation of cadres by means of, 52 ff.; Confucius and Pavlov in background of technique, 55. *See also* Cadre training

Britain, 103, 312–14; assets seized, 239. *See also* British Labor party

British Labor party, 238, 312; delegation to China, 214, 232, 249, 313

Buck, J. L., 21, 131 f.

Buddhists, 188–9

Bukharin, N. I., 120

Bureaus: Northeast, 85; Northwest, 85; Public Security, 224; State Statistical, 119, 203. *See also* Federal Bureau of Investigation

Cadre(s), 2, 11, 19, 21, 27, 46 f., 49 ff., 79 ff., 87 ff., 94, 102, 118, 121, 123 f., 134 f., 137 ff., 142, 162, 165, 182, 185, 187, 206, 217, 257, 274, 281 f., 287; definition, 51 and n.; changing thought pattern of, 51; creation through brain-washing, 52 ff.; trainees, 52–72; assignment, 72; as teachers and organizers, 73; abuse of power, 86; as targets of criticism, 85–6, 140, 144–5, 149, 166, 173, 186. *See also* Activists, Brain-washing, Cadre training

Cadre training, 27; success with, 53–4, 74–5; educational centers for, 53–4, 57; origins, 54; role of Liu Shao-ch'i, 54; Party Reform Movement in, 54–5; in Moscow, 54; as blend of Confucius, Pavlov, and Liu Shao-ch'i, 55; criticism and self-criticism

Cadre training *continued*
as key weapons in, 56; attitude toward individual, 57; six factors (controlled area, 57–8, fatigue, 58, tension, 58, sense of isolation and uncertainty, 58, vicious language, 58, seriousness, 58); six techniques (discussion groups, 59, group meetings, 59–60, writing of autobiographies and diaries, 60, questioning, 60, volunteering, 61, isolation, 61); Ai Ssu-ch'i as one of key ideologists, 61–2; the "Organization" as infallible, 61; as all powerful, 63 ff.; three Marxist theories as background, 62; themes stressed (unimportance of individual, 63, power and force of the Organization, 63, old versus new, 63, patriotism, 63, inevitability, 63, class consciousness and class struggle, 63–4, "steeling," 64); five stages (physical control, 65–7, intense indoctrination, 67–70, emotional crisis, 70–1, final convincing, 71–2, assignment, 72); typical daily schedule, 68. *See also* Brainwashing, Cadre(s)

Campaigns. *See* Drives

Canton, 12, 79, 94, 107, 124, 162, 192, 220

Censorate, 47

Census, 18, 21, 46, 97 f., 111–12

Central Committee, 21, 25 ff., 33 f., 42, 81, 88, 114, 120, 186, 206, 216, 254 f., 275, 286 f.; Administration Office, 34; Organization Department, 34; Propaganda Department, 29, 34 f.; Social Affairs Department, 34; United Front Work Department, 34

Central Conservatory of Music, 199

Central Nationalities College, 186

Central People's Government of the People's Republic of China. *See* CC government

Ceylon, 113, 234, 240

Chains of command, 27, 28–9, 43; government organization, 29–31; military, 31–2; party, 32–4; mass

media of communication, 34–6; mass support organizations, 36–43; effect on individuals, 43 ff.; control of individuals, 43 ff.

Chang, C. M., 139

Chao, K. C., 39

Chao Tsi-chen, 190 f.

Chekiang University, 202

Ch'en Ming-shu, 188

Ch'en Tuan-hsiu, 90

Ch'en Tu-hsiu, 211

Ch'en Yüan, 208

Chen Yu-ming, 74

Ch'en Yün, 26, 156

Chi Chien-hua, 204

Ch'i Pai-shih, 199 f.

Chiang Kai-shek, 220, 257, 273, 295, 305, 316 f., 320

Ch'ien Mu, 95

Ch'ien Tuan-sheng, 210

China: as test case for Communism, x; influence of its remoteness on U.S. planning, x–xi; importance of lessons to be learned from, xi; world position in *1949* and *1954*, 1; relations with U.S., 1; remolding of Chinese society, 6; literacy, 6; role of Stalinism in future of, 23; as totalitarian dictatorship, 24; population, 4, 6; U.S. aid to, 104; *1949* industrial production, 104; rural problems, 130; ownership of rural land, 131; chances for Chinese Titoism, 293–300. *See also* CC government

China Agriculture Fortnightly, 147

China Monthly Review, 195

China News Analysis, 119, 229 f.

China Pictorial, 248

China Reconstructs, 244

China Technical Development Company, 124

China Today, 243

China Youth, 85 f., 204

Chinese, overseas, 116, 262, 263–5; blackmailed, 250–1

Chinese Communist government: fundamental character of Communist changes, xii; permanency of changes, xii–xiii; wealth of data on,

Drives *continued*
Reform, 54 f., 177 f., 180; Party
Unity, 98; Peace, 79, 98; Production
Increase and Austerity, 98; to propagandize benefits of Marriage Law,
19; to publicize party line, 97; Resist
America, Aid Korea, 48, 78, 80, 91–
2, 97, 188, 195; Sanitation, 98; Sino-
Soviet Friendship, 79; Stakhanovite,
41, 122; 3-anti, 33, 37, 74 and n.,
81, 95–6; 3-anti 5-anti, 14, 95–7,
98, 167; to volunteer extra work,
122
Dulles, John Foster, 253

"East Shines Red," 181
Economic control, 101–27; as key to all
control, 101; *1952* basis for state
monopoly, 106; elimination of private enterprise, 107 ff.; nationalization of rural handicrafts and village
stores, 109; and population, 111 f.;
industrialization problems, 113; export problems, 113 ff.; increase of
food production and export as
means of raising capital, 113–15;
other means of raising capital, 116;
statistics on industrial investment,
126; result of tightened control,
126–7; of peasants, 128–53; state
food monopoly, 152; of workers,
157–8. *See also* Five-year plan
Economist (London), 249
Eden, Anthony, 295
Education, 53–4, 57 ff., 182; linked with
psychological mass coercion, 52;
problems of technical training, 117–
18; of workers, 158 f.; mission
schools, 192; student deportment,
201; theory, 201; primary schools,
202; institutions of higher learning,
202; technical training, 202; study
of Russian, 202; number of students, 203; teachers, 203; policy
changes toward, 203; quantity before quality, 203–4; graduate place-
ment, 204; a major *1954* goal to
serve industrialization, 204; and
literacy, 204–5. *See also* Cadre

training, Culture, Drives (Ideolog-
ical Remolding), Intellectuals, Lit-
eracy
Ehrenburg, Ilya, 199
Einstein, Albert, 180
Eisenhower, D. D., 284, 305
Elections, 18 f., 21 f., 29, 46, 97 f.
Engels, Friedrich, 56, 180, 255

Fainsod, Merle, 214
Famine (*1953*), 17, 148, 151; wild
beasts blamed, 148; value of, in edu-
cating people, 231
Federal Bureau of Investigation, 305
Federations: All China, of Coopera-
tives, 124; All China, of Democra-
tic Youth, 39; All China, of Indus-
trial and Commercial Circles, 41,
108; All China, of Trade Unions,
18, 28, 40–1, 85, 155 ff., 160, 164,
169, 174; All China Students', 39;
Chinese, of Labor, 225; Women's
International Democratic, 9; World,
of Christian Associations, 190;
World, of Trade Unions, 155.
See also All China Democratic
Women's Federation
Fedorenko, N., 283
Fei Hsiao-t'ung, 185–6
Feudalism, 63, 66, 129 f., 133 f., 138,
140, 182, 206, 209. *See also* Land
Reform program
Five-year plan, 17, 20, 23, 98, 106,
108 f., 169, 175, 204, 231, 281, 286;
beginning, 101; adherence to Soviet
model, 101–2; goals, 102; development of heavy industry, 102–3; distinction between colonial and industrialized economy, 93; three
major tasks completed before
launching, 103; educational shift in
launching, 110; reduction of original goals, 110; early difficulties,
111; problem of increasing heavy
industry, 113; of increasing agriculture, 113; of increasing exports,
113–15; increasing capital through
enforced savings, 116; through increased rate of production, 116;

Propaganda: embracing all activity, 35; all news as political news, 35; through unions, 155; to enhance workers, 160; toward workers, 174; toward youth, 196; in foreign relations, 242–6; typical NCNA handouts, 245. *See also* Central Committee, Mass media of communication
Propaganda Handbook, 35, 48
Provisional Measures for Capital Construction Work, 101
Provisions for the Suppression of Counterrevolutionaries, 93
Psychological control, 50–76. *See also* Brain-washing, Cadre(s), Cadre training, Psychological mass coercion
Psychological mass coercion, 214; as dimension of political power, 52, 75; import, 57; as means of mobilization, 75; of producing conformity and unity, 75–6; dehumanization, 76
Public Security forces, 43–4
Purges, 14, 21, 33, 171

Railroads, 15 f., 18, 121, 225–6, 273, 279; woman worker on, 40; nationalization, 106; lack, 117; hours of workers, 163; doctored books, 170
Read method of childbirth, 277
Recantations. *See* Confessions
Red Cross, International, 231
Red Flag over Tsuikang, 285
Regional divisions, 30, 31–2
Regulations: for the Control of Publications, Printing, and Distribution Enterprises, 194; Governing the Organization of Peasants' Associations, 134; Labor Insurance, 169, 174; Provisional, Governing the Organization of Security Committees, 15; for the Punishment of Counterrevolutionaries, 11, 45, 216
Religion: subordinate to state, 12; as "opiate for the masses," 187. *See also* under names of religions
Roads, 18; construction, 226

Roosevelt, F. D., 241
Rosenbergs, 306
Rostow, W. W., 103, 126, 159
Runev, 43
Russia, October Revolution, 9

Sacred Heart Home for Children, 191
St. John's University, 305
San-fan Movement. *See* Drives (3-anti)
Schönberg, Arnold, 199
Schwartz, Benjamin, 274, 380
Second World War. *See* World War II
Secret police, 27. *See also* Social Affairs Department
Security police, 87, 138
Self-criticism. *See* Criticism
Shah, K. T., 244
Shanghai, 81, 107, 162, 192 f., 207, 217, 219 f., 232, 305
Shanghai General Labor Union, 165
Shanghai News, 195
Short Course, 126
Sino-Korean Agreement on Economic and Cultural Cooperation, 267
Sino-Soviet Aviation Company, 123
Slave labor, 12, 23, 122, 220–7; as punishment and "education," 221, 222–4; statistics, 222; camp schedule, 223; deaths, 224; projects involving, 224–8. *See also* Counterrevolutionaries, Labor, forced, Terror
Socialism, as goal of Communism, 4, 79, 139, 186
Socialism—Utopian and Scientific, 62
Songs, 200–1
Soong Ching-ling (Mme. Sun Yat-sen), 29, 76, 308
Southeast Asia Treaty Organization, 313
Southern Daily, 107, 147, 218, 220, 302
Soviet Encyclopedia, 284
Soviet Union: as model, ix, 3, 4 ff., 14, 16, 22 f., 25 f., 30, 32 ff., 37, 39, 44, 51, 54 f., 57, 95, 101–2, 120, 121–2, 138, 142 f., 145 f., 150, 151 ff., 158, 160 ff., 168, 170, 175–6, 177 f., 183, 184–5, 192, 202, 210, 213, 224,